NURTURING CREATIVITY IN THE CLASSROOM

Deciding how best to nurture creativity in our schools has become more complicated as interest in creativity has exploded. There are controversial Common Core strictures in many states; at the same time, the classroom has become increasingly digital, making it easier to access information, communicate ideas, and learn from people across the world. Many countries now include cultivating creativity as a national educational policy recommendation, yet there is still debate over best practices. Many well-intentioned educators may be instituting programs that do not reach the desired outcome, and the notion that schools "kill creativity" has become widespread. This belief is both hyperbolic and problematic: it allows us to recognize a problem but not solve it. In this book, an international group of experts in the field addresses these issues, discussing theories and research that focus on how to nurture creativity in both K–12 and college-level classrooms.

RONALD A. BEGHETTO is Professor of Educational Psychology in the Neag School of Education at the University of Connecticut. Prior to joining the faculty at UConn, Dr. Beghetto served as the College of Education's Associate Dean for Academic Affairs and Associate Professor of Education Studies at the University of Oregon. He is the Editor-in-Chief for the *Journal of Creative Behavior* and serves as an associate editor for the *International Journal of Creativity and Problem Solving*. He also serves on the editorial boards of *Psychology of Aesthetics, Creativity, and the Arts*; the *Journal of Educational Research; Gifted Child Quarterly*; and *Creativity Studies*. Dr. Beghetto is a Fellow of the American Psychological Association and the Society for the Psychology of Aesthetics, Creativity, and the Arts (Division 10, APA). He has also received numerous awards for excellence in research and teaching.

JAMES C. KAUFMAN is Professor of Educational Psychology at the University of Connecticut. An internationally recognized leader in the field of creativity, he is the author or editor of more than 35 books, including *Creativity 101* and *The Cambridge Handbook of Creativity*. Kaufman is a past president of the American Psychological Association's Division 10, devoted to creativity. He coedits the *International Journal of Creativity and Problem Solving* and cofounded two APA journals. He has won the Torrance Award from the National Association for Gifted Children, the Berlyne and Farnsworth Awards from the APA, and Mensa's Award for Excellence in Research.

CURRENT PERSPECTIVES IN SOCIAL AND BEHAVIORAL SCIENCES

Current Perspectives in Social and Behavioral Sciences provides thought-provoking introductions to key topics, invaluable to both the student and scholar. Edited by world's leading academics, each volume contains specially commissioned essays by international contributors, which present cutting-edge research on the subject and suggest new paths of inquiry for the reader. This series is designed not only to offer a comprehensive overview of the chosen topics but also to display and provoke lively and controversial debate.

Also in this series:

Reflections on the Learning Sciences edited by MICHAEL A. EVANS, MARTIN J. PACKER, AND R. KEITH SAWYER

Mindfulness and Performance edited by AMY L. BALTZELL

Creativity and Reason in Cognitive Development, Second Edition edited by JAMES C. KAUFMAN AND JOHN BAER

Forthcoming titles:

Research and Theory on Workplace Aggression edited by NATHAN A. BOWLING, AND M. SANDY HERSHCOVIS

Genetics, Ethics and Education edited by SUSAN BOUREGY, ELENA L. GRIGORENKO, STEPHEN R. LATHAM, AND MEI TAN

Teacher Motivation edited by HELEN WATT, PAUL RICHARDSON, AND KARI SMITH

The Cambridge Companion to Culture, Mind, and Brain: Emerging Concepts, Methods, Applications edited by LAURENCE J. KIRMAYER, MARIE-FRANÇOISE CHESSELET, SHINOBU KITAYAMA, CAROL M. WORTHMAN, AND CONSTANCE A. CUMMINGS

NURTURING CREATIVITY IN THE CLASSROOM

SECOND EDITION

RONALD A. BEGHETTO

University of Connecticut

JAMES C. KAUFMAN

University of Connecticut

CAMBRIDGE
UNIVERSITY PRESS

CAMBRIDGE
UNIVERSITY PRESS

One Liberty Plaza, 20th Floor, New York, NY 10006, USA

Cambridge University Press is part of the University of Cambridge.

It furthers the University's mission by disseminating knowledge in the pursuit of education, learning, and research at the highest international levels of excellence.

www.cambridge.org
Information on this title: www.cambridge.org/9781107103153

© Cambridge University Press 2017

First edition printed 2010
Reprinted 2011 (thrice), 2012
Second editon first published 2017

Printed in the United States of America by Sheridan Books

A catalogue record for this publication is available from the British Library.

ISBN 978-1-107-10315-3 Hardback
ISBN 978-1-107-50130-0 Paperback

For Ms. Sheryl VanPelt,
Thank you for inspiring and expecting creativity
from all *of your students!*
– Ronald A. Beghetto

For Zorana Ivcevic Pringle,
Passionate about creativity, schools, and children,
and one of my dearest friends for many years
– James C. Kaufman

Contents

Preface
Continuing to Nurture Creativity in the Classroom

The first edition of *Nurturing Creativity to the Classroom* was published in 2010. Although less than a decade has passed, much has happened in the worlds of education and creativity. We've seen the Common Core Standards implemented in many states, eliciting emotional reactions both in favor of and against these ideas. The classroom (and world) has become increasingly digital; it is easier than ever to access information, communicate ideas, and learn from people across the world. New voices have emerged and new research and theories have added to the discussion.

We have also seen interest in creativity explode over the past few years. Creativity has become an international educational priority. Many countries have included cultivating creativity in their national educational policy recommendations. This recognition of the importance of creativity has also come with increased concern that many schools are ill-equipped to nurture students' creative potential. In fact, the notion that schools "kill creativity" has become a widespread social meme. We view such beliefs as both hyperbolic and problematic. Although it is true that some educational contexts might suppress students' willingness to take the risks necessary for creativity, schools can't really kill creativity. Indeed, opportunities for supporting creativity are ever-present. Often what is needed is simply recognizing and capitalizing on those opportunities.

The ideas shared in the new addition of this book have the goal of helping educators and researchers nurture creativity in K–12 and college-level classrooms. The chapters in this edition represent a blend of old and new. Some of the chapters are updated from the first edition, some are vastly rewritten, and some are brand-new chapters written expressly for the second edition. We also have four new brief essays to open the book from educators working in the field who have accomplished remarkable feats at incorporating creativity into the classroom. The book concludes with a rewritten coda of both classic and new take-home points.

As we wrote in the first preface, we have dual roles of being professors and fathers. As we have watched Olivia, Jacob, and Asher explore and develop their own creativity, the importance of an educational system that values creativity has become increasingly salient. Our children have an advantage in that their fathers value creativity (perhaps too much!). Like so many other parents, we are committed to providing diverse learning opportunities for our children. However, this commitment is not enough.

Sometimes the well-intended parenting and educational practices backfire or get in the way of supporting creativity. In some cases, more guidance and structure is needed to help young people anchor their originality to the given set of task constraints for a particular activity. In other cases, it may be most helpful to get out of the way and allow young people to express their originality in their own unique way. Striking this balance is an ongoing challenge. There are no simple recipes for how best to accomplish it. One key is recognizing that it is a dynamic process. It is a process that often requires blending timely support and encouragement with guidance and awareness of real-world constraints.

It is our hope that this book inspires educators, parents, and researchers to ensure that all students have an opportunity to find, nurture, and sustain their creative potential. We are excited to present an updated and revised edition of this book. We hope that you will enjoy and draw as much insight and inspiration from these essays as we have.

Acknowledgments

The authors would like to give very special thanks David Repetto of Cambridge University Press for his interest, patience, encouragement, and constant support; Paul J. Barnett for editorial assistance; and our colleagues and friends at the University of Connecticut. Love to Jeralyn and Olivia and to Allison, Jacob, and Asher.

PART I

Voices from the Field

CHAPTER I

Changing the Subject

Larry Rosenstock and Rob Riordan

High Tech High

What should students learn in the 21st century? At first glance, this question divides into two: What should students know, and what should they be able to do? Knowledge and skills. For more than a century, policy makers and educators have drawn a sharp distinction between the two – between college preparatory and technical education. John Dewey argued against this division early in the 20th century. It is now way past time to integrate hands and minds, as the skills and knowledge required for "college" and "career" have become virtually identical.

But there is more at issue than knowledge and skills. For the innovation economy, dispositions come into play: learning to learn, readiness to collaborate, seeing from multiple perspectives, initiative, persistence, and curiosity. While the content of any learning experience is important, the *particular* content is irrelevant. What matters is how students apply it, react to it, or shape it. The purpose of learning in this century is not simply to recite inert knowledge, but rather to transform it. It is time to change the subject.

This is no small matter. For more than a century, the whole point of schooling has been to restrict the curriculum, specify the content, keep it inert, and limit the entry points to it – often by means of a watered-down, already obsolete text, mediated by a manager tasked with transmitting the content to 30 or more individuals of diverse backgrounds, experiences, and resources. This is particularly true of the "big four" core subjects that the Carnegie Commission decided, nearly a century ago, are the subjects that matter. English, math, science (biology, chemistry, and physics), and social studies count, and the fine and practical arts are irrelevant.

Why not study anthropology, zoology, or environmental science? Why not integrate art with calculus, or chemistry with history? Why not pick up skills and understandings in all of these areas by uncovering and addressing real problems and sharing findings with authentic audiences? Why not study a nearby estuary, invent a useful product that uses electricity, or devise solutions to community problems, all the while engaging in systematic observation, collaborative design, and public exhibitions of learning?

If we are to change the subject in this way, then we must change the trappings within which we educate our youth. It is a fool's errand to expect teachers to model 21st-century skills in a 19th-century work environment. Instead, situate them where they can collaborate with other teachers – and with their students – to pose problems, engage expert assistance, and design products and performances of lasting value. Embrace a cohort model, where teams of teachers and students work together. Build professional collaboration and development time into the daily schedule, so that teachers can meet variously in teaching teams, academic departments, and study groups to reflect on and refine their day-to-day practice.

The aim is to unleash teachers – and their students – to design learning experiences that are applied, integrated, situated, expeditionary, and alternatively assessed.

It has long been axiomatic to separate students according to perceived academic ability, to separate academic from technical teaching and learning, and to isolate adolescents from the adult world they are about to enter.

Instead, our aim should be to integrate students by eliminating tracking, integrate the subjects via problem-focused experiences, and integrate school with the world beyond through fieldwork, service learning, and internships.

What might student do in such schools, in the absence of prescribed subject matter? They might work together to build robots, roller coasters, gardens, and human-powered submarines. They might write and publish a guide to the fauna and history of a local estuary, or an economics text illustrated with original woodcuts, or a children's astronomy book. They might produce original films, plays, and spoken-word events on adolescent issues, Japanese internment, cross-border experiences, and a host of other topics. They might mount a crime scene exhibition linking art history and DNA analysis, or develop a museum exhibit of World War I as seen from various perspectives. They might celebrate returning warriors, as did the skop or bard in Beowulf, by interviewing local veterans and writing poems honoring their experiences. The possibilities are endless.

In executing such projects, students develop deep understandings by making something new of their subject matter. Of necessity, they learn how to collaborate, how to plan, how to give and accept critique, how to revise, how to self-assess. They read complex texts and write a wide range of pieces, from personal reflections to news articles, project proposals, memos, research reports, stories, and essays. They interview community members, learning to listen and appreciate diverse perspectives. As they present their work to important audiences, they begin to understand what it means to be a member of the human community. And the irony is that as students pursue their passions and interests, we rediscover the living curriculum.

"Changing the subject" in this way means deriving the curriculum from the lived experience of the student, which becomes a text to be "read" and interpreted, just as any print or video text might be. In this view, rather than a fixed text, the curriculum is more like a flow of events, accessible through tools that help students identify and extract rich academic content from the world: guidelines and templates for project-based development, along with activities and routines for observation and analysis, reflection, dialogue, critique, and negotiation.

When we learn – really learn – we transform the self, the content, and the very context for learning. This is what it means to change the subject. We can do this. If we value our future, we must.

CHAPTER 2

Creativity and the Invention Convention

Jake Mendelssohn
Connecticut Invention Convention

I am living my boyhood dream – and no, it's not the one involving Raquel Welch.

When I was 16, like many young people, I wanted to have an impact and to change the world. I became an engineer in order to design and build things that would change the world. But then I became a teacher so that I could educate hundreds of students who would then themselves change the world. Now I am working with the Connecticut Invention Convention where I am supporting hundreds of teachers who are educating thousands of students who will change the world.

I love every day of it.

The Connecticut Invention Convention (CIC) is the largest and oldest continuously operating student invention program in the United States. Last year more than 16,000 students in grades K through 8 from 246 schools across the state experienced this program, which brings creativity and problem solving into the classroom in the form of an invention education curriculum and competition.

When I first started out teaching, it was something of a personal mandate for me. I wanted to be able to take my years of engineering experience and inspire young people toward those same wonders. If there ever was a STEM-focused problem-solving teacher, it was I. In fact, I would not tell my kids I was a teacher because in my heart of hearts I was still an engineer. So I would tell the students that I was hired to be a problem solver. "In the beginning of the year, the School Board gives me a curriculum and a school room of empty heads, and I have until the end of the year to get that knowledge into your heads. The teaching and homework is about me trying to solve the problem of how to get all the cool information into your heads. All those quizzes and tests we take? You think those are for you? No, they're for me – to help me see if I am doing a good job and if I am solving the problem."

Being creative in a traditional school situation is actually very difficult. Creativity and education are, in some ways, almost contradictory. A standard education system is based on a fixed curriculum and delivering that curriculum. It is approved and set. Teachers are creative and innovative themselves, but limited by what they can do. I've known many very creative and wonderful teachers, but schools are governed by a lot of constructs that are anything but creative – standard curricula, schedules, assessment testing, and so on. Teachers and schools really do want to be creative, but how can they do that while still delivering a set standard education curriculum? Given the pressures and directives a school operates under – and I understand why those are necessary – I would not want to be a Superintendent of Education; it is a tough job.

This is why working with the CIC as a program is so fulfilling. I'm helping all these great teachers and principals do what they really would love to be doing – being really creative – but within the constraints of also fulfilling their curriculum-based systems.

The CIC is a K–8 invention education curriculum that aligns to the Connecticut Common Core standards and Next Generation Science Standards. It helps teach creativity and problem solving to kids by allowing them to seek out and identify a problem that they feel passionate about – and lets them craft a solution to solve that problem. The program starts in the Fall with Professional Development sessions where teachers can learn cutting-edge ways to teach creativity by using the invention process in their classrooms. There are basic sessions for first-time CIC teachers and advanced sessions for returning ones. In the early part of the year, teachers start an introductory program to help the students seek out and identify problems in the world around them, document a possible solution, and then undertake an Invention Process to refine that concept into a working prototype. Students present their projects – with accompanying display boards and Invention Logs – at their local school Invention Convention. Selected students then progress to higher competitions, up to the State Finals event held at the University of Connecticut's Gampel Pavilion – home of the UCONN Huskies basketball team.

For many students, everything about the CIC is a life-changing experience. It is one of the few opportunities in school where the kids can take what they have learned in math, English, science, art, and other courses and apply it to a real-world problem that they themselves relate to on some personal level. It is not the teacher's problem, but rather an issue in their own world that they are addressing and solving. I have spoken with hundreds of student inventors, and there always is a great story about why they invented what they did. And it is usually quite empathic. "My grandma has so much trouble reaching high places." "My best friend is blind." "My dad travels a lot and misses my ballet performances." Some of them are quite personal. "I always hit my head on the bathroom door." "My ball gets lost in the storm drain when we play street ball." "I hate having to get up from bed to shut off the light when I've just about read myself to sleep." This is their world, and where else in school can they use their knowledge to make their own world better?

The students learn that inventing solutions to problems is what the real world is all about. Take, for example, electricians – they solve energy problems with wires and electrical outlets. Doctors use medicines and surgery. Plumbers use pipes and solder. But whatever the technology or the materials used, the basic process of problem discovery, goal determination, and evaluation of the result is the same. That is the experience students have at the Invention Convention. The curriculum is problem solving articulated. The Invention Log that the student creates is essentially a step-by-step cookbook for how to solve problems, any problems. And like in real life, the students have to be able to explain what the problem is and how their solution works. "People need to have faith in what you did . . . that's the real world," we tell them.

Students use all types of creativity at the Invention Convention. The program allows the student to apply what they have learned in school to issues in their own world. They are going to think the facts – measure, do calculations, get something to balance. They apply their learning about the center of gravity, moment of inertia, and electricity circuits. When they make their display board, they are using the concepts of aesthetic design, contrasting colors, and drawing skills. When they write, they are using the techniques of grammar, composition, and storytelling that they have learned.

When I was in elementary school, I was an annoying child. I was always raising my hand and asking, "Why do I have to know this?" I hated the usual response: "Because the school says so." It turned me off. But if I could see a relevance to my life, some value to me about what the teacher was presenting, then I would be interested in it. The Invention Convention takes this one step further. The students think to themselves, "If the facts I learned last year can be applied to a problem in my life this year then maybe stuff I'm learning this year will help me in the future, too!" The CIC actually changes the way students view school.

Perhaps most amazing to me is that in the CIC experience, the students seem to forget their limitations. I cannot tell you how many times I've had a teacher or parent come up to me and tell me that we've brought a child out of their own narrow world. Numerous times, after a student has explained their invention to me, I have been told that the student has Asperger's Syndrome and they have never been so animated or engaged before. All I can do is say, "Well, if they did it once, they can do it again!" The Invention Convention is all about the students finding and discovering themselves. It is their world, and they get to do what is important to them. Students get a chance to find other ways to express themselves, and this stays with them the rest of their lives.

Let's be honest: almost none of these students are going to win a Nobel Prize or achieve some other type of global acclaim. Most will stay in Connecticut and lead relatively ordinary yet meaningful lives. The students who end up in the Invention Convention State Finals are the ones who have done something in a way that adults think is appropriate. The display board is pretty and filled with info; the Invention Log is complete; the prototype actually works as advertised. So it is still an adult's view of the world, even if that adult is open and creative. In any given year, you can find inventions that will range from a simple netted bag to prevent socks from being lost in the wash to RFID sensors on hearing aids to prevent them from being accidentally washed at all. But the reality is that the students who really benefit are not the classic ones that always do well in school, but rather the real outliers. They might not do especially well in math or English, and on quizzes and tests. But in the world of their own problems that they can solve themselves, they see a whole new future. "I really like my invention. I thought what I did was good, I can do this." Especially for the inner city, low-income kids, it changes their outlook. Of these kids that do make it to the State Finals, they usually had no idea that UConn looked like that – they are only used to seeing a basketball court on TV. "It's like a CITY." "There are so many things to do." "I spoke with a real professor who showed me what engineers do!" For many students, it is their first opportunity to realize there is something to their life beyond the four walls they are living in.

The most telling evidence of this is the reaction when other people find out about what I do for a living. The CIC is in its 34th year now, and so we've had plenty of time for children to come full circle and grow up well beyond their school years. We have more than 300,000 adults who were in the CIC at some time in their childhood. They may not remember anything else they did in fourth grade, but they do remember the details of what they invented for the Invention Convention (and even what their friend invented). Some days I feel like a small-town doctor who has delivered everyone in town over 34 years.

For the teachers, the CIC is the most fun thing they do all year. Would you rather teach students to memorize spelling words or help them build something of their own design? CIC gives the teachers an opportunity to bring creativity into the classroom, and as such our program has always been teacher driven. Our curriculum enables teachers to address the needs of a standard education while bringing true creativity into the classroom. The CIC program allows teachers to "have their cake and eat it too."

What is different about the CIC program is that while we have a lot of rules and guidelines – shape, format, policy for how it works – we don't enforce any of them. We have suggestions and advice, but not mandates. Those putting on the program interpret the program as is best for their own school's circumstances and environment.

In school, before school, after school, weekends.

One grade, some grades, all grades.

One of the unique approaches of the CIC is its Judging Circles – peer review by other students as the inventors present their projects. We have materials that prescribe how to do the Judging Circle in their local school Invention Convention. But the reality? Some schools do it our way, in a tight U-shaped table format, some have it is scattered all over the cafeteria, some invite parents to take part, some invite other non-inventing students to ask questions during judging. Sometimes it is a circus and chaotic, but the parents love it, judges love it, and importantly, students love it; the inventors always get to show off their stuff, and to the people who matter the most to them. For this reason the CIC program works in every school. We give them the North Star, but they can choose their own path to it.

In the end, the strength of the Invention Convention is not the invention itself, but in the process the student goes through to create the invention. Since the inventions are designed and made by children, 99% of them are silly. No one would ever buy them. The real value is that we are teaching children how to solve problems. All good jobs for humans in the future are about problem solving. If you only push a button to do a task, robots will take that job. In the schools that run CIC programs, it is typically a science teacher coordinating it, but sometimes a history teacher, or an art teacher, and I've even seen a band leader in charge. I met with the band leader before he signed on and explained what we do: "We take things from all over the place and put them together in a way that solves a problem." His reply? "OMG, this is exactly what I do. I have all these kids making their own sounds that we put together into a composition, something that is great sound. We are inventing music. This is what I do all the time." Now he is running the CIC program in the music room and I am going to take credit for everything that his students will ever do in their lives.

I am very happy!

The Connecticut Invention Convention (CIC) is an award-winning, internationally recognized, 501(c)(3) educational organization started in 1983 as part of the Connecticut Educators Network for the Talented and Gifted. The program is open to K–8 students statewide, and is designed to develop, encourage, and enhance critical thinking skills through invention, innovation, and entrepreneurship. For more info, please visit www.ctinventionconvention.org

CHAPTER 3

Creativity and Shifting Roles of an Educational Leader
A Reflection of What Creativity Used to Mean to Me and What It Means Now

Larry Audet

Throughout my adult life I have inherently known that I possess qualities that are less prevalent in others. I am more comfortable with risk-taking, always curious, and have the ability to quickly and effectively assess an individual. Along with these traits, I have several dispositions. I have attraction to complexity, refrain from judgment, rely on my intuition, and have a willingness to accommodate opposite or conflicting points of view. It was not until I began to study creativity that I realized these traits and dispositions were subjects of creativity research (Amabile & Khaire, 2008; Barron & Harrington, 1981; Puccio & Grivas, 2009; Shalley & Gilson, 2004; Sternberg, 2007). As I gained knowledge about creativity, I began to understand that creativity was an important and natural part of me and affected my work as a school superintendent.

I was creative in my formative years, the time when I was learning to be a school leader. I was able to convert old ideas into new processes and products by testing my rhetoric on school principals and asking for their feedback. At some point, however, I realized that the reliance on the superintendent as the lone inventor was insufficient for solving the myriad of problems within a school district. Principals and teachers were closest to ideas about student learning and they were better equipped to help shape a system that expected creative outcomes in others. After making the decision to count on creative contributions from others, I began to offer creative leadership, the ability to lead for creativity in others.

I accepted responsibility for learning outside of the mainstream of traditional leadership because creativity could not be found in the department of educational leadership syllabi. I learned to become fluent in disparate discourses including motivational theory, creative leadership in the private sector, and traditional leadership in the public sector, all of which took years of experience to develop (C. Shalley & Gilson, 2004; Sternberg, 2007). My learning trajectory in acquiring skills necessary for creative leadership was at times painful and rewarding, laden with pitfalls and promise. The journey was not one that I would have chosen, the arc of this journey was not something I self-selected, but it was through learning from suffering and celebrating that I gained the wisdom necessary to become a thoughtful executive leader of creativity (Sternberg, 2006). I suffered from being isolated from my peers, being rejected by school boards, and feeling anxious about my relationships with those I supervised.

However, the more I learned about creativity, motivational theory, and myself, the more I noticed a change in the people who worked under my care. The most noticeable differences were my relationships with others and their psychological relationship with their work environment (Amabile, Conti, Coon, Lazenby, & Herron, 1996; Ekvall, 1983). Leaders throughout the district seemed more invigorated, and they became better at multiple aspects of their practice because their confidence and attitudes improved. Because I was counting on their creative contributions, they began acting on the belief that teachers were willing and capable of providing self-leadership, the intrinsically motivated behavior necessary for creativity. My personal passion for creativity began to scale to a district-wide value, cascading down to each level in the organization, and eventually found its way to students. The few principals and teachers in the district who were not able to authentically lead and teach for creativity made the decision to look for employment in other districts that remained steeped in the dogma of traditional education.

We became more intentional in the hiring process by offering employment contracts to people who possessed traits and dispositions of creative individuals. We offered provisions for individuals to work in groups and engage in problem-solving processes (Brophy, 2006; Choi & Thompson, 2005; Cooper & Jayatilaka, 2006; Cranston, 2011). We expected people to communicate with each other, to be open to new ideas, constructively challenge each other's work, trust and help each other, and feel committed to the work they were doing (Amabile, Burnside, & Gryskiewcz, 1995). These design teams worked together on a number of projects and solved important organizational problems. One creative idea included imagining, designing, and implementing a new schooling experience within our existing high school. The new school was named *My Life School.*

Several students were nominated to participate in this new schooling process based on their creative personality traits and dispositions. Teachers were allowed to take a principled risk by providing students with a large amount of autonomy in deciding what to do and how to go about accomplishing their work. They explained and helped our students understand the constraints between novelty (new ideas) and utility (appropriateness to the task at hand) (Runco, 2004). Students were initially asked to think about creativity in their lives and learn for the purpose of being prepared for life rather than for the sole purpose of test taking.

Teachers struggled with the shift from teacher to coach in their new relationship with students. Coaching was about supporting students and finding ways to encourage creativity and removing obstacles that impeded creativity. However, high expectations and continuous support yielded impressive results. Within the first eight days of school, students completed the small project: they developed a website and listed their interests and passions and cataloged required subject curriculum goals for graduation.

Before students began designing their long-term projects, teachers directed students to practice completing a simple project that required creative ideation. Once students came to grips with the shift in their learning, they began imagining a number of possibilities. Some students wanted to become social entrepreneurs and create new opportunities for student gatherings with the purpose of giving back to their schools and community. Others wanted to become small business entrepreneurs by designing new ways to increase commerce and add capital to the student body fund. Three students decided to build a skateboard park. My Lifer School's students, to the surprise of some teachers, took full responsibility for bridging their personal passions with prescribed learning goals.

Most students shifted their view on the role of the teacher. Teachers were viewed as a resource even if they were unable to coach students because of their lack of knowledge in domain-specific areas. The coaches who were unfamiliar with skateboard parks asked mentors in the local and larger community for help. Community mentors provided relevant feedback, and students' ideas became more clear and creative with additional feedback opportunities. Students were positively stimulated and their desire to solve problems became more interesting, involving, and personally challenging. Students reported that by integrating their passions with course curriculum and making their learning visible, they were more intrinsically motivated to persevere through challenging work. However, these students were not enrolled in a suburban school or charter school, nor did they come from families of wealth. Rather, these were rural students who were truly disadvantaged.

All students in this school district qualify for free lunch. Many students had low self- and creative efficacy and were in need of increasing their self-agency. One student came to the project feeling undereducated, with a broken spirit. As teachers learned to teach for creativity (Beghetto, 2010), the same creativity-enhancing forces described in the business sector stimulated students to take a conscious act that required a leap from the known to alternatives (Pickard, 1990). One student, who was heading toward failure, designed and built a skateboard park and earned all the requirements for graduation by integrating required learning standards into his project. By the end of the year, he applied for and was accepted into a business college and is currently enrolled in the department of innovation and entrepreneurship. The shift within this student seems to be scalable because everyone has creative potential.

Organizational creativity is a phenomenon that relies on commitment rather than compliance. It begins at the top and relies on a leader who acts with an enduring belief in the goodness of people and is willing let go of control. Creativity is built on being able to explore, which is a crucial thing to remember when considering students, their classroom, their school, and across their district. Organizational creativity can occur in schools with populations of the affluent and the poor, rural and urban. If the same provisions were available for those who learn and teach in other schools, you would see the same eventual blossoming of ideas.

REFERENCES

Amabile, T. M., Burnside, R. M., & Gryskiewcz, S. M. (1995). User's guide for KEYS: Assessing the clmate for creativity. The Center for Creative Leadership.

Amabile, T. M., Conti, R., Coon, H., Lazenby, J., & Herron, M. (1996). Assessing the work environment for creativity. *The Academy of Management Journal*, **39**(5), 1154.

Amabile, T. M., & Khaire, M. (2008). Creativity and the role of the leader. *Harvard Business Review*, **86**(10), 100–109.

Barron, F., & Harrington, D. M. (1981). Creativy, intelligence, and personality. *Annual Review of Psychology*, **32**(1), 439–476.

Beghetto, R. A. (2010). Creativity in the classroom. In *The Cambridge Handbook of Creativity* (pp. 447–463). New York: Cambridge University Press.

Brophy, D. R. (2006). A comparison of individual and group efforts to creatively solve contrasting types of problems. *Creativity Research Journal*, **18**(3), 293–315.

Choi, H.-S., & Thompson, L. (2005). Old wine in a new bottle: Impact of membership change on group creativity. *Organizational Behavior and Human Decision Processes*, **98**(2), 121–132.

Cooper, R., & Jayatilaka, B. (2006). Group creativity: The effects of extrinsic, intrinsic, and obligation motivations. *Creativity Research Journal*, **18**(2), 153–172.

Cranston, J. (2011). Relational trust: The glue that binds a professional learning community. *Alberta Journal of Educational Research*, **57**(1), 59–72.

Ekvall, G. (1983). Climate, structure and innovativeness of organizations: A theoretical framework and experiement. The Swedish Council for Management and Work Life Issues.

Pickard, E. (1990). Toward a theory of creative potential. *Journal of Creative Behavior*, **24**(1), 1–9.

Puccio, G., & Grivas, C. (2009). Examining the relationship between personality traits and creativity styles. *Creativity and Innovation Management*, **18**(4), 247–255.

Runco, M. A. (2004). Creativity. *Annual Review of Psychology*, **55**(1), 657–687.

Shalley, C., & Gilson, L. (2004). What leaders need to know: A review of social and contextual factors that can foster or hinder creativity. *The Leadership Quarterly*, **15**(1), 33–53.

Sternberg, R. J. (2006). Creative leadership: It's a decision. *Leadership*, 36–37.

Sternberg, R. J. (2007). *Wisdom, Intelligence, and Creativity Synthesized* (1st ed.). New York: Cambridge University Press.

CHAPTER 4

What I Used to Think about Creativity in Schools

Tim Patston

Geelong Grammar School

Life can take you on strange and interesting journeys. When I was at an all-boys state school in Australia in the 1960s and 1970s, life seemed predetermined. The smart kids went to a place called university to be smart, and the dumb kids (there were only two types of child at my school) went and did a trade. Knowing now how much it costs to get an electrician or plumber these days, I wonder about this system . . .

Creativity happened in the Art Department, where a very exotic woman, with long hair and flowing robes, smelling of an exotic substance called patchouli oil, entranced those who were "gifted" with her ability to make pictures or pots out of thin air. As I had no aptitude for pottery or drawing, I accepted that this would always be so. There seemed to be a correlation between art and surfing at my school, or perhaps between art and long hair, I was not certain. My form of expression at school was to be in the school musical. This was not seen as being creative, unless you painted the sets. Learning dialogue and songs was hard, dedicated work, as was learning choreography. I never thought of this as a creative activity, merely a process from learning to performance which was a lot of fun.

Upon leaving school I began to participate in amateur musicals, meeting, for the first time, the "creative types." These highly idiosyncratic individuals seemed to spend their days as accountants or public servants, only to transform twice a week, in the evening, into what seemed to me to be parodies of the characters we were portraying – flamboyant and exotic, with extravagant hand gestures, and highly affected voices with an indeterminate accent which was part Royal Shakespeare, part working-class Australian with pinched vowels. Creativity seemed to belong in the local halls of Australian suburbia, an outlet from the banality of the workplace, unchanged from the industrial revolution in its conformity to the norm.

What I Now Think about Creativity in Schools

In 2016 my life has (fortunately) moved on. I hold the position of Coordinator of Creativity and Innovation at one of this country's oldest and most prestigious private schools. Such a job could not have existed even five years ago; I am the first person to hold this position. What then are the parameters of my work?

Firstly, I am not in the Art Department, nor Drama or Music (or the department which builds and paints sets). I do not wear a loud suit and spinning bowtie to work. I am at pains to appear neither flamboyant nor exotic. I am, in fact, in no department, yet every department. My role is threefold:

1. to research current theories of creativity and innovation, and determine their relevance to school education;
2. to observe and analyse creative and innovative practices currently in place;
3. to introduce, trial and assess creativity and innovation in the school environment, both in terms of a workplace and in teaching and learning.

My current understanding is as follows:

Published theories of creativity currently lie predominantly in four areas; the Arts, Engineering, Business and Psychology. There is currently no dominant model of creativity in education. While there is some common ground between the aforementioned disciplines, there is a lack of definitional congruence. Accordingly, there is no standardised measure of creativity. Creativity is yet to develop its own version of the IQ test (and all of the problems associated with such a measure).

Accordingly, I am at the start of a new journey, with some maps written by others, often in a language I don't understand, taking me to a destination which is, as yet, undetermined. In other words, my job is the perfect metaphor for creativity and innovation.

At this early stage I am looking at how creativity can be utilized throughout the education process. Teachers in this school are exploring. They are exploring creative ways to develop curriculum, beginning by focusing on their strengths as a teacher – their style, their personality and their preferred modalities of delivery. They then expand their orbit to look at the same aspects of their students, and tailor a curriculum which complements. Creativity and innovation can be applied to matters as diverse as timetabling, teaching spaces, the costs and benefits of trying vertical and horizontal peer instruction, and forms of assessment.

Teachers can begin asking questions such as "Is there a 'creativity slump' between primary and secondary schools, and, if so, is it caused by standardised testing, teaching by separate subjects, or simply a reflection of the psychosexual development of the students?" or "If a middle school classroom looked like a teenager's bedroom, would students learn more effectively?" They can then explore the answers to such pressing questions.

There is consensus in the creativity literature that risk taking is a necessary part of the creative process. Teachers are, for the most part, conservative, particularly in private education. A creative school requires two major shifts in teacher thinking. Teachers need to accept that risk and failure are as much a part of teaching as they are a part of learning. A lesson which does not go well should be explained to, rather than hidden from, students. Secondly, all teachers need to become experts in reflective practice. Most teachers are comfortable observing and critiquing students. They are comfortable observing and critiquing other teachers. They are significantly less comfortable at observing and critiquing themselves. The idea of creative self-critique needs to be explored.

A creative school has many facets. It should be flexible and responsive, not bound by dogma and standardised testing. It should acknowledge the humanity of teachers and students in terms of both creativity and fallibility. Creativity is for all students at all levels, and for all teachers in all subjects. Schools can only graduate creative students if they have creative teachers.

PART II

Voices from the Research

CHAPTER 5

Developing Creativity Across All Areas of the Curriculum

Joseph Renzulli

Imagination grows by exercise.

W. Somerset Maugham

This chapter will deal with two aspects of providing teachers with guidance about encouraging more creative thinking in their classrooms. The first part will focus on a few basic principles and strategies underlying creativity training and how these principles and strategies can lead us in the more practical task of developing creativity- training exercises. This section uses a "learn-by-doing" approach and will prepare you for the more advanced challenge of developing your own activities.

The second part of the chapter focuses on using the basic principles of creative thinking to develop your own activities. In this section you will be asked to examine any and all topics that are part of the regular curriculum or prescribed curricular standards and to design and infuse creative thinking activities into standards based curricular topics. This section is purposefully designed to develop your own creativity, and by so doing you will not only be enriching the regular curriculum for your students but also modeling the creative process for them.

PART 1: BASIC PRINCIPLES AND START-UP ACTIVITIES

Three Major Starting Points. Although a great deal has been written about fostering creativity in classrooms, relatively few basic teaching strategies have been effective in encouraging creative development. The starting point for teachers who would like to promote more creative behaviors in their students is a basic understanding of the difference between convergent and divergent production. In most traditional teaching-learning situations, major emphasis is placed on locating or *converging* on correct answers. Teachers raise questions and present problems with a predetermined response in mind, and students' performance is usually evaluated in terms of the correctness of a particular answer and the speed and accuracy with which youngsters respond to verbal or written exercises. Thus, the types of problems raised by the teacher or textbook and the system of rewards used to evaluate student progress cause most youngsters to develop a mindset that is oriented toward zeroing in on the "right" answer as quickly and efficiently as possible. Although this ability has its place in the overall development of the learner, most teachers would agree that impressionable young minds also need opportunities to develop their rare and precious creative thinking abilities.

Divergent production provides these opportunities, as it is a kind of thinking that is characterized by breaking away from conventional restrictions on thinking and letting one's mind flow across a broad range of ideas and possible solutions to a problem. These are the kinds of thinking that literally have enabled people to change the world, and we can do more in our schools to prepare young people to bring about changes in small or large ways.

The real problems humanity confronts do not have the kinds of predetermined or "pat" answers on which a great deal of traditional instruction focuses. Yet we give our students very few opportunities to practice letting their minds range far and wide over a broad spectrum of possible solutions to open-ended questions or problems. The philosopher Alan Watts (1964) has talked about these two kinds of thinking in terms of what he calls the "spotlight mind" and the "floodlight mind." The spotlight mind focuses on a clearly defined area and cannot see the many alternative possibilities or solutions to a problem that may exist outside that well-defined area.

Floodlight thinking, on the other hand, reaches upward and outward without clearly defined borders or limitations. The floodlight thinker is free to let his or her imagination wander without the confinements or limitations that usually lead to conformity. Both types of thinking are valuable, and to pursue one at the expense of the other is clearly a disservice to the young people for whose development we are responsible. This description of divergent thinking should not lead teachers to believe that opportunities for creative thinking are undisciplined or disorderly. Meeker (1969) has pointed out that "divergent generation does not proceed willy-nilly; the divergent thinker is not a scatterbrain; the worthwhile generation of information requires discipline and guidance" (p. 32).

A second starting point to providing teachers with guidance about encouraging more creative thinking in their classrooms is crafting a classroom atmosphere where divergent thinking is valued, where teachers model divergent thinking by asking open-ended questions and encouraging their

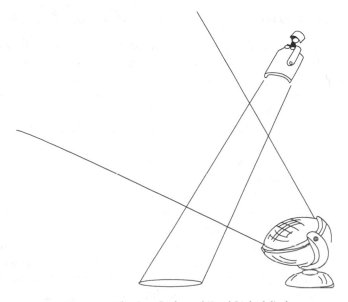

Figure 5.1 The Spot Light and Food Light Mind

students to do the same thing. In describing the role of teachers in this regard, Starko (1995) emphasized the distinction between teaching for the development of creativity and creative teaching. She concluded that effective teachers who develop students' creative thinking know how to use techniques that "facilitate creative thinking across disciplines and provide a classroom atmosphere that is supportive of creativity" (p. 17). Other studies, including a meta-analysis study by Rose and Lin (1984) and a research synthesis by Torrance (1987), indicate that training in divergent thinking is associated with increased creativity, involvement in creative activities, and positive feelings toward school.

The third and perhaps most important starting point is that teachers themselves must become more creative, not in the sense of becoming artists or poets or inventors (which they very well might want to pursue), but in *the creative act of teaching*. Therefore, a focus of this chapter is on applying the basic strategies of creativity training to curriculum modifications in their classrooms. Gandhi once said, "You must be the change you wish to see in the world." I would like to modify this quote slightly by saying that: "You [the teacher] must be the change that you wish to see in your students." In other words, the things you do in your teaching will reflect examples of the creative process in action.

A Quick Overview of the Basic Principles and Strategies

In most cases, the first thought that comes to mind in seeking the solution to a difficult problem is seldom the most original idea. Therefore, *fluency*, defined as the ability to produce several ideas or possible solutions to a problem situation, is an important condition for creative production. The fluency principle, which underlies the development of most creativity training, maintains that fluency is a necessary, though not sufficient, condition for originality. Although there are some cases on record of highly creative products that have resulted from sudden inspirations, research on creativity in both children and adults strongly supports the fluency principle. Studies by Archambault (1970), Paulus (1970), and Baer (1996) have shown that initial responses to a given problem tend to be the more common or ordinary ones, and that the greater the number of responses generated in a problem-solving situation, the higher the probability of producing an original response (*original* in the sense that fewer students come up with that response). Therefore, a hypothetical curve of creativity for a given task or activity would show a gently sloping incline, with an increase in originality being related to an increase in the number of responses. For example, if we asked a group of students to list all of the utensils that people *might* use to eat with, their initial responses would no doubt include common utensils such as forks, spoons, and knives. But if we encouraged them to increase their lists by using their imaginations ("Suppose you didn't have any forks or spoons. What *could* you use?"), students would begin to explore some possible alternatives. They might suggest such items as sharpened sticks, shells, and bottle caps. If we compared the lists of several youngsters, we would find that most of the initial answers are quite common and that most of the students have given the same responses. As the lists grow longer, we would find more divergence occurring, and the probability of a youngster's producing an original response increasing. In other words, quantity generates quality, and research has shown that individuals who produce a large number of ideas are more likely to produce ideas that are more original (Bousfield & Barclay, 1950; Derks & Hervas, 1988; Runco, 1986). Originality is defined in research and, indeed, in most real-life situations as a statistical rarity. If everyone in our example above says that knife, fork, and spoon are eating utensils, we would not consider these responses to be statistically rare. But if only one student said that a bottle cap could be used as an eating utensil, we can consider this response creative because of its statistical infrequency in this particular problem-solving situation.

The questions you raise in your classroom can capitalize on the fluency principle by including a number of activities that generate a large number of responses. In opposition to the techniques of convergent production discussed earlier, these exercises should have no "right" or predetermined correct answer. Rather, they should be designed to encourage the student to produce a large quantity of responses, and hopefully, practice in this mode of thinking will help free the learner from previously acquired habits of mind, which predispose him or her to rely mainly on recall and convergent thinking.

The basic technique for increasing fluency of expression is called *brainstorming*. The first step in this process is to provide students with a problem that has many possible alternative solutions. Brainstorming can be carried out individually or in group sessions. During the early stages of a brainstorming activity, students should write or verbalize *all* thoughts and ideas that come to mind, no matter how silly, way-out, or wild the ideas may be. The best way to promote free-wheeling and offbeat thinking is to value quantity and withhold criticism and evaluation until students have exhausted their total supply of ideas related to a given problem. At that time you may then ask students to explain a response if you are unclear about the relevance of the response to the problem being addressed. This practice, known as the principle of deferred judgment (or unevaluated practice), simply means that judgment is deferred until the individual has had an opportunity to explore several possible answers or solutions to a given problem. The principle of deferred judgment, first elaborated on by Osborn (1963), has consistently been shown to be an essential ingredient for creative thinking. Several researchers (Amabile, 1985; Baer, 1996) have found evidence to support this claim. The main purpose of unevaluated practice is to free children from the fear of making mistakes.

The following is a list of general questions (adapted from Arnold 1962) that can be used to spur students' thinking during brainstorming sessions:

Other Uses
> Can it be put to other uses as is?
> Can it be put to other uses if it is modified?

Adaptation
> What else is like it?
> What other ideas does it suggest?
> What could you copy?
> Whom could you imitate?

Modification
> What new twist can you make?
> Can you change the color, size, shape, motion, sound, form, and odor?

Magnification
> What could you add?
> Can you add more time, strength, height, length, thickness, value?
> Can you duplicate or exaggerate it?

Minification
> Can you make it smaller, shorter, lighter, lower?
> Can you divide it up or omit certain parts?

Substitution
> Who else can do it?
> What can be used instead?
> Can you use other ingredients or materials?
> Can you use another source of power, another place, another process?
> Can you use another tone of voice?

Rearrangement
> Can you interchange parts?
> Can you use a different plan, pattern, or sequence?
> Can you change the schedule or rearrange cause and effect?

Reversibility
> Can you turn it backward or upside down?
> Can you reverse roles or do the opposite?

Combination
> Can you combine parts or ideas?
> Can you blend things together?
> Can you combine purposes?

These are only some of the questions that teachers and students can use to stimulate creative thinking during brainstorming. Once students have learned the basic brainstorming technique, you should encourage them to approach each activity with an idea-finding frame of reference. As a general rule, you should always encourage students to go as far as they can to come up with many answers to an open-ended question and use probing questions such as the above to extend brainstorming activity.

Getting Started

If you have not previously carried out creativity training activities, a good way to get started is to walk students through an activity that demonstrates the difference between convergent and divergent thinking. The following sample activity has been purposefully designed to teach this distinction.

> *Today we are going to begin practicing a different kind of thinking. This kind of thinking will help us learn how to explore many different kinds of solutions to a given problem. Some problems and questions have only one right answer, but there are also many problems and questions that have hundreds of possible answers.*
>
> *Suppose I asked you, "Who was the first president of the United States?"* (Wait for an answer and write it on the white board.)
>
> *Are there any other possible answers to this question?* (General conclusion should be negative.)
>
> *Now suppose I were to ask you, "What are all of the possible ways that you might have come to school this morning?"* (Call on youngsters and list responses on the white board.)
>
> Students will probably give some fairly common responses ("walk," "bus," "car," "bicycle"). At this point, you might say:

Remember, I said all of the possible ways that you might have come. Use your imagination. Let your mind wander, even if you think the method for coming to school is silly or unusual. How about by donkey or pogo stick? (Add these to the list on the board.) You can emphasize this point by grabbing a yardstick (conveniently placed nearby beforehand) and improvise with a few hops to demonstrate a pogo stick. Students will no doubt become a little noisy and even express some laughter, but it is very important to tolerate these reactions. If you hush them, the whole atmosphere of freedom you want to create will be lost, and they will subjectively think that this new kind of thinking is the same old "right answer" game.

This point is extremely crucial to introducing creativity training to your students. By suggesting the donkey and the pogo stick, you have accomplished three very important objectives. First, you have conveyed the idea that answers need not be feasible, practical, or realistic. Second, you have let youngsters know that you will accept these kinds of answers. Third and perhaps most important, you have let the youngsters know that you are capable of some way-out ideas.

After your examples, students may give a wide variety of answers. Let them call out their answers (rather than raising hands) as you write them on the board. Prompt students if necessary:

> *Are there any other ways that you might come to school?*
> *How about on an airplane or in a rocket?*

A second crucial factor at this point is the generous use of praise on your part. Enthusiastic comments such as "good," "great," and "fantastic" will help youngsters open up. Do not call on students who are not taking part. It takes some youngsters longer than others to trust the teacher and their classmates in this type of atmosphere. The main idea is to let students know that you like what is going on and that you are having fun. When the flow of responses begins to slow down, say:

> *Let's go one step farther. Suppose you could change your size or shape. Can you think of some other ways that you might possibly come to school?*

If no one responds, say: *Could you make yourself very tiny and come in your brother's lunch box? Could you change to a drop of water and come in through the drinking fountain? Could you come in as an app in your friend's cell phone?*

Continue to fill the board as long as the youngsters are generating responses. When you finally call a halt, say:

> *I guess there really are many questions and problems that have several possible answers. Is the question different from the one about the first president of the United States? Do you think this kind of thinking is fun?*

This activity is an excellent way of teaching students the difference between convergent and divergent thinking without dwelling on the rituals of a formal definition.

Next, you might want to say: *From time to time, we are going to be working on some activities like the one we just did. The main purpose of these activities will be to practice answering questions and solving problems that have many possible answers. We will be using our imaginations to come up with some clever new ideas.*

The Principle of Mild Competition

Although a great deal has been written about the dangers of high-pressure competition in the classroom, research with various curricular materials has shown that *mild* competition is a positive nutrient in motivating students to become involved in learning activities. The use of simulations and learning games to promote learning is based on the finding that game-like activity is one of the child's preferred ways of learning (Connolly, Boyle, MacArthur, Hainey, & Boyle, 2012). Several researchers have investigated the relationship between children's play and creativity. For example, Li (1985) found significant gains in preschool children's creativity after being exposed to play training. Mellou (1995) examined the literature on the relationship between dramatic play and creativity and concluded that most of the research supports a positive relationship between them, noting the alternative symbolic constructions and flexibility common to both. In a research synthesis on creativity processes in children that are predictive of adult creativity, Russ (1996) also concluded that the relationship between children's play and creativity is strong.

We have made an attempt to capitalize on the motivational benefits of game-like activity by suggesting that certain exercises be carried out under mildly competitive conditions. This approach will introduce an element of excitement into the program and give youngsters an opportunity to pursue classroom activities in their preferred manner of learning. To avoid the dangers associated with high-pressure competition, you should use caution when employing the mildly competitive mode. You should observe the following general rules whenever you introduce competition into creativity training activities.

1. Group competition should be used rather than individual competition.
2. Grades or other material rewards should never be associated with competitive activities. Students will derive satisfaction from the competitiveness itself and the excitement of winning or trying to win.
3. Teams should continually be rearranged in a way that allows all youngsters an opportunity to be on a winning team.

You will, of course, have to experiment to determine the best ways for operating in the mildly competitive mode. A good deal of the art of teaching is in knowing your students and in using classroom management procedures that are especially applicable to a given group.

A general strategy that you can use in follow-up discussions is intergroup competition. Prior to assigning a particular exercise or after an exercise has been completed, divide the class into several small groups that can then compete with each other on the basis of: (1) the greatest number of team responses, and (2) the most original responses (i.e., statistically rare responses that other teams did not think of). A team's score would consist of one point for the total number of responses generated by all team members (including duplications) minus a given number of points for each response that appears on another team's list. Slowly increasing the number of points for unusual responses will encourage the students to strive for originality as well as quantity of responses. Students might like to keep a scorecard on the bulletin board to record team progress. Competitive follow-up activity of this type is probably most appropriate for exercises that emphasize the quantity of responses rather than the production of a story, invention, or piece of artwork.

The Principle of Cooperation

Researchers have found that activities involving team collaboration help youngsters increase their creative productivity (Fleming, Mingo, & Chen, 2007). You should allow students to work on some activities in pairs or in small groups, and students should direct their efforts toward the production of group as well as individual responses. Group activities provide an opportunity for youngsters to "piggyback"[1] on other students' responses and learn cooperation and the benefits of bringing several minds to bear on a particular problem. They also provide opportunities for you to develop leadership skills and help less creative youngsters experience success by working cooperatively with more highly creative individuals. Since you can use many of the activities in the data base mentioned above for both individual and group work, it is important for you to review each activity before using it with students. Field tests have shown that the teacher is the best judge of the conditions under which the class works best, and therefore the teacher should decide when it is best to use creativity training activities with individuals, groups, or both.

The Importance of Classroom Atmosphere

The success of any creativity training program depends on the amount of freedom and flexibility that exists in the classroom. The very nature of creativity requires that students be allowed to express their thoughts and ideas in a warm and open atmosphere. Teachers should encourage their students to play with ideas, laugh, and have fun without worrying about being graded and evaluated when they are engaged in creativity-training activities. Rogers (1969) emphasized the importance of freedom from the threat of evaluation and asserted that creativity can be fostered by establishing psychological safety through the unconditional acceptance of each individual's worth. When you encourage youngsters to express themselves in an uninhibited manner, it is extremely important that you also provide them with a climate that is free from external evaluation and the critical judgments so often associated with schoolwork. The importance

---

[1] "Piggybacking" simply means that the response of one person gives rise to a response(s) on the part(s) of others.

of providing this free climate is supported by the research of Amabile (1996) and Lepper, Greene, and Nisbet (1973) who found that extrinsic motivation undermines students' creativity, and Amabile identified factors of intrinsic motivation that impact students' performance on creative tasks. Since no right answers are prescribed for this type of creativity training, students have the opportunity to work in an open atmosphere without the constant threat of failure hanging over their heads.

The most effective way to open up the classroom atmosphere is to minimize formal evaluation and lead students in the direction of self-evaluation. In the real world, people often judge things in terms of self-satisfaction and the degree to which they, as individuals, like or dislike the things they do, the products they purchase, the books they read, or the products they produce. The only way that we can teach students to become self-evaluators is to give them numerous opportunities to judge their own work and to modify their work when they are not satisfied with it. On occasion, peer reactions may spur further originality. For example, you might say: *"Of all the examples about the best ways to come to school today, which one(s) do you think were the most original?"*

As mentioned earlier, unevaluated practice simply means that judgment is deferred until the individual has had an opportunity to explore several possible answers or solutions to a given problem. Creating such an atmosphere in the classroom is far easier said than done, but there are some specific strategies that teachers can use to help promote an environment that is more supportive of creativity. The most important strategy is to be tolerant and respectful of children's ideas, questions, and products. You should show interest, acceptance, and excitement toward student responses and avoid expressions of shock, surprise, annoyance, or disinterest. Above all, never laugh at or make light of a youngster's responses, and try to discourage teasing and laughter from other students. Healthy amusement and friendly competition will help promote a supportive atmosphere, but ridicule and scowls will have a negative effect. Each student must come to believe that his or her ideas are as valuable as the ideas of others. One of the hardest things to control in the classroom is the spontaneous laughter that may arise when a student says something that is somewhat unusual. A good way to overcome this problem is to legitimatize laughter by showing students that you also have some way-out ideas and that you do not mind if the students laugh when you express them. If you demonstrated an improvised pogo stick as suggested in the Getting Started section earlier in the chapter, you undoubtedly noted an expressive reaction on the parts of your students. This activity has been found to be an extremely effective way to legitimatize laughter and show students that you are not afraid to express unusual ideas or actions. Whenever possible, participate in written and oral activities and set the pace by contributing your own unusual responses. Your contributions will help students realize that you are a human being and that you are not afraid to express yourself freely. Remember, you set the limits on student behavior. If you actually participate in creative activities, students will learn that you value your own creative behavior, and they will quickly begin to display their own creative thoughts.

Another strategy aimed at promoting an environment that encourages students to be creative involves the principle of rewarding desired types of responses. If you show generous praise for quantity and unusualness of responses, students will quickly recognize the types of behavior that you value and they will strive to achieve these types of behaviors.

You can increase creative production by combining the fluency principle with the reward principle and the principle of unevaluated practice. In follow-up discussions to creativity-training activities, you should praise individual responses and give generous praise to the sheer quantity of response. Remember that an increase in fluency will almost always result in a corresponding increase in flexibility and originality. Consequently, you should develop a repertoire of enthusiastic fluency-producing comments, such as: *"That's really good. Can you think of a few more?"* and *"Let's see who can come up with five more possible titles for Bill's picture."* Don't be afraid to make up a few new words (for example, *"fantabulous,"* *"super-great"*) to show your enthusiasm. Gently probing youngsters for more and more responses will help them develop a fluency mindset, and hopefully, practice in this mode of thinking will carry over to other areas of learning and experience.

You should make every effort to avoid using phrases or expressions that are natural "killers" of creativity. Examples of such phrases include:

> Don't be silly.
> Let's be serious.
> That's ridiculous.
> Quiet down.
> The principal won't like it.
> Let's be practical.
> You should know better.
> What's the matter with you?
> That's not our problem.
> We've tried that before.

That's not part of your assignment.
That's childish.
A good idea but . . .
It won't work.
Don't be so sloppy.

One of the underlying purposes of creativity training is to help youngsters learn how to evaluate their own creative products. One of the great tragedies of traditional school instruction is that students almost always look to the teacher for evaluation and approval. By so doing, they fail to develop a system of internal self-evaluation. And yet, psychological studies have revealed that each person has a need to be his or her own primary evaluator. The nature of creativity is such that the individual produces something that is new, unique, or novel for him or her at a particular point in time (Beghetto & Kaufman, 2007). To break away from social pressure toward ordinary and common production, a person must place his or her own opinions and feelings above those of others. He or she must be satisfied with his or her products and feel that they express a part of his or her feeling, thoughts, and ideas.

One of the primary goals of developing creativity is for teachers to prepare young people to learn how to make judgments about their own work. This task is undoubtedly one of the most difficult challenges of teaching, but there are a few simple guides that you can use to help students evaluate their own work. When students look to you for judgment, you might ask:

What do you think about it?
Do you feel good about it?
Would you like to work on it some more?
Why do you like (or dislike) it?
What things (criteria) are important to you?
How would you compare it to the work you did last time?

Encourage students to compare their own products by ranking them and selecting the ones they like best. Students should learn that you respect their judgment and will not overrule that judgment by placing your evaluation above their own. This behavior does not mean that you should not comment and make suggestions, especially about the relevance of a student response to the problem or question being addressed. Students should always be given an opportunity to explain relevance in their own words. But they should also understand that you are stating your opinion and there is no reason to assume that it is more important than theirs. Since there are no right answers to creativity exercises, and since students should not be graded on their creativity or creative products, training activities provide a real opportunity for students to develop self-evaluation techniques. The key word in this process is *trust*. If students think that you will consider their creative activities in their final grades, they will constantly look to you for what they believe to be the ultimate source of judgment.

Peer evaluation can also provide students with a source of feedback. This feedback should always be informal, and it should be related to the type of product involved. For example, in writing a humorous ending for an unfinished story activity or a cartoon caption-writing activity designed to stimulate humor, the amount of laughter the student elicits from the class is the best kind of real-world assessment that one can receive. You should encourage students to add their own praise to other children's responses, and their spontaneous reactions should be a regular part of all follow-up discussions.

A final consideration in the creation of a free and open classroom atmosphere is the acceptance of humor and playfulness. When you purposefully ask youngsters to strive for clever and unusual responses, a good deal of healthy noise and whimsical behavior is likely to result. The creative adult has the same uninhibited expressiveness and spontaneity found in happy and secure children. Creativity time should be a fun time, and playfulness, impulsiveness, humor, and spontaneity are all part of having fun.

PART 2: CREATIVITY APPLIED: DEVELOPING YOUR OWN ACTIVITIES THROUGH AN INFUSION-BASED APPROACH TO CURRICULAR MODIFICATION

This section deals with an *infusion*-based approach to promoting creativity within the context of the standards-based or "regular curriculum." We do not criticize or recommend throwing out basic curriculum, current practices, programs, or projects if they are currently producing positive results in *both* achievement and joyful learning. Rather, the approach recommended here attempts to strike a balance between traditional approaches to learning and approaches that promote creative thinking skills, hands-on learning, and original thinking on the parts of all students. Our goals are to minimize boredom and school "turn-offs" and to improve achievement and creative productivity by infusing what I call the Three E's – Enjoyment, Engagement, and Enthusiasm for learning – into the culture and atmosphere of a school, the tool bags of teachers and administrators, and the mindsets of students.

An Infusion-Based Approach simply means that teachers will (1) examine opportunities to create and select highly engaging *open-ended activities* related to particular topics; (2) infuse these activities into the curriculum to make the topics more interesting; and (3) provide support and encouragement for individuals and small groups who would like to extend their pursuit of the teacher-designed activities. The infusion process described here is your opportunity to apply the material described earlier in the chapter to your own challenge of becoming a more creative teacher.

A few examples will show how this Infusion-Based Approach works. A Creative Idea Generator that uses the following guidelines is distributed to individuals or small groups of teachers, and they are asked to focus on a topic within their prescribed curriculum that is generally based on acquiring and memorizing facts, concepts, or other forms of received knowledge. Teachers are asked to keep in mind the concepts listed above (Other Uses, Adaptation, Modification, etc.)[2] and apply as many of the following criteria as possible to the brainstorming process.

1. The activity has a relationship to one or more regular curriculum topics.
2. There is not a single, predetermined correct answer or solution to the problem raised in the activity.
3. The activity consists of something students do rather than sit and listen to.
4. The activity is fun for most students.
5. The activity should lead to some form of product development on the parts of students who show an interest in the topic.
6. The activity has various levels of challenge to which interested students can escalate if they would like to creatively extend the interest through follow-up activity.

The examples that follow illustrate how the generator has been used by teachers to infuse creative activities into regular curricular topics. Figure 5.2 is an example of how a group of teachers used the Creative Idea Generator to brainstorm interesting creativity and thinking skills activities that could be infused into a typical memory-oriented curricular topic in geography.

The teachers in this example were required to have their students memorize the names of all the states and capitals in the United States. To make the assignment more interesting, they brainstormed potential activities related

[2] It is a good idea to have printed copies or a poster with these concepts readily available while brainstorming.

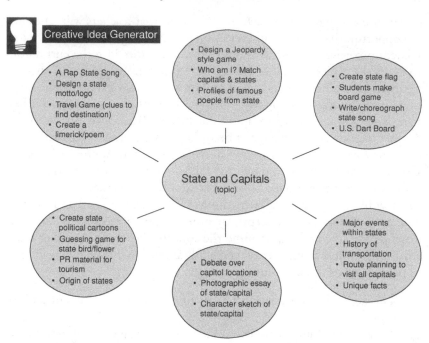

Figure 5.2 Creative Idea Generator (Geography).

to this topic and gave their students an opportunity to select an activity that the latter would like to pursue based on their interests and learning styles. One group of students interested in music chose to develop a rap song for their state's official anthem. Another group interested in history decided to develop historic site maps, posters, and travel brochures for a state they had visited or would like to visit some day. A third group used state-shaped cookie cutters to make an edible map of the United States, using chocolate bits to designate the locations of each state's capital. This group was so enthusiastic that they extended their work by starting a small cookie-making business. They visited other classrooms, accepted donations that were used to buy supplies for the school store, and provided brief historical facts and points of interest about some of the states in which other students expressed an interest. This follow-up is a good example of the creative extension mentioned in Guideline No. 6 above.

A second example of how the Creative Idea Generator was used by a group of primary grade teachers to make the topic of teaching the alphabet more interesting and creativity oriented is presented in Figure 5.3. In this

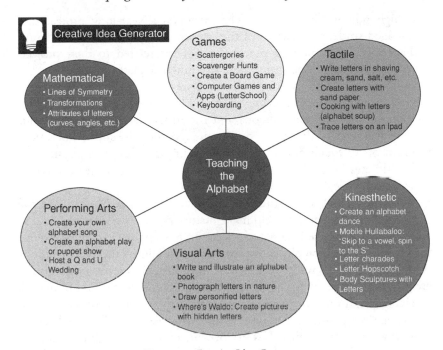

Figure 5.3 Creative Idea Generator.

case the teachers were in a school that had adopted Howard Gardner's well-known work on Multiple Intelligences (Gardner's, 1983) as a school-wide theme. Note that the suggested activities listed in Figure 5.3 range across several levels of complexity, but that all activities provide students with an opportunity to engage in some level of the creative process related to learning the alphabet. Also note how the several intelligences of Gardner's theory are accommodated.

Additional examples can be found in the brief descriptions of teachers who used the Creative Idea Generator to infuse open-ended activities into various subject areas at different grade levels. A middle grade math teacher had her students develop fictional fantasy baseball cards and analyze the players' statistics to facilitate the drafting and trading of players while building their own teams. One group of students drew caricatures of their players and a "Player Wheel" with geometric representations of player's strengths and weaknesses was created, and they used the player wheel to play against other students' teams. A regular season schedule was set for the class, ending with a World Series game to decide the classroom champion.

A high school AP Physics teacher assigned a year-long project that encouraged students to use all of the concepts they covered in each unit of his course to addressing practical problems related to their project. A recent project by one group was to launch a platform containing a video camera, a GPS tracking unit, and weather data-gathering instruments into space. The platform was carried high above the Earth's surface by helium-filled weather balloons and the instruments gathered various types of atmospheric data while the camera recorded the entire experiment from lift off to touch down. Numerous examples of applied physics and real-world creative problem solving took place throughout the duration of this year-long project.

A middle school social studies teacher covering U.S. history used the Creative Idea Generator to help make history come alive. Her idea was to ask students to use the Internet to select and portray one person of interest for a Night of The Notables showcase event highlighting the lives of famous Americans from all walks of life (art, government, sports, pop culture, etc.). Students were required to research the life of the person, develop a 30-second "Who Am I" guessing game about their famous person, design a costume, prepare artifacts representing the person's life, and become that person for the evening. History became more meaningful as students created scenarios about their assumed identities, answered questions for parents and other students attending the showcase, and related information about the lives of the persons they selected to portray. They were not allowed to step out of character for the entire evening. This creative idea was so successful that other teachers in the school district adopted it for use in their own classrooms.

Using Technology to Enhance the Infusion Process

We now have the tools to easily infuse engaging material and creative activities into the curriculum because of changes taking place in technology that have given us the potential to make formal learning a different process than it was a decade or two ago. Today's young people are digital learners and emerging masters of interactive media technology. Traditional ways of learning, even under the best of circumstances, cannot compete with students who find texting under their desks more engaging than listening to their teachers and professors or memorizing factual material for a forthcoming test.

Another development in technology that will aid infusion is the almost unlimited amount of information that is now available through the

Internet. Thousands of free course-related materials are easily accessible through organizations such as the Khan Academy, which has produced more than 4,000 videos on topics across all grade levels and several curricular areas. The Massive Open Online Courses sponsored by some of the best-known universities in the country, including MIT's Open Courseware program and Coursera, have produced thousands of courses that can be widely accessed without cost.

Changing the learning process and infusing more creativity development opportunities have now become a reality because of the almost unlimited access to the knowledge sources mentioned above. Teachers can also become creative contributors to the resource stockpile and the producers of their own televised lectures, course-related material, and media events. Free or inexpensive software now allows teachers to prepare and upload their own lectures and assignments, as well as creative activities for student use anytime and anywhere through the application of easy-to-use screen-casting software (e.g., Camtasia Studio 8, Screenflow Software). They can also become creative contributors to the profession by sharing their innovative activities with other teachers through various forms of social media. A program called Juno (http://gofrontrow.com/en/products/frontrow-juno) enables easy recording of high-quality audio/video clips without adding any extra work to a teacher's day. The program automatically adds titles, prepares files for uploading, and they can be accessed by computers, tablets, smart phones, or interactive white boards. And, as mentioned earlier, content recorded by others is readily available in all subject areas. These tools enable teachers to easily turn their lectures, creative activities, and related lesson-planning material into audio and video podcasts and printed course and video materials that can be easily uploaded for student access. We can capitalize on students' fascination and skills with technology and the availability of vast amounts of online material by giving teachers the license and the skills to infuse creativity and thinking skills activities into standards-driven curriculum.

While it is not practical to use infusion for every topic or course, the value of this approach is to make learning more engaging and to create an enthusiasm for learning that seldom results from merely covering the material in traditional ways. Finding activities for infusion is now easier than ever. Internet-based search engines allow teachers to search for topics, subtopics, and sub-subtopics by subject area, grade level, and difficulty level. A program called GoQuest (https://compasslearning.com/goquest/), developed at the University of Connecticut (Renzulli & Reis, 2007) and now marketed by Compass Learning, provides an electronic profile of each student's interests, achievement levels, learning styles, and preferred modes of expression. A search engine then scans through thousands of resources and matches these resources with individual student profiles. Teachers can also use the GoQuest program to identify literally thousands of high-engagement activities that direct them to an almost endless array of exciting open-ended enrichment activities. By using the aforementioned six guidelines when selecting activities that are specifically designed to promote creativity, especially the one that relates to "no single, predetermined correct answer," teachers can rest assured that these strategies serve as important criterion for selecting or developing creativity infusion activities.

Conclusion

I first became interested in creativity in the 1960s when I ran across a mimeographed copy of the Minnesota Test of Creative Thinking, later to become known worldwide as the TTests of Creative Thinking (TTCT, Torrance, 1998). I began experimenting with my middle school students using activities that I designed to promote the kinds of divergent thinking measured by the TTCT, and later collaborated with Carolyn Callahan (Callahan & Renzulli, 1974) to conduct a research study that showed that we could indeed improve test scores through the use of these activities. The 250 activities, along with teacher's guides, were originally published as a five-book series (Renzulli, 1972) but are now available at no cost on our Web site: www.gifted.uconn.edu/sem/ndc.html.

Among the hundreds of articles about creativity that I have read over the years, the one contribution that has been the most influential to my present way of viewing this complex concept is the previously cited article by Beghetto and Kaufman (2007). This article reinforces the intuitive belief that I have over time had that (1) creativity exists along a continuum, from small to larger manifestations, and that (2) providing young people with training activities will not only improve divergent thinking, but that some people, both young and older, will "climb up the scale" from mini-c to more advanced manifestations of creative output.

Society advances through innovation and the economic, social, and cultural success of any country based on the creativity of its people. Recent popular press commentaries about chief executive officers at major corporations worldwide identified creativity as the most important leadership quality of the future. The demand for creativity and innovative thinking is increasing and will fuel the economies and cultural growth of the future, yet historically, the education establishment has not focused on preparing all of our young people to become the innovative thinkers of tomorrow. There is a vast amount of research that clearly and unequivocally shows these skills can be enhanced and taught. There is a young Thomas Edison, Rachel Carson, and George Washington Carver in every school in the world, and the kinds of teaching discussed in this chapter describe easy-to-learn instructional practices that will find and nurture the creative potential that is so desperately needed to make the world a better place. Teachers must become the change they wish to see in their students, and administrators must value this kind of teaching by giving teachers the license to blend creativity development into a curriculum that has traditionally focused on acquiring received knowledge. New and better ideas lead to the kinds of innovation that address the requirements of a rapidly changing world, and education leaders and policy makers are finally realizing that what happens in classrooms on a daily basis can play an important part in contributing to the world's reservoir of creative and productive people.

REFERENCES

Amabile, T. M. (1985). Motivation and creativity: Effects of motivational orientation on creative writing. *Journal of Personality and Social Psychology*, **48**, 393–399.

Amabile, T. M. (1996). *Creativity in context*. Boulder, CO: Westview Press.

Anderson, H. H. (Ed.). (1959). *Creativity and its cultivation*. New York: Harper & Brothers.

Archambault, F. X. (1970, March). *A computerized approach to scoring the Torrance tests of creative thinking*. Paper presented at the annual meeting of the American Educational Research Association, Minneapolis, MN.

Arnold, J. E. (1962). Useful creative techniques. In S. J. Parnes and H. F. Harding (Eds.), *A Source Book for Creative Thinking* (pp. 63–105). New York: Charles Scribner's Sons.

Baer, J. (1996). The effects of task-specific divergent thinking training. *Journal of Creative Behavior*, **18**(1), 11–22.

Beghetto, R. A., & Kaufman, J. C. (2007). Toward a broader conception of creativity: A case for "mini-c" creativity. *Psychology of Aesthetics, Creativity, and the Arts*, **1**(2), 73–79.

Bousfield, W. A., & Barclay, W. D. (1950). The relationship between order and frequency of occurrence of restricted associated responses. *Journal of Experimental Psychology*, **40**, 643–647.

Callahan, C. M., & Renzulli, J. S. (1974). Development and evaluation of a creativity training program. *Exceptional Children*, **41**, 44–55.

Connolly, T. M., Boyle, E. A., MacArthur, E., Hainey, T., & Boyle, J. M. (2012). A systematic literature review of empirical evidence on computer games and serious games. *Computers & Education*, **59**(2), 661–686.

Derks, P., & Hervas, D. (1988). Creativity in humor production: Quantity and quality in divergent thinking. *Bulletin of the Psychonomic Society*, **26**(1), 37–39.

Fleming, L., Mingo, S., & Chen, D. (2007). Collaborative brokerage, generative creativity, and creative success. *Administrative Science Quarterly*, **52**(3), 443–475.

Gardner, H. (1983). *Frames of mind: The theory of multiple intelligences*. New York: Basic Books.

Lepper, M., Greene, D., & Nisbet, R. (1973). Undermining children's intrinsic interest with extrinsic rewards: A test of the "overjustification" hypothesis. *Journal of Personality and Social Psychology*, **28**, 129–137.

Li, A. K. F. (1985). Correlates and effects of training in make-believe play in preschool children. *Alberta Journal of Educational Research*, **31**(1), 70–79.

Meeker, M. N. (1969). *The structure of the intellect: Its interpretation and uses*. Columbus, OH: Charles E. Merrill.

Mellou, E. (1995). Review of the relationship between dramatic play and creativity in young children. *Early Child Development and Care*, **112**, 85–107.

Osborn, A. F. (1963). *Applied imagination* (3rd ed.). New York: Charles Scribner's Sons.

Paulus, D. H. (1970, March). *Are sub-tests of the Torrance test independent?* Paper presented at the annual meeting of the American Educational Research Association, Minneapolis, MN.

Renzulli, J. S. (1972). *New directions in creativity* (Vols. 1–5). New York: Harper and Row.

Renzulli, J. S., & Reis, S. M. (2007). A technology based program that matches enrichment resources with student strengths. *International Journal of Emerging Technologies in Learning*, **2**(3), 1–12.

Rogers, C. (1969). *Freedom to learn*. Columbus, OH: Charles E. Merrill.

Rose, L. H., & Lin, H. T. (1984). A meta-analysis of long-term creativity, training programs. *Journal of Creative Behavior*, **18**(1), 11–22.

Runco, M. A. (1986). Flexibility and originality in children's divergent thinking. *Journal of Psychology: Interdisciplinary and Applied*, **120**, 345–352.

Russ, S. W. (1996). Development of creative processes in children. *New Directions in Child Development*, **72**, 31–42.

Starko, A. J. (1995). *Creativity in the classroom: Schools of curious delight*. White Plains, NY: Longman Publishers.

Torrance, E. P. (1987). Teaching creative and gifted learnings. In S. G. Isaksen (Ed.), *Frontiers of creativity research: Beyond the basics* (pp. 189–215). Buffalo, NY: Bearly Limited.

Torrance, E. P. (1998). *The Torrance tests of creative thinking norm – technical manual figural (streamlined) forms A & B*. Bensenville, IL: Scholastic Testing Service, Inc.

Watts, A. (1964). A psychedelic experience: Fact or fantasy? In D. Solomon (Ed.), *LSD: The Consciousness- Expanding Drug* (pp. 78–86). New York: G. T. Putnam's Sons.

CHAPTER 6

Accountability, the Common Core, and Creativity

John Baer and Tracey Garrett
Rider University

Must Content Standards and Accountability Be in Conflict with Creativity?

The past two decades have seen a major and unrelenting call for more test-ing of students and more explicit and more detailed content standards that form the framework for such assessment. Although No Child Left Behind legislation has played a prominent role in recent educational policy formu-lations, federal mandates have not been the only force pushing for greater accountability (Fuhrman, 2001; Ladd, 1996). This movement includes both state initiatives and nongovernmental, nationwide efforts such as the Core Knowledge Foundation's Core Knowledge Sequence (Core Knowl-edge Foundation, 1998; Hirsch, 1987, 1991, 1996) and, most recently, the Common Core State Standards. Although this latter initiative, which has been adopted by almost all the states, was started and promoted heavily by the National Governors Association for Best Practices and the Coun-cil of Chief School Officers (2014a, 2014b, 2014c), it has become a very divisive political issue, even within the ranks of its supporters (American Federation of Teachers, 2013; Beghetto, Kaufman, & Baer, 2015; Porter, McMaken, Hwang, & Yang, 2011; Strauss, 2013). We will not argue the merit (or lack thereof) of either an increasing reliance on standardized test-ing or the wisdom of fine-grained, grade-by-grade content standards. That debate is ongoing, and for the moment we will take the current situation, and a near-term future that seems to be heading toward ever more explicit content standards, as a given that any educational goals or activities must acknowledge and (to some extent at least) accommodate. We will argue that these initiatives (both the focus on explicit and detailed content standards and the standardized test-based accountability to which these standards are often closely linked) need not doom the teaching and promotion of creativity in the classroom. Teaching for creativity and detailed required content standards can coexist quite comfortably, and although they may

seem at times to be working at cross purposes (and indeed, this is sometimes the case), they just as often work synergistically, such that teaching
for creativity helps meet content standards goals, and teaching detailed
content knowledge can reinforce and enhance student creativity.

At first glance, creativity and accountability do indeed seem to be at
odds. Most educators readily associate creativity with divergent thinking (coming up with many possible ideas in response to an open-ended
prompt). For example, Woolfolk (2001) noted that "[e]ncouraging creativity in a classroom means to accept and encourage divergent thinking"
(p. 102). They may also associate accountability with convergent thinking
(finding a single correct or best answer to a problem) and/or evaluative
thinking (judging whether an answer is accurate, consistent, or valid). The
concepts of divergent, convergent, and evaluative thinking originated in
Guilford's Structure of the Intellect Model, and because divergent thinking is widely believed to be an important component of creative thinking,
the improvement of divergent thinking skills has often been the goal of
creativity training (Baer, 1997a; Baer & Kaufman, 2012; Guilford, 1956;
Woolfolk, 2007). In addition, the most widely used tests of creativity – the
Torrance Tests of Creative Thinking – are actually not tests of creativity,
but rather tests of divergent thinking (Kim, 2006; Torrance, 1966, 1974,
1990; Torrance & Presbury, 1974). So these common associations are not
unexpected.

But creativity is not just about divergent thinking; it also requires evaluative and convergent thinking, as well as a great deal of domain knowledge
and skills (Kaufman & Baer, 2006; Runco, 2003; Simonton, 1999, 2006).
For example, one of the best studied and most influential models of creativity, Campbell's blind variation and retention model, requires a combination
of chance variation to produce new ideas (divergent thinking) and selective retention of more workable ideas (evaluative and convergent thinking)
to produce creative breakthroughs (Campbell, 1960; see Simonton, 1994,
1998, 2004 for more recent versions of this model). The CPS model of creative problem solving, which is perhaps the most well-validated practical
approach to creativity enhancement on the level of more everyday creativity
and problem solving, also requires both divergent thinking and evaluative
judgment as part of each and every step in the process (Baer, 1988, 1997a;
Isaksen & Treffinger, 1985; Puccio, Murdock, & Mance, 2007; Treffinger,
Isaksen, & Dorval, 2006). So although divergent thinking might be the
first thing to come to mind when one thinks of creative thinking, it is not
all there is to creativity by any means. Judgment, evaluation, skills, and
knowledge all play important roles.

So creativity and content knowledge and skills are not (or need not be) orthogonal variables. They interact, and creativity is dependent on domain knowledge and skills. Nonetheless, the pressures of accountability and testing naturally impact the ways teachers teach, and one common fear is that creativity may be lost in the shuffle (Baer, 1999, 2002; Beghetto, 2013; Beghetto, Kaufman, & Baer, 2015; Beghetto & Plucker, 2006; Fasko, 2001).

The effort to devise and implement detailed content standards has had many critics, many of whom have charged that attention to such content standards will detract from student thinking and creativity. Several have suggested that adherence to content standards like those exemplified by the Core Knowledge Sequence will result in the unthinking, uncritical, and uncreative absorption of knowledge (Orwin & Forbes, 1994; Schear, 1992; Vail, 1997). One critic called students in Core Knowledge schools "informational blotters" (Paul, 1990, p. 431) and claimed that these students would be able to do very little interesting or productive thinking with the knowledge that they obtained in Core Knowledge schools.

Recent criticisms of content standards and the testing of student achievement based on those standards have naturally focused on the new Common Core Standards, which are currently going into effect across the country. Some of this criticism has even come from supporters of the new standards. According to a recent poll, "Three-quarters of public school teachers surveyed support the Common Core State Standards, yet just 27 percent said their district has provided them with the tools and resources necessary to teach the standards" (American Federation of Teachers. 2013, p. 1). Lack of training and a distrust of the tests being developed have led to calls for a moratorium on any consequences for schools or teachers based on Common Core testing from a wide range of educators (American Federation of Teachers, 2014; Finn, Levesque, Phillips, & Skandera, 2014; National Education Association, 2014; Ravitch, 2014; Rich, 2014).

Our focus is not on that controversy or on the Common Core Standards in particular, but rather on the impact of content standards (be they Common Core, Core Knowledge, or other state standards) on students' creativity. There is a sense among many educators that the push for stricter content standards will decrease the amount of time teachers can allocate to the teaching of thinking skills. There is also a concern that content standards will encourage teachers to limit their instruction to that which will be tested (Beghetto, 2010; Berliner, 2011; Jones, Jones, & Hargrove, 2003; Olson, 2000, 2001; Tucker, 2002). Teaching to the test, many fear, will drive creativity from the classroom.

We cannot deny that this can and sometimes does happen. We argue, however, that it should not and need not happen. There is significant evidence that the introduction of explicit content standards does not lessen students' creativity; in fact, it may do just the opposite. In the one large study (N = 540) to date that has looked directly at this issue (Baer, 2003), students in Core Knowledge middle schools had as high or higher creativity ratings than matched students in non–Core Knowledge middle schools. This study looked at actual performances of students on creativity-relevant tasks (such as writing stories and poems), not simply scores on divergent thinking tests. Contrary to the predictions of critics such as Paul (1990), students in schools with detailed content standards and a strong focus on teaching to those content standards were not less creative than similar students in schools with less detailed content standards. They were several creativity measures in this study, and the Core Knowledge students were by some judged to be more creative, while in others there was no statistically significant difference between the two groups. In none of the creativity assessments was the Core Knowledge group judged to have lower creativity than the matched non–Core Knowledge group.

The possibility that teaching for creativity and emphasizing content knowledge may be in conflict is part of the larger question about the relationship between learning content and learning to think more effectively (see, e.g., Chi, Glaser, & Farr, 1988; Feldhusen, 2006; Glass & Holyoak, 1986; Hirsch, 1996; Johnson-Laird, 1983; Karmiloff-Smith, 1992; Kaufman & Baer, 2006; Mayer, 2006; Paul, 1990; Simon & Chase, 1973; Woolfolk, 2007). It is also related to questions about the possibilities of transfer of learning and of teaching to promote such transfer (see, e.g., Gage & Berliner, 1992; Mayer, 1987; Perkins & Salomon, 1988; Salomon & Perkins, 1989; Woolfolk, 2007). It has become increasingly clear that thinking depends quite heavily on knowledge; that mistakes in everyday critical thinking are more often the result of faulty premises (i.e., incorrect factual knowledge) than a lack of general problem-solving skills; and that teaching for transfer requires a great deal of context-specific training or practice in any domain to which transfer is desired (Ashcraft, 1989; Baer, 1993, 1996; Kaufman & Baer, 2006; Weisberg, 1988, 1999, 2006; Willingham, 2001; Woolfolk, 2007). It seems that content knowledge is essential to serious thinking, that teaching content-free thinking skills is not possible, that higher-level thinking requires the automatization of lower-level skills, and that to improve students' thinking in a given domain, students must acquire an understanding of much factual content about that domain as well as a variety of domain-specific cognitive skills.

So we must teach students content knowledge if we want to improve their thinking. Conversely, often the best way to teach content knowledge is to get students to think about it in some way – to become actively engaged with the content to be learned (Ashcraft, 1989; Craik & Lockhart, 1972; Hirsch, 1987, 1996; Lockhart & Craik, 1990; Mayer, 1987; Woolfolk, 2007; Zimbardo & Gerrig, 1999). Being actively engaged with the content to be learned means being actively engaged *cognitively*, of course. Simply being physically active or emotionally engaged is not what is required (and may even get in the way of meaningful cognitive engagement). An emphasis on the acquisition of content knowledge does not conflict with an emphasis on active processing of information; in fact, the former requires the latter.

For these reasons, an emphasis on content standards need not hinder those who wish to emphasize the development of students' thinking skills, and this is true for creativity just as it is for other kinds of thinking. Having richer and more extensive content knowledge and skills should support, not detract from, creative thinking, just as such knowledge and skills support other kinds of thinking (Beghetto, Kaufman, & Baer, 2015). There is a consensus among creativity researchers and theorists that creative genius in particular requires extensive content knowledge (Gruber, 1981; Gruber & Davis, 1988; Simonton, 1994, 1998, 1999, 2004, 2006; Weisberg, 1988, 1999, 2006), and there is much evidence to support what has come to be known as the "ten-year rule," which claims that it generally takes at least ten years of extensive work and/or study in a field before truly creative work is even possible (see, e.g., Chase & Simon, 1973; Hayes, 1989; Kaufman & Baer, 2002; Weisberg, 1999).

This is not to suggest that all is well and that there is no conflict between content standards (and test-based accountability) and teaching for creativity. There are very real problems, problems that are in most cases avoidable, but very real problems because they are often not avoided. In fact, teachers' misperceptions of how best to meet accountability standards often results in the worst possible outcomes: lower test scores and lessened creativity. Teachers who feel pressured to raise test scores may drop anything resembling divergent thinking from their lesson plans. They may also emphasize rote memorization at the expense of thinking about and understanding the content they are teaching. But dropping divergent thinking activities and focusing on memorization is not only bad for creativity – it is also bad for the acquisition of skills and content knowledge. As will be argued later in the chapter, the most effective ways to teach skills and content knowledge often involve the very same activities one would emphasize to promote creative thinking. When teachers banish divergent thinking and replace it with rote memorization, they are creating the worst of all possible educational worlds, one in which both creativity and content knowledge suffer. Although there are situations in which these two goals are at odds, they are more often synergistically linked. More creativity will often lead to more content knowledge, and more content knowledge will generally lead to more creativity. But there are a few bumps on the road to this educational nirvana, as explained in the following.

How to Emphasize Acquisition of Skills and Content Knowledge *and* Enhance Creativity

Teaching Divergent Thinking

The most widely used teaching techniques for improving student creativity are brainstorming activities (e.g., "List as many different possible uses for a brick as you can" or "How many different ways can you think of to get people to use less petroleum?"). The rules of brainstorming are fairly simple:

- *Defer judgment.* The goal of brainstorming is to come up with unusual and original ideas. When ideas are being judged, most people will take fewer risks and self-censor many ideas. Judgment can come later, after all the ideas are on the table. This includes both negative judgments and positive ones.
- *Avoid ownership of ideas.* When people feel that an idea is "theirs," egos sometimes get in the way of creative thinking. They are likely to be more defensive later when ideas are critiqued, and they are less willing to allow their ideas to be modified.
- *Feel free to "hitchhike" on other ideas.* This means that it is okay to borrow elements from ideas already on the table, or to make slight modifications of ideas already suggested.
- *Wild ideas are encouraged.* Impossible, totally unworkable ideas may lead someone to think of other, more possible, more workable ideas. It is easier to take a wildly imaginative bad idea and tone it down to fit the constraints of reality than to take a boring bad idea and make it interesting enough to be worth thinking about. (Baer, 1997a, p. 43)

There are many programs designed to enhance creativity that are used in schools, such as Synectics (Gordon, 1961), Talents Unlimited (2007), CPS (Eberle & Stanish, 1980), and the Odyssey of the Mind creative problem solving competition (formerly known as the Olympics of the Mind;

Micklus, 1986; Micklus & Micklus, 1986). In all these program the development of divergent thinking skills is paramount and brainstorming (or a variant of brainstorming) is employed as a primary tool for encouraging and improving divergent thinking. Brainstorming can be used as part of a broader program of creativity training (as in CPS) or it can stand alone as a way to improve divergent thinking.

For many teachers, these kinds of divergent thinking activities are both fun and worthwhile, but not essential – and there certainly are not going to be any divergent thinking questions on the state's standardized assessments of student learning. When accountability push comes to testing shove, therefore, teachers may be quick to stop asking students to "think of many varied and unusual ways to do X" and use that time to drill math facts or practice reading comprehension strategies.

It is hard to argue with the reasoning behind such a decision. Helping children improve their divergent thinking skills may have long-term value – it may help them become more creative thinkers – but it is hard to see how listing 100 interesting and unusual ways to use egg cartons will help Johnny improve his scores on state-mandated achievement tests.

We agree that doing daily brainstorming activities using "How many uses can you think of for X?" kinds of questions is probably not a good use of class time. In fact, it is not even clear that such activities will have much impact on students' creativity, because unusual uses kinds of brainstorming activities exercise only a very limited number of divergent thinking muscles. Divergent thinking, like creativity more generally, varies from domain to domain, and even from task to task within a given domain. Doing the same kind of brainstorming activity every day would be rather like going to the gym every day and doing a single exercise, the same exercise, every day. One set of muscles would get stronger, but the rest would atrophy (Baer, 1993, 1996, 1997a, 1998a; Baer & Kaufman, 2005; Kaufman & Baer, 2005).

Using brainstorming only in response to unusual uses kinds of prompts, while perhaps a good way to improve one's score on a divergent thinking test, is nonetheless a very unimaginative and unproductive way to use brainstorming in the classroom. Even if improving students' creative thinking were a teacher's only goal, she would still be well advised to use brainstorming in a wide range of contexts and with as diverse a set of prompts as possible. But the benefits of brainstorming need not be limited to improving divergent thinking skills. They can also be used to help students acquire content knowledge and develop skills. (It is perhaps worth noting that unusual uses kinds of prompts *can* be an excellent choice the very first time a group is introduced to brainstorming, because they are very easy to understand. But after that, one needs to branch out.)

Here is a very simple example of a way to use brainstorming in class to help students learn content knowledge. At the beginning of a lesson, teachers can ask students to brainstorm what they already know about the topic the class is about to study. Let's say a third-grade class is about to read a book about Abraham Lincoln. Students might be asked to brainstorm everything they know about Lincoln, with the teacher recording their responses on the board. (Remember the *Defer Judgment* rule while doing this. If someone says that Lincoln was the first president, the teacher should just write it down, and if another student tries to correct this, she might remind him that time for judging or commenting on the ideas will come later. Judging ideas in the middle of brainstorming will short-circuit the process, because if students worry that their ideas might be criticized, they will hold back and take fewer risks expressing ideas about which they might not be fully confident.) Soon the board will be filled with ideas – some correct, some incorrect, some important, some tangential – about Lincoln. What has been accomplished?

1. The students have activated their own background knowledge about Lincoln. It is therefore more likely that the new information they are about to learn will be encoded in long-term memory and linked in a propositional network with other things they know about Lincoln, making it much easier to recall the information later (even on a test!).
2. The students will be learning new things about Lincoln from the ideas offered by other students.
3. The teacher will get a quick reading of what students know about Lincoln, a kind of formative assessment that can help guide the lesson that will follow.
4. The teacher will quickly become aware of misconceptions students may have about Lincoln and have an opportunity to correct these mistaken ideas. Getting those incorrect ideas (such as Lincoln being the first president) on the board provides an opportunity to deal with those misconceptions straightforwardly (but only *after* brainstorming ends). Some such mistaken notions can be corrected easily (e.g., in response to a brainstorming response that Lincoln was the first president, the teacher might explain that "Sometimes students confuse Lincoln, who was president during the Civil War, with George Washington, who was our leader during the Revolutionary War and who later became our first president"). Other misconceptions may be more subtle and better

dealt with later in the lesson (e.g., it might take a while to explain why the claim that "Lincoln started the Civil War to free the slaves" is not exactly true).

5. Students will get practice doing divergent thinking.

Brainstorming can be used in many other ways to help students develop skills and acquire content knowledge that meet state content standards. Here is an example taken from the New Jersey Core Curriculum Content Standards (New Jersey Department of Education, 2004). Standard 6 states (among other things) that students will be able to "Analyze the impact of various human activities and social policies on the natural environment and describe how humans have attempted to solve environmental problems through adaptation and modification," "Apply spatial thinking to understand the interrelationship of history, geography, economics, and the environment, including domestic and international migrations, changing environmental preferences and settlement patterns, and frictions between population groups," and "Analyze why places and regions are important factors to individual and social identity."

One of us designed a middle school social studies project some time ago that is directly related to this standard and that employs divergent thinking as a way to learn skills and content while at the same time developing creative thinking skills. Students were asked to create a new continent somewhere on the globe and to explain how this continent might have developed culturally. This was a project that lasted about two weeks with several lessons on different topics along the way, but the general goal was to help students understand how geography and human history interact (e.g., how such things as climates, landforms, and natural resources influence how people live, and how the ways people live are adapted to their differing geographical settings).

The unit started off with some exercises designed to improve some divergent thinking skills that students might find useful as they worked on the project. Here are three abilities that were thought were important and that would help them make their projects more creative:

1. Ability to think of specific cultural elements that might be influenced by geography.
2. Ability to think of ways that geography might influence general features of a culture.
3. Ability to think of ways that a society's culture might lead them to adapt different geographical elements to a given purpose.

Each of these provided the content for a brainstorming exercise. For example, after learning what the expression "specific cultural elements" means, students brainstormed and created lists of things that might count as cultural elements. Later they brainstormed cultural elements that might be influenced by geography. Evaluation of their ideas can follow these brainstorming sessions, providing another chance to grapple with important knowledge and skills. These activities – and similar activities related to abilities 2 and 3 above – were designed to increase students' divergent thinking skill in these particular social studies content areas. Development of these particular divergent thinking skills supported the larger create-a-continent activity, and it also addressed New Jersey Core Curriculum Content Standard 6.9. (For more information on other divergent thinking activities that support various curricular objectives, see Baer, 1997a; Baer & Kaufman, 2012.)

Balancing Intrinsic and Extrinsic Motivation

Teaching for creativity and teaching for content tend to go in opposite directions when it comes to motivation. (Recall that at the beginning of this chapter we acknowledged that at times creativity and content standards really *do* work at cross purposes.) Student motivation is one place that is particularly true, as will be explained later in the chapter. But the situation is not hopeless.

Amabile's (1983, 1996) intrinsic motivation theory has been one of the most powerful and productive ideas to come out of the last quarter-century of creativity research. This theory says that people are more creative when they do something simply because they find it intrinsically interesting – because it is something they have chosen to do just because they derive pleasure, or even joy, from doing it – and they are less creative when they do something because they are extrinsically motivated, such as to earn a reward.

This idea probably seems pretty harmless, but it is not just saying that being intrinsically motivated leads to more creative behavior. It is also saying that when people do things to earn rewards, or when they expect that their work will be evaluated, they become *less* creative; and when they do things primarily to please someone else, they also become less creative. It is somewhat distressing to many teachers to hear that the things they do everyday – offer rewards to students (that is, bribe students to do things they might not do otherwise) and evaluate their work – tend to decrease students' creativity. But troubling though it may be, it is nonetheless true.

Intrinsic and extrinsic motivations tend to compete with each other, and when we experience both at the same time, extrinsic motivation tends to drive out intrinsic motivation. When a teacher offers students rewards for doing things, or when they evaluate their students' work, they do indeed increase their motivation – their extrinsic motivation – but at the same time they are diminishing their students' intrinsic motivation for those activities. And by reducing intrinsic motivation, they are also causing their students to be less creative. (For more information about this theory and the evidence supporting it, see Amabile, 1983, 1996; Hennessey, 2010a, 2010b; Hennessey & Amabile, 1988; Hennessey & Zbikowski, 1993. The negative impact of extrinsic motivation on creativity is especially powerful for girls; see Baer, 1997b, 1998b.)

But we must evaluate students' work – if for no other reason (and there are other and better reasons, to be discussed later in the chapter) than that we must give grades of some kind. And sometimes if we couldn't offer rewards – if we couldn't bribe students – we simply wouldn't be able to get them to do some things that they really need to do. For better or worse, some of the same things that we know tend to diminish creativity are the very things that tend to increase competence. Students *need* feedback (a.k.a. evaluation) on their performance if they are to improve their skills, and they sometimes need some kind of extrinsic motivation – rewards – to keep working when they would otherwise simply stop. They need extrinsic motivation to learn, and teachers need extrinsic motivation (bribes and evaluations) to teach them. And so teaching for creativity and teaching to learn content do seem to part company when it comes to motivation. This sometimes forces us to make difficult choices.

One way out of this fix would be to argue that even though doing something for a reward, or working harder because one wants to earn a better evaluation, may lower one's creativity in the short run, it is this extrinsically motivated learning that makes it possible to acquire the skills and knowledge that one will need in the future to do something in a more creative way than would be possible at present. The skills and knowledge that our students are acquiring (with the help of evaluation and occasional rewards) will allow them to be more creative in the future, because they will need considerable amounts of both skills and knowledge to do anything truly creative. And this is true. But it is only one part of the story. The other part – the intrinsic-motivation-reducing effects of evaluation and rewards – does not just go away because they may also have some other positive effects. And if students lose their intrinsic motivation, they may have the skills and knowledge they need to be creative, but they may no longer have any interest in doing anything creative with those skills and that knowledge. And if you do not do anything, you do not do anything creative.

Teachers thus find themselves between a rock and a hard place, needing evaluations and rewards but knowing they also have negative effects. The way out of this dilemma is first to keep in mind one's goals for a given lesson. If one's focus is on skill development or knowledge acquisition, then one needs to use extrinsic motivation and (at least temporarily) risk depressing creativity. To the extent that evaluation is viewed by students as empowering, there is even some evidence that it may not negatively impact creativity at all (Byron & Khazanchi, 2012; Eisenberger, Pierce, & Cameron, 1999; Eisenberger & Rhoades 2001; Eisenberger & Shanock, 2003); and if the focus is on the student's work (rather than on the student's abilities), this should also lessen the negative impact (Amabile, 1983, 1996). But the fact that under some conditions and for some students the creativity-dampening, intrinsic motivation–killing effects of rewards and evaluations might be mitigated does not mean there are no negative effects. They are real and they should not be ignored.

Sometimes a teacher's goal is not skill development, however. For some lessons or activities, the primary goal may well be to encourage both intrinsic motivation and creativity, and in those cases one needs to avoid doing things that will increase extrinsic motivation and try to do whatever one can to increase intrinsic motivation. For example, when teaching writing, we want students to learn a number of skills, and sometimes we want them to write imaginatively. These goals are sadly at odds because one requires an emphasis on extrinsic motivation – evaluative feedback, in this case – and the other just the opposite (a focus on intrinsic motivation, which would require one to avoid evaluation). If one tries to do a little of each, it will not work, because extrinsic motivation will win – it will tend to drive out students' intrinsic motivation. But a teacher can do both if she does them at *different times*. When working on skill development in writing, she can let students know the criteria or rubric she will use to evaluate their work (to promote skill development), and at other times she can tell them that although they must do the writing assignment, they will get credit simply for doing it and there will be no further evaluation (to promote intrinsic motivation and creativity). Teachers often evaluate work in different ways for different purposes (and may evaluate the same piece of writing in different ways, depending on the stage of the writing process), and it is appropriate to evaluate different aspects of students' performance when emphasizing different goals. Consider, for example, how for very young writers it may be helpful to ignore spelling errors and have students use invented spelling rather than have them completely shut down every time they need a word they cannot spell, while at other times teaching spelling directly and expecting students to learn to spell the words that they have studied correctly. Teachers using this strategy can emphasize both correct spelling and fluency in writing, but at different times, with the long-term goal of fluent and correct writing (Bank Street College, 1997; Burns, Griffin, & Snow, 2000).

Some teachers object that this is unrealistic and students will not believe it anyway, but if one actually follows through on the promise not to evaluate, students will (gradually) come to believe this promise. This will allow them to concentrate on skills and focus on doing things "right" when they expect evaluation and it will free them up to write more imaginatively (albeit often with less technical correctness) when the no-evaluation promise is in effect. One cannot simultaneously make extrinsic and intrinsic motivation salient (because extrinsic motivation will win and drive out intrinsic motivation), but one can do both at different times. This allows both skill development and a nurturing of interest in creative writing.

Will some kids abuse the license that a no-evaluation promise provides? Of course they will. But sometimes we need to allow the students who want to do as little as possible to get away with it, in order not to punish those students who do have the kind of intrinsic motivation that we wish all our students had.

But what about content standards and accountability? Won't this take time away from learning content? Probably so. (Remember, sometimes content standards and accountability *do* come into conflict with creativity. There is no free lunch here.) But probably not as much as one might fear. If students spend a few hours each week doing activities that will not be evaluated but which will be likely to increase students' intrinsic motivation, it will not take a huge amount of time away from learning the content knowledge on which they will be tested, and these activities may help students acquire important content knowledge and skills, even without evaluations or rewards, simply because they allow and encourage students to think about that content knowledge and apply those skills in different, and sometimes even original, ways. Thinking deeply about content is a highly effective way to retain it – more effective in the long term than many short-term strategies such as flashcards – so teacher might think of divergent thinking or other creativity-relevant activities as an investment in their students' long-term acquisition of content knowledge (Beghetto, 2013; Beghetto, Kaufman, & Baer, 2015; Woolfolk, 2007). In addition, these kinds of activities may simply help getting students to show up in class – psychologically as well as physically. And without that, all the great content knowledge and skill-focused lessons cannot do them any good anyway.

Using Both Teacher-Centered and Student-Centered Learning

There are many continua on which different teaching approaches can be located, such as constructionist/transmissive, progressive/traditional, and teacher-centered/student-centered. These are at best fuzzy guides because they are often on the most extreme cases that are easy to classify, but they are often used to describe different teaching approaches.

Schuh (2003), an advocate of student-centered and constructivist teaching, defines the teacher-centered/student-centered distinction in a way that also encompasses the constructivist-transmissive and progressive-traditional continua:

> In a teacher-centered model of instruction, the instructor's role is seen as imparting knowledge to students, and instruction proceeds from the instructor's point of view... The teacher decides for the learner what is required... by defining characteristics of instruction, curriculum, assessment, and management... in which the information... is moved into the learner.... In contrast, learner-centered instruction (LCI) fosters opportunities for learners to draw on their own experiences and interpretations.... LCI proposes that teachers need to understand the learner's perspective and must support capacities already existing in the learner to accomplish desired learning outcomes. Learning goals are then achieved by active collaboration between the teacher and learners who together determine what learning means and how it can be enhanced within each individual learner by drawing the learner's own unique talents, capacities, and experiences. (p. 427, quoted in Beghetto & Plucker, 2006, pp. 319–320)

Student-centered (also known as learner-centered) approaches have been associated with creativity (Beghetto & Plucker, 2006; Fasko, 2001), although this is a prediction, not a tested empirical claim. It is not difficult to see why teaching for creativity seems to fall into the student-centered side of this continuum. How can an idea be new or original – how can it be creative? – if it has been "moved into the learner" by an outside force (the teacher)? It is perhaps almost as obvious why teaching students content knowledge – the stuff of state content standards and the stuff that will be on the state-mandated tests – seems to fall on the teacher-centered instructional side (certainly it is the state, and its employee, the teacher, that "decides for the learner what is required").

What often gets lost when thinking about student- and teacher-centered instruction (and similar schemes for comparing modes of instruction) is that this is a continuum, not a dichotomy. Most teachers do not use exclusively the rote memorization strategies that are typically invoked when teacher-centered instruction is attacked (see, e.g., Jones, Jones, & Hargrove, 2003, who argue that high-stakes testing leads to more teaching via rote memorization in schools serving low-scoring, disadvantaged populations; but see also the review by Pletka [2005] of their book, which contends that they provide no statistics to support this assertion). Similarly, most teachers do not use the pure discovery, unguided or minimally guided instructional approaches that Kirschner, Sweller, and Clark (2006) have shown to be significantly "less effective and less efficient than instructional approaches that place a strong emphasis on guidance of the student learning" (p. 75), that is, more teacher-centered approaches.

Teachers are more likely to use techniques that fall at neither extreme of this continuum, but rather employ approaches that fall closer to the middle (or to use a mix of approaches). There is a conservatism in teaching that results in teachers rarely adopting the more extreme stances of reformers (Kennedy, 2006). There is certainly reason for the concerns raised by Jones, Jones, and Hargrove (2003) that accountability concerns may lead teachers to adopt ineffective teaching methods, because rote memorization is not only bad for creativity – it is also a poor way to learn content (Woolfolk, 2007). As Beghetto and Plucker (2006) contend in their plea that creativity not be forgotten in our schools,

> We argue that student understanding develops from a balance between the pursuit of efficient methods to attain viable solutions *and* opportunities to engage in the creative process of developing the personal knowledge of when, why and how to arrive at those solutions. This includes allowing students the time and experiences necessary to develop an understanding of what those solutions mean in the context of the particular problem as well as a more general set of problems. Conversely, when teachers simply teach the most efficient method they may actually short-circuit the creative process necessary for the development of meaningful understanding. Again, this is not to say that students should never be taught the most efficient method, but rather they should be given opportunities to work through the problems in their own way such that they develop an accurate yet personally meaningful understanding. (p. 324)

As with divergent thinking, so with teacher-centered vs. student-centered learning. The most effective way to teach for the knowledge and under-standing that will result in good scores on state accountability measures dovetails quite nicely with effective methods for teaching for creativity. Misunderstanding how students learn (and going to either extreme of the teacher- or student-centered continuum) will result in both less skill and knowledge acquisition and less student creativity.

Teaching for creativity in an era of content standards does, at times, force teachers to make difficult choices, as the section on intrinsic and extrinsic motivation in this chapter describes. But if teachers avoid (a) mistaken notions that teaching academic skills and content knowledge requires them to abandon creativity-relevant skills like divergent thinking or (b) retreating into rote memorization strategies that drain learning of meaning, they can successfully meet both accountability standards and promote creativity in their classrooms.

REFERENCES

Amabile, T. M. (1983). *The social psychology of creativity*. New York: Springer-Verlag.

Amabile, T. M. (1996). *Creativity in context: Update to the social psychology of creativity*. Boulder, CO: Westview.

American Federation of Teachers. (2013, May 2013). AFT poll of 800 teachers finds strong support for Common Core Standards and a moratorium on stakes for new assessments until everything is aligned (Press Release). Retrieved June 3, 2016 from www.aft.org/newspubs/press/2013/050313.cfm

American Federation of Teachers. (2014, April 30). AFT's Weingarten calls for moratorium on high-stakes consequences of Common Core tests: Tests should be decoupled from decisions that hurt students, teachers and schools until standards are properly implemented and field-tested. Retrieved August 3, 2014 from www.aft.org/newspubs/press/2013/043013.cfm

Ashcraft, M. H. (1989). *Human memory and cognition*. New York: Harper Collins.

Baer, J. (1993). *Creativity and divergent thinking: A task-specific approach*. Hillsdale, NJ: Lawrence Erlbaum Associates.

Baer, J. (1996). The effects of task-specific divergent thinking training. *Journal of Creative Behavior*, **30**, 183–187.

Baer. J. (1997a). *Creative teachers, creative students*. Boston: Allyn and Bacon.

Baer, J. (1997b). Gender differences in the effects of anticipated evaluation on creativity. *Creativity Research Journal*, **10**, 25–31.

Baer, J. (1998a). The case for domain specificity in creativity. *Creativity Research Journal*, **11**, 173–177.

Baer, J. (1998b). Gender differences in the effects of extrinsic motivation on creativity. *Journal of Creative Behavior*, **32**, 18–37.

Baer, J. (1999). Creativity in a climate of standards. *Focus on Education*, **43**, 16–21.

Baer, J. (2002). Are creativity and content standards allies or enemies? *Research in the Schools,* **9**(2), 35–42.

Baer, J. (2003). Impact of the Core Knowledge Curriculum on creativity. *Creativity Research Journal,* **15**, 297–300.

Baer, J., & Kaufman, J. C. (2005). Bridging generality and specificity: The amusement park theoretical (APT) model of creativity. *Roeper Review,* **27**, 158–163.

Baer, J., & Kaufman, J. C. (2012). *Being creative inside and outside the classroom.* Rotterdam: Sense Publishers.

Bank Street College. (1997). America reads: Bank Street College's approach to early literacy acquisition. Retrieved April 28, 2008 from www.paec.org/david/reading/amreads.pdf

Beghetto, R. A. (2010). Creativity in the classroom. In *The Cambridge handbook of creativity* (pp. 447–463). New York: Cambridge University Press.

Beghetto, R. A. (2013). *Killing ideas softly? The promise and perils of creativity in the classroom.* Charlotte, NC: Information Age Publishing.

Beghetto, R., Kaufman, J., & Baer, J. (2015). *Teaching for creativity in the common core classroom.* New York: Teachers College Press.

Beghetto, R. A., & Plucker, J. A. (2006). The relationship among schooling, learning, and creativity. In J. C. Kaufman & J. Baer (Eds.), *Reason and creativity in development* (pp. 316–332). Cambridge: Cambridge University Press.

Berliner, D. C. (2011). Narrowing curriculum, assessments, and conceptions of what it means to be smart in the U.S. schools: Creaticide by design. In D. Ambrose & R. J. Sternberg (Eds.), *How dogmatic beliefs harm creativity and higher-level thinking* (pp. 79–93). New York: Routledge.

Burns, M. S, Griffin, P., & Snow, C. E. (Eds.), (2000). *Starting out right: A guide to promoting children's reading success.* Washington, DC: National Academy Press.

Byron, K., & Khazanchi, S. (2012). Rewards and creative performance: A meta-analytic test of theoretically derived hypotheses. *Psychological Bulletin,* **138**, 809–830.

Campbell, D. T. (1960). Blind variation and selective retention in creative thought as in other knowledge processes. *Psychological Review,* **67**, 380–400.

Chase, W. G., & Simon, H. A. (1973). The mind's eye in chess. In W. G. Chase (Ed.), *Visual information processing* (pp. 215–281). New York: Academic Press.

Chi, M. T. H., Glaser, R., & Farr, M. (Eds.). (1988). *The nature of expertise.* Hillsdale, NJ: Erlbaum.

Core Knowledge Foundation. (1998). *Core knowledge sequence: Content guidelines for grades K–8.* Charlottesville, VA: Core Knowledge Foundation.

Craik, F. I. M., & Lockhart, R. S. (1972). Levels of processing: A framework for memory research. *Journal of Verbal Learning and Verbal Behavior,* **11**, 671–684.

Eberle, B., & Stanish, B. (1980). *CPS for kids: A resource book for teaching creative problem-solving to children.* Buffalo, NY: D.O.K. Publishers.

Eisenberger, R., Pierce, W. D., & Cameron, J. (1999). Effects of reward on intrinsic motivation: Negative, neutral, and positive. *Psychological Bulletin*, **125**, 677–691.

Eisenberger, R., & Rhoades, L. (2001). Incremental effects of reward on creativity. *Journal of Personality and Social Psychology*, **81**, 728–741.

Eisenberger, R., & Shanock, L. (2003). Rewards, intrinsic motivation, and creativity: A case study of conceptual and methodological isolation. *Creativity Research Journal*, **15**, 121–130.

Fasko, D. (2001). Education and creativity. *Creativity Research Journal*, **13**, 317–327.

Feldhusen, J. F. (2006). The role of the knowledge base in creative thinking. In J. C. Kaufman & J. Baer (Eds.), *Reason and creativity in development* (pp. 137–144). Cambridge: Cambridge University Press.

Finn, C., Levesque, P., Phillips, V., & Skandera, H. (2014, June 18). A Common Core accountability moratorium. The Thomas B. Fordham Institute. Retrieved August 3, 2014 from http://edexcellence.net/articles/a-common-core-accountability-moratorium

Fuhrman, S. H. (Ed.). (2001). *From the capital to the classroom: Standards-based reform in the states.* Chicago: National Society for the Study of Education.

Gage, N. L., & Berliner, D. C. (2012). *Educational psychology* (5th ed.). Boston: Houghton Mifflin.

Glass, A. L., & Holyoak, K. J. (1986). *Cognition* (2nd ed.). New York: Random House.

Gordon, W. J. J. (1961). *Synectics.* New York: Harper & Row.

Gruber, H. E. (1981). *Darwin on man: A psychological study of scientific creativity* (2nd ed.). Chicago: University of Chicago Press.

Gruber, H. E., & Davis, S. N. (1988). Inching our way up Mt. Olympus: The evolving-systems approach to creative thinking. In R. J. Sternberg (Ed.), *The nature of creativity* (pp. 243–270). New York: Cambridge University Press.

Guilford, J. P. (1956). The structure of intellect. *Psychological Bulletin*, **53**, 267–293.

Hayes, J. R. (1989). Cognitive processes in creativity. In J. A. Glover, R. R. Ronning, & C. R. Reynolds (Eds.), *Handbook of creativity* (pp. 135–145). New York: Plenum.

Hennessey, B. A. (2010a). The creativity-motivation connection. In J. C. Kaufman & R. J. Sternberg (Eds.), *The Cambridge handbook of creativity* (pp. 342–365). New York: Cambridge University Press.

Hennessey, B. A. (2010b). Intrinsic motivation and creativity in the classroom: Have we come full circle? In J. C. Kaufman & R. A. Beghetto (Eds.), *Nurturing creativity in the classroom* (pp. 329–361). New York: Cambridge University Press.

Hennessey, B. A., & Amabile, T. M. (1988). Conditions of creativity. In R. J. Sternberg (Ed.), *The nature of creativity* (pp. 11–38). Cambridge: Cambridge University Press.

Hennessey, B. A., & Zbikowski, S. (1993). Immunizing children against the negative effects of reward: A further examination of intrinsic motivation techniques. *Creativity Research Journal,* **6**, 297–308.

Hirsch, Jr., E. D. (1987). *Cultural literacy: What every American needs to know.* Boston: Houghton Mifflin.

Hirsch, Jr., E. D. (Ed.). (1991–1997). *The core knowledge series: Resource books for kindergarten through six.* New York: Doubleday.

Hirsch, Jr., E. D. (1996). *The schools we need and why we don't have them.* New York: Doubleday.

Isaksen, S. G., & Treffinger, D. J. (1985). *Creative problem solving: The basic course* Buffalo, NY: Bearly Limited Press.

Johnson-Laird, P. N. (1983). *Mental models.* Cambridge, MA: Harvard University Press.

Jones, G., Jones, B., & Hargrove, T. (2003). *The unintended consequences of high-stakes testing.* Lanham, MD: Rowman & Littlefield.

Karmiloff-Smith, A. (1992). *Beyond modularity: A developmental perspective on cognitive science.* Cambridge, MA: MIT Press.

Kaufman, J. C., & Baer, J. (2002). Could Steven Spielberg manage the Yankees? Creative thinking in different domains. *Korean Journal of Thinking and Problem Solving,* **12**, 5–14.

Kaufman, J. C., & Baer, J. (2005). The amusement park theory of creativity. In J. C. Kaufman & J. Baer (Eds.), *Creativity across domains: Faces of the muse* (pp. 321–328). Hillsdale, NJ: Lawrence Erlbaum Associates.

Kaufman, J. C., & Baer, J. (Eds.). (2006). *Reason and creativity in development.* New York: Cambridge University Press.

Kennedy, M. M. (2006). *Inside teaching: How classroom life undermines reform.* Cambridge, MA: Harvard University Press.

Kim, K. H. (2006). Can we trust creativity tests: A review of the Torrance Tests of Creative Thinking. *Creativity Research Journal,* **18**, 3–14.

Kirschner, P. A., Sweller, J., and Clark, R. E. (2006). Why minimal guidance during instruction does not work: An analysis of the failure of constructivist, discovery, problem-based, experiential, and inquiry-based teaching. *Educational Psychologist,* **41**(2), 75–86.

Ladd, H. F. (1996). *Holding schools accountable: Performance-based reform in education.* Washington, DC: Brookings Institution Press.

Lockhart, R. S., & Craik, F. I. M. (1990). Levels of processing: A retrospective commentary on a framework for memory research. *Canadian Journal of Psychology,* **44**, 87–122.

Mayer, R. E. (1987). *Educational psychology: A cognitive approach.* Boston: Little, Brown and Company.

Mayer, R. E. (2006). The role of domain knowledge in creative problem solving. In J. C. Kaufman & J. Baer (Eds.), *Reason and creativity in development* (pp. 145–158). Cambridge: Cambridge University Press.

Micklus, C. S. (1986). *OM-AHA! Problems to develop creative thinking skills.* Glassboro, NJ: Creative Competitions.

Micklus, C. S., & Micklus, C. (1986). *OM program handbook*. Glassboro, NJ: Creative Competitions.

National Education Association. (2014, June 12). NEA welcomes Gates Foundation moratorium on Common Core high-stakes tests. Retrieved August 3, 2014 from www.nea.org/home/59364.htm.

National Governors Association Center for Best Practices, & Council of Chief State School Officers (2014a). Common Core state standards initiative. Retrieved June 3, 2016 from www.corestandards.org/

National Governors Association Center for Best Practices, & Council of Chief State School Officers (2014b). English language arts standards: Common Core state standards initiative. Retrieved June 3, 2016 from www.corestandards.org/ELA-Literacy/

National Governors Association Center for Best Practices, & Council of Chief State School Officers (2014c). Mathematics standards: Common Core state standards initiative. Retrieved June 3, 2016 from www.corestandards.org/Math/

New Jersey Department of Education. (2004). New Jersey Core Curriculum Content Standards. Retrieved May 10, 2007 from: www.state.nj.us/njded/cccs/index.html

Olson, L. (2000). Worries of a standards "backlash" grow. *Education Week*, **19**(30), 1, 12–13.

Olson, L. (2001). Education alliance calls for corrections to standards-based systems. *Education Week*, **20**(19), 6.

Orwin, C., & Forbes, H. D. (1994). Cultural literacy: A Canadian perspective. *International Journal of Social Education*, **9**(1), 15–30.

Paul, R. W. (1990). Critical thinking and cultural literacy: Where E. D. Hirsch goes wrong. In R. W. Paul (Ed.), *Critical thinking: What every person needs to survive in a rapidly changing world* (pp. 429–435). Rohnert Park, CA: Center for Critical Thinking and Moral Critique, Sonoma State University.

Perkins, D. N., & Salomon, G. (1988). Teaching for transfer. *Educational Leadership*, **46**(1), 22–32.

Pletka, B. (2005, March 26). Review of *The unintended consequences of high-stakes testing. Education Review*. Retrieved May 12, 2007 from http://edrev.asu.edu/reviews/rev369.htm

Porter, A., McMaken, J., Hwang, J., & Yang, R. (2011). Common Core Standards: The new U.S. intended curriculum. *Educational Researcher*, **40**, 103–116.

Puccio, G. J., Murdock, M. C., & Mance, M. (2007) *Creative leadership: Skills that drive change*. San Diego, CA: Sage.

Ravitch, D. (2014, June 10). New York Times: Gates Foundation calls for a moratorium on high stakes attached to Common Core tests. Diane Ravitch's blog. Retrieved August 3, 2014 from http://dianeravitch.net/2014/06/10/new-york-times-gates-foundation-calls-for-a-moratorium-on-high-stakes-attached-to-common-core-tests/

Rich, M. (2014, June 10). Delay urged on actions tied to tests by schools. *The New York Time*, June 10, 2014. Retrieved August 3, 2014 from www.nytimes.com/2014/06/11/education/gates-foundation-urges-moratorium-on-decisions-tied-to-common-core.html

Runco, M. A. (Ed.). (2003). *Critical creative processes*. Cresskill, NJ: Hampton Press.

Salomon, G., & Perkins, D. N. (1989). Rocky roads to transfer: Rethinking mechanisms of a neglected phenomenon. *Educational Psychologist*, **24**(2), 113–142.

Schear, E. L. (1992). Cultural literacy and the developmental student: Whose culture and what kind of literacy? *Research and Teaching in Developmental Education*, **8**(2), 5–14.

Schuh, K. L. (2003). Knowledge construction in the learner-centered classroom. *Journal of Educational Psychology*, **95**, 426–442.

Simonton, D. K. (1994). *Greatness: Who makes history and why*. New York: Guilford Press.

Simonton, D. K. (1998). *Scientific genius: A psychology of science*. Cambridge: Cambridge University Press.

Simonton, D. K. (1999). *Origins of genius: Darwinian perspectives on creativity*. Oxford: Oxford University Press.

Simonton, D. K. (2004). *Creativity in science: Chance, logic, genius, and zeitgeist*. Cambridge: Cambridge University Press.

Simonton, D. K. (2006). Creative genius, knowledge, and reason. In J. C. Kaufman & J. Baer (Eds.), *Reason and creativity in development* (pp. 43–59). Cambridge: Cambridge University Press.

Strauss, V. (2013, July 24). New Common Core tests: Worth the price? *The Washington Post*. Retrieved November 8, 2013 from www.washingtonpost.com/blogs/answer-sheet/wp/2013/07/24/new-common-core-tests-worth-the-price/

Talents Unlimited, Inc. (2007). *Talents Unlimited*. Retrieved May 9, 2007 from www.mcpss.com/websites/MCPSS/MCPSS/Default.asp?PN=PagesLevel1&L=0&DivisionID='23'&DepartmentID='95'&SubDepartmentID="&PageID='510'

Torrance, E. P. (1966). *The Torrance Tests of Creative Thinking – Norms-Technical Manual Research Edition – Verbal Tests, Forms A and B – Figural Tests, Forms A and B*. Princeton, NJ: Personnel Press.

Torrance, E. P. (1974). *The Torrance Tests of Creative Thinking – Norms-Technical Manual Research Edition – Verbal Tests, Forms A and B – Figural Tests, Forms A and B*. Princeton, NJ: Personnel Press.

Torrance, E. P. (1990). *The Torrance tests of creative thinking: Norms-technical manual*. Bensenville, IL: Scholastic Testing Service.

Torrance, E. P. (1998). *The Torrance Tests of Creative Thinking Norms-Technical Manual Figural (Streamlined) Forms A & B*. Bensenville, IL: Scholastic Testing Service, Inc.

Torrance, E. P., & Presbury, J. (1984). The criteria of success used in 242 recent experimental studies of creativity. *Creative Child & Adult Quarterly*, **9**, 238–243.

Treffinger, D. J., Isaksen,, S. G., & Dorval, K. B. (2006) *Creative problem solving: An introduction* (4th Ed.). Waco, TX: Prufrock Press.

Tucker, M. S. (2002). The roots of backlash. *Education Week*, **21**(16), 76, 42–43.

Vail, K. (1997). Core comes to Crooksville. *American School Board Journal*, **184**(3), 14–18.

Weisberg, R. W. (1988). Problem solving and creativity. In R. J. Sternberg (Ed.), *The nature of creativity* (pp. 148–176). New York: Cambridge University Press.

Weisberg, R. W. (1999). Creativity and knowledge: A challenge to theories. In R. J. Sternberg (Ed.), *Handbook of creativity* (pp. 226–250). New York: Cambridge University Press.

Weisberg, R. W. (2006). Expertise and reason in creative thinking. In J. C. Kaufman & J. Baer (Eds.), *Reason and creativity in development* (pp. 7–42). Cambridge: Cambridge University Press.

Willingham, D. B. (2001). *Cognition: The thinking animal*. Upper Saddle River, NJ: Prentice-Hall.

Woolfolk, A. (2001). *Educational psychology* (8th ed.). Boston: Allyn and Bacon.

Woolfolk, A. (2007). *Educational psychology* (10th Ed.). Boston: Allyn and Bacon.

Zimbardo, P. G., & Gerrig, R. J. (1999). *Psychology and life* (15th ed.). New York: Addison Wesley Longman.

CHAPTER 7

Ever-Broadening Conceptions of Creativity in the Classroom

Ronald A. Beghetto and James C. Kaufman

University of Connecticut

In the time since we wrote the first version of this chapter, conceptions of creativity in the classroom have continued to broaden. These include both our own conceptions and those of others. Whereas it was once safe to say that creativity in the classroom seemed to belong on the endangered species list (next to the Mantled howler monkey), we have seen changes in recent years. Many people now recognize that classroom creativity is much more than a distracting tangent, something to be explored "later," or even a behavior problem. Indeed, creativity has become a hot topic in education (Beghetto & Kaufman, 2013).

This, of course, does not mean that creativity has become the center-piece of the everyday curriculum. There are still instances where creativity is squeezed out of the curriculum. Indeed, this can happen anytime schools turn to extreme measures such as scripted or "teacher-proof" curricula (Sawyer, 2004) in pursuit of boosting performance on standardized learning assessments. Although persistent concerns remain, creativity has been recognized as a core 21st Century skill (J. C. Kaufman, 2016). Moreover, there is growing understanding of how creativity can compliment external content standards and enhance academic learning (Beghetto, Kaufman, & Baer, 2014).

Some advocates of creativity, however, have perhaps gone too far in making claims about creativity. Consider, for instance, the claim that "creativity now is as important in education as literacy" (Robinson, 2006). Such claims strike us as rhetorically compelling but problematic in practice. One problem is that they can result in conceptions that separate creativity from academic subject matter and academic skills. Instead of stressing the importance of how teachers might teach literacy more creatively or how teachers can support students' creative learning of literacy, they effectively split creativity and literacy into two separate, competing, and even interchangeable goals. Imagine a second grade teacher saying, "I'm not going to develop my students' literacy skills this year. But don't worry, I'll be cultivating their creative imagination instead." Would you want your child to have this teacher?

We would argue that creativity now occupies an even more interesting and potentially perilous position in education. On one hand, overly narrow emphasis on academics can result in squeezing creativity out of the classroom. On the other hand, overemphasizing the importance of creativity may ironically undermine teachers' ability to meaningfully incorporate it into the curriculum. Our purpose in revisiting this chapter is to reexamine, and in some cases reinforce, conceptions of creativity that can support educators in nurturing student creativity and, at the same time, allow them to fulfill curricular requirements.

Creativity Compliments Academic Constraints

Teachers commonly find themselves caught between contradictory demands of externally imposed mandates and supporting the needs of their students (Ingersoll, 2003). In a time of heightened school accountability (largely propelled by the No Child Left Behind Act of 2001), teachers may feel that they cannot nurture student creativity within the constraints of the required curriculum – particularly when they feel increased pressure to cover standardized curricula and prepare students for standardized learning assessments.

Indeed, as Aljughaiman and Mowrer-Reynolds (2005) have reported, many teachers feel "overwhelmed" with curricular pressures, and consequently, nurturing creativity takes a backseat to more convergent, skill-and-drill approaches to teaching the curriculum. Even prospective teachers seem to feel this pressure. For instance, Beghetto (2007a) found that prospective middle and secondary school teachers generally preferred more expected (and less unique) student responses during class discussions. This preference was frequently underwritten by a concern that unexpected student responses, while potentially promising, would take class discussions "off-task."

When creativity is viewed as an "add-on" to the curriculum or expression of unconstrained originality, it makes sense that teachers might feel ambivalent about supporting creativity in their classroom. This may help explain why so many teachers, from around the globe, have been found to hold negative views about creative students. For instance, researchers (e.g., Cropley, 1992; Dawson, 1997; Scott, 1999) have found that teachers sometimes prefer less creative students in their classroom, in part because they associate creativity with nonconformity, impulsivity, and disruptive behavior. Similar findings have been reported by researchers outside of the United States. Tan (2003) found that prospective teachers in Singapore favored students who had pleasant dispositions (e.g., kind, friendly, etc.) over students who they viewed as more creative and risk-taking. Chan and Chan (1999) found that Chinese teachers associated socially undesirable traits with student creativity – explaining that in Chinese culture, nonconforming or expressive behavior can be interpreted as arrogant or rebellious. Güncer and Oral (1993) reported similar beliefs held by Turkish teachers. Even poetry teachers, who one might think would value creativity, were found to resist assessing creativity in their students' work, and doubted it was possible to measure creativity at all (Myhill & Wilson, 2013).

Not all studies have found that teachers hold negative views about creative students (e.g., Runco, Johnson, & Bear, 1993). However, subsequent studies have indicated that teachers who hold more favorably views about creativity are not fully clear on what creativity actually means. For example, in one study (Westby & Dawson, 1995), teachers reported that they enjoyed working with creative students, yet when given adjectives that are typically used to describe creative people, they rated students who possessed those adjectives as their least favorite type of student (see also Aljughaiman & Mowrer-Reynolds, 2005). In another study, teachers and parents in the United States and India reported favorable views of creativity but also linked several words associated with mental illness (emotional, impulsive) with creativity (Runco & Johnson, 2002).

When teachers develop negative or conflicted views about creativity, it can result in missed opportunities for teachers to develop students' creative potential and even result in the systematic suppression of students' creative expression in the classroom (Beghetto, 2013). This need not be the case. Indeed, we would argue that teachers (like most people) value creativity, but likely have a problem with it when it is expressed at the wrong time or in the wrong place (e.g., a student coming up with a wildly original story of the life of plants instead of reporting her scientific observations in her science lab notebook). Teachers who successfully support creativity in their classroom help students learn when and how to be creative (J. C. Kaufman & Beghetto, 2013b; J. C. Kaufman, Beghetto, & Watson, forthcoming) and understand that in order for an idea, product, or behavior to be considered creative it must combine originality *and* appropriateness in the context of a particular task or activity (see Plucker, Beghetto & Dow, 2004, for a review). A few hypothetical (yet representative) examples might help clarify.

Tessa teaches mathematics, and she assigns her students a series of algebraic equations. She looks for originality in how a student chooses different strategies to get to the solution, but she also considers appropriateness (do the strategies reach the correct solutions?). Markus is a poetry teacher, and he asks his class to write Haikus. His goals for originality revolve around the students' use of language, word choice, imagery, and metaphor – but he also expects students to be appropriate and follow the specific rules for writing a Haiku. A student who hands in a free verse poem would not be considered creative in this instance (because the poem does not meet the conventions of Haiku or task constraints of the assignment). Laura is a creative shop teacher who asks her students to construct wooden birdhouses. She expects originality in their designs and decorations (students use a variety of unique architectural designs and decorate them with a variety of novel materials, including shells and beads), but the appropriateness (can a bird roost there?) is key.

The definition of creativity can therefore be represented in the following notation (adapted from Beghetto & Kaufman, 2014; Simonton, 2012):

$$C = O \times TA$$
$$\text{(Context)}$$

In this notation, creativity (C) requires both originality (O) and Task-appropriateness (TA) as defined within a particular context (e.g., eighth grade language arts). If something is original ($O = 1$), but not task appropriate ($TA = 0$), then it can be said to be original but not creative. When teachers recognize that creativity is not simply unconstrained originality – but actually requires a combination of originality and task appropriateness as defined in a particular context – they can see the value of curricular standards and conventions. Indeed, curricular constraints provide necessary evaluative criteria for judging whether student's original ideas, novel products, and unique accomplishments are appropriate (and therefore creative) within the constraints of particular curricular task, activity, or assignment.

Teachers who have a clear understanding of the nature of creativity – particularly with respect to the necessary combination of originality and task appropriateness – are able to avoid negative stereotypes and myths about creativity and, thereby, make room in for creativity in their curriculum (Beghetto & Plucker, 2006). Moreover, they can help students understand that there is a time and a place for creativity (J. C. Kaufman & Beghetto, 2013b). Even with this understanding it is sometimes still difficult to image how creativity might be supported as part of everyday curriculum.

Do Curricular Constraints Suppress Teachers' Ability to Support Creativity?

The Role of Creativity in the Day-to-Day Curriculum

When most people think of creative individuals, two types of images generally come to mind. The first image includes legendary pathfinders who have produced amazingly novel accomplishments (e.g., the jazz of John Coltrane, the poems of Emily Dickenson, the scientific brilliance of J. Robert Oppenheimer, or the social justice of Martin Luther King, Jr.). The other type of image is that of the more everyday creative person (e.g., the teacher down the hall who always has the most unique classroom decorations and bulletin boards, the front office secretary who makes original woven baskets, or the facilities crewmember who consistently comes up with novel solutions to broken classroom equipment).

These two types of images are often described as Big-C (legendary) and little-c (everyday) creativity. This Big-C/little-c dichotomy, at first blush, seems to offer broad enough categories for classifying creativity. However, as with most dichotomies, these categories are too restrictive – particularly in the context of the classroom. Consider, for instance, a junior high school student who has several unique and personally meaningful insights about how she might arrange graphics and text for her school's yearbook. If the little-c category is the only alternative to Big-C, this student's creative insights might be overlooked or unfairly compared to those of college student enrolled in a graphic arts degree program or even a professional graphic artist who is giving a guest lecture on graphic design at a local university. Or consider the veteran teacher who has been consistently creative in her approach to teaching – it would be somewhat insulting to equate this teacher's creativity with a student-teacher who has developed one or two creative ideas about how he would like to teach a lesson. It seems equally unhelpful to compare her teacher with the transformative pedagogical approaches pioneered by Maria Montessori. If there is no middle ground between Big-C and little-c creativity, then where does this teacher's creativity fit? Neither category seems appropriate.

In an effort to address the limitations of the Big-C/little-c dichotomy, we developed the Four-c Model of Creativity (Beghetto & Kaufman, 2007; J. C. Kaufman & Beghetto, 2009, 2013a), which includes interpretive (mini-c) creativity and professional (Pro-c) creativity. We believe that this model can help teachers understand the developmental trajectory of

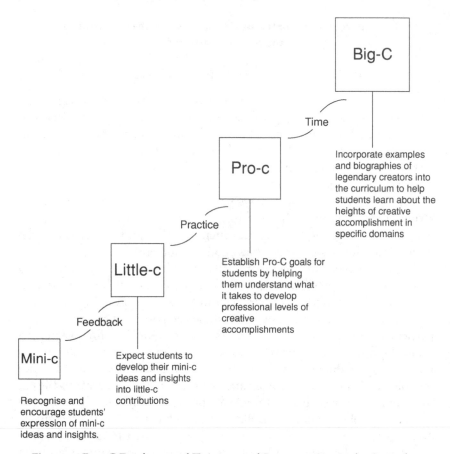

Figure 7.1 Four-C Developmental Trajectory and Representations in the Curriculum

creativity (Beghetto & Kaufman, 2014) and help teachers recognize how the different levels of creativity can be represented in their curriculum (see Figure 7.1).

Mini-c Creativity

The first level of creativity is mini-c creativity. Mini-c creativity represents conceptions of creativity that have focused on more "subjective" (Stein, 1953), "personal" (Runco, 1996), "universal" (Cohen, 1989), and developmental (Moran & John-Steiner, 2003) conceptions of creativity. We have defined mini-c creativity as *the novel and personally meaningful interpretation of experiences, actions, and events* (Beghetto & Kaufman, 2007, p. 73). Mini-c creativity occurs during the process of learning (e.g., a student having a new and personally meaningful insight about how to incorporate design principles she learned in art class in her PowerPoint presentation on the Civil War). In this way, learning can be thought of as a creative act (Beghetto, 2015). Our conception of mini-c creativity is informed by a Vygotskian (or sociocultural) view of knowledge that stresses the transactional relationship between the individual and social world. This sociocultural emphasis underscores how internal (mini-c) insights and interpretations are influenced by interactions and experiences with domain-relevant knowledge and how, under the right conditions, those internal (mini-c) insights can potentially develop into external (larger-C) contributions. In this way, creativity and learning have an interdependent relationship (Beghetto, 2016a).

A real-life example (as reported by Lofing, 2009) may help illustrate this process. Navel orangeworms are a major pest of almond and pistachio growers. Growers commonly use bait made with almonds to attempt to control this pest. However, Gabriel Leal, a sixth-grade student and son of an entomology professor at University of California at Davis, had the mini-c insight that orangeworms might actually prefer pistachios over almonds. This insight was based on his own experiences (pistachios tasted better to him) and interpretation of the problem (if he preferred the taste of pistachios, then perhaps the orangeworms would also prefer pistachios). Although Gabriel's mini-c insight ran counter to prior research (and the practice of growers), he was supported in testing this idea in a controlled experiment, using his dad's University of California at Davis lab, under the supervision of one of his father's colleagues. The results of the experiment shocked researchers and confirmed Gabriel's mini-c insight. The findings have subsequently been reported at a professional conference by his father, thereby influencing the work of researchers and impacting professional knowledge and practice.

This example illustrates how mini-c creativity can, under the right conditions, lead to larger-c contributions. Of course, most students do not have access to the kinds of supports, domain-relevant knowledge, and resources to take their mini-c ideas directly to real-world contributions (as Gabriel, the sixth-grader, did). Still, with respect to creativity in the classroom, awareness of mini-c creativity can help educators recognize that not only do students' mini-c insights have the potential to develop into external expressions of creativity but also such insights and interpretations can (and should) be considered creative in their own right.

As Vygotsky (2004) argued, "Any human act that gives rise to something new is referred to as a creative act, regardless of whether what is created is a physical object or some mental or emotional construct that lives within the person who created it and is known only to him" (p. 7). Thus, whatever the creative product (be it an idea, paintings, or performance) or the magnitude of that product (be it little-c or Big-C), it all starts with the imaginative and personal interpretations of mini-c.

Recognizing Mini-c Insights

Teachers can go a long way in supporting students' creative potential by recognizing the mini-c insights that students have as part of their every-day learning of academic subject matter. Instead of dismissing students' unexpected (yet potentially creative) ideas, teachers who support creative expression will help their students clarify, re-voice, and, when necessary, reconsider their novel ideas and interpretations.

Recognizing and encouraging the expression of students' mini-c insights serve at least three purposes. First, it helps students develop confidence in their own creative potential. For instance, Beghetto (2006) found that positive teacher feedback about students' creativity was the strongest unique predictor of students' confidence in their own creativity. Such confidence is critical as it increases the likelihood that students will take the intellectual risks necessary to share their mini-c insights, interpretations, and ideas (Beghetto, 2008; Nickerson, 1999).

Second, encouraging students to share their unique ideas is necessary if teachers what to help students develop their ideas mini-c (personal) inter-pretations into socially vetted ideas and understandings. Teachers who support the development of students' creative potential do so, in part, by helping their students become aware of academic subject matter conven-tions and constraints, teaching students how to articulate the relevance of their mini-c ideas in light of those conventions and constraints and, when necessary, helping them realize that it is sometimes necessary to let go of some ideas in search of more generative ones.

Finally, encouraging students to share their mini-c insights – and pro-viding informative feedback on those insights – can enrich other students' learning and understanding. When students have an opportunity to share their unique and meaningful strategies for solving problems in mathemat-ics, for instance, other students can develop a more nuanced understanding of the nature of mathematical reasoning. The same can be said for most any subject area (be it unique interpretations of an historical event, novel insights about a scientific phenomenon, or a new way of interpreting the meaning of a poem). Providing students with opportunities to find their own path through problems and share their unique ideas is a sign of a powerful learning environment (Duckworth, 1996) – a learning environment that supports the development of creative potential.

In sum, teachers who support the creative potential of their students welcome and work with – rather than dismiss and suppress – students' unexpected interpretations and insights. This involves taking the time to hear and attempt to understand students' mini-c interpretations, helping students recognize when their contributions are not making sense given the curricular constraints of a particular activity or task and providing multiple opportunities for students to practice developing the skills of a particular domain or task (Beghetto, 2007b). These strategies, like other practical suggestions for supporting creativity (highlighted in various chapters throughout this book), stress the importance of teachers recognizing students' creative potential while at the same time introducing students to the conventions, standards, and existing knowledge of the various academic subject areas. As a result, students can develop the requisite academic subject matter knowledge necessary for moving from mini-c interpretations to little-c expressions of creativity.

Little-c Creativity

Everyday, or little-c, creativity refers to the creativity accessible to most anyone (Richards, 2007). Examples of little-c creativity include a fourth-grader's drawing displayed at the local grocery store, a group of high-school actors' unique interpretation of *The Crucible*, and a middle-school teacher's original way of teaching grammar. Little-c creativity rarely garners the same level of pop culture attention as Big-C creativity, with the exception of sometimes highlighting cute and clever comments of a young child being interviewed on a televised talk show or the unique twist put on classic recipes submitted by readers of a popular cooking magazine.

Although pop culture pays only passing attention to little-c creativity, several theories of creativity have focused on this more everyday level of creative accomplishment. The Investment Theory of Creativity (Sternberg & Lubart, 1996), for instance, argues that the key to being creative is to buy low and sell high in the world of ideas. Amabile's (1996) Componential Model of Creativity is another example of a theory that has relevance for more everyday or classroom-level creativity. This theory highlights three components that seem necessary for creative accomplishments to occur: domain-relevant skills (e.g., learning how to play a musical instrument), creativity-relevant skills (i.e., the ability to synthesize and combine musical notes and scales in unique ways), and task motivation (i.e., the requisite commitment to put in the hard work and sustain that effort in the face of challenges).

Little-c Expectations

The little-c category is a reminder that creative expression is possible for most any student, in almost any curricular subject area, on almost any given day. Teachers who support little-c creativity in their classroom recognize that creative expression is not a distal goal or extracurricular activity, but rather a seamless part of their everyday curriculum. Moreover, they recognize that by encouraging and providing feedback on students' mini-c insights, such insights can grow into little-c contributions that, in turn, have a positive impact on the learning of others (Beghetto, 2016a). Indeed, as illustrated in Figure 7.1, one of the key factors in moving from mini-c to little-c is feedback.

Elena Grigorenko and her colleagues (Grigorenko, Jarvin, Tan, & Sternberg, 2008), for instance, demonstrated how little-c creativity can be "naturally integrated into teaching and assessing domain-specific knowledge" (p. 304). Their work is particularly compelling because it focuses on the use of curriculum-based assessments of creativity, which offer teachers ways to monitor and support creative thinking proficiency as part of their regular teaching of the academic curriculum.

Teachers who integrate creativity into their regular curriculum do so by including little-c expectations in their everyday learning activities, assignments, and assessments (Beghetto, 2013; Grigorenko et al., 2008) – including academic content standards such as the Common Core (see Beghetto, Kaufman, & Baer, 2014). As Grigorenko et al. (2008) have explained,

> The learning of new content in all areas lends itself to creative exercises. For example, when learning new math applications, students can be asked to imagine new, futuristic, or fantastical uses of such an application. Facts learned in a science exercise can be employed in visual creations (pictures and illustrations, e.g., Draw a scenario in which some typical behaviors of a sea anemone are included); in verbal creations (sentences or stories, e.g., Write a sentence or story about sea anemones employing some facts that you have learned); as well as in numerical creations (mathematical equations or relationships, e.g., Come up with some equations that describe quantitative relationships that are important in the life cycle or in the environment of a sea anemone). (p. 305)

In addition to integrating expectations for creative expression in everyday assignments and assessments, creativity researchers have also stressed the importance of monitoring the motivational messages sent by common teaching and assessment practices. Recommendations based on a summary of this work (see Beghetto, 2005) include (1) focusing students attention on interesting and personally meaningful aspects of tasks; (2) providing students with opportunities to generate a wide array of novel ideas and then helping them focus their attention on selecting the most promising and appropriate ideas for a given task; (3) minimizing the pressures of assessments, grades, and other forms of evaluation; (4) encouraging students to focus on self-improvement, increased effort, and seeking help from skilled others when necessary; (5) helping students frame mistakes as a natural and necessary part of learning; and (6) helping students focus on what grades mean with respect to what they did well and how they might improve in the future.

In this way, little-c creative expression becomes part of (rather than an add-on to) the curriculum. Teachers who include little-c expectations as part of the regular curriculum not only provide students with an opportunity to develop confidence and competence in their creative expression but also help debunk entrenched myths and stereotypes about creativity (such as, only certain people can be creative, creativity is only appropriate in the arts, and so on – see Plucker et al., 2004, for an overview).

Pro-c Creativity

Pro-c creativity represents developmental and effortful progression beyond little-c that has not yet attained Big-C status. Consider the hypothetical case of Wanda, who earned her doctorate in science education. Her dissertation explored methods for teaching aquatic science to youth attending high-poverty schools along the Pacific Coast. She later received a small grant and conducted a study on how science teachers used both in-class activities and outdoor excursions to reach their students. After publishing this research in a peer-reviewed journal, her next project (on scientific reasoning in elementary classrooms) won an award for the best paper published that year on that topic.

If we stick to little-c/Big-C distinction, where do we place Wanda? Categorizing her efforts in the little-c category diminishes everything she has accomplished. Yet placing Wanda in the Big-C category is equally inappropriate. Her work is creative and has attained a level of creative acumen in a professional field, but she has not made the kind of contribution that will place her in the history books. The Pro-c category offers accomplished creative individuals, such as Wanda, their own category.

Anyone who attains professional-level expertise in any creative area is likely to have attained Pro-c status. Not all working professionals in creative fields will necessarily reach Pro-c (a street artist at *Disneyland* who draws quick caricatures of tourists, for example, may make a good living but may not necessarily be Pro-c level creative in his or her craft). Similarly, some people may reach Pro-c level without being able to quit their day jobs. Some areas of creative expression may not provide enough monetary sustenance to allow financial freedom from other responsibilities. Yet many "amateur" artists are being creative at the Pro-c level, even if it is not their primary means of support. Most poets, for example, earn the majority of their income from teaching (or other work). A poet who has published in many top literary magazines may be highly respected yet unable to make a living solely from writing. Similarly, many renowned stage actors, even those who have been on Broadway, may have a hard time paying New York City–level rents.

Although many creativity theories have focused on Big-C or little-c, there is at least one that seems more suited for Pro-c levels of creativity: the Propulsion Theory of Creative Contributions (Sternberg, Kaufman, & Pretz, 2002; Sternberg & Kaufman, 2012). This theory highlights eight different types of creative contributions. The first type, *replication*, primarily keeps the status quo of earlier creations by reproducing past work (e.g., movie sequels, such as the seemingly endless, yet slightly different, string of *Friday the 13th* horror movies). The remaining seven types of creativity, in contrast, highlight more profound contributions. *Reinitiation*, for instance, represents contributions that move some field to a new starting point and then progresses from there (e.g., the development and progression of American jazz music). And *creative integration*, which merges two diverse domains, can result in new genres and transformative paradigms (e.g., George Lucas combining samurai movies, ancient myths, and science fiction to create *Star Wars*). Pro-c is often seen in and across these various types of creative contributions.

Of the eight types of contributions in the theory, *replication* is perhaps most relevant for the classroom (e.g., a high-school student writing a sonnet in the style of Shakespeare). The other types of contributions speak to large scale innovations that usually take many years of intensive study and expert skill development and, therefore, are not feasible or directly relevant for the typical classroom.

The movement from little-c to Pro-c therefore requires many years of deliberate practice (see Figure 7.1). In this way, the concept of Pro-c is consistent with the expertise acquisition approach of creativity (Ericsson, 1996, 2014), which stresses that creative expertise results from many years of deliberate practice in a particular domain. Typically a decade (or more) of intensive preparation is necessary to become an international performer in a broader range of domains including chess, sports, the arts, and science (Hayes, 1989). These years are not necessarily spent simply learning and following standard protocol, but rather actively experimenting and exploring (Gardner, 1993). There is also evidence that it may take even longer than ten years of active acquisition. For example, S. B. Kaufman and Kaufman (2007) analyzed contemporary fiction writers and found that there was a further time lag (also approximately ten years) between an author's first publication and a peak publication. This finding is consistent with Simonton's (2000) work with classical composers, which suggests that although it does take about ten years to learn a field, it may take additional time to reach a level of eminence. Some domains that focus more on consistently strong performance (such as chess, sports, and medicine) may only need ten years, whereas domains that require a variety of styles and ranges may take longer (Martindale, 1990).

Pro-c Goals

Although most K–12 students will not be in a position to produce Pro-c creations, including examples of Pro-c level creativity in the curriculum can still offer long-range goals for which students can strive. Teachers can support the development and students' movement toward attaining such goals by developing assignments and activities that highlight the specific skills, knowledge, dispositions, and strategies necessary for creative work in and across various academic disciplines (see also Piirto, 2004).

Science teachers, for instance, can have their students investigate the types of knowledge, training, and creative aspects of developing and conducting scientific inquiry. Students in language arts classes might be asked consider the creative and imaginative aspects involved in writing (including everything from novel uses of language and grammar to how story ideas are generated and represented in various types of narratives). Math teachers might help their students explore the more creative and imaginative aspects of mathematics – everything from how mathematicians work with highly abstract concepts to the aesthetics of visual representations of quantitative data.

Teachers can also support students' understanding of creativity in the professions by inviting visits from local Pro-c professionals (e.g., architects, scientists, professional artists, novelists, and so on) who can help youngsters understand what it takes to be creative in various professions and academic disciplines. This might include everything from the type and amount of professional training required to how creativity is judged in that particular profession (e.g., peer review, critics, co-insures, etc.). Providing students opportunities to hear from and ask questions of Pro-c professionals can go a long way in sparking (and sustaining) students' interest in how creativity might be expressed in and across various professions.

Big-C Creativity

As we have already mentioned, legendary creative accomplishments occupy a great deal of attention, both in the scholarly literature and pop culture representations. Indeed, many of the iconic images of creators come from television, film, and other sources of media. Consider for instance, the *A&E Biography* television program, which highlights well-known creators from history, or movies such as *Pollack*, *Amadeus*, or *Capote*, which offer fictionalized portrayals of genius-level creators. Big-C creativity has also garnered a great deal of attention among creativity scholars, including Simonton's (2009) work on greatness; Gruber's (1981) compelling case study of Darwin's notebooks; Gardner's (1993) case histories of Freud, Einstein, Picasso, Stravinsky, Eliot, Graham, and Gandhi; and Nandy's (1995) studies of creative scientists and mathematicians, including the great Srinivasa Ramanujan. Many of the most prominent theories of creativity also focus on the most highly accomplished creators but also highlight how creativity can differ both by domain (e.g., artistic versus scientific) and type of contribution (incremental versus transformative).

Csikszentmihalyi's (1999) Systems Model, for instance, describes how accomplishments in a particular domain (such as art) are judged to be creative by gatekeepers of that domain (critics, curators, collectors, and fellow artists). This theory highlights how eminent levels of creativity are different across domains (partly because accomplishments are being judged by different criteria, conventions, and constraints).

Big-C creativity is largely out of the hands of individual creators as historians, critiques, and connoisseurs typically bestow this "legendary" status upon them long after they have made their contributions. In this way, the passing of time is a key factor in movement from Pro-c to Big-C (see Figure 7.1).

Big-C Exemplars

Although nurturing students' smaller-c creativity is what teachers can most readily incorporate into their curriculum, legendary creators can serve as important illustrations of the highest levels of creative achievement that have occurred in various disciplines. Such Big-C exemplars can serve as particularly powerful illustrations for students when they are considered in light of the full trajectory of creative development – exploring not only how these creators progressed from having mini-c insights to producing Big-C breakthroughs but also what kinds of supports, setbacks, and chance occurrences were involved along the way. Including Big-C biographies in the curriculum can help capture students' imagination, raise important questions, and even dispel misconceptions about major creative contributions in particular fields and professions.

When sharing legendary biographies, educators need to be careful that they are not reinforcing persistent and pernicious myths about creativity (e.g., only certain people have creative potential), but rather use these biographies to illustrate the domain knowledge, access to resources, confidence, effort, and chance opportunities necessary to go from mini-c insights to trend setting breakthroughs (see also Simonton, 2004).

Making Room for Creativity in the Classroom: Now and for the Future

As we finish this revised chapter and reflect on the changes we have seen since the first version, we remain optimistic about the recognized importance and role that creativity teaching and learning can (and does) play in the day-to-day curriculum. We still harbor some concerns about the pressures that have been placed on teachers to meet content standards. We also view some of the policy initiatives aimed at promoting creativity in schools with a raised eyebrow – hoping that policy makers will not make the mistake of trying to mandate creativity. Our hope is that policy makers will step back from attempting to control the creative teaching, learning, and lives of teachers and students. A more viable approach is to provide opportunities for teachers, students, and instructional leaders to learn meaningful ways to use their creativity to support the day-to-day teaching, learning, and school leadership practices in their particular school context (e.g., Beghetto, 2016b, J. C. Kaufman & Beghetto, 2013b). We see great promise in more self-directed efforts, supported by insights gleaned from the field of creativity studies.

The future of creativity in schools and classrooms is no more certain now than it was the first time we addressed this topic. What has remained the same is our optimism and confidence that whatever the future holds there will always be creative teachers who are committed to finding ways to teach for and with creativity. We continue to hope that the ideas we have revisited in this chapter help current and future educators develop new and more powerful ways to support the development of students' creative potential within the curricular constraints of the various academic disciplines.

We also continue to believe that one of the most important factors to supporting student creativity is caring teachers and their allies (be they school leaders, parents, researchers, or fellow educators) who are truly committed to providing opportunities for students to develop their creative learning potential – from the mini-c level upward. We stand with all teachers who are committed to this effort and hope that our ideas can continue to support your important and creative work.

REFERENCES

Aljughaiman, A., & Mowrer-Reynolds, E. (2005). Teachers' conceptions of creativity and creative students. *Journal of Creative Behavior*, **39**, 17–34.

Amabile, T. M. (1996). *Creativity in context: Update to the social psychology of creativity*. Boulder, CO: Westview.

Beghetto, R. A. (2005). Does assessment kill student creativity? *The Educational Forum*, **69**, 254–263.

Beghetto, R. A. (2006). Creative self-efficacy: Correlates in middle and secondary students. *Creativity Research Journal*, **18**, 447–457.

Beghetto, R. A. (2007a). Does creativity have a place in classroom discussions? Prospective teachers' response preferences. *Thinking Skills and Creativity*, **2**, 1–9.

Beghetto, R. A. (2007b). Ideational code-switching: Walking the talk about supporting student creativity in the classroom. *Roeper Review*, **29**, 265–270.

Beghetto, R. A. (2008). Correlates of intellectual risk taking in elementary school science. *Journal of Research in Science Teaching*, **46**, 210–223.

Beghetto, R. A. (2009). In search of the unexpected: Finding creativity in the micro-moments of the classroom. *Psychology of Aesthetics, Creativity, and the Arts*, **3**, 2–5.

Beghetto, R. A. (2013). *Killing ideas softly? The promise and perils of creativity in the classroom*. Charlotte, NC: Information Age Publishing.

Beghetto, R. A. (2015). Learning as a creative act. In T. Kettler (Ed.), *Modern curriculum for gifted and advanced learners*. Waco, TX: Prufrock.

Beghetto, R. A. (2016a). Creative learning: A fresh look. *Journal of Cognitive Education and Psychology*, 15, 6–23.

Beghetto, R. A. (2016b). *Big wins, Small steps: How to lead for and with creativity*. Thousand Oaks, CA: Corwin Press.

Beghetto, R. A., & Kaufman, J. C. (2007). Toward a broader conception of creativity: A case for "mini-c" creativity. *Psychology of Aesthetics, Creativity, and the Arts*, **1**, 13–79.

Beghetto, R. A., & Kaufman, J. C. (2013). Fundamentals of creativity. *Educational Leadership*, 70, 10–15.

Beghetto, R. A., & Kaufman, J. C. (2014). Classroom contexts for creativity. *High Ability Studies*, **25**, 53–69.

Beghetto, R. A., Kaufman, J. C., & Baer, J. (2014). *Teaching for creativity in the common core classroom.* New York: Teachers College Press.

Beghetto, R. A., & Plucker, J. A. (2006). The relationship among schooling, learning, and creativity: "All roads lead to creativity" or "You can't get there from here?" In J. C. Kaufman & J. Bear (Eds.), *Creativity and reason in cognitive development* (pp. 316–332). Cambridge: Cambridge University Press.

Chan, D. W., & Chan, L. K. (1999). Implicit theories of creativity: Teachers' perception of student characteristics in Hong Kong. *Creativity Research Journal*, **12**, 185–195.

Cohen, L. M. (1989). A continuum of adaptive creative behaviors. *Creativity Research Journal*, **2**, 169–183.

Cropley, A. J. (1992). *More ways than one: Fostering creativity.* Norwood, NJ: Ablex.

Csikszentmihalyi, M. (1999). Implications of a systems perspective for the study of creativity. In R. J. Sternberg (Ed.), *Handbook of human creativity* (pp. 313–338). New York: Cambridge University Press.

Dawson, V. L. (1997). In search of the Wild Bohemian: Challenges in the identification of the creatively gifted. *Roeper Review*, **19**, 148–152.

Duckworth, E. (1996). *The having of wonderful ideas and other essays on teaching and learning* (2nd ed.). New York: Teachers College Press.

Ericsson, K. A. (Ed.). (1996). *The road to expert performance: Empirical evidence from the arts and sciences, sports, and games.* Mahwah, NJ: Erlbaum.

Ericsson, K. A. (2014). Creative genius: A view from the expert-performance approach. In D. K. Simonton (Ed.), *The Wiley handbook of genius* (pp. 321–349). Oxford: Wiley.

Gardner, H. (1993). *Creating minds.* New York: Basic Books.

Grigorenko, E. L., Jarvin, L., Tan, M., & Sternberg, R. J. (2008). Something new in the garden: Assessing creativity in academic domains. *Psychology Science Quarterly*, **50**, 295–307.

Gruber, H. (1981). *Darwin on man.* Chicago: University of Chicago Press.

Güncer, B., & Oral, G. (1993). Relationship between creativity and nonconformity to school discipline as perceived by teachers of Turkish elementary school children, by controlling for their grade and sex. *Journal of Instructional Psychology*, **20**, 208–214.

Hayes, J. R. (1989). *The complete problem solver* (2nd ed.). Hillsdale, NJ: Erlbaum.

Ingersoll, R. M. (2003). *Who controls teachers' work? Power and accountability in America's schools.* Cambridge, MA: Harvard University Press.

Kaufman, J. C. (2016). *Creativity 101* (2nd ed.). New York: Springer.

Kaufman, J. C., & Beghetto, R. A. (2009). Beyond big and little: The Four C Model of creativity, *Review of General Psychology*, **13**, 1–12.

Kaufman, J. C., & Beghetto, R. A. (2013a). Do people recognize the Four Cs? Examining layperson conceptions of creativity. *Psychology of Aesthetics, Creativity, and the Arts*, **7**, 229–236.

Kaufman, J. C., & Beghetto, R. A. (2013b). In praise of Clark Kent: Creative metacognition and the importance of teaching kids when (not) to be creative. *Roeper Review*, **35**, 155–165.

Kaufman, J. C., Beghetto, R A., & Watson, C. (forthcoming). Creative metacognition and self-ratings of creative performance: A 4-C perspective. *Learning and Individual Differences*.

Kaufman, S. B., & Kaufman, J. C. (2007). Ten years to expertise, many more to greatness: An investigation of modern writers. *Journal of Creative Behavior*, **41**, 114–124.

Lofing, N. (2009, January 10). Davis sixth-grader's science experiment breaks new ground. *Sacramento Bee* (Sacramento, CA). Retrieved January 13, 2009 from www.sacbee.comeducationv-printstory1530953.html.

McNeil, L. M. (2000). *Contradictions of school reform: Educational costs of standardized testing*. New York: Routledge.

Martindale, C. (1990). *The clockwork muse: The predictability of artistic change*. New York: Basic Books.

Moran, S., & John-Steiner, V. (2003). Creativity in the making: Vygotsky's contemporary contribution to the dialectic of development and creativity. In R. K. Sawyer, V. John-Steiner, S. Moran, R. J. Sternberg, D. H. Feldman, J. Nakamura, et al. (Eds.), *Creativity and development* (pp. 61–90). New York: Oxford University Press.

Myhill, D., & Wilson, A. (2013). Playing it safe: Teachers' views of creativity in poetry writing. *Thinking Skills and Creativity*, **10**, 101–111.

Nandy, A. (1995). *Alternative sciences: Creativity and authenticity in two Indian scientists*. Delhi: Oxford University Press.

Nickerson, R. S. (1999). Enhancing creativity. In R. J. Sternberg (Ed.), *Handbook of human creativity* (pp. 392–430). New York: Cambridge University Press.

No Child Left Behind Act of 2001, Pub. 1, No. 107–110, 115 Stat. 1425 (2002).

Piirto, J. (2004). *Understanding creativity*. Scottsdale, AZ: Great Potential Press.

Plucker, J. A., Beghetto, R. A., & Dow, G. T. (2004). Why isn't creativity more important to educational psychologists? Potentials, pitfalls, and future directions in creativity research. *Educational Psychologist*, **39**, 83–96.

Richards, R. (2007). Everyday creativity: Our hidden potential. In R. Richards (Ed.), *Everyday creativity and new views of human nature* (pp. 25–54). Washington, DC: American Psychological Association.

Robinson, K. (2006). Do schools kill creativity? [Transcript]. Retrieved from www.ted.com/talks/ken_robinson_says_schools_kill_creativity/transcript?language=en

Runco, M. A. (1996). Personal creativity: Definition and developmental issues. *New Directions for Child Development*, **72**, 3–30

Runco, M. A. (2005). Motivation, competence, and creativity. In A. Elliott & C. Dweck (Eds.), *Handbook of achievement motivation and competence* (pp. 609–623). New York: Guilford.

Runco, M. A., & Johnson, D. J. (2002). Parents' and teachers' implicit theories of children's creativity: A cross-cultural perspective. *Creativity Research Journal*, **14**, 427–439.

Runco, M. A., Johnson, D. J., & Bear, P. K. (1993). Parents' and teachers' implicit theories of children's creativity. *Child Study Journal*, **23**, 91–113.

Sawyer, R. K. (2004). Creative teaching: Collaborative discussion as disciplined improvisation. *Educational Researcher*, **33**, 12–20.

Scott, C. L. (1999). Teachers' biases toward creative children. *Creativity Research Journal*, **12**, 321–337.

Simonton, D. K. (2000). Creative development as acquired expertise: Theoretical issues and an empirical test. *Developmental Review*, **20**, 283–318.

Simonton, D. K. (2004). *Creativity in science: Chance, logic, genius, and zeitgeist.* Cambridge: Cambridge University Press.

Simonton, D. K. (2009). *Greatness 101.* New York: Springer.

Simonton, D. K. (2012). Citation measures as criterion variables in predicting scientific eminence. *Measurement: Interdisciplinary Research and Perspectives*, 10, 170–171.

Stein, M. I. (1953). Creativity and culture. *The Journal of Psychology*, **36**, 311–322.

Sternberg, R. J., & Kaufman, J. C. (2012). When your race is almost run, but you feel you're not yet done: Application of the Propulsion Theory of Creative Contributions to late-career challenges. *Journal of Creative Behavior*, **46**, 66–76.

Sternberg, R. J., Kaufman, J. C., & Pretz, J. E. (2002). *The creativity conundrum.* New York: Psychology Press.

Sternberg, R. J., & Lubart, T. I. (1996). Investing in creativity. *American Psychologist*, **51**, 677–688.

Tan, A. G. (2003). Teaching the Chinese learner: Psychological and pedagogical perspectives. *International Journal of Educational Development*, **23**, 233–240.

Vygotsky, L. S. (2004). Imagination and creativity in childhood. (M. E. Sharpe, Inc., Trans.). *Journal of Russian and East European Psychology*, **42**, 7–97.

Westby, E. L., & Dawson, V. L. (1995). Creativity: Asset or burden in the classroom? *Creativity Research Journal*, **8**, 1–10.

CHAPTER 8

Creativity in Mathematics Teaching
A Chinese Perspective (An Update)

Weihua Niu

Pace University

Zheng Zhou

St. John's University

Introduction

In a recent BBC documentary, five teachers from China were invited to create a "Chinese school" within a British public school (Bagnall, Quaglieni & Rumney, 2015). In four weeks, a group of 50 ninth graders fully experienced the "Chinese way of learning," which include a large classroom setting with 50 students of mixed abilities, longer school hours (12 hours per day), a descriptive teaching style featured with lectures from the teachers and note-taking from the students, and grueling learning materials and homework. By the end of the four-week experiment, they then competed with the rest of students of their age group from the same school to test the results of their learning. Despite constant rebellion from the students and chaotic classroom at least in the first two and half weeks, students from the "Chinese school" outperformed their counterparts from the "British school" in mathematics and sciences by 10%.

The results shocked both the school and the Chinese teachers, as they all felt the Chinese classroom would not fit to the British students. Before the experiment, the school headmaster, Neil Strowger, visited public schools in Shanghai and made comments to the 2012 Programme for International Students Assessment (PISA) results that put Chinese students from Shanghai on the top of test in mathematics and sciences among 65 countries and economies.

> It is, however, abundantly clear to me that Chinese parents, culture and values are the real reasons that Shanghai Province tops the oft-cited Pisa tables rather than superior teaching practice. No educational approach or policy is going to turn back the British cultural clock to the 1950s. Nor should it seek to. (BBC News Magazine, August 4, 2015)

Mr. Strowger's view probably represents most Western observers' perspective regarding cross-national differences in academic achievement. The results from the experiment, however, challenge the view. There ought be something valuable about the Chinese way of teaching, or the way of teaching was in the West few decades ago, which is worthwhile to examine further. The documentary sparked a new round of global interest from both the general public and educational professionals to reflect their own educational systems. What have we done well and what can we learn from others? Are there true objective and universal criteria to examine the quality of education in a global context at least from the competence levels in subject areas all school try to delivery?

Mathematics is one of core areas often subjected to cross-cultural comparisons. There are a considerable number of studies in the past few decades demonstrating that, when compared to students from Eastern Asian countries (e.g., China, Japan, Korean, and Singapore), U.S. students not only fall behind in their basic knowledge and skills in mathematics across all age levels but also show less interest in learning and appreciating the subject (Stevenson et al., 1990; Stevenson & Stigler, 1992; U.S. Department of Education, 1996). The results of some large-scale cross-national comparative studies on mathematics achievement, such as the International Association for Evaluation of Educational Achievement (IEA) Studies, the Third International Mathematics and Science Study (TIMSS) studies, and the Organization for Economic Cooperation and Development (OECD) Studies (Fan & Zhu, 2004), suggest that math education programs in the United States are uninspiring compared to those of other industrial countries.

PISA, created by OECD, following the tradition of IEA and TIMSS, became a popular international standardized test in the 21st century, assessing basic literacy in reading, mathematics, and sciences of 15-year-old students across nations who are nearing the end of their compulsory schooling period. The first round of PISA results were published in 2000 and then updated every three years. The results have been consistent in the past 15 years. When looking at the average score of all participating students from 65 countries and economics, the first group of educational systems are all from East Asia, such as China, Korea, and Japan, followed by a group of Northern European countries, such as Switzerland, Netherlands, and Finland. United States is often listed in the middle, almost the lowest among all developed countries (OECD, 2013).

How can this gap in mathematics achievement and students' attitudes toward learning mathematics be explained? There seems to be no straightforward answer to this question, especially when examining the Chinese mathematics classrooms from a Western perspective. The average class size in China is almost twice as large as that in the United States (40–50 students) (Cortazzi & Jin, 2001). Moreover, Chinese teachers widely adopt expository and explanatory pedagogy and use norm-referenced assessments to assist their teaching and ensure student learning. Nevertheless, this apparent counterproductive pedagogy does not seem to prevent Chinese students from acquiring a deeper, more meaningful problem solving–oriented approach to learning. Chinese students also seem to develop higher levels of understanding of mathematics and show increased levels of intrinsic motivation toward learning mathematics compared to their American counterparts. These phenomena were captured and examined by Watkins and Biggs (1996, 2001) as the "paradox of the Chinese learners."

In order to understand the paradox of Chinese learners, it is important to examine the effectiveness of the Chinese method of teaching mathematics. This chapter focuses on examining the Chinese approach to mathematics instruction from a creative teaching perspective. We purport that teaching mathematics in Chinese classrooms is like engaging in the performing arts. As in any other performing arts, the creative products – the mathematics lessons in this case – are often carefully crafted and executed by Chinese teachers. During this process, the teachers are also frequently observed and critiqued formally and informally by colleagues to achieve perfection in teaching. Paine (1990) describes this method of teaching as the "virtuoso model" in which teachers take center stage, providing lectures and leading students in various activities.

Using Amabile's Componential Framework of Creativity, we analyze how Chinese teachers achieve high levels of creativity in their teaching by focusing on the analyses of the critical components in the Framework. These components are observed in Chinese teachers' teaching of mathematics: (1) developing domain-specific knowledge, (2) promoting creativity-related processes by developing strategies of teaching with variation, and (3) nurturing intrinsic motivation to learn mathematics by providing well-crafted, interesting, and meaningful activities. In this chapter we first present Amabile's componential framework and a discussion of how such a framework coincides with the Chinese conception of good teaching, supported by teaching examples of how Chinese teachers facilitate creative problem-solving strategies in teaching mathematics. We then introduce the Chinese teacher-training model and the concept of the model lesson. Finally, we discuss how Chinese teachers acquire creative teaching techniques through the three approaches discussed previously. We conclude with a discussion of the implications of learning Chinese approaches to the teaching of mathematics.

Theoretical Framework of Creative Teaching

The theoretical consideration of creative teaching is based on Amabile's Componential Framework of Creativity. The theory was first proposed in 1983, and has since been revised many times. According to Amabile (1996), three major components are necessary and sufficient for individuals to produce creative productions in any domain. These components include: (1) domain-relevant skills (i.e., factual knowledge about the domain, technical skills, and special domain-relevant talents; (2) creativity-related processes (i.e., cognitive styles, personality characteristics, implicit and explicit knowledge of heuristics for generating novel ideas, and conducive working styles); and (3) task motivation (i.e., attitude toward the task and perceptions of one's own motivation for undertaking the task). We generalize this model for creativity to math teaching. In essence, in order to teach creatively in mathematics, a teacher must have in-depth background knowledge in the subject area of mathematics as well as skills in and knowledge about mathematics instruction. He/she also needs to develop creativity-related processes in the area of mathematics teaching. Lastly, a teacher must also enjoy teaching and know how to motivate his or her students to learn mathematics. All three aspects are important in achieving a high level of creative teaching in mathematics.

The core features of creativity in teaching mathematics in Chinese classrooms are embedded in a set of cultural beliefs and manifested in the cultural practice. These beliefs are an integral part that guides teaching behaviors in the Chinese mathematics classrooms. The Chinese sayings of "Famous master brings out excellent apprentice 名师出高徒" and "one problem solved with three variations 举一反三" highlight the characteristics of a good teacher. The purpose of such teaching is to instill a passion for learning.

Domain-Relevant Knowledge

There is very little cross-cultural research on teacher expertise in mathematics that addresses the question of whether Asian teachers are more knowledgeable and skilled in teaching mathematics than U.S. teachers are. Shulman (1986, 1987) proposed that expertise in teaching is based in the development of three knowledge bases: subject matter knowledge (SMK – ideas, facts, and concepts of the field, as well as their relationships), pedagogical content knowledge (PCK – the ways of representing and formulating the subject that makes it comprehensible to others), and general pedagogical knowledge (GPK – psychological and pedagogical aspects of teaching and learning). Guided by Shulman's theoretical framework, Zhou, Peverly, and Xin (2006) compared 162 U.S. and Chinese third grade mathematics teachers' expertise in teaching fractions. Results show that U.S. teachers lag significantly behind Chinese teachers in SMK (concepts, computations, and word problems) and in some areas of PCK (e.g., such as identifying important points of teaching the fraction concepts and how to ensure students' understanding). Findings from Zhou et al.'s study revealed deficits in U.S. teachers' knowledge of fractions (SMK) and their ability to communicate their fraction knowledge to students (PCK). These deficits could underlie a "teaching gap" (Stigler & Hiebert, 1999) between American and Chinese teachers that parallels the "learning gap" in mathematics. Thus, it is likely that U.S. mathematics teachers' domain knowledge and their teaching of fractions (and possibly of other areas of mathematics as well) are not sufficient for the purposes of developing a deep understanding of these concepts in their students. Similarly, Ma (1999) compared American and Chinese elementary school teachers' knowledge of mathematics (SMK) in four areas: subtraction with regrouping, multi-digit multiplication, division by fractions, and the relationship between perimeter and area. She found that Chinese teachers had a significantly deeper understanding of these concepts than did American teachers.

How do Chinese mathematics teachers develop solid subject knowledge and pedagogical content knowledge? The within-cultural research in China compared the effectiveness of teachers trained in Teaching-Regulated Ability (TRA) to a control group of teachers not trained in this model (Lin, 1992; Shen & Xin, 1998; Xin, Shen, & Lin, 1999/2001. The results indicated that students taught by TRA-trained teachers showed greater competence in mathematical thinking and learning than did students taught by teachers who use more traditional drill-and-memorization methods.

In TRA, teachers are trained by experts from Beijing Normal University (BNU) in TRA theory and expert teachers selected from schools in the same school district to (1) construct lesson plans, (2) evaluate their own teaching, (3) modify their activities based on their own self-evaluations and the evaluations of BNU experts and expert teachers, and (4) develop students' thinking using Lin's "Five Traits of Thinking" model (Lin, 1992). The latter includes instruction that promotes depth (analysis and synthesis of relationships between number and quantity), flexibility (divergent thinking), creativity (creating unique solutions to existing problems), self-criticism (evaluating arguments and proofs), and fluency (speed and accuracy in using the most efficient problem solutions).

More specifically, new teachers are placed in a teaching apprenticeship with a more experienced teacher who regularly conducts observations of the novice's teaching. Novice teachers give demonstration lessons, observe model teachers' teaching, and discuss teaching methods, among other activities. Novice teachers are taught how to evaluate themselves and also are given feedback by their mentors. In the TRA group, new teachers meet once every two weeks for three years. Trainees give demonstration lessons, observe each other teach, and discuss teaching methods. Trainees are taught how to evaluate themselves and also are given feedback by experts, students, and colleagues verbally and through video case studies and tests. For several years thereafter, teachers' skills are periodically evaluated to ensure that the quality of their implementation of the TRA principles continues to be high. This "cognitive apprenticeship" is described by Stevenson and Stigler (1992): "Asian [Japanese and Chinese] lessons are so well crafted that one can notice a very systematic effort to pass on the accumulated wisdom of teaching practice to each new generation of teachers and to keep perfecting that practice by providing teachers the opportunities to continually learn from one another" (p. 46). In comparison, American teachers are rarely offered opportunities for collaborative deliberations and can teach for many years without having the opportunity to deepen their understanding of the content they teach (Fullan, 1991; Ma, 1999). A detailed TRA training cycle with descriptions of purpose and activities is presented in Appendix 8A.

Questions have been raised about the relationship between content knowledge and creativity. Would "too much" content knowledge sometime become detrimental to one's creativity? Psychologists used to believe that a tension existed between knowledge and creativity, in the sense that too much experience within a field might sometimes restrict one's creativity and make it hard for people to break out of the boundaries set by that knowledge. Some laboratory studies confirm this belief by showing that when solving different sets of problems, participants could be so "fixated" on strategies developed in solving previous questions that they overlooked new clues that would have allowed them to become efficient problem solvers – an effect termed "negative transfer" (Luchins & Luchins, 1959).

However, the tension view is not supported in real life when examining knowledge acquisition versus the creative contribution of eminent individuals in different domains, and the relationship between knowledge and creativity seems to be much more straightforward than people used to believe – that is, knowledge is positively related to creativity (Weisberg, 1999). In other words, domain-specific knowledge is a necessary prerequisite or foundation for creativity. One must possess ample knowledge in a certain domain in order to become creative in that field.

Such a view is more easily embraced by the Chinese. In a review of people's implicit theory of creativity, Niu & Sternberg (2002, 2006) demonstrates that compared to the Western conception of creativity, there is more emphasis on learning from old and existing knowledge systems in Eastern people's views of creativity. Rooted in Confucian tradition, the Chinese have historically believed that acquiring basic knowledge and skills is the key to achieving a high level of excellence (Niu, 2012). It is therefore not surprising that the Chinese mathematics curriculum gives eminent status to acquiring fundamental knowledge in mathematics. In practice, Chinese teachers also put a significant amount of effort into improving their own domain-related knowledge and skills in mathematics by studying the curriculum and teaching technology at various levels of teacher training.

In a study comparing Chinese and American views of effective mathematics teaching, Cai and Wang (2007) found that whereas U.S. mathematics classrooms are student-centered, mathematics instruction is more content-based in Chinese classrooms. In this study, Cai and Wang interviewed 9 Chinese and 11 American distinguished mathematics teachers, and found that one striking differences between the Chinese and U. S. views of effective teachers is that Chinese teachers emphasize the teachers' strong mathematics knowledge, especially a thorough understanding of the pedagogy, whereas U.S. teachers pay more attention to the teachers' personal traits like a sense of humor and an enthusiasm about mathematics. Chinese teachers also stress the ability to provide clear and precise mathematics information to students, but the U.S. teachers stress the ability to listen to students and adjust teaching for individual student needs.

Creativity-Related Learning Process

Contrarily to the Westerners' perception of Chinese learners' "rote-drill" style of passive learning, systematic and in-depth observations (e.g., Lopez-Real, Mok, Leung, & Marton, 2004, p.382) have revealed a picture strikingly different from this stereotypical image of how mathematics is learned and taught in China. For the past two decades, the Chinese mathematics education reform has been emphasizing children's development of mathematical abilities. Commensurate with the child's cognitive structure, the core feature of the development of children's mathematical thinking centers on cultivating children's understanding of mathematical problem structures, logical thinking, flexible thinking, and ability to analyze and synthesize mathematical information. Such learning process nurtures creativity in mathematics learning.

Creativity can be illustrated in teacher's use of multiple methods to solve a problem. Students approach the problem from various angles, using different methods to analyze the problem situation and find the solutions to the problem. The purpose is to facilitate students in their flexibly integration of the mathematical knowledge in depth and breadth, thus cultivating their mathematical creativity. The following is an example given by a master teacher guiding her third grade students solving one multi-step word problem involving distance, time, and speed.

The main purpose of the lesson is to (1) actively engage students in mathematical thinking in order to promote their ability to synthesize what they have learned in the past and apply the acquired knowledge in solving a novel problem, (2) facilitate student's flexibility in thinking, and (3) expand their breadth of thinking and guide them in connecting prior knowledge across domains to promote creativity in problem solving. The practice of solving one problem with many variations is illustrated in the following. The teacher encourages her students to come up with as many solutions as possible in solving the following problems:

> Problem: The distance of a railway between the south and north of a city is 357 kilometers. An express trained started from the north; simultaneously a local train started from the south. The two trains were running toward each other. In 3 hours, the two trains met. The speed of the express train is 79 kilometers per hour. How many kilometers less does the local train travel per hour than the express train on average?

$$\text{Student 1}: [357 - (79 \times 3)] \div 3$$
$$= [357 - 237] \div 3$$
$$= 120 \div 3$$
$$= 40(\text{km})$$

The local train travels 40 km/hour. We already know that the express train travels 79 km/hour; therefore,

$$79 - 40 = 39(\text{km})$$

Local train travels 39 km less per hour on average than the express train.

$$\text{Student 2}: 79 - (357 \div 3 - 79)$$
$$= 79 - (119 - 79)$$
$$= 79 - 40$$
$$= 39(\text{km})$$

Student 3: Suppose the local train travels χ km per hour,

$$79 \times 3 + 3\chi = 357$$
$$3\chi = 120$$
$$X = 40$$
$$79 - 40 = 39(\text{km})$$

Student 4: Suppose the local train travels χ km per hour,

$$(79 + \chi) \times 3 = 357$$
$$237 + 3\chi = 357$$
$$3\chi = 357 - 237$$
$$3\chi = 120$$
$$X = 40(\text{km})$$
$$79 - 40 = 39(\text{km})$$

Student 5: Suppose the local train travels χ km per hour,

$$3\chi = 357 - 79 \times 3$$

$$\cdots \cdots \cdots$$

Student 6: Suppose the local train travels χ km per hour,

$$359 - 3\chi = 79 \times 3$$

$$\cdots \cdots \cdots$$

Student 7: Suppose the local train travels χ km per hour,

$$79 + \chi = 357 \div 3$$

$$\cdots \cdots \cdots$$

Student 8: Suppose the local train travels χ km per hour,

$$357 \div 3 - \chi = 79$$

$$\cdots \cdots \cdots$$

Student 9: Suppose the local train travels χ km less than the express train per hour,

$$(79 - \chi) \times 3 + 79 \times 3 = 357$$
$$474 - 3\chi = 357$$
$$3\chi = 117$$
$$\chi = 39(\text{km})$$

Student 10: Suppose the local train travels χ km less than the express train per hour,

$$(79 - \chi + 79) \times 3 = 357$$

. . . .

Student 11: Suppose the local train travels χ km less than the express train per hour,

$$(79 - \chi) \times 3 = 357 - 79 \times 3$$

. . . .

Student 12: Suppose the local train travels χ km less than the express train per hour,

$$357 - (79 - \chi) \times 3 = 79 \times 3$$

Student 13: Suppose the local train travels χ km less than the express train per hour,

$$79 + (79 - \chi) \times 3 = 357 \div 3$$

Student 14: Suppose the local train travels χ km less than the express train per hour,

$$357 \div 3 - (79 - \chi) = 79$$

. . . .

Student 15: Suppose the local train travels χ km less than the express train per hour,

$$79 - \chi = 357 \div 3 - 79$$

An interview with this master math teacher reveals her view on how to cultivate student's development of mathematical creativity. According to the teacher, the purpose of solving a problem with variations is not for the sake of solving the problem per se. It is the way of promoting students' flexibility in thinking and broadening their logical reasoning skills. By encouraging students to think of all possible ways of problem solving deepens their understanding of mathematical knowledge structures within and across domains. Solid foundation and skills in mathematics are indispensable to the development of mathematical creativity. If there is no mastery of relevant knowledge and skills, there will be no flexibility, depth, and speed in problem solving.

From this example it is apparent that in order to understand or appreciate student's problem solving with variations, the teacher must have a solid understanding of the subject matter. Sternberg and Horvath (1995) identified three differences between expert and novice teachers. Expert teachers' knowledge is more extensive, accessible, and organized for use in teaching than that of novice teachers. Expert teachers solve problems more efficiently within their domain of expertise and do so with little or no cognitive effort. They engage more readily in high-order metacognitive or executive processes such as planning, monitoring, and evaluating ongoing efforts at problem solving. Finally, expert teachers have more insight. They are more likely to identify information that is relevant to the solution of problems, and are able to reorganize domain knowledge to reformulate problem representations. Often the solutions they arrive at are both novel and appropriate. Wilson, Shulman, and Rickert (1987) observed that teachers who had more subject matter knowledge were more likely to detect misconceptions, deal effectively with general class difficulties in the content area, and correctly interpret students' insightful comments.

Another determining factor in teaching mathematics creatively is the teacher's knowledge of the "longitudinal coherence" (Ma, 1999). Zhou et al. (2006) study shows that in comparison to their American counterparts, Chinese math teachers demonstrated a better understanding of their students' prior mathematics knowledge relevant to learning new fraction concepts (i.e., dividing a whole into equal parts, part-whole relationships, knowledge of geometric shapes relevant to understanding fractions). This is a necessary prerequisite to determining what teaching strategies to use to facilitate students' deeper understanding of these concepts. In addition, the Chinese teachers' responses suggested that their knowledge was not limited to the grade they were teaching. Rather, it seems that they knew when each piece of knowledge is introduced in the whole elementary mathematics curriculum, and its relationship with knowledge taught in previous and future grades. In other words, from what we observed, it appeared likely that they knew what students would be taught in later grades that would build on what they were teaching now. Our observations are consistent with Ma's (1999) notion of "longitudinal coherence," the term she used to describe Chinese mathematics teachers' curricular knowledge. Ma observed that Chinese teachers "are ready at any time to exploit an opportunity to review crucial concepts that students have studied previously. They also know what students are going to learn later, and take opportunities to lay the foundation for it" (p. 122). Furthermore, the Chinese teachers' performance we observed were similar to that of the teachers observed by Ma – they all seemed to have a "knowledge package," a network of procedural and conceptual topics supporting or supported by the learning of the topic in question. In comparison, the U.S. teachers in the present study rarely displayed "longitudinal coherence" or the "knowledge package" so readily articulated by the Chinese teachers.

Task Motivation

Chinese teachers regard intrinsic motivation as the core in academic learning. They believe that if students demonstrate intrinsic interest in the subject matter, they will be more actively involved in the learning process that enhances observation, thinking, reasoning, and memory. For example, in the elementary school, mathematical games are often used to stimulate young children's interest in mathematics learning. The games often have specific focus on the development of particular mathematical concepts. For example, in teaching the first grade students geometric shapes, the teacher puts various shapes of different sizes and materials in a bag. The students are divided into two groups. When the teacher calls out a particular shape, one student from each group will compete to grab the correct shape as fast as he/she can. The fastest group that gets the most shapes correct wins the game. In order to perform the tasks with accuracy and speed, the students need to ignore the irrelevant features of the objects (i.e., size and materials) and focus on the critical features of the shape.

In addition to the games, another method that Chinese teachers use to stimulate student's motivation and interest in learning math is to arouse the curiosity among the students so that they are eager to figure out the problems. This is achieved through solving mathematical riddles and finding solutions to intricate mathematical stories. The following story was presneted to a third grade class when the concept of "rounding up and rounding down" (四舍五入) is introduced.

Long time ago, there was a miser named Li who loved to eat eggs. On the market, 10 eggs weighed about 500 kg, which cost ¥1.54. Li came up with an idea that he thought would save him money. He gave his servant ¥1.50 and insisted that he buy 500 kg of eggs. If the servant did not bring back 500 kg of eggs, he would keep his salary. Can you think of a way to help the servant?

This problem stimulated a great deal of interest and curiosity among the students. After much discussion among the students, a solution was born: "The servant will buy one egg at a time for ten times. Each egg costs *¥0.154.* By applying the "rounding down" principle, 500 kg eggs (10 eggs) cost a total of ¥1.50."

The Chinese believe that the motivation in learning is developed from the constant resolution of conflicts entailed in the mathematics problems. The teacher's role is to deliberately and carefully present the critical elements in the mathematics problems in order to challenge student's thinking through discovery and exploration of various solutions. As Amabile (1996) put it, "the intrinsically motivational state is conducive to creativity" (p. 107). As such, the math problem presentation above exemplifies the Chinese way of motivating students to learn by effectively controlling student's attention and stimulating interest, curiosity, and satisfaction during problem solving.

The relationship between some forms of extrinsic motivation and creativity has been examined extensively, and it has been shown that some extrinsically motivated activities can actually enhance individual's creativity. These forms of extrinsically motivated activities include a direct instruction to be creative (Chen, Kasof, Himsel, Dmitaieva, Dong, & Xue, 2005; Chen, Kasof, Himsel, Greenberger, Dong, & Xue, 2002; Niu & Liu, 2009; Niu & Sternberg, 2001, 2003; O'hara & Sternberg, 2000–2001; Runco, Illies, & Eisenman, 2005) and performance-contingent rewards (Esenberger & Armeli, 1997; Esenberger, Armeli, & Pretz, 1998; Eisenberger & Cameron, 1996; Horelik, 2007). For example, contrary to common belief, in a study to examine different types of instructions on creativity, Niu & Liu (2009) showed that Chinese students showed more creativity when given instructions explicitly detailing how to be creative rather than merely reminding the students to be creative. Such a result may suggest that, at least in Chinese classrooms, teachers' explicit instruction may have beneficial effects on student creativity. It may also reflect the fact that in Chinese classrooms, there is a significant amount of activities that are teacher-led; it is therefore important for Chinese teachers to be able to design activities to promote individuals' task motivation to learn mathematics, both intrinsically and extrinsically.

Creativity and "Good Teaching"

The concept of creativity is expressed in a set of cultural beliefs about what makes "a good teacher" in Chinese society. Confucius, a great thinker in 500 BCE, whose theories and philosophy have profoundly influenced how people view the world not only in Chinese societies, but also in neighboring countries such as Korea, Japan, and Vietnam, believes one's important life goal is to have the enjoyment and the continuous passion to learn. The original Chinese character of "to learn" is actually the same as "to teach." Therefore, a good teacher is a role model of his or her students, who enjoys learning and is able to bring out the good nature of his or her students through teaching and self-cultivation. A good teacher is someone who is very knowledgeable, loves learning, and who knows how to stimulate students' passion to learn and to promote students' divergent thinking. Teachers have historically received an eminent social status in Chinese society. The relationship between a teacher and a student is often regarded to be as important and close as the relationship between a father and a son. The title of "good teacher" is very special in Chinese societies and can be a life-long goal for literati to achieve. In fact, Confucius was himself a teacher. In his life, Confucius accepted more than 3,000 students. Of these, 72 became outstanding scholars whose commentaries on Confucian theories and teaching later became doctrines of Chinese classic literature and philosophy and exerted tremendous impact on Chinese political and social structures for the next 2,500 years. Confucius was vocal in his interaction with his students about the true meaning of teaching and learning and what makes a good teacher. For example, in Analects, book VII, section 2, Confucius said to his students, "Pleasure is not a means but the goal in itself," so that "to learn is pleasure." In this passage, Confucian emphasized the importance of intrinsic motivation in one's learning. Confucian also believed and demonstrated through his own life the importance of self-cultivation and the ability of continuing to learn in teaching. For example, in Analects, book II and section 1, it was recorded that Confucius once said, "a man is worthy of being a teacher who gets to know what is new by keeping fresh in his mind what he is already familiar with" (Lao, 1983). In this passage, Confucius gave a high status of being a "teacher," who possess good qualities and can be a role model of others. He also illustrated the importance of acquiring old knowledge when developing new skills. Therefore, being a good teacher is not easy according to his model, as Confucius believed everyone possessed a tremendous amount of potential, and it was the teacher's responsibility and privilege to bring out this potential. Confucius also believed and practiced individualized teaching to each individual's need. Confucius considered becoming a good teacher to be a life-long goal, and he indeed achieved such a goal. Today, Confucius is regarded as "the teacher of ten thousand generations." Following Confucius' tradition, many famous Chinese scholars pursued the same goal of becoming a good teacher throughout their lives.

The importance of good teachers in the development of students' creativity is also recognized by Western scholars. John Baer, for example, in his *Creative Teachers, Creative Students* (Baer, 1997a), says it is important to develop teachers' creativity in the domain of teaching in order to promote students' creative potential in that subject area. Exactly how do Chinese teachers develop their potential to become good teachers in mathematics classrooms? We believe it may be largely attributable to the Chinese mathematics teaching system and its unique teacher-training model.

Chinese School System and Its Teacher-Training Model

Unlike in the United States, teachers in most Chinese schools only teach one (sometimes two) subject areas from the level of elementary school up to high school, and they teach significantly fewer lessons per week than do their American counterparts (Cortazzi & Jin, 2001; Tan & Mcinerney, 2008). Chinese schools also put more effort into helping their teachers improve their classroom teaching skills, and put more emphasis on teachers' continuing education, compared to their American counterparts (Cavanagh, 2007). An important mechanism that Chinese schools adopt in helping their teachers develop expertise in one subject area is called the "model lesson" (Guan Mo Ke 观摩课). It is a special form of peer observation of a classroom lesson. Typically, when a teacher is asked to teach a model lesson, he or she will be required to first come up with a detailed lesson plan, and the actual delivery of the lesson will be observed and evaluated by a group of colleagues at various levels such as a school, a district, a city, a province, or even nationwide. The number of audience members can therefore range between several and hundreds of people. The model lesson is a popular form of research for teaching in China with regards to teachers' training and it can heavily impact decisions about promotion. A good model lesson can help a teacher improve their own teaching, secure a promotion, and even achieve fame. Those who teach excellent model lessons to large audiences may go on to become distinguished teachers, who enjoy superstar status at teachers' conferences and whose model lessons are sought after not only by other teachers but also by parents and students as extra learning material.

The mechanism of the model lesson makes teaching mathematics in Chinese schools more like a performing art, such as dancing. Teachers pursue excellent teaching in their classrooms much like a dancer pursues a flawless performance on stage. In this pursuit, Chinese teachers strive to develop all three components illustrated by Amabile (1996) that are necessary to the development of creative teaching abilities.

Conclusions

Guided by Amabile's Componential Framework of Creativity, we discussed how creativity is facilitated in math classrooms in China. We began by introducing the fact that Chinese students not only achieve well in mathematics by any international standard; they also demonstrate a greater level of interest in learning the subject than do their U.S. counterparts. We also introduced the "paradox of the Chinese learner" coined by Watkins and Biggs (2001), specifically that some seemingly unfounded instructional practices such as large class sizes and content-based, teacher-centered teaching strategies adopted by Chinese schools could actually produce higher achievers in mathematics in China. We examined these issues from a creative teaching perspective. We argued that, contrary to prevailing popular belief that Chinese mathematics teachers adopt many counterproductive activities such as having their students engage in rote learning, drills, and studying exam-related materials, Chinese teachers actually spend a great deal of effort developing their creative teaching skills. Using teaching math problem solving as examples, this chapter also showed the three major approaches Chinese teachers have adopted in developing their creative teaching skills, which include (1) developing profound understanding of the domain knowledge in mathematics and learning how to teach mathematics effectively; (2) promoting their creative-related processes through developing strategies of teaching with variation; and (3) nurturing intrinsic motivation to learn mathematics in both themselves and their students by providing well-crafted, interesting, and meaningful activities. The Chinese approach to mathematics instruction coincides with modern creativity theories such as Amabile's componential framework of creativity. There are at least two reasons why teaching creatively in mathematics is a desirable goal for many Chinese teachers. First, it is a long-standing cultural belief that a good teacher is someone who is knowledgeable, flexible in using various teaching skills, and able to stimulate student interest to learn, a belief that is consistent with modern theories of creativity such as the componential framework of creativity that emphasizes the importance of knowledge, creativity-related process, and task motivation. Second, the Chinese teacher-training model and system of promotion encourage teachers to learn from the collective wisdom of their peers with regards to creative teaching strategies. More specifically, the system of exercising the "model lesson" makes Chinese teachers treat classroom teaching as a performing art, and it is both socially and economically desirable for novice teachers to learn and exercise in order to master the teaching of mathematics.

What are some implications of studying the Chinese approach to mathematics instruction in the United States? There are at least three major lessons to be taken from this research. The first and most important is the "cognitive apprenticeship" that the Chinese math teachers receive in their teaching career. In this chapter we elaborated on how this process is carried out. For example, the mechanism of the model lesson allows distinguished teachers to showcase their creative teaching abilities and novice teachers to learn firsthand how seemingly abstract concepts are effectively taught in a way that will stimulate student interest in learning.

The second lesson is the practice of having specialization in a teaching subject area. The system of having teachers concentrate on just one or two subject areas, even at the elementary school level, allows teachers to develop a high level of expertise. In the Chinese concept of creativity, knowledge is the key element, therefore Chinese schools exert a great effort to make sure their teachers are well equipped with subject matter knowledge and pedagogical content knowledge.

The final implication is at the societal level. American schools are not producing the math excellence for global economic leadership and homeland security in the twenty-first century. The lack of access to quality education, and more specifically a quality mathematics education, has the possibility of limiting human potential and individual economic opportunity. In many other countries, including the United States, knowledge of mathematics acts as an academic passport for entry into virtually every avenue of the labor market and higher education. As the global market moves forward, the pressure to advance the mathematical skills of workers across the world will increase. If the United States hopes to remain competitive in the world economy, the mathematics education of its future generation must be taken seriously and have to be addressed early in students' academic life.

Appendix: Teaching Regulated Ability (TRA) Training Cycle

TRA Cycle	Objective	Joint Activity between Expert & Teacher

Lesson Study	Develop coherent lesson plans based on teacher's understanding of the curriculum content and knowledge of student thinking to facilitate conceptual understanding among students of the topics being taught.	1. Develop an overarching goal to achieve with students
		Identify the gaps between students' knowledge
		— discuss weaknesses they see in their students
		— look at past test scores
		— conduct informal assessments to determine student weaknesses
		2. Set specific goals for each lesson based on knowledge of students' prior learning
		3. Review teacher's instructional guide to clarify the goals of the lesson, formulate ideas about how to teach the lesson, consider how this particular lesson relates to other lessons, and locate where this lesson fits within the entire unit of lessons to be taught
		4. Develop teaching-learning activities for each lesson in four domains
		  a) Grasping the problem setting (sequence of tasks and key questions planned to ask)
		  b) Expected student reactions
		  c) Teacher response to student reactions (how she relates responses to the ideas she wants children to think about/Things to remember (why a question is included/what teachers are working toward)
		  d) Evaluation for determining the success of each step in the lesson

Implementation and Observation	Observe whether the intended goals are successfully implemented; assess the strengths and weaknesses during instruction	Observations by expert teachers, peers, and researchers:
		  a) Use the lesson plan with extra space as a ready-made tool to record observations as the lesson unfolds
		  b) Observe students' understanding and solution process by recording their strategies and questions asked
		  c) c) Observe teacher's responses to students questions and his/her evaluation of students' strategies in problem solving

(cont.)

(cont.)

TRA Cycle	Objective	Joint Activity between Expert & Teacher
Reflection and Improvement	Improve teaching strategies and principles that can carry over into their everyday lessons	1. Follow-up meeting on the same day in order to keep memory fresh 2. Videotape of the lesson is used for analysis 3. Teacher who taught begins with his/her own reflection on the lesson 4. Observers follow discussion with comments 5. Teacher can accept or reject suggestions 6. Teacher takes notes and asks questions in order to facilitate lesson improvement 7. Lesson plan will be revised and the necessary instructional materials will be prepared
Reflective Reports	Create a record of deep and grounded reflection about the complex activities of teaching that can then be shared and discussed with other members of the profession	Lesson plans developed during the TRA cycle are filed away along with comments recorded during the post-lesson discussions

REFERENCES

Amabile, T. M. (1996). *Creativity in context: Update to the social psychology of creativity*. Boulder, CO: Westview Press.

Amabile, T. M., Hennessey, B. A., & Grossman, B. S. (1986). Social influences on creativity: The effects of contracted-for reward. *Journal of Personality and Social Psychology*, **50**, 15–23.

Baer, J. (1997a). *Creative teachers, creative students*. Needham Heights, MA: Allyn & Bacon A Viacom Company.

Baer, J. (1997b). Gender differences in the effects of anticipated evaluation on creativity. *Creativity Research Journal*, **10**, 25–31.

Baer, J. (1998). Gender differences in the effects of extrinsic motivation on creativity. *Journal of Creative Behavior*, **32**, 18–37.

Bagnall, S., Quaglieni, G., & Rumney, B. (2015). *Are our kids tough enough? Chinese school*. London: BBC2.

BBC News Magazine (2015, August 4). Would Chinese-style education work on British kids? Retrieved from www.bbc.com/news/magazine-33735517.

Cai, J., & Wang, T. (2007). Conceptions of effective mathematics teaching within a cultural context: Perspectives of teachers from China and the United States. Paper presented at the Annual Meeting of the American Educational Research Association, Chicago, IL, April 9–13.

Cavanagh, S. (2007). Asian equation. *Education Week*, **26**, 22–26.

Chen, C., Kasof, J. Himsel, A., Dmitrieva, J. Dong, Q., & Xie, Q. (2005). Effects of explicit instruction to "be creative" across domains and cultures. *Journal of Creative Behavior*, **39**(2), 89–110.

Chen, C., Kasof, J. Himsel, A., Greenberger, E. Dong, Q., & Xie, Q. (2002). Creativity in drawings of geometric shapes: A cross-cultural examination with the consensual assessment technique. *Journal of Cross-Cultural Psychology*, **33**, 171–187.

Cortazzi, M., & Jin, L. (2001). Large classes in China: "Good" teachers and interaction. In D. A. Watkins & J. B. Biggs (Eds.), *Teaching the Chinese Learners: Psychological and Pedagogical Perspectives* (pp. 115–134). Hong Kong and Victoria, Australia: Comparative Education Research Centre and The Australian Council for the Educational Research.

Eisenberger, R., & Armeli, S. (1997). Can salient reward increase creative performance without reducing intrinsic creative interest? *Journal of Personality & Social Psychology*, **72**, 652–663.

Eisenberger, R., Armeli, S., & Pretz, J. (1998). Can the promise of reward increase creativity? *Journal of Personality and Social Psychology*, **74**, 702–714.

Eisenberger, R., & Cameron, J. (1996). Detrimental effects of reward: Reality or myth? *American Psychologist*, **51**(11), 1153–1166.

Eisenberger, R., & Shanock, L. (2003). Rewards, intrinsic motivation, and creativity: A case study of conceptual and methodological isolation. *Creativity Research Journal*, **15**, 121–130.

Fan, L., & Zhu, Y. (2004). How haven Chinese students performed in mathematics? A perspective from large-scale international mathematics comparisons. In L. Fan, N.-Y. Wong, J. Cai, & S. Li (Eds.), *How Chinese learn mathematics: Perspectives from insider*. Series on Mathematics Education, Vol. 1 (pp. 3–26). Hackensack, NJ: World Scientific.

Fullan, M. G. (1991). *The new meaning of educational change*. New York: Teachers College Press.

Hennessey, B. A. (2001). The social psychology of creativity: Effects of evaluation on intrinsic motivation and creativity of performance. In S. Harkins (Ed.), *Multiple perspectives on the effects of evaluation on performance: Toward an integration* (pp. 47–75). Norwell, MA: Kluwer Academic Publishers.

Horelik, I. K. (2007). Rewards and creativity: Building a bridge between two theories. Unpublished doctoral dissertation, Pace University, New York.

Lao, D. C. (1983). *Confucius: The Analects*. London: England Penguin Putnam.

Lin, C. (1992). *Xuexi yu fazhan* [Learning and developing]. Beijing: Beijing Education Publisher.

Lopez-Real, F., Mok, A. C. I., Leung, K. S. F., & Marton, F. (2004). Identifying a patter of teaching: An analysis of a Shanghai Teacher's Lessons. In L. Fan, N.-Y. Wong, J. Cai, & S. Li (Eds.), *How Chinese learn mathematics: Perspectives from insider*. Series on Mathematics Education, Vol. 1 (pp. 382–410). Hackensack, NJ: World Scientific.

Luchins, A. S., & Luchins, E. H. (1959). *Rigidity of behavior*. Eugene: University of Oregon Press.

Ma, L.-P. (1999). *Knowing and teaching mathematics: Teachers' understanding of fundamental mathematics in China and the United States*. Mahwah, NJ: Erlbaum.

Niu, W. (2012). Confucian ideology and creativity. *Journal of Creative Behavior*, **46**(4), 274–284.

Niu, W., & Liu, D. (2009). Enhancing creativity: A comparison between effects of an indicative instruction "to be creative" and a more elaborate heuristic instruction on Chinese student creativity. *Psychology of Aesthetics, Creativity, and the Arts*, 3(2), 93–98.

Niu, W., & Sternberg, R. J. (2001). Cultural influences on artistic creativity and its evaluation. *International Journal of Psychology*, **36**(4), 225–241.

Niu, W., & Sternberg, R. J. (2002). Contemporary studies on the concept of creativity: The east and the west. *Journal of Creative Behavior*, **36**, 269–288.

Niu, W., & Sternberg, R. J. (2003). Societal and school influence on students' creativity. *Psychology in the Schools*, **40**, 103–114.

Niu, W., & Sternberg (2006). The philosophical roots of western and eastern conceptions of creativity. *Journal of Theoretical and Philosophical Psychology*, **26**, 1001–1021.

OECD. (2013). PISA 2012 Results in Focus: What 15-year-olds know and what they can do with what they know: Key results from PISA 2012. www.oecd.org/pisa/keyfindings/pisa-2012-results-overview.pdf

O'Hara, L. A., & Sternberg, R. J. (2000–2001). It doesn't hurt to ask: Effects of instructions to be creative, practical, or analytical on essay-writing performance and their interaction with students' thinking styles. *Creativity Research Journal*, **13**, 197–210.

Runco, M. A., Illies, J. J., & Eisenman, R. (2005). Creativity, originality, and appropriateness: What do explicit instructions tell us about their relationship? *Journal of Creative Behavior*, **39**(2), 137–148.

Paine, L. W. (1990). The teachers as virtuoso: A Chinese model for teaching. *Teachers College Record*, **92**(1), 49–81.

Shulman, L. S. (1986). Those who understand: Knowledge growth in teaching. *Educational Researcher*, **15**, 4–14.

Shulman, L. S. (1987). Knowledge and teaching: Foundations of the new reform. *Harvard Educational Review*, **57**(1), 1–22.

Shen, J., & Xin, T. (1998). Luen Jiaoshi de jiankong nenli [On teachers' teaching-regulated ability]. *Keti Yianjiou Tongxun Zhuan Kang*, 38–46.

Sternberg, R. J., & Horvath, J. A. (1995). A prototype view of expert teaching. *Educational Researcher*, **24**(6), 9–17.

Stevenson, H. W., Lee, S., Chen, C., Lummis, M., Stigler, J. W., Liu, F., & Fang, G. (1990). Mathematics achievement of children in China and the United States. *Child Development,* **61**, 1053–1066.

Stevenson, H. W., & Stigler, J. W. (1992). Mathematics classrooms in Japan, Taiwan, and the United States. *Child Development,* **58**, 1272–1285.

Stigler, J. W., & Hiebert, J. (1999). *The teaching gap: Best ideas from the world's teachers for improving education in the classroom.* New York: The Free Press.

Sun, Y., Zheng, X., & Kang, L. (1999/2001). Twenty discoveries of public school students' learning and development [Electronic version]. *China Education and Research Network, 2001–05–15.* www.edu.cn/20010827/208598.shtml.

Tan, O. S., & Mcinerney, D. M. (Eds.). (2008). *What the West can learn from the East: Asian perspectives on the psychology of learning and motivation.* Charlotte, NC: Information Age Publishing.

U.S. Department of Education, National Center for Education Statistics. (1996). *Pursuing excellence: A study of U.S. eighth-grade mathematics teaching and leanring* (pp. 127–146). New York: Macmillan.

Watkins, D. A., & Biggs, J. B. (Eds.). (1996). *The Chinese learner: Cultural, psychological and contextual influences.* Hong Kong and Victoria, Australia: Comparative Education Research Centre and The Australian Council for the Educational Research.

Watkins, D. A., & Biggs, J. B. (Eds.). (2001). *Teaching the Chinese learner: Psychological and pedagogical perspectives.* Hong Kong and Victoria, Australia: Comparative Education Research Centre and The Australian Council for the Educational Research.

Weisberg, R. W. (1999). Creativity and knowledge: A challenge to theories. In R. J. Sternberg (Ed.), *Handbook of creativity* (pp. 226–250). New York: Cambridge University Press.

Wilson, S. M., Shulman, L. S., & Richert, A. E. (1987). "150 different ways" of knowing: Representations of knowledge in teaching. In J. Calderhead (Ed.), *Exploring teachers' thinking* (pp. 104–124). London: Cassell Educational Limited.

Xin, T., Shen, J.-L., & Lin, C.-D. (2000). Renwu zhixiangxin ganyu shoduan duai xiaoshijiaxue jiankong nenli de jinxian [The effect of task-oriented intervention on teachers' teaching regulated ability]. *Xinli Kexue,* **23**(2), 129–132.

Zhang, M. (2007). *Xinli Zhisheng – Yiwei Xinlixuejia de Jiaoyu Faxian [Achieving psychological success: The educational discovery of a psychologist].* Beijing: Sinopec Press.

Zhou, Z., Peverly, S. T., & Xin, T. (2006). Knowing and teaching fractions: A cross-cultural study of American and Chinese mathematics teachers. *Contemporary Educational Psychology,* **31**, 438–457.

CHAPTER 9

Roads Not Taken, New Roads to Take
Looking for Creativity in the Classroom*

*Thomas Skiba, Mei Tan, Robert J. Sternberg and
Elena L. Grigorenko*

A river runs through a village somewhere. And for many years, it is just a river, feeding the rice paddies, carrying away waste, silt, pebbles, and the occasional dog or cat. But one day, without even consciously trying, someone realizes that it is a road, a way out. And later that someone wonders why he or she did not see it before – that the river is a road and that the road can be a river – even though it had been there all along.

And so we are beginning to realize with creativity that it has always been in the classroom but hidden in plain sight. It is not that creative behavior, creative thinking, and creative learning never existed before in classrooms. A colleague recalls once proposing an unconventional subject of study for a senior project in high school. While his classmates took up the ubiquitous topics of various sports, medicine, feminism, and other well-recycled subjects, he decided to review the history and legitimacy of parapsychology. His topic was firmly rejected. However, being a persistent fellow, he undertook it anyway, approached it seriously, and presented an interesting and worthy paper in the end that earned a high mark. But why was his innovation and unconventional thinking not recognized initially as a form of creativity?

In this chapter, we examine the evolving and exploratory relationship between teachers and creativity in the classroom. Our emphasis in the chapter is that teachers' implicit theories of creativity are often at variance with explicit theories of creativity – that is, what the teachers may value as creative behaviors are actually noncreative, and what they devalue as not creative behaviors may be creative. As a result, teachers may think they are developing creativity when, in fact, they are suppressing it. In the hands and minds of researchers and theoreticians, creativity has been viewed through many lenses and explored in a variety of lights for the last 60 years. But what effect has this had on teaching in the classroom?

* This work, in part, was supported by a generous gift from Karen Jensen Neff and Charlie Neff.

And has it helped teachers identify and nurture creative behavior in the context of school? In the pages that follow, we will consider the importance of creativity in education, why it warrants a place in the classroom. We will then summarize the various definitions and perspectives on creativity, specifically with respect to how they fit approaches to teaching. Teachers' various understandings (or misunderstandings) of creativity will then be examined by comparing and contrasting them to researchers' views, and implementations of teaching and assessment strategies will be briefly summarized. We will then discuss the practical aspects of fitting theoretical notions from research into classroom practice. How can creativity research fruitfully and effectively inform lessons and learning? Finally, we will propose for consideration some tools and strategies based on the theory of successful intelligence (Sternberg, 1999) and its accompanying investment theory of creativity (Sternberg & Lubart, 1991).

Why Does Creativity Matter in Schools?

In Western society, the public fascination with creativity dates back to iconic artists of the sixteenth century, such as Leonardo da Vinci and Michelangelo (Abuhamdeh & Csikszentmilhalyi, 2004). This fascination continued to expand through the Enlightenment and into the inception of cognitive science in the mid-twentieth century, exalting romantic ideals and artistic geniuses who were depicted as conjuring up their creative inner spirits to create imaginative and remarkable works of art (Coyne, 1997). In part as a result of the pioneering work of Guilford (1950) and Torrance (1962), scientists began to rationalize creativity – to study it in its various manifestations – and to develop ways of assessing it and cultivating it in classrooms. Yet, despite this long history of valuing creativity, it is only in recent years that developing creative thinking in all people has been discussed as a necessity in the classroom (Csikszentmihalyi & Wolfe, 2014; Henderson, 2004).

This change in educational values is related to the expansion of telecommunications and technology in the 1990s, which changed global marketplaces and put a special emphasis on innovation and thus increased international attention on the ineffectiveness of traditional pedagogies in preparing students for the demands of the next century (Hartley, 2003; Henderson, 2004). The economies of countries like the United States have, over the years, become knowledge and innovation based, reducing the emphasis on their industrial foundation and relying on the invention of products and technologies that provide desirable services for an increasingly technologically advancing society (Florida, 2003). There has been a new cry for so-called twenty-first-century skills, which include creative and innovative ways of thinking, along with skills in metacognition, communication, collaboration, information technology, and citizenship (Binkley et al., 2012). Hence, there is a recent demand for creative employees who can, while being constantly immersed in new information, display mental flexibility, innovation, complex problem-solving abilities, and productive collaborations with others (Schoen & Fusarelli, 2008). However, it is important to note that the momentous attention being placed on the economic incentives of fostering creativity in students by policy makers (Craft, 2006) is only part of a more general understanding that creativity has many distinct and pronounced benefits for people's personal lives as well as for society as a whole (for reviews, see Plucker, Beghetto, & Dow, 2004; Runco, 2004). For example, the use of creative abilities to solve relevant problems in one's life can contribute to one's overall success, both personal and financial (Sternberg & Lubart, 1999). Yet, often these general realizations contradict the reality of the accountability-oriented, No Child Left Behind–driven classrooms of U.S. public schools (Hennessey & Watson, 2016; Sternberg, 2015).

Defining Creativity: An Embarrassment of Riches

There is a saying that one can have too much of a good thing. Many might debate this, but it would seem to be the case right now with conceptions of creativity. That is, as one begins to work on a new frontier of research, one is compelled to explore, speculate, hypothesize, experiment, and create theories. However, when it comes to applying the research to useful practice, one realizes the need to sort, classify, collapse together, and even possibly discard or at least put aside some theories that cannot be applied. Conceptions of creativity direct people's approaches to creativity. For example, researchers' varying perspectives and definitions of creativity affect the selection of participants and behaviors for their studies, as well as their research methodology and data analytical techniques (Fishkin & Johnson, 1998). Similarly, educators hold different implicit views of creativity, which they should then be aware of when they choose assessment and teaching tools (Fishkin & Johnson, 1998). The numerous definitions, conceptions, and theories of creativity appropriately reflect the complexity of the construct, but they can also blur one's vision with their myriad views.

It has been noted by more than one researcher that creativity has four major facets or avenues of approach: personality, process, press (situation), and product (MacKinnon, 1961). That is, in studying creativity, one can focus on creative people, their personality, motivation, or cognitive abilities; or the creative process, the stepwise progress that results in the making of something new; or the mental or environmental conditions that facilitate the creation of new things. Or, finally, in studying creativity, one may examine creative products – the actual physical outcomes, such as works of art or inventions, or the nonphysical outcomes, like ideas – pondering their qualities such as originality, relevance to the situation or problem at hand, or their aesthetics. Yet, when following any of these roads, one inevitably finds that they cross each other at multiple junctions. And so it seems that it is the interplay between two or more of these four facets, either explicitly or implicitly stated, that has shaped many subsequent definitions over the years (see, for example, Murdock & Puccion, 1993; Rhodes, 1987 [1961]). At a more recent intersection, the study of personality and process in creativity has led to the development of theories of creative styles, such as problem-solving styles with respect to creative problem solving, turning the major question from *How much creativity?* to *How was it accomplished?* (Treffinger, Selby, & Isaksen, 2008). All of this is further complicated by the fact that creativity – whether an idea, product, or mental process – is judged and identified within the specific sociocultural context within which it occurs. Therefore, something recognized as creative in one place or time may not be considered so in another place and time (Csikszentmihalyi & Wolfe, 2014). All of these avenues of creativity research have been fruitful and of interest, but where do they all lead?

One systematic survey of the research literature (Plucker et al., 2004) has charted the extent to which researchers' explicit definitions of creativity varied, and found that clear definitions of creativity are rarely consistent. Definitions ranged from things such as "openness to ideas" (Edwards, 2001) to "the ability to form remote ideational associations to generate original and useful solutions" (Atchley, Keeney, & Burgess, 1999) to "the bringing into existence of something new" (Hasse, 2001). This lack of consensus has two recognized drawbacks. First, when it comes to understanding the field as a whole, one finds oneself attempting to juggle a basket of different "fruits," comparing apples to oranges and bananas to avocados. Second, without a clear definition, those who are most interested in understanding the construct of creativity and conveying it to others (i.e., educators and other practitioners) are left confused or discouraged by the conflicting views. It has been noted that one of the factors limiting the progress of educational implementation of creative thinking lessons and assessment is the lack of a coherent definition of creativity that can be agreed on widely

(Plucker et al., 2004). In some respects, the field of creativity has in fact become fragmentary; the big picture on the larger meaning and value of creativity has been split by the multiple facets, approaches, and goals of all of the various creativity research studies (Hennessey & Watson, 2016).

Which Definitions of Creativity Are Most Useful for the Classroom?

Having considered the problems of multiple definitions of creativity, we turn our attention to issues of definition pertaining specifically to creativity in the classroom, including teachers' implicit views and the definitions that have been based on or have shaped creativity assessment in schools. Our purpose here is to hone in on the importance of focusing on the demands of educational settings and considering a definition that works within the activities of the general classroom.

An initial dichotomy that has improved the clarity and utility of definitions has been the distinction between "Big-C" and "little-c" creativity. Big-C, or eminent creativity, involves the study of famous contributors to society (e.g., Charles Darwin and Toni Morrison) and the factors that led to their achievement (Simonton, 1994, 2004). The Big-C approach is not optimal for developing a theory for educational practice because of the low number of samples and high level of subjectivity regarding the products being evaluated, such as notes, journal entries, and creative products (Beghetto & Kaufman, 2007). Studies and theories based on little-c creativity investigate everyday creativity, including implicit definitions held by people and cognitive processes involved in ordinary people's creative thinking and behaviors (for a review, see Sternberg, Grigorenko, & Singer, 2004). Little-c creativity can be empirically tested in large samples and applied to the general population. Consequently, a theory of creativity that will work in the classroom requires a little-c approach. (Further models of creativity involving "mini-c" and "Pro-c" have also been proposed – see Kaufman & Beghetto, 2009 – but Big-C vs. little-c is an adequate distinction for the scope of this chapter.)

Furthermore, the debate between domain-specific and domain-general creativity has complicated the discussion of translating creativity theory into practice. This is because both perspectives, if applied, have very limiting educational implications (Baer, 2013). It has been stated (Plucker et al., 2004) that domain-specific approaches discourage students' openness to applying their creative abilities to solving problems in all areas of their life when enhancement of creative abilities are closely linked to particular areas of expertise. Conversely, domain-general approaches ignore task-specific growth and interests, which may in fact provide the most effective ways for students to develop creativity. Consequently, it would seem that defining creative approaches that allow flexibility across domains and encouragement of both domain-general and domain-specific creative skills, thinking, or problem solving is best for the classroom setting.

A definition of creativity that is grounded in little-c observable characteristics, that can be evaluated across domains and in all students, and that can be differentiated from other abilities appears to be the most pragmatic solution. When synthesized, elements of many recurring definitions fit these requirements and generally suggest that creativity is an interaction of one's aptitudes, processes, and environment, resulting in a relevant, novel, and useful product (Plucker et al., 2004). Developing a working definition with specific goals is a necessary step in effectively translating creativity theory into educational practice. Without a comprehensive and precise definition, creativity remains a soft construct, susceptible to pervasive myths related to the obsessive romanticism of Big-C creativity and creative eccentrics, rather than an important facet of education and our everyday lives.

Bending the Rules

As if it were not difficult enough to extract a working definition of creativity from theorists, the next step, injecting it into the classroom, has its own complexities. As the intricacies of systematically changing school pedagogies and policy are too broad for this chapter, we are concerned here instead with the demands that creativity education places on individual teachers. How do teachers view creativity, and what challenges must educational psychologists and educators be aware of to properly implement and assess creativity education or education for creativity?

For educational psychologists, preparing teachers to enhance and assess creative thinking skills across many subjects involves both theoretical and pragmatic challenges. Despite the value placed on creativity and a half-century's worth of research, and the explosion of teacher-targeted books and articles on teaching for creativity in the classroom, there seems to remain an awkward quietude on the topic in most classrooms (Sternberg, 2015). It is possible that, lacking formal training, teachers interested in creativity may feel left with only intuitive approaches to enhancing creativity that have not been empirically validated. Also, teachers who are uncomfortable with novel approaches to learning or thinking may inhibit creative thinking and discourage creativity in students. Therefore, consideration of preexisting teacher perceptions of creativity and potential challenges/biases that may hinder effective teaching and accurate assessment is warranted. Yet we must make a brief acknowledgment of the systemic and traditional demands that may conflict with a teacher who would like to incorporate creativity into his or her class.

Priorities and Weighing High-Stakes Assessments: Creativity Gets in Line

First, teachers have incentives to promote student conformity in the classroom, both to reduce disruption and to focus on fulfilling the demands of standardized assessment (Kim, 2008). The traditional classroom environment is goal oriented and mainly evaluates students' analytical and memory skills; the main idea is to transmit knowledge in specifically socially sanctioned domains (Csikszentmihalyi, 2014). Creativity is suppressed in traditional classrooms in part as a result of lack of opportunity and encouragement based on this narrow approach (Sternberg, 2006). Students may even experience punishment for displaying creativity in the classroom (Guncer & Oral, 1993).

Educators' reluctance to teach for creativity is reinforced by high-stakes standardized testing, which has promoted narrow and well-defined standards for achievement (Beghetto, 2005; Hennessey, 2015; Kim, 2008; Sternberg, 2015). Typical standardized tests that are used to set standards of accountability for schools and teachers encourage identification of the "right answer," which diminishes the value of divergent approaches to problem solving (Sternberg, 2006). For highly creative students whose preference for novel approaches to learning and thinking may be perceived as inappropriate, negative responses by teachers may lead to discouragement, underachievement, and even dropping out of school (Kim, 2008).

Consequently, teachers play an instrumental role in moderating the effects of traditional practices and standardized assessments on limiting creative thinking in the classroom (Beghetto, 2005). Yet, the literature argues that teachers currently lack the training and incentives needed to promote and assess creative thinking (Beghetto, 2005). Teachers interested in the development of creative thinking in their students often rely on intuitive approaches or assume that creative thinking can be most effectively nurtured in a handful of subjects, such as visual arts, music, and creative writing. Thus, often, there is an attitude of promoting creativity in "artsy" classes and "getting serious about the work" in classes on subjects for which the knowledge mastered may be assessed with standardized tests. In the face of standardized test preparation and the overwhelming importance of students' scores, creativity can appear irrelevant or simply out of place (Kaufman & Sternberg, 2007; Rubenstein, McCoach, & Siegle, 2013).

Teacher Perceptions of Creativity

Given the apparent conflicts of integrating creativity into an educational system that emphasizes traditional standards of behavior, teaching approaches, and assessment, developing an accurate understanding of teacher perceptions of creativity is important before considering how creativity might best be incorporated into the classroom environment. Although education has historically ignored or even undermined creative thinking, most teachers claim to value creative students and a creative classroom atmosphere (Runco & Johnson, 2002). In fact, using a scale developed to assess teachers' perceptions of creativity, Rubenstein and colleagues found that teachers appeared to believe that creativity was extremely valuable for society (Rubenstein et al., 2013). The discrepancy between teachers' claims of valuing creativity and the realities of the classroom can be explained by one or all of the following phenomena:

1. Teachers are not aware that their behaviors in the classroom actually inhibit creativity (Dawson, Andrea, Affinito, & Westby, 1999). Occupational pressures may overwhelm even well-intentioned teachers, who feel compelled to fall back on traditional authoritarian teaching methods (Besançon & Lubart, 2008) to preserve order and efficiency in the classroom.
2. It is socially desirable for teachers to claim they value creativity in the classroom even if they do not (Runco & Johnson, 2002).
3. Teachers' implicit definitions of creativity and creative behavior are uniquely different from the behaviors exhibited by students whom experts would define as creative (Dawson et al., 1999).

To understand the discrepancy between the value placed on creativity and its role in classroom environments, teachers' definitions of creativity needed to be gauged. Parents' and teacher's perceptions of what characteristics describe creative and uncreative children were collected from a set of 300 adjectives (Runco & Johnson, 1993). There was a high level of agreement (67%) between parents and teachers over creative traits. The differentiating traits for teachers' preferences were adjectives describing socially desirable characteristics (e.g., *cheerful, friendly,* and *easygoing*). Parents mentioned more personality-driven traits (e.g., *industrious, impulsive,* and *self-confident*). The rest of the definitions were as expected and described typical favorable traits that illustrate creative children.

For a more in-depth understanding of teachers' perceptions of creative children, teachers were asked to rate their favorite and least favorite student according to twenty terms – ten of the most and ten of the least prototypical characteristics of creative children (Westby & Dawson, 1995). The teachers were also asked to rate which of the twenty characteristics described creative and uncreative children. The traits describing the teachers' favorite students were negatively correlated with the creative traits; as expected, the least favorite students were positively correlated with the creativity prototype. But more telling was the finding that teachers only agreed with 45% of the adjectives defining creative/uncreative characteristics in previous literature. Several of the traits (i.e., *good-natured, reliable,* and *sincere*) unique to teachers' perception of creative students were also socially desirable characteristics; this finding resonates with the finding of a previous study (Runco & Johnson, 1993). Also, teachers rated "nonconformist" as one of the least creative traits, in contrast to almost every expert definition of creativity (Westby & Dawson, 1995).

Thus, although teachers may support the idea of creativity in the classroom (Runco & Johnson, 2002), they appear to prefer students who exhibit socially desirable traits, which they then label as creative. At the same time, they hold negative views of students displaying creative traits (Westby & Dawson, 1995). Furthering our understanding of this complex teacher-student dynamic, another study (Scott, 1999) evaluated college students' ($n = 133$) and teachers' ($n = 144$) assumptions about the potential disruptiveness of students based on four fictitious profiles that gave information about age, grade, and reading, language, and math proficiency, as well as scores on divergent thinking and creative tasks. Each participant rated the four student profiles, which differed in creative aptitude, according to twenty-one characteristics teachers may observe in students that define disruptiveness and creativity. Teacher predictions of behaviors for highly creative students were positively correlated with disruptive characteristics. The teachers' ratings also indicated that they viewed creative students as more disruptive than did the college students' ratings. Furthermore, ratings differed according to sex, suggesting that gender bias plays a role in teacher perceptions of creativity.

Consider the in-class dynamics that may result from teachers' perceptions of creative students. A mixed-method study of prospective middle and high school teachers' preferences toward unique and unexpected comments during class discussion (Beghetto, 2007) demonstrated that most teachers, especially math and high school teachers, perceived the comments as potentially disruptive. In written responses, teachers did express their desire to facilitate unique discussions to make lessons engaging but preferred relevant comments. They expressed the need to maintain relevance to start a conversation topic and feared unique comments might result in the class's getting "off task." The preference of math teachers for strictly relevant comments suggests that teachers who deal with certain subjects may have more difficulty adopting creativity-enhancing practices. Another study (Beghetto, 2008) also concluded that prospective teachers believe that in the primary school grades, memorization should be emphasized over imaginative thinking to establish a necessary foundation for future learning. The preference of memorization was also linked to the view that unique comments are disruptive. These studies help identify how teachers' educational approaches influence their preferences for specific uncreative classroom behaviors.

In addition to research in the United States, several studies (Chan & Chan, 1999; Diakidoy & Kanari, 1999; Guncer & Oral, 1993; Kampylis, Berki, & Saariluoma, 2009; Kwang & Smith, 2004; Lee & Seo, 2006; Runco & Johnson, 2002; Seo, Lee, & Kim, 2005) that have been conducted in other countries illustrate cross-cultural differences in implicit views of creativity and approaches to teaching for creativity. Runco and Johnson (2002) repeated their study on parent versus teacher implicit views of creativity (1993, see earlier) with samples from the United States and India. Similar to the previous U.S.-based study, parent and teacher views did not differ significantly, but there was a significant difference between the two cultures' definitions of *creativity* and ratings of the desirability for certain creative traits, showing that cross-cultural differences do exist. Specifically, the U.S. sample significantly favored the two clusters of attitudinal (e.g., *humorous, dreamy,* and *independent*) and intellectual (e.g., *imaginative* and *clever*) definitions of creativity compared to the Indian sample. The desirability ratings of creativity did not suggest a significant cross-cultural difference overall. In a Chinese study, researchers (Chan & Chan, 1999) asked teachers to identify creative traits and differed from the U.S. studies (Runco & Johnson, 1993, 2002) in identifying creative traits as socially undesirable (e.g., nonconformity) but related to high intellectual ability. Korean teachers have also been found to hold similar perceptions about the social undesirability of creativity due to cultural emphases on conformity, while also holding the view that creativity is related to high intellectual abilities (Seo et al., 2005).

At the University of Cyprus, researchers (Diakidoy & Kanari, 1999) analyzed the beliefs of 49 prospective teachers regarding their perceptions of creativity. The student teachers viewed creativity as a general characteristic that can be enhanced in anyone through environment and that involves novel thinking. However, they did not believe creative products necessarily demanded task appropriateness, which contradicts most definitions of creativity (Sternberg & Lubart, 1999). Creativity was seen as being more relevant to artistic and literary work (i.e., domain specific). The participants also emphasized knowledge acquisition in school as the primary reason for the lack of creativity in education. Thus, traditional methods of education are seen as inhibitors of creativity in other countries. So, while the previous studies are clearly not a summation of the international perspectives on creativity, it is important to understand that creativity exists largely in the context of a specific culture (see Kaufman & Sternberg, 2006, for further review).

It has been important for researchers to establish evidence that teachers hold a variety of views toward creativity, including negative perceptions toward creative students. These negative perceptions suggest that teachers currently may commonly fail to identify and then value creative students. To highlight this point, researchers (Dawson et al., 1999) tested third- and fourth-grade teachers' predictions of student creativity via ratings for traditional concepts of creativity (Sternberg, 1985) and teacher concepts of creativity (Westby & Dawson, 1995). The predictions were compared with the students' performance on verbal and figural creativity tasks. Students who were identified as highly creative by teachers and fit the teachers' concepts of creativity received high scores for the verbal creativity task and low scores for the figural task but did not display high levels of traditional creative personality traits. Conversely, students who were rated less creative by teachers had high scores on the figural creativity task and closely reflected traditional creative personality traits. While the findings display some of the limitations in performance assessment of creativity (i.e., lack of correlation between figural and verbal creativity tasks), the researchers noted that teachers continued to favor students with creative abilities related to social domains (Dawson et al., 1999).

Research also suggests that teachers not only have differing views of creativity (Dawson et al., 1999; Runco & Johnson, 1993, 2002; Westby & Dawson, 1995) but also show some biases in favor of uncreative behavior in the classroom (Beghetto, 2007). Psychologists have provided evidence of the current barriers to the display of creativity in the classroom. While education policy and teacher training will need to be developed, providing an adequate definition and set of assessments for creativity represents important first steps in promoting classrooms that will enhance creative thinking. Suggestions for a useful theoretical foundation for teaching and classroom assessment are discussed in the following sections.

Teaching and Assessing Creativity in the Classroom

There are now a number of papers and books that provide comprehensive overviews of ways of nurturing creativity and types of creativity assessment (e.g., Beghetto, Kaufman, & Baer, 2014; Esquivel, 1995; Feldhusen & Goh, 1995; Gregerson, Snyder, & Kaufman, 2012; Houtz & Krug, 1995; Jordan & Carlile, 2013; Starko, 2013). Here, we only briefly summarize them before describing a new approach that attempts to integrate the practice of creativity into classroom curricula.

Based on the research findings on the elements of creativity, a survey of approaches can be based on the so-called Four P model, focusing on people, processes, press, and products. First, there are several proposed models for teaching creativity in the classroom, and these tend to incorporate the development of personality factors (e.g., tolerance of ambiguity, flexibility, risk-taking, persistence, and motivation) and cognitive skills (e.g., problem defining, original thinking, elaboration, finding new connections) with process. Esquivel focuses on three examples of such teaching models that emphasize creative process enrichment, problem solving, and productivity: Torrance's Incubation Model of Teaching, Renzulli's Enrichment Triad Model, and Treffinger's Creative Problem-Solving Model. These models describe systematic, research-based approaches that promote creativity in individuals at various developmental stages. These models describe systematic, research-based approaches that promote creativity in individuals in a stepwise fashion.

The Torrance Incubation Model of Teaching (Torrance & Safter, 1990) is a generally applied three-stage model that creates opportunities for creativity in any area of learning by encouraging the mental states that seem to lead to creative thinking – such as being motivated and imaginative, desiring to pursue ideas or knowledge, and being persistent in this pursuit. Renzulli's Enrichment Triad Model (Renzulli, 1977) presents three progressive stages of activities or exercises that can develop creative thinking processes. Type I activities involve general exploratory exercises, which may be field trips or other open-ended experiences that invite exploration. Type II activities emphasize training in particular thinking skills, such as reflective thinking, divergent thinking, and problem solving. They involve such specific activities as brainstorming, elaboration, the practice of flexibility, fluency, and originality. Type III activities involve work with real problems. Treffinger's model describes three levels of instruction toward building creative problem-solving skills (Treffinger, 1991). Level 1 teaches the basic tools for creative and critical thinking. Level 2 promotes extending the basic tools to learning and practicing systematic approaches to problem solving. Level 3 involves applying creative problem-solving processes to real-life problems. In this model, the learning process and the application of systematic efforts toward creative solutions and ideas (the products) are emphasized. These models illustrate how many elements of creativity can be systematically developed within the classroom setting in long-term curriculum-based projects.

Other proposed models are classroom atmosphere based, such as establishing a sense of openness, fun, and a safe environment for personal expression (Amabile, 1989), or activity based, such as teaching creativity explicitly and using various instructional activities, media, and teaching methods (Desailly, 2012; Feldheusen & Treffinger, 1977), or they focus on teaching styles, such as not always lecturing, taking into account students' interests, encouraging questions and opinions, and soliciting students' ideas (McGreevy, 1990). Teachers who enhance student creativity are more humanistic in their approach to students – that is, they value interpersonal relationships, want to understand individual students, are open-minded and flexible, have a sense of humor, and can be spontaneous in the classroom (Esquivel, 1995).

In addition to these more generally formulated models, there are other approaches that integrate creativity as a skill that can be practiced within a positive learning environment as part of learning a given curriculum (Beghetto, 2013; Beghetto & Kaufman, 2014; Beghetto et al., 2014; Grigorenko, Jarvin, Tan, & Sternberg, 2008; Grigorenko & Tan, 2009). Based on the understanding that creativity is an inherent part of much of our everyday experience, Beghetto and colleagues outline ways in which teachers may adjust their classroom environments to be more supportive of student creativity, for example by recognizing and fostering students' internal motivations for learning, and by encouraging students' creative metacognition (self-awareness of their own creativity) (Beghetto & Kaufman, 2014). Teachers may also learn to capitalize on the "creative micro-moments" that students may experience within the context of everyday lessons on various subjects. These may take the form of unexpected and seemingly off-task insights (Beghetto, 2013). By understanding that deep conceptual knowledge is a necessary precursor to creative thinking, Beghetto and colleagues argue that teaching creativity may be a natural and completely compatible aspect of teaching in accordance with the Common Core State Standards (Beghetto et al., 2014).

Similarly, Grigorenko and colleagues propose identifying and fostering creative skills through understanding how these skills manifest themselves in curriculum-related activities. Building on the distinction between Big-C and little-c creativity, the authors define *little-c creativity* as a skill that may be used in approaching and successfully addressing novel problems and situations, generally requiring abilities such as imagining, designing, inventing, and dealing with unfamiliar contexts. As a skill, it can then be developed to a level of competency within any number of academic domains. The authors then present a study in which reading comprehension is assessed using traditional means (asking the student to use analytical and memory-based skills) versus creative means (asking the student to use creative skills). These results showed the presence of content/comprehension in both sets of answers but reflected the exertion of two very different sets of skills, both of which can be developed with practice. The value of this view of creativity in the classroom is that it allows for the integration of creative thinking and its exercise and assessment in multiple domains of a curriculum – that is, it can be practiced and developed in the course of teaching content.

What about Formal Assessment in the Classroom?

Under the purview of research, hundreds of tests have been developed to consider the many aspects of creativity (Houtz & Krug, 1995). The more well known of these are The Torrance Tests of Creative Thinking (Torrance, 1974 [1966]), Guilford's Alternative Uses Test (Guilford, 1967), Flanagan's Ingenuity Test (Flanagan, 1976), and the Remote Associates Test (Mednick, 1967). A more recent assessment attempting to incorporate the best among these methods is the Evaluation of Potential for Creativity (EPoC; Barbot, Besançon, & Lubart, 2011). All of these consider mostly the creative components of cognitive ability, such as flexibility and fluency, as well as creative production, such as originality and novelty, and problem-solving skills. In addition to these tests, lists of personality traits and rubrics for judging creative products (artwork or writings) have been developed as useful tools for looking at certain aspects of creativity (associated personalities, behaviors, and productive outcomes). However, the need for practical applications and teacher assessment tools to consider creativity specifically within the classroom begs the question of what is a viable and useful view of creativity so that it may be recognized, addressed, and nurtured within the context of schooling. That is, what is the most useful way for teachers to view creativity in the classroom so that it can be nurtured productively within that particular context, and what are some appropriate tools for assessing creativity within the classroom that can inform teachers and help them shape their teaching of creativity?

One specific classroom-based example is given by Proctor and Burnett, who developed a Creativity Checklist (Proctor & Burnett, 2004) for teachers to use within the classroom. Based on the collective literature on the personal characteristics of creative individuals, the list comprises nine items that describe various behaviors characteristic of creative individuals. It is designed to be used as an observational tool by teachers to focus on the creative personality traits displayed by students as they are engaged in a creative endeavor. These are traits such as "A fluent thinker," "An original thinker," and "An intrinsically motivated student," combining both personal dispositional and cognitive traits. This set of traits reflects one type of tool for teachers in the classroom, useful for identifying and characterizing the creative individual. However, other tools have been developed to be integrated directly into the curriculum. These rely on even more generally applicable definitions of creativity. What follows is a description of a theory of intelligence and creativity that has formed the basis for developing a classroom assessment of creativity.

Integrating Theory and Classroom Assessment

Robert Sternberg proposed a theory of intelligence (Sternberg, 1996, 1999) that explicitly incorporates creativity as one of the three main abilities that make up intelligence. This theory of intelligence, called the theory of successful intelligence (or triarchic theory of successful intelligence), combines three subtheories that address the meta-components, performance components, and knowledge acquisition components of conventional intelligence (i.e., analytical intelligence), an experiential component of intelligence (i.e., creative intelligence), and a contextual component of intelligence (i.e., practical intelligence). Summed up, the theory puts forth that intelligence is the ability to achieve one's goals in life, whatever one's context, by adapting to, shaping of, or selecting of one's environment, through a balance in the use of one's analytical, creative, and practical abilities. Within this theory, creative abilities are described through active verbs, such as *imagining, designing, finding new solutions,* and *inventing.* This verbal anchoring in everyday activities keeps the theory close to the observable classroom behaviors that may be exhibited in the course of class work. But a further elaboration on this view of creativity provides an even broader foundation for applications in the classroom.

Sternberg and Lubart (1991, 1995) then conceived the "investment theory of creativity" to capture the nature of creativity as an act of conscious decision making – generally speaking, the decision to buy low and sell high in the realm of ideas. According to their conception, creativity depends on a confluence of six resources: intellectual skills, knowledge, styles of thinking, personality, motivation, and environment (Sternberg, 2006, 2012). Each of these resources presents an individual with choices concerning whether to act creatively: whether to use one's intellectual skills to pursue unpopular ideas; whether to build on or be limited by one's set of knowledge; whether to view situations globally rather than locally; whether to take risks or to tolerate ambiguity; whether to seek out creativity-motivating factors in a situation; whether to seek out environments that support one's ideas; and whether to defy the challenges the environment may pose against acting creatively. In other words, the power to be creative rests largely within the individual. Creativity, this theory implies, can be activated by providing more encouraging and supportive environments that reward rather than punish the choice to be creative. Creativity can also be nurtured and developed within these environments. Another useful aspect of this view is that it focuses on creativity as something that happens in the real world, in the classroom and in the course of everyday life. This view can be built on in the classroom setting.

One classroom tool currently under construction (Aurora-*r*) is part of an assessment battery for intelligence in students aged 9 to 12 (The Aurora Project) that is based on Sternberg's theory (Sternberg, 1996, 1999). Aurora-*r* is a rating scale designed for teachers to rate an individual student's abilities in these areas, as well as in memory. The scale was developed specifically to tap into teachers' observations of their students executing typical classroom activities, for example, approaching their work in differentiated ways, asking questions, solving problems, and socializing. Using Aurora-*r*, teachers rate their students on a five-point scale – almost always, often, sometimes, rarely, never – responding to questions such as: "This child retains/remembers for long periods of time the following types of information . . ." (memory); "In the course of class discussion, this child asks questions that are . . ." (analytical abilities); and, "This child is able to persuade others of his/her opinion points of view . . ." (practical abilities). The creative portion of this rating scale asks teachers to focus on how often the child comes up with new or unique ideas to solve problems, whether the child responds to open-ended situations by creating new things, whether the child exhibits independence in completing a task, and how the child responds to new materials or methods for doing things. These questions presuppose that the teacher provides opportunities for these behaviors to occur; however, even if they are not occurring, the scale provides the opportunity to think about each student with respect to these behaviors.

In a small study, teachers whose students had taken both Aurora's paper-and-pencil test, which looks at analytical, practical, and creative abilities, and the CogAT (Lohman & Hagen, 2001), a general cognitive abilities test that focuses primarily on analytical thinking, filled out Aurora's rating scales on these same students. Correlations indicated that teachers' ratings of their students' analytical, practical, and creative abilities matched more closely the students' performance on the CogAT than an indication of students' respective skill levels on Aurora-*a*, a maximum-performance assessment of student's analytical, practical, and creative abilities. Why would this be?

One explanation is that teachers have been taught to look for conventional indicators of abilities. That is, they tend to rate highly those students they perceive as "high performing" in general, according to conventional practices of assessment, no matter what a given rating scale asks them to do. Thus, they demonstrate a halo effect in their ratings. Also of note in the results was a marked negative correlation between teachers' ratings of students' creative abilities with students' performance on the creative subtests of Aurora-*a*: four open-ended productive tasks generally calling for the student to generate original answers to novel stimuli, and one multiple-choice receptive task asking a student to respond appropriately to unusual uses of language. That is, students who did well on Aurora-*a*'s creative subtests were not rated as exhibiting creative behaviors by teachers according to Aurora-*r*'s teacher rating scale. This result could indicate that students who perform creatively on a test do not (or are not encouraged to) behave creatively within the general context of the classroom – in discussions, in open-ended activities, in novel problem-solving situations. Or they are not often given these opportunities. Another explanation is that the teachers might not have a clear understanding of what creativity in classrooms might be like. Clearly, if they do not know what it is, they cannot teach it or teach for it.

What all of this underlines is the importance of approaching the assessment of creativity in multiple ways. What one assessment may miss (e.g., a maximum performance test or even a one on one exercise) another may capture. What one context discourages may be elicited in another. A child who finds it difficult to concentrate on her studies in the classroom may go home and immerse herself in writing stories or plays – all of which she dreamed up while staring out of the window during class time. Thus, a parent's input might be important to discover a creative child's engagement in such an activity. At the same time, creative behavior that may be observed by an educator may be missed by a parent. Or something a student may keenly realize about himself may be overlooked by both adults, arguing the usefulness of self-scales. And yet, assessment is only a focal point in a much larger, more important, and more varied picture that has to do with possibility and promise: If creativity (or its seed) exists in everyone, can it be nurtured and grown? And further, can it be developed in the context of the classroom?

Conclusion

We must respond emphatically "yes" – creativity can be developed in the context of the classroom! But first, clarity must be established as to what does and does not constitute creative skills and competencies as well as creative behavior in the classroom. We have argued that the most useful definition of creativity for the classroom describes cognitive skills that can be identified in everyday school activities, while mastering literacy, numeracy, and science. However, equally valid classroom methods for teaching and assessing creativity may be developed based on yet to be agreed-on terms between researchers and practitioners concerning the observable and measurable indicators, such as personality traits and classroom products (e.g., ideas, discussion offerings, written and figural products), that truly indicate creative potentials. Views of creativity need to be merged and refocused. For teachers, a proper definition, training, and assessment strategy should help. They need guidance in understanding what creativity is, why this skill is important in the new emergent global economy, and how it can be taught. Concepts such as little-c creativity, creativity as a skill, and the universal possibilities for creativity in almost any context or subject matter can and should support creativity in the classroom. Building on these concepts and ongoing creativity research, teachers can create tools to implement creative thinking systematically, even within the curriculum requirements established by standardized assessment.

REFERENCES

Abuhamdeh, S., & Csikszentmilhalyi, M. (2004). The artistic personality: A systems perspective. In R. J. Sternberg, E. L. Grigorenko & J. L. Singer (Eds.), *Creativity: From potential to realization* (pp. 31–42). Washington, DC: American Psychological Association.

Amabile, T. (1989). *Growing up creative: Nurturing a lifetime of creativity*. New York: Crown.

Atchley, R. A., Keeney, M., & Burgess, C. (1999). Cerebral hemispheric mechanisms linking ambiguous word meaning retrieval and creativity. *Brain & Cognition*, **40**, 479–499.

Baer, J. (2013). Teaching for creativity: Domains and divergent thinking, intrinsic motivation, and evaluation. In M. B. Gregerson, H. T. Snyder & J. C. Kaufman (Eds.), *Teaching creatively and teaching creativity* (pp. 175–181). Dordrecht, Germany: Springer Science & Business Media.

Barbot, B., Besançon, M., & Lubart, T. I. (2011). Assessing creativity in the classroom. *The Open Education Journal*, **4**, 124–132.

Beghetto, R. A. (2005). Does assessment kill student creativity? *The Educational Forum*, **69**, 254–263.

Beghetto, R. A. (2007). Does creativity have a place in the classroom? Prospective teachers' response preferences. *Thinking Skills and Creativity*, **2**, 1–9.

Beghetto, R. A. (2008). Prospective teachers' beliefs about imaginative thinking in K–12 schooling. *Thinking Skills and Creativity*, **3**, 134–142.

Beghetto, R. A. (2013). Nurturing creativity in the micro-moments of the classroom. In K. H. Kim, J. C. Kaufman, J. Baer & B. Sriraman (Eds.), *Creatively gifted students are not like other gifted students: Research, theory, and practics* (pp. 3–15). New York: Springer.

Beghetto, R. A., & Kaufman, J. C. (2007). Toward a broader conception of creativity: A case for "mini-c" creativity. *Psychology of Aesthetics, Creativity, and the Arts*, **1**, 73–79.

Beghetto, R. A., & Kaufman, J. C. (2014). Classroom contexts for creativity. *High Ability Studies*, **25**, 53–69.

Beghetto, R. A., Kaufman, J. C., & Baer, J. (2014). *Teaching for creativity in the common core classroom*. New York: Teachers College Press.

Besançon, M., & Lubart, T. I. (2008). Differences in the development of creative competencies in children schooled in diverse learning environments. *Learning and Individual Differences*, **18**, 381–389.

Binkley, M., Erstad, O., Herman, J., Raizen, S., Ripley, M., Miller-Ricci, M., & Rumble, M. (2012). Defining twenty-first century skills. In P. Griffin, B. McGaw & E. Care (Eds.), *Assessment and teaching of 21st century skills* (pp. 17–66). Dordrecht, The Netherlands: Springer.

Chan, D. W., & Chan, L. (1999). Implicit theories of creativity: Teachers' perception of student characteristics in Hong Kong. *Creativity Research Journal*, **12**, 185–195.

Coyne, R. (1997). Creativity as commonplace. *Design Studies*, **18**, 135–141.

Craft, A. (2006). Fostering creativity with wisdom. *Cambridge Journal of Education*, **36**, 337–350.

Csikszentmihalyi, M., & Wolfe, R. (2014). New conceptions and research approaches to creativity: Implications of a systems perspective for creativity in education. In *The systems model of creativity* (pp. 161–184). Dordrecht, Germany: Springer Science and Business Media.

Dawson, V. L. D., Andrea, T., Affinito, R., & Westby, E. L. (1999). Predicting creative behavior: A reexamination of the divergence between traditional and teacher-defined concepts of creativity. *Creativity Research Journal*, **12**, 57–66.

Desailly, J. (2012). *Creativity in the primary classroom*. London: Sage.

Diakidoy, I. N., & Kanari, E. (1999). Student teachers' beliefs about creativity. *British Educational Research Journal*, **25**, 225–244.

Edwards, S. M. (2001). The technology paradox: Efficiency versus creativity. *Creativity Research Journal*, **13**, 221–228.

Esquivel, G. B. (1995). Teacher behaviors that foster creativity. *Educational Psychology Review*, **7**, 185–202.

Feldheusen, J. F., & Goh, B. E. (1995). Assessing and accessing creativity: An integrative review of theory, research and development. *Creativity Research Journal*, **8**, 231–247.

Feldheusen, J. F., & Treffinger, D. T. (1977). *Teaching creative thinking and problem solving*. Dubuque: KendallHunt.

Fishkin, A. S., & Johnson, A. S. (1998). Who is creative? Identifying children's creative abilities. *Roeper Review*, **21**, 40–46.

Flanagan, J. C. (1976). *Flanagan Aptitude Classification Tests (FACT Battery)*. Chicago: Science Research Associates.

Florida, R. (2003). *The rise of the creative class: And how it's transforming work, leisure, community and everyday life*. New York: Basic Books.

Gregerson, M. B., Snyder, H. T., & Kaufman, J. C. (2012). *Teaching creatively and teaching creativity*. Dordrecht, Germany: Springer Science & Business Media.

Grigorenko, E. L., Jarvin, L., Tan, M., & Sternberg, R. J. (2008). Something new in the garden: Assessing creativity in academic domains. *Psychology Science Quarterly*, **50**, 295–307.

Grigorenko, E. L., & Tan, M. (2009). Teaching creativity as a demand-led competency. In O. S. Tan, D. M. McInerney, A. D. Liem & A.-G. Tan (Eds.), *What the West can learn from the East: Asian perspectives on the psychology of learning and motivation (Vol. 7)*. Greenwich, CT: Information Age Press (IAP).

Guilford, J. P. (1950). Creativity. *American Psychologist*, **5**, 444–454.

Guilford, J. P. (1967). *The nature of human intelligence*. New York: McGraw-Hill.

Guncer, B., & Oral, G. (1993). Relationship between creativity and nonconformity to school discipline as perceived by teachers. *Journal of Instruction Psychology*, **20**, 7.

Hartley, D. (2003). New economy, new pedagogy? *Oxford Review of Education*, **29**, 81–94.

Hasse, C. (2001). Institutional creativity: The relational zone of proximal development. *Culture & Psychology*, **7**, 199–221.

Henderson, S. J. (2004). Inventors: The ordinary genius next door. In R. J. Sternberg, E. L. Grigorenko & J. L. Singer (Eds.), *Creativity: From potential to realization* (pp. 103–126). Washington, DC: American Psychological Association.

Hennessey, B., & Watson, M. (2016). The defragmentation of creativity: Future directions with an emphasis on educational applications. In G. E. Corazza & S. Agnoli (Eds.), *Multidisciplinary contributions to the science of creative thinking* (pp. 21–31). Singapore: Springer.

Hennessey, B. A. (2015). If I were secretary of education: A focus on intrinsic motivation and creativity in the classroom. *Psychology of Aesthetics, Creativity, and the Arts*, **9**, 187–192.

Houtz, J. C., & Krug, D. (1995). Assessment of creativity: Resolving a mid-life crisis. *Educational Psychology Review*, **7**, 269–300.

Jordan, A., & Carlile, O. (2013). *Approaches To Creativity: A Guide For Teachers*. Maidenhead, Berkshire: McGraw-Hill Education.

Kampylis, P., Berki, E., & Saariluoma, P. (2009). In-service and prospective teachers' conceptions of creativity. *Thinking Skills and Creativity*, **4**, 15–29.

Kaufman, J. C., & Beghetto, R. A. (2009). Beyond big and little: The four c model of creativity. *Review of General Psychology*, **13**, 1–12.

Kaufman, J. C., & Sternberg, R. J. (2007). Creativity. *Change*, **39**, 55–58.

Kaufman, J. C., & Sternberg, R. J. (Eds.). (2006). *The international handbook of creativity*. New York: Cambridge University Press.

Kim, K. H. (2008). Underachievement and creativity: Are gifted underachievers highly creative? *Creativity Research Journal*, **20**, 234–242.

Kwang, N. A., & Smith, I. (2004). The paradox of promoting creativity in the Asian classroom: An empirical investigation. *Genetic, Social, and General Psychology Monographs*, **130**, 307–330.

Lee, E. A., & Seo, H. (2006). Understanding of creativity by Korean elementary school teachers in gifted education. *Creativity Research Journal*, **18**, 237–242.

Lohman, D. F., & Hagen, E. P. (2001). Cognitive Abilities Test (CogAT). Rolling Meadows, IL: Riverside Publishing.

MacKinnon, D. W. (1961). The study of creativity. In D. W. MacKinnon (Ed.), *The creative person* (pp. 1-1–1-15). Berkeley: Institute of Personality Assessment Research, University of California.

McGreevy, A. (1990). Tracking the creative teacher. *Momentum*, **21**, 57–59.

Mednick, S. A. (1967). *The Remote Associates Test*. Boston, MA: Houghton-Mifflin.

Murdock, M. C., & Puccion, G. J. (1993). A contextual organizer for conducting creativity research. In S. G. Isaksen, M. C. Murdock, R. L. Firestien & J. D. Treffinger (Eds.), *Understanding and recognizing creativity: The emergence of a discipline* (pp. 249–280). Norwood, NJ: Ablex.

Plucker, J. A., Beghetto, R. A., & Dow, G. T. (2004). Why isn't creativity more important to educational psychologists? Potentials, pitfalls, and future directions in creativity research. *Educational Psychologist*, **39**, 83–96.

Proctor, R. M. J., & Burnett, P. C. (2004). Measuring cognitive and dispositional characteristics of creativity in elementary students. *Creativity Research Journal*, **16**, 421–429.

Renzulli, J. S. (1977). The enrichment triad model: A guide for developing defensible programs for the gifted and talented. Wethersfield, CT: Creative Learning Press.

Rhodes, M. (1961/1987). An analysis of creativity. In S. G. Isaksen (Ed.), *Frontiers of creativity research: Beyond the basics* (pp. 216–222). Buffalo, NY: Bearly Limited.

Rubenstein, L. D., McCoach, D. B., & Siegle, D. (2013). Teaching for Creativity Scales: An instrument to examine teachers' perceptions of factors that allow for the teaching of creativity. *Creativity Research Journal*, **25**, 324–334.

Runco, M. A. (2004). Creativity. *Annual Review of Psychology*, **55**, 657–587.

Runco, M. A., & Johnson, D. J. (1993). Parents' and teachers' implicit theories on children's creativity. *Child Study Journal*, **23**, 91–109.

Runco, M. A., & Johnson, D. J. (2002). Parents' and teachers' implicit theories of children's creativity: A cross-cultural perspective. *Creativity Research Journal*, **14**, 427–438.

Schoen, L., & Fusarelli, L. D. (2008). Innovation, NCLB, and the fear factor. *Educational Policy*, **22**, 181–203.

Scott, L. C. (1999). Teachers' biases toward creative children. *Creativity Research Journal*, **12**, 321–328.

Seo, H., Lee, E., & Kim, K. H. (2005). Korean science teachers' understanding of creativity in gifted education. *Journal of Secondary Gifted Education*, **2**, 98–105.

Simonton, D. K. (1994). *Greatness: Who makes history and why*. New York: Guilford Press.

Simonton, D. K. (2004). *Creativity in science: Change, logic, genius, and zeitgeist*. New York: Cambridge University Press.

Starko, A. J. (2013). *Creativity in the classroom: Schools of curious delight*. New York: Routledge.

Sternberg, R. J. (1985). Implicit theories of intelligence, creativity, and wisdom. *Journal of Personality and Social Psychology*, **49**, 607–627.

Sternberg, R. J. (1996). *Successful intelligence*. New York: Simon & Schuster.

Sternberg, R. J. (1999). The theory of successful intelligence. *Review of General Psychology*, **3**, 292–316.

Sternberg, R. J. (2006). The nature of creativity. *Creativity Research Journal*, **18**, 87–98.

Sternberg, R. J. (2012). The assessment of creativity: An investment-based approach. *Creativity Research Journal*, **24**, 3–12.

Sternberg, R. J. (2015). Teaching for creativity: The sounds of silence. *Psychology of Aesthetics, Creativity, and the Arts*, **9**, 115–117.

Sternberg, R. J., Grigorenko, E. L., & Singer, J. L. (Eds.). (2004). *Creativity: From potential to realization*. Washington, DC: American Psychological Association.

Sternberg, R. J., & Lubart, T. I. (1991). An investment theory of creativity and its development. *Human Development*, **34**, 1–31.

Sternberg, R. J., & Lubart, T. I. (1995). *Defying the crowd*. New York: Free Press.

Sternberg, R. J., & Lubart, T. I. (1999). The concept of creativity: Prospects and paradigms. In R. J. Sternberg (Ed.), *Handbook of creativity* (pp. 3–15). New York: Cambridge University Press.

Torrance, E. P. (1962). *Guiding creative talent*. Englewood Cliffs, NJ: Prentice Hall.

Torrance, E. P. (1974 [1966]). *The Torrance Tests of Creative Thinking*. Bensenville, IL: Scholastic Test Services.

Torrance, E. P., & Safter, H. T. (1990). *The incubation model of teaching*. Buffalo, NY: Bearly.

Treffinger, D. J. (1991). Creative productivity: Understanding its sources and nurture. *Illinois Council for the Gifted Journal*, **10**, 6–9.

Treffinger, D. J., Selby, E. C., & Isaksen, S. G. (2008). Understanding individual problem-solving style: A key to learning and applying creative problem solving. *Learning and Individual Differences*, **18**, 390–401.

Westby, E. L., & Dawson, V. L. (1995). Creativity: Asset or burden in the classroom? *Creativity Research Journal*, **8**, 1–10.

CHAPTER 10

The Five Core Attitudes and Seven I's of the Creative Process

Jane Piirto

Ashland University

When I began working in the field of the education of the gifted and talented, as a county coordinator in Ohio, in 1977, I looked at the categories of giftedness as described in the Marland Report of 1972. These were superior cognitive ability, specific academic ability, *creativity*, visual and performing arts ability, and psychomotor ability. With regard to the inclusion of creativity as a type of giftedness, I asked myself, "Aren't smart people creative? Aren't people good at academic subjects creative? Aren't visual and performing artists creative? Aren't athletes creative? Why is there a separate category for creativity?" Over the next 13 years I was a county coordinator in two states, and the principal of a school for gifted children. I am now a college professor who runs a graduate program for certification for teachers of the gifted and talented. I am unusual, I suspect, because in my inner life, my real life, I am and have been an artist – a published novelist and a poet – and I see the world not only through the eyes of a researcher in education and psychology but also through an artist's eyes. I have also been what is called a *teaching artist* (Oreck & Piirto, 2014), as I also worked for four years as a Poet in the Schools in the National Endowment for the Arts "Artist in the Schools" program during the late 1970s and early 1980s.

I got myself trained in many of the current (and still ongoing – not much has changed in the creativity training arena since the 1970s) creativity training programs – Creative Problem-Solving, Future Problem-Solving, and Odyssey of the Mind. I began to think about my own creative process. I learned firsthand from California's Mary Meeker about the Structure of the Intellect (Meeker, 1977; Piirto & Keller-Mathers, 2014), and became one of her first advanced trainers, going around the country giving workshops on Guilford's theory of intellect, as well as on divergent production–fluency, flexibility, elaboration, synthesis, and the like (Guilford, 1950, 1967). Then I would go home and write my literary works, send them out for possible publication, receiving many rejections and enough acceptances to keep me going. I was separating my life as an educator from my life as an artist. My own creative life contained little brainstorming, SCAMPERing, generating of alternative solutions, or creative problem solving, as described by the flowchart handouts I had been given at the many workshops I attended.

I wrote the textbook for the creativity studies course in our gifted endorsement, and I began to construct exercises and activities that reflected the creative process for the eminent creators that I was discovering in my reading and reflection. Most creative adults who had biographies written about them, who had written memoirs, who had been interviewed and researched, talked about their creative process in more organic terms. One of the finest essays on that topic was poet Brewster Ghiselin's, written in 1952, as an introduction to his anthology, *The Creative Process,* where he collected essays by creative people describing what they do before, during, and after they create. My artistic self (Piirto, 1985, 1995c, 2008b) gravitated toward accounts such as Ghiselin's introduction to this anthology, even though cognitive psychologists have disparaged such accounts, which they call anecdotal and retrospective, therefore untrustworthy, saying that you cannot trust what people say about their creative processes, because they cannot know what is really happening inside (c.f. Perkins, 1981; Sternberg & Lubart, 1999). Such disparaging of the biographical is a common practice for scientifically oriented psychologists who distrust any findings that are not made with double-blind experiments. But my literary background, which dwelt on the poetic way of knowing that embraces the psychoanalytic and the depth psychological viewpoints of Freud (1976 [1908]), Jung (1976 [1923]), and Hillman (1975), caused me to doubt the purely scientific and to search for the experiential, the affective in these biographical descriptions.

I found no mention of the words *creative problem solving, fluency, flexibility, brainstorming,* or *elaboration* in the essays, memoirs, biographies, and interviews I used to formulate the theory I am elucidating in this chapter, even though the creative process as practiced by creative productive adults has engaged thinkers of the world from prehistoric times. For example, mythological and classical perspectives on the creative process have viewed inspiration as the visitation of the Muse (Calame, 1995; Plato, *Dialogues*). Historically, the creative process has been tied with the desire for spiritual unity, and with the desire for personal expression. The creative process can be viewed in the context of a person's life and the historical milieu. Contemporary psychological and religious thought have emphasized that the creative process has universal implications. What is popularly called right-brain thinking, as well as visualization, metaphorization, and imagery, seems to help people in the creative process. The concept of the two sides of the brain – one for creativity and one for plodding intellect – persists (cf. Pink, 2006), although we need the whole brain for creative production. The creative process is a concern of humanists as well as of scientists. While scientific experimentation has sought to demystify many popular creative process beliefs, even the most recent biographical accounts described experiences similar to those of yore. I reluctantly concluded that the repertoires of those who teach about creativity in the classroom, who often use only the Creative Problem Solving (CPS) and Guilford's cognitive aspect of divergent production in enhancing creativity, should be expanded.

Many of the creative and productive adults whose lives I read about seemed to have creative processes that could be divided into three themes, with several subthemes: (1) they seemed to have certain core attitudes toward creativity; (2) they experienced what I came to call the Seven I's (Inspiration, Insight, Intuition, Incubation, Improvisation, Imagery, Imagination); and (3) they engaged in certain general practices – a need for solitude and for rituals, they had formally studied their domains, they liked meditative practices, they were part of a community of people working in the same domain, and their creativity was part of a lifestyle, a lifelong process. I collapsed these into what I have called the Five Core Attitudes for Creativity, the Seven I's for Creativity, and the General Practices for Creativity, and I began to translate these concepts into lessons. One caveat is that all of these have not been found in all creators, but many of them have been found in most creators.

By now, I have assembled a full course – nay, more than that – of activities that tap into the mysterious, nebulous, dreamy, solitary quietness of the creative process as it has been written about and talked about by adult creators (Table 10.1). My graduate students, teachers training to achieve an 18-semester-hour endorsement for teaching the gifted in our state, have translated these principles into their own practices. In the course we use my books as primary texts (Piirto, 2004, 2007b, 2011). Over 25 years, students have completed biographical studies seeking to confirm or deny my findings; to date, more than 1,200 biographical studies have been conducted, and those findings have been mostly confirmatory.

However, although the exercises can enhance and direct the students to the creative process as creators practice it, the creators have what is absolutely necessary and nonnegotiable to creative production – they have a desire, a motivation, a passion to do the work in the domain they have

Table 10.1 *Piirto Model for Creativity Course for Five Core Attitudes, Seven I's, and General*

Concept	Subconcept	Type	Exercise
Five core attitudes	Naiveté		• Raisin meditation (taste, touch, and smell) • Draw a detail (sight) • Listen closely (hearing)
	Risk-taking Self-discipline Group trust Tolerance for ambiguity		• Princess and the Pea • Thoughtlogs • Field trips – bonding • Caveat about confidentiality and respect • Storytelling • Janusian • Escher • Mock debate
Seven I's	Inspiration		
		Muse	• Write a sonnet • Sculpt a holder
		Nature	• Nature walk
		Substances	• Focus question
		Travel	• Field trips– bookstore/library, a museum, a concert, a play, a movie, a reading or lecture, a place
		Dreams	• Dream interpretation
	Insight		• Grasping the Gestalt • Aha! • Zen sketching
	Incubation		• Individual creativity project
	Imagination		• Myth creation with costumes
	Imagery		• Ten-minute movie • Guided imagery
	Imagination		• Acting • Fingerpainting • Clay • Poetry • Fiction
	Intuition		• Intuition probe • Psychic intuition • Dream work
	Improvisation		• Jazz • Theater • Word rivers • Writing practice • Creative movement • Rhythm and drumming • Scat singing • Doodling

Table 10.1 *(cont.)*

Concept	Subconcept	Type	Exercise
General	Creativity rituals		• Thoughtlogs • Biographical study
	Meditation		• Meditate on beauty (15 minutes before a work of art; aesthetics; archetypes) • Meditate on the dark side (a visit to a cemetery; the shadow) • Meditate on God (bring a sacred text class; literature) • Meditate on nature (i am a naturalist; this is the day which the Lord hath made; Gaia)
	Knowledge about demands/ training in the domain		• Noticing oceanic consciousness (flow) • Biographical study
	Salon		• Field trip • Biographical study
	Exercise		• Run, walk, exercise, swim, noticing when creative thoughts come
	Process of a life		• Whole course • Biographical study

chosen. And so in the beginning of the course, we focus on my notion of the thorn of fiery passion as explicated in my model of the Pyramid of Talent Development (Figure 10.1). In describing the Pyramid of Talent Development, I (Piirto, 1994, 1995a, 1995b, 1998, 1999, 2000, 2002, 2004, 2006, 2007a, 2007b, 2008a, 2009, 2011, 2014; Reynolds & Piirto, 2007) used the image of the thorn as a metaphor for the motivation to develop one's inborn talent. Although absolutely necessary, the presence of talent for work in the chosen domain is not sufficient. Many people have more than one talent and wonder what to do with their talents. What is the impetus and what and what is the reason for one talent taking over and capturing the passion and commitment of the person with the talent? Which talent a person with multiple talents will choose is evident by its insistence and its continuous presence.

Much evidence exists to show that the creative person decides to pursue the development of his or her talent after some catalyst reveals what must and can happen. It may be winning a contest, receiving praise, or becoming so pleasantly engrossed in what is being created that the person realizes

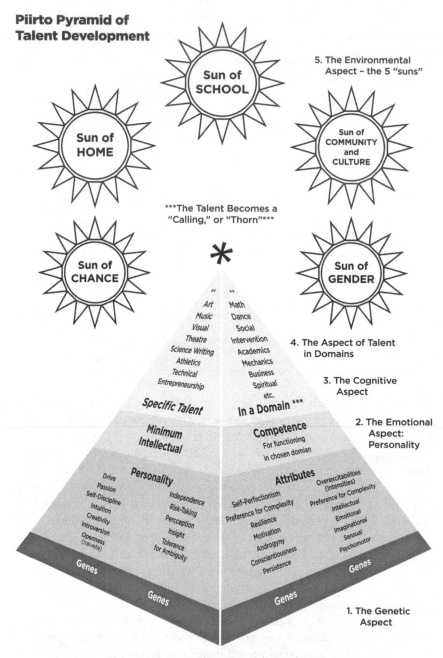

Figure 10.1 The Pyramid of Talent Development

that it is what he or she must do at all costs. It may be a depression that is assuaged by making or creating, such that the self-healing that occurs when one is creative warns the person that he or she must create in order to prevent illness. It may come after a long period of thought and meditation. The creative person recognizes that the thorn is pricking and the call must be answered. Reynolds and Piirto (2005, 2007) presented a philosophical and theoretical rationale and many activities that can be used by teachers to identify and nurture the thorn.

In the creativity class, students are encouraged to honor their domains of passion – that which they can't *not* do.

My students who are becoming teachers of the gifted and talented tell me that yes, indeed, the K–12 students that they work with can begin to see the creative process as something that is, at base, more a transformational journey than a cognitive one. Every week they try out the activities I created, modifying them for their own use. For a student to devise an activity at the Application level on the Bloom's Revised Taxonomy (Anderson, Krathwohl, & Bloom, 2001) for the students one teaches is where the true creativity of the teacher is shown, and that is my goal as a professor. After each exercise, I ask the students to tell about a way this concept could be applied. The sections that follow are organized as follows: first the concept is defined; then biographical examples are given; and, finally, a class activity is described. An outline of the course activities is given in Table 10.1, and examples of a few of the activities teachers have developed are given in Box 10.1.

Five Core Attitudes

Core Attitude of Openness to Experience

Openness is one of the Big Five personality attributes, and some studies are finding that creators score highest in openness on such instruments as the NEO-PI-R (Costa & McRae, 1992). Openness as a core attitude refers to the fact that creative people pay attention to the small things and are able to view their fields and domains by seeing the old as if it were new; that is, they see the world with naiveté. As an example, the artists Arshile Gorky and Willem de Kooning used to walk the streets of New York at night, pointing out the reflections of the few neon lights in paper thrown on the streets, remarking on the shapes and shadows, seeing the obvious as if new (Spender, 1999). Igor Stravinsky (1990) remarked on the creator's "gift of observation." He said, "The true creator may be recognized by his

Box 10.1 Examples from Teachers of 5 Core Attitudes and 7 I's

NAIVETÉ (OPENNESS TO EXPERIENCE)

1. Do not provide an example; share an experience using sensory details.
2. Since some children rush through things to move onto something else, I would do the relaxation technique and then have them draw an object and commit them to a time (20–30 min) during which only that activity can be worked on.
3. Bring in objects that are unfamiliar to the students. Play 20 Questions on what the purpose of the object is. Example: old kitchen utensils.
4. Students who test out of a math unit can look at the concept through "new" eyes and create a game that would require a demonstrated mastery of the skill/concept.
5. Taste the hardtack in simulation of a Civil War soldier's life.

INSPIRATION OF LOVE

1. For middle schoolers we would focus on a variety of choices with a gentle push in the direction of love for mankind, friends, schoolmates, teachers, etc.
2. Share meaningful picture books about love: *Thank you Mr. Falker*; Patricia Polacco books (she uses family tales). Have students share meanings or do a write off of an idea. Relate text to self, to other text, to world. Pose: How would the world change with love of all cultures?
3. Teach your students about the types of love (agape, eros, filios). Teach them (especially boys) that it is okay to tell someone you love them, whether it is a family member, a friend, or significant other.
4. With fourth, fifth, and sixth graders, the poetry, the music, or the clay sculpture would all work. They have strong feelings of love at their young ages. I know from reading their journals. Some have a passion for animals, some for young children, many for a parent, grandparent, aunt, or uncle. One has a strong bond with a neighbor.
5. When teaching Shakespeare, love always pops up. Write sonnets when studying Shakespeare.

IMAGERY

1. Imagery could be used to set the stage for an event in history. Students would close their eyes and listen as the teacher painted a word picture of the scene. Descriptions of the place, the people, the emotion, the action gives a clear sense of what it was like to be there.
2. My students always write better and more naturally after I show them video excerpts concerning the historical facts and commentary from the time and place that we are studying. This is partly due to them acquiring background knowledge, but more because the images in the film connect

with the images in their own minds and blend to form new images in their writing.

3. Use imagery when studying bees. By using cups with different scents, the students will explore how bees use their senses to find the pollen that needs to be collected. By using their sense of sound, students will listen to the flight of the bumblebee to imagine the sounds of a busy beehive. Connections made from human to nature help understand life.

4. Before reading Susan B. Anthony's speech, "Are Women Persons," create an imagery exercise about women and men coming to hear her speak. Maybe a woman with her child in arms. Jeers in the background. Loud noise. Posters on both sides of issue. After giving a chance to imagine setting, I will read the speech.

5. Forming the semi-regular polyhedra from the regular polyhedra; imagine the truncation of the vertices – see the new faces. Using images to predict and then concretely verify those images.

ability always to find about him, in the commonest and humblest thing, items worthy of note" (p. 11).

The raisin meditation is an exercise in taste and smell. Students eat, slowly, two raisins, noticing the taste, texture, and smell. Other exercises follow, in the senses of sight (draw a detail of this classroom), hearing (listen carefully to this music and to this noise), and so on. After initial exercises in openness and observation, students wrote about how they would apply this principle to their own practice. Box 10.1 shows some examples.

Core Attitude of Self-Discipline

When one studies the lives of creators, one often finds they have created many, many works, even though they are only known for one, two, or a few (Simonton, 1995). This self-discipline leads to the great productivity of creators. Van Gogh (1937) wrote to Theo, "I am daily working on drawing figures. I shall make a hundred of them before I paint them" (p. 45). Choreographer Agnes deMille (1991) noted that "all artists – indeed all great careerists – submit themselves, as well as their friends, to lifelong, relentless discipline, largely self-imposed and never for any reason relinquished" (p. 124). Most well-known creators are known for only a few of their voluminous numbers of creative works, produced through great self-discipline over a period of years. Expertise research says that one cannot contribute anything new to a domain unless one has been working in the domain for at least 10 years and performed at least 10,000 repetitions (Ericsson, 1996).

In creativity class, the thought logs are solitary creative practice, as well as practice in the core attitude of self-discipline. The students must make marks for 10 minutes a day. "Making marks" means anything – not only writing; sometimes, literally, the page for the day has consisted of one pencil slash. These are not judged or commented on. For example, this is not a dialogue between teacher and student as journals often are, but rather an attempt to imitate the creative practice of creators, who all make marks about their products. They do not hold them in their heads and produce them full blown, as Venus rises from the sea, from the sperm of Zeus. It takes about 21 days to 2 months to form a habit, according to popular Internet sources. This requirement has had various results – one student used the sketches in her thoughtlog for her senior art show; others have not continued the practice but have looked back on the 15 weeks of creativity class and find there a portrait of their lives at that time.

Core Attitude of Risk-Taking

Risk-taking in creative people has been noticed since creativity began to be studied at the Institute of Personality Assessment and Research in the 1950s (Barron, 1968; Mackinnon, 1978). Risk-taking enables one to try new things. While introverted and shy creators may eschew physical risk-taking, professional risk-taking in creators may be manifested in trying new forms, styles, or subjects. The kind of courage they have is the courage to stumble, fail, and, after rejection, try again. May (1975) called it *creative courage*, which is finding the new, providing the vanguard's warning of what is about to happen in the culture and showing in image and symbol, through their imaginations, what is possible. The creative artists and scientists threaten what is. That is why, in repressive societies, those creators who speak out in image and in symbol are jailed or exiled. Courage is required in the presence of censure and rejection. For example, take the case of Nikola Tesla, the inventor of alternating current. He fought and won, fought and lost, trusted and was betrayed, and still remained steadfast to his principle that alternating current would eventually be preferred over direct current (Cheney, 1981). The biographical literature is rife with examples of how creators stepped into the river of their domains and became, through the years, the leader through groundbreaking risk-taking work.

The exercise used for illustrating risk-taking is called "The Princess and the Pea." Students list about five personal acts that would be risk-taking for them. They then fold this into a "pea" and place it upon their body (in a shoe, in a pocket, in a bra), where it will bother them and where they will notice it. They then take a vow to try ("I will try, Jane") to do one of the risks that semester. One student, whom I had the year before, came to me at a conference and said, "I took my risk. I finished a quilt and entered it into a quilt show. I didn't win, but I did it." This is a common result. Each class period has a time set aside to discuss progress on risk-taking.

Core Attitude of Tolerance for Ambiguity

The term *tolerance for ambiguity* comes from the research done by the IPAR (Institute for Personality Assessment and Research) group in the 1950s, especially that of the late Frank Barron. Likewise, psychiatrist Albert Rothenberg (1979), in his research, thought that creators used a Janusian process in creating, referring to the two-faced god Janus, who was able to face in opposite directions. In fact, few research findings are cut and dried – true without any doubt. The researcher must set out the study's method, participants, and findings according to a prescribed way and then must take into account the arguments that would be opposing. Albert Einstein was described by biographer Isaacson thus: "He retained the ability to hold two thoughts in his mind simultaneously, to be puzzled when they conflicted, and to marvel when he could smell an underlying unity" (Isaacson, 2007, location 536, Kindle). Tolerance for ambiguity is necessary to not focus on one solution too soon. It is related to the "I" of Incubation. Abstract expressionist Mark Rothko would lie on a couch in his studio for hours and days, contemplating the placement of the shades and stripes and colors of his mammoth abstract paintings, rising ambiguous forms (Breslin, 1993). Tolerance for ambiguity is illustrated in the creativity class through a discussion of critical thinking and its various forms. We conduct a mock debate about current issues, for example, the shootings by police of unarmed black men, with some people taking the role of the police and others taking the roles of the African-American community activists.

Core Attitude of Group Trust

In collaborative creativity, which is the kind that is usually encouraged in business and manufacturing, theater, dance, athletics, and music, the members of the group who is creating have to trust each other. Leaders make sure that the people in the group feel comfortable taking risks, are open and naive, have acceptance for differing views and for incomplete answers, and do the work with regularity and discipline. From the raucous team in a closed room writing the jokes for a talk show or situation comedy, to the football team studying the game mistakes after losing the big one, members of a group must be confident enough and have enough trust in the process and in the group to be able to move on, to take criticism, and to do more. Working in a group creates interdependency, as each member has a role to play and a job to do, and they cannot be egotistical or selfish, or the whole project will suffer. One person cannot dominate; everyone must play and experience together. Trust is necessary among the members of the group. Each team or ensemble has its own culture. One must look for a "good fit." Sawyer (2007) called it "group genius," and he chronicled studies where the creative community had more juice than the individual. However, even when the creator creates alone, he or she is really not alone, for what I have called the "Sun of Community and Culture" on my Pyramid of Talent Development (see Figure 10.1) is operative; the work is judged by peers and connoisseurs of the domain, and the creator socializes with and learns from other creators in the domain. No creator is isolated from the domain's rules, laws, and members.

The American Abstract Artists group in the 1930s gave each other problems at their meetings, as they experienced rivalry as to who would be the best teacher of abstract art, and who was the best abstract artist:

> Gorky suggested that they all go off and produce a painting restricted to the colors black and red. At the next meeting they would decide whose was the best. Or else they could produce a communal painting, choosing from among themselves who was the beset draftsman, who is the best colorist, who the best in textures, and so forth. They would produce a masterpiece in which each would set his hand to a different task, and they would exhibit the result, naturally, unsigned. Or – craziest idea of all – they should go home to their studios and come back next week with an object made from a light bulb and a piece of string. That would surely determine who was best qualified to teach abstraction. (Spender, 1999 p. 159)

Group trust in the creativity course is developed through affective activities, whereby students feel that they can take risks without being ridiculed or teased. The class begins with a caveat based on the advertisement for Las Vegas – "What is said in creativity class stays in creativity class" – to encourage confidentiality and no gossip about what people said. At each course meeting, students must read their essays about focus questions aloud. I also take students on field trips, where they see and meet each other outside of the classroom and travel together, sharing personal experiences.

It is called *meditation day* – we visit a nature preserve early in the morning in the dew and colored leaves, to meditate on nature and its inspiration for creative work; we go to a cemetery, where we reverently and quietly contemplate the dark side and its inspiration for creativity; we lunch at the art museum, where we practice "salon conversation" about the news, the arts, books read, and issues about the world; we then visit the museum, with the rule for the day being that students must simulate solitude – that is, they do the activities alone, writing notes in their thoughtlogs, with a time for sharing afterward. Students realize the difficulty of organizing field trips, with fund raising, permissions, and the like, but this activity inspires them to try and to develop group trust among their own students through the affective.

The Seven I's

Here are some further aspects of the creative process as really practiced by real creators in the arts, sciences, and business (Piirto, 1992, 1998, 2002, 2004). I have called them the Seven I's – several types of (1) Inspiration, (2) Imagery, (3) Imagination, (4) Intuition, (5) Insight, (6) Incubation, and (7) Improvisation. I have developed exercises for each of these aspects so that my students can teach them in their classes and practice them in their lives.

Inspiration

All creators talk about inspiration. Literally, inspiration is a taking in of breath. In terms of creativity, inspiration provides the motivation to create. Inspiration is a breathing or infusion into the mind or soul of an exaltation. Creators in domains discuss several types of inspiration, including the inspiration of love, of nature, through substances, by others' works, from dreams, from travel, and so on.

The Visitation of the Muse: The Inspiration of Love

Being inspired by regard for another – by the gaze of desire – has been called the visitation of the muse. Muse originally meant "reminder." The Muses were inspirations for creators in various domains. Each muse had her own province in music, literature, art, and science. Calliope was the muse of epic poetry; lyric poetry had Clio (as portrayed in *The Allegory of Painting* by Vermeer); and Euterpe, Thalia, Melpomene, Terspichore,

Polyhymnia, and Thalia inspired tragedy, comedy, choral singing, dance, and poetry celebrating the divine, respectively. Erato was the muse of love poetry. The person experiencing the inspiration of the muse is inspired by that feeling and seeks to impress the object of desire by making something or showing something. The whole industry of greetings related to February 14 is an example of the pervasive inspiration of love. One need only study art history to see the myriads of works dedicated to desire. The paintings of Gerome (the Pygmalion and Galatea series), Tura, Poussin, Chagall (*Apparition: Self Portrait with Muse*), Picasso's many models and several wives, Dali – the list is infinite. Listening to popular radio songs also illustrates the power of desire and erotic love to inspire songwriters. The desire inspires longing and the longing leads to the creative work.

Inspiration by the muse also has a mystical aspect. The people who are inspired often say that they are possessed. This idea is an ancient one, with a broad literature that is seldom referred to by psychologists working on the creative process. The Platonic view puts forth that the work comes from elsewhere than the intellect. The surrealists elaborated on this idea to theorize that the inspiration is from the unconscious, the unknown within (Maritain, 1953; Plato, *Dialogues*) – thus, "visitation" of the Muse. Creators often speak as if what they write was sent from something within yet afar. Inspirations "come."

Some creators feel as if they are go-betweens, mediums. Some mysterious force impels them, works through their hands, wiggles through them, shoots from them. This type of inspiration also applies in theater. For example, some actors speak of being receptacles for their characters' souls, of being possessed. Today actors talk about "getting into" character. Athletes talk of putting on their "game face," an oblique reference to the mask, echoing the masks of Greek theater. They often have pre-performance rituals for entering the state of mind necessary. This might include putting on their makeup, meditating, or being alone for a period of time.

When I teach about the inspiration of love for creativity, I discuss the Greek terms for love – *agape* (love of God), *storge* (love of family), *filios* (brotherly love), *eros* (sexual love), and *patrios* (love of country or tribe). After I speak about how the 14-line sonnet imitates human breath through the meter of iambic pentameter, students write a love sonnet. Students sculpt a holder for this powerful love, out of clay. Clay is ground, earth, a way to contain strong emotion. Students have shared ideas about the influence of love and how to include it into their practice as teachers. Some of their ideas are given in Table 10.1.

The Inspiration of Nature

The inspiration of the natural world, from mountains, plains, animals, landscapes, insects, snakes, and all things natural, pervades much creative work, and creators are frank in their gratitude to nature. One of the most telling differences between scientists and mathematicians is that scientists are inspired by the opportunity to solve mysteries of nature, whereas mathematicians seek to solve theorems and abstract problems. Mathematics is a tool for scientists, a tool that helps them understand nature. The inspiration of nature was particularly pervasive in the works of the nineteenth-century British and American transcendentalists and romantics, writers such as Wordsworth, Coleridge, Shelly, Byron, Emerson, Dickinson, and Thoreau. They decried the industrial revolution and sought to return to simpler times when nature was preeminent, and not the conquering of nature.

The meditation day field trip mentioned earlier crystallizes the influence of nature on human beings, as we silently walk in a park in solitude, with only a camera, drawing materials, and a thoughtlog, thinking about things. This is often the favorite part of meditation day for the students, and they in turn take their own students out of the school buildings to meditate on nature.

Inspiration through Substances

The use of substances – alcohol, drugs, herbs – has a long and respectable reputation within the literature on the creative process in writers, artists, musicians, and others. Aldous Huxley wrote about the influence of mescaline; Samuel Taylor Coleridge about the influence of opium; Jack Kerouac about amphetamines; Edgar Allen Poe about absinthe; the seventh-century Chinese Zen poet Li Po about wine; Fyodor Dostoevsky about whiskey; Allen Ginsberg about LSD; Michael McClure about mushrooms – peyote – and also about heroin and cocaine.

The list of substances used could go on and on. The altered mental state brought about by substances has been thought to enhance creativity – to a certain extent. The partaker must have enough wits about self to descend into the abyss to reap what is learned there, but also to be able to return and put it aside. The danger of turning from creative messenger to addicted body is great, and many creators have succumbed, especially to the siren song of alcohol. After taking drugs, Allen Ginsberg had a vision of William Blake. "I had the impression of the entire universe as poetry filled with light and intelligence and communication and signals. Kind of like the top of my head coming off, letting in the rest of the universe connected to my own brain" (Miles, 1989, p. 79). Ginsberg viewed the initial vision as the most important, most genuine experience he ever had, and he spent many years trying to recapture it through drugs and, after he gave up drugs, through meditation.

This is a difficult and often illegal way to illustrate inspiration, so I just mention it in my book (Piirto, 2004), and many students choose this focus question ("Discuss the role of substances [alcohol, drugs, hormones for sports, etc.] in the creative process" [Piirto, 2004, p. 456]), but we all know our duty about substances in the school setting. Nevertheless, the presence of substances in the creative process is duly noted.

Inspiration by Others' Creativity, Especially Works of Art and Music

Many creators are inspired by others' creativity, especially by works of art and music produced by other artists. Art inspires. Music also inspires. Friendships between artists of different genres abound in biographical literature.

The Canadian artists called The Group of Seven made history by creating an art that was truly Canadian, of the Canadian landscapes. They were Tom Thomson, Arthur Lismer, F. H. Varley, A. Y. Jackson, Arthur Lismer, and Lawren Harris. Harris was one of the leaders. The onset of World War I and his brother's death led Harris to a nervous breakdown and early discharge from the army. While recovering, he traveled to the Algoma region north of Sault Ste. Marie, Ontario, where he experienced a spiritual reawakening that led him to paint local landscapes, unique to Canada and the north (Harris, 1964; Murray, 2003). Several other Canadian artists were feeling the same way. They influenced each other as they painted across Canada, and they admitted one woman to their number, Emily Carr of British Columbia, who also had a passion for painting and writing about western Canada (Carr, 1971; Crean, 2001; Walker, 1990). Carr had felt isolated and persecuted. Harris called Carr "one of us," and though she was very frank and independent, he encouraged to her in her solitary attempts to paint what she saw in the West.

In physics, the creation of the Manhattan Project put scientist Neils Bohr, Joseph Carter, Enrico Fermi, Richard Feynman, Hans Bethe, and J. Robert Oppenheimer, among others, together in a remote location in New Mexico, where they inspired each other to perfect the atomic bomb that was later dropped on Hiroshima and Nagasaki. Bird and Sherwin (2005) biographers of Oppenheimer, said, "Wartime compelled some mild-mannered men to contemplate what was once unthinkable" (p. 222).

Inspiration from Dreams

Dreams have inspired many creative works. Dreams often have personal meanings that solve problems that the dreamers are incubating. Dreams can also present images that entice creators to make their works. The Surrealists encouraged creators to use their dreams as inspiration. Freudian psychology had a great influence on the Surrealists. Both Freud and Jung wrote extensively on the significance of dreams. Freud believed that dreams are wish fulfillment, and Jung asserted that dreams capture the collective unconscious – the primitive archetypes lost to us in our waking state. The Indian-born and wholly naturally talented mathematical genius, Ramanujan said that his genius came in dreams from a goddess named Namagiri (Hoffman, 1998). Sculptor David Smith said that dream images were "exchange" images; that is, even though he didn't "consciously use either signs or symbols . . . they've arrived in my mind as exchange images," that is, "dream images, subconscious images, after-images" (Kuh, 1990, p. 219). Einstein received an image for field theory from his dreams; Ingmar Bergman's films are notoriously based on dreams; the prophets of the Old and New Testaments were inspired by dreams (cf. the story of Joseph and the 7 plagues of Egypt); the list goes on and on.

Students are encouraged to begin to write down their dreams in their daily thoughtlogs, and several dream interpretation sessions are held, during which a student shares a dream and we all use techniques from dream psychologists Reed (1988) and Aizenstadt (2004).

The Inspiration of Novel Surroundings: Travel

Travel makes it easy to maintain openness and naiveté. Being in a new setting, seeing new places makes everyone burn with the fire of apprehending what is new, novel. Often the traveler awakens to deep insight about his or her own reality, his or her own life. Oftentimes the subject of the creative work is the creator's homeland. Picasso and Miró traveled to Paris and painted Spain. The presence of American writers and artists in Paris in the 1920s is another example. We do not do much with this in the creativity class, but we do mention it, and students are encouraged to recall how they felt when they first saw and apprehended the strange wonders of new places.

Other types of inspiration not elaborated on here, but which are experienced in creativity class, are the inspiration of the dark side (of tragedy, death, mysterious goings-on), of the "I'll show you" or personal, and of just plain curiosity about a phenomenon.

Imagery

Imagery is also part of the creative process. The term *imagery* is psychological, the ability to mentally represent imagined or previously perceived objects accurately and vividly. Imagery is an attribute of imagination. Imagery is not only visual, but also auditory, tactile, olfactory, and gustatory. Three types of studies of creativity and imagery have been done: (1) biographical and anecdotal studies of creators telling about their personal imagery and how it inspired them; (2) studies that compared people's ability to create imagery and their scores on certain tests of creative potential; and (3) studies about creative imagery and creative productivity (Houtz & Patricola, 1999).

Guided imagery training goes on in schools, in athletics, and in business and industry. This training attempts to help people learn to manipulate images in their minds. Imagery is essentially spatial, and as such, concrete evidence of the mind's power to construct. Coaches teach athletes to image their performances before they do them; they visualize the ski run, the football play, or the course for the marathon. Studies have shown that athletes who use imagery perform better (Murphy & Martin, 2002).

In creativity class, an example of guided imagery from the seminal book on classroom imagery (Bagley and Hess, 1983) is practiced. Students then think of ways they could use imagery in their own practice (see Box 10.1). One student wrote:

> I love the imagery exercise. It feels so real – helps create so much in my mind. It also makes me feel so calm and centered. I would like to do more with my students in this area. Setting a scene is a great way to make students think visually. I also might have my students take turns describing a place while the other students draw that place. I also like closing my eyes. Using the mind's eye is a great skill. I think we should all develop the ability to create in our heads.

Imagination

Imagination in the creative process refers to a mental faculty whereby one can create concepts or representations of objects not immediately present or seen. The philosopher Aristotle considered works of the imagination such as poetry, drama, and fiction more true than history, because the artist could fabricate truth from the elements of history rather than exhaustively tell all the facts. The artist is able to tell the truth on a deep level, being able to see the patterns, and the overarching themes, using the imagination. Working from the imagination is both stimulating and entertaining. Visual imagination is not the only kind that creators use. Composers imagine works in their "mind's ear," and mechanics imagine problems in their physical, spatial array. Imaginative thought is also called daydreaming, and may be called night dreaming, as well as being called fantasy.

Inventor Nicoli Tesla had, from his childhood, an imagination that could create images of inventions, without the help of drawings (Cheney, 1981). Tesla wrote in a 1919 essay about his inventions:

> When I get an idea I start at once building it up in my imagination. I change the construction, make improvements and operate the device in my mind. It is absolutely immaterial to me whether I run my turbine in my thought or test it in my shop. I even note if it is out of balance. (Cheney, 1981, p. 12)

In creativity class, the students rummage through my costume trunk, choose a costume, and form teams whereby they imagine a myth of creation for a mask I randomly hand out. They then act out the myth. This exercise ends up in hilarity, as well as profundity, and illustrates, in a short concrete way, how the imagination, when permitted, is used in creating literary works and works of the body such as theater and dance.

Intuition

Intuition means having a hunch, "just knowing," having a gut feeling. Creative people trust and prefer to use their intuition. Everyone has intuition, but many do not trust it. Intuition is ambiguous, nebulous. Biographical information, testing, historical and archival research, and experimental studies have shown that creative people use intuition (as operationally defined in instruments such as the Myers-Briggs Type Indicator [MBTI], which is based on Jung's work on types) in doing their work. For example, skipping steps in mathematics is an indicator that intuition is being used. Paul Erdös frustrated even his fellow mathematicians with his tendency to skip steps and then expect people to understand him (Hoffman, 1998). Those who prefer the intuitive often prefer not to read technical manuals, but jump straight to the tasks, using trial and error to solve the problems.

Intuition is not verifiable by scientific or empirical means. Intuition seems to be a personality preference on the MBTI for artists, scientists, and writers, entrepreneurs, mathematicians, actors, inventors, and composers (Barron, 1968; Mackinnon, 1978; Myers & McCaulley, 1985). The place of intuition in creating has long been honored. Jung (1971) defined intuition as "neither sense nor perception...a content presents itself whole and complete, without our being able to explain or discover how this content came into existence" (p. 453).

The importance of intuitive perception of the world, of a non-concrete but still tangible apprehension of underlying truth, informs the creator's view of life. Another exercise that we do in class is Zen sketching, after Franck (1983). I project a series of artworks on the screen in a darkened room, and students quickly sketch the outlines. This helps them see the big picture, a characteristic of the intuitive perceiver. One of the teachers said, about intuition:

> Intuition is something that children recognize. They already know it and are comfortable with whatever it is that they know. Therefore, they should be allowed to explore it fully. Intuition will be the base, and from it will extend elaboration, fluency, and the development of their gifts.

Examples of how teachers would use intuition in their teaching practice are given in Box 10.1.

Insight

Insight in the creative process is the ability to see and understand clearly the inner nature of things, especially by intuition. Cognitive psychologists have researched several types of insight. The studies have shown that insight has the appearance of suddenness, requires preparatory hard work, relies on reconceptualization, involves old and new information, and applies to ill-structured problems.

Insight involves restructuring the problem so that it can be seen in a different way. Many notable creative works have originated from insights. When insight happens, we just have to say, "Aha! So that's how it works. So that's the answer. So that's what it's all about. So that's what the pattern is." The "Aha!" comes after knowing the field really well, and after incubation.

Physicist J. Robert Oppenheimer was known as an idea man, a man with insight. He would publish a small paper, just ahead of the scientists who would develop the elegant solutions to the problems. He published about black holes before anyone, but then moved on to another insight and another, having no patience for developing the problem further (Bird & Sherwin, 2005).

Insight is demonstrated in the creativity class with the drawing exercise, after Franck, explained earlier in the chapter. Students also record their creative process in their thoughtlogs as they decide on their individual creativity project, which is the culminating activity of the course. They cite their dreams, their walks, their drives, and such, as the moments when it all came together – their "aha!" experiences.

Incubation

Incubation as a part of the creative process occurs when the mind and the body are at rest and the creator has gone on to something else. The problem is percolating silently through the mind and body. But somewhere inside, deep below the conscious surface, the dormant problem is arising. A solution is sifting. Incubation was one of the steps in Wallas's (1926) four-part description of problem solving. Psychologists speak of an "incubation effect," which may be caused by conscious work on the problem, followed by overwhelming fatigue, during which period what does not work will have been forgotten (Navarre, 1979; Smith & Dodds, 1999). While resting, the mind works on putting non-alike things together. Then awareness comes – and the answer is there. Experiments have shown that if people are given a problem and told to solve it right away, they solve it less successfully than if they are given the problem and told to go away and think about it. People often incubate while driving, sleeping, exercising, even showering. Kary Mullis, a Nobel Prize winner, came up with the polymerase chain reaction (PCR) while driving (Mullis, 1997).

In creativity class, incubation is illustrated by the individual creativity project, which is the final product. While some know right away what they will do, many students spend days, weeks, even months thinking about what they will do for this project. Then, when they choose their subject or topic, they incubate the ideas on how to proceed to completion and on how to present it.

Improvisation

The importance of improvisation in the creative process cannot be under-stated. To play your musical instrument without music in front of you is frightening to some who have learned to trust in their reading ability and not in their intuition and musical memory. The idea of "play" in improvisation is a necessity. Think of children making up the game as they go along, lost in imagination, forming teams and sides in a fluid all-day motion generated by the discourse of the moment.

Improvisation seems to be a key part of the creative process. Visual artist Edward Hopper relied on improvisation as he painted: "More of me comes out when I improvise" (Kuh, 1990, p. 131). The poet James Merrill used automatic writing as an improvisational technique: William Butler Yeats used automatic writing as inspiration for work. In music and theater, the performer cannot revise the work as writers or painters can. Improvisation in theater and music is almost always collaborative, and requires instant communication between people in the improvisation group. Improvisation reveals inner truth. Dance choreographers rely almost universally on improvisation in order to begin to make a dance. Martha Graham would begin to dance, outlining the pattern she wanted, and her dancers would imitate her. Then she would work on fixing the gestures so that the dancers would be moving together.

In creativity class, we also do several exercises from improvisational theater, such as "What Are You Doing?" (Newton, 1998), and we dance improvisationally to videos by dancer Gabrielle Roth (1992). We also dance to *Where the Hell Is Matt?* (www.youtube.com). We also form a drum circle.

General Aspects of the Creative Process

In the studies, biographies, and memoirs, several other aspects of the creative process seem apparent (Piirto, 2002; 2004): (1) the need for solitude; (2) creativity rituals; (3) meditation; (4) the need for community and culture; and (5) creativity as the process of a life.

The Need for Solitude

The creative process in domains such as creative writing, music composition, mathematics, and visual arts requires solitude. Solitude is not loneliness, but a fertile state where the creator can think and work freely. Poet Amy Clampitt said, "I think the happiest times in my childhood were spent in solitude – reading . . . Socially, I was a misfit" (Hosmer, 1993, p. 80). Today, those who seek solitude are often looked at askance, for people are supposed to be in society, and to crave companionship. The Internet abounds with sites for dating, comradeship, gaming, and commenting instantaneously via Twitter or posting one's every location via

Facebook or Instagram. People who do not share on such vehicles, who prefer to be alone, who have few human relationships, who are not married, or in love, or in a family, are viewed as leading an unhealthy lifestyle. But in creative people's lives, their work is often the most important thing. The iPod may be playing, but the work is often done while in solitude. Creative people may be solitary, but that does not make them neurotic or unhappy. There is something transcendental about such experiences. When the person is suddenly alone and able to concentrate, she is able to decipher what may have seemed too puzzling, and to unite ideas that may have seemed too different. Not being able to achieve solitude is frustrating for many creative people.

Solitude induces reverie. The state between sleeping and waking is relaxed, allowing images and ideas to come so that attention can be paid. What is important is a state of passivity and receptivity. Some people achieve this while cooking, exercising, cleaning, sewing, walking in the woods, or during a long, boring drive. It is in solitude that, as Buber (1985) said, "We listen to our inmost selves – and do not know which sea we hear murmuring" (p. 11).

The thoughtlogs are companions on the meditation day the full day field trip – as well. During each visit (woods, cemetery, museum), students must do the activity alone, reflecting on themselves and their thoughts. They are not permitted to speak to their classmates, and as they pass each other silently, in solitude, they just nod in acknowledgement to their classmates, without other communication. This is simulated solitude, and student evaluations have said, "I am such a busy person; mother, teacher, student; this day gave me a chance to reflect within, in solitude. I am grateful." Others said, "The thoughtlogs made me realize what a creative person I really am; as I made my marks each day for 10 minutes, the alone time really made me focus. I thought about things I hadn't thought about for years." Students have translated the thoughtlog experience for their students of various ages.

Creativity Rituals

Ritual is repetitive practice. Ritual involves special places, special procedures, and special repetitive acts during or before creating. Rituals are sometimes personal. The artist Arshile Gorky would, every week, scrub the parquet floor of his studio with lye, and keep his hallway dark so he could see who was knocking without being observed. According to his biographer, "His working day was governed by ritual. A certain state of dreamy

exhaustion was necessary, he used to say, to create freely and spontaneously"
(Spender, 1999, p. 83).

Ritual serves to remove the creator from the outer and propel her to
the inner. Some people walk or exercise before creating, and they often
get their best ideas while doing it. Some people go for a long drive. Some
arrange their rooms or desks a certain way. Some like to work at a certain
time of day. The approach to the work is ritualistic, and the work itself
could be called, perhaps, the ceremony. Rituals are individually prescribed
and performed.

In creativity class, students are encouraged to create their own rituals
for their own work and within their classrooms; for example, enacting a
gathering ceremony before beginning the day; having everyone clean their
desks before they do finger-painting; or having everyone breathe silently
with eyes closed before writing.

Meditation

Meditation is a part of the creative process in all domains. Whether or not
it is formal, tied to a religion like Buddhism, or informal, tied to a need for
inner quiet, creators meditate. Visual artist Morris Graves said of painting:
"The act is a meditation in itself" (Kuh, 1990, p. 116). A 1991 anthology of
poetry contained works by contemporary poets who practice Buddhism
(Johnson & Paulenich, 1991). In his introduction, poet Gary Snyder
stated:

> In this world of onrushing events the act of meditation – even just a
> "one-breath" meditation – straightening the back, clearing the mind for
> a moment – is a refreshing island in the stream . . . it is a simple and plain
> activity. Attention; deliberate stillness and silence . . . the quieted mind has
> many paths, most of them tedious and ordinary. Then, right in the midst of
> meditation, totally unexpected images or feelings may suddenly erupt, and
> there is a way into a vivid transparency. (Johnson & Paulenich, 1991, p. 1)

The vehicles for discovering one's self are breathing, sitting still, and waiting. Often the creative work follows the meditation, and the meditation
is a preparatory ritual for the creative work.

Wonder. Beauty. Dissolving. Disintegrating. Ecstasy. What "unscientific" words these are! What language used by those who treasure precision
in language! In more prosaic terms, the experimental research psychologists
have categorized such responses and examples as the "mystical" approach
(Sternberg & Lubart, 1999, p. 3).

Creativity as Defined by Community and Culture

Recent television reality shows such as *American Idol, So You Think You Can Dance, America's Got Talent, The Voice,* and the like have featured excruciatingly embarrassing auditions by people who consider themselves to be singers or dancers with enough talent and background to become professionals. These people lack the criticism of the professional community, and are often unable to take the criticism and rejection of the judges, as they stumble, sing off-key, and blindly assume they are able to jump into the field without, as they say, "paying their dues." In fact, no domain exists where higher and higher-level practice is not required. Each domain has its rules that are enforced by the domain's gatekeepers. For creators who want to enter a domain not to become aware and to follow the prescribed rules of the domain is folly, for their changes of reaching a place of respect and influence are almost nil. Space does not permit an explication of the rules for proceeding in the various domains, but prospective creators must know them. Creativity class is but an attitudinal, emotional, and illustrational venue; if a student wants to achieve in a domain, the thorn must pierce, and the schooling must be undertaken.

The "Sun" of Community and Culture above the Piirto Pyramid of Talent Development (see Figure 10.1) is an environmental necessity in the development of talent. Almost all creators formally belong to professional associations and groups dedicated to the pursuit of creativity in their domain of choice. That said, the creativity can also be what Csikszentmihalyi (1995) called "little-c" creativity – creativity as an enjoyable way to live life.

Creativity as the Process of a Life

The creative process is viewed these days as the province of every human being, and not just of the Einsteins, O'Keeffes, or Darwins of the world. People's lives are their creative products. In the past few years, the creative process has gained cachet. Best-selling books have detailed how creativity is The Way. Florida (2003) described a "creative class," which is predicted to provide the most growth in jobs and salaries for the future.

In enhancing people's creativity, teachers sometimes use methods such as visualization, imagery, metaphorization, chanting, and the formulation of affirmations. People hold sacred objects such as quartz crystals and sit beneath pyramids. They go on vision quests and bang drums, chant in tones, and dance like dervishes, seeking inner peace and the guidance for living a creative life. Creativity is intertwined in the feeling of awe, of closeness to the essential that results.

Other, less exotic methods such as writing in journals (Cameron, 1992; Goldberg, 1986; Progoff, 1980, drawing (Edwards, 1979), crooning and engaging with the Mozart effect (Campbell, 1997), or dancing (Roth, 1992) are also employed in teaching people to be more creative, and thus to enhance the process of their lives. Again, the educational psychology of divergent production is notably absent.

An outgrowth of the humanistic psychology movement and of the work of such humanistic psychologists as Rogers (1976), Maslow (1968), and Perls (Amendt-Lyon, 2001), this quest for inner meaning has even made it to public television stations, where fund-raising is led by former guidance counselor, Wayne Dyer (2006). Public television has also hosted the Bill Moyers Creativity series (1982), and the series called *The Creative Spirit* (Goleman, Kaufman, & Ray, 1992). The Open Center and the Omega Institute in New York offer creativity-focused sessions such as intensive journal workshops, dream, singing, empowerment, improvisational theater, and dance workshops. Almost all the teachers of these workshops have written books that tell us how to enhance our creativity. All have in common the probing of the inner psyche, making one's life a work of art, and the attainment of inner peace through auto-therapy done by making creative products.

Thus, the nurturing of creativity in the classroom is a partnership between the professor and the students who are themselves teachers, with the professor providing concepts and theories and the students providing the practical applications to their own practices with their own K–12 students. Along the way, the students might also make the core attitudes, seven I's, and general practices part of their own lives.

REFERENCES

Adorno, T., Frenkel-Brunwik, E., Levinson, D., & Sanford, N. (1950). *The authoritarian personality: Studies in prejudice series* (Vol. 1). New York: W. W. Norton.

Aizenstadt, S. (2004, August 25). *Dream tending: Techniques for uncovering the hidden intelligence of your dreams. Workshop handout.* Pacifica Graduate Institute. Santa Barbara, CA.

Amendt-Lyon, N. (2001). Art and creativity in gestalt therapy. *The Gestalt Review*, 5, 225–248.

Bagley, M., & Hess, K. (1983). *200 ways of using imagery in the classroom.* New York: Trillium.

Barron, F. X. (1968). *Creativity and personal freedom.* New York: Van Nostrand.

Bird, K., & Sherwin, M. J. (2005). *American Prometheus: The triumph and tragedy of J. Robert Oppenheimer.* New York: Vintage Books.

Breslin, J. E. B. (1993). *Mark Rothko: A biography.* Chicago: University of Chicago Press.

Buber, M. (1985). *Ecstatic confessions.* Trans. by P. Mendes-Flohr. New York: Harper & Row. Original published in German *as Ekstatische Konvessionen*, 1909.

Calame, C. (1995). *The craft of poetic speech in ancient Greece.* Trans. by Janice Orion. Ithaca, NY: Cornell University Press.

Cameron, J. (1992). *The artist's way: A spiritual path to higher creativity.* Los Angeles, CA: Jeremy Tarcher.

Campbell, D. (1997). *The Mozart effect: Tapping the power of music to heal the body, strengthen the mind, and unlock the creative spirit.* New York: Avon.

Carr, E. (1971). *Klee Wyck.* Toronto, CA: Clark Irwin.

Chency, M. (1981). *Tesla: Man of our time.* New York: Barnes & Noble Books.

Chilvers, I. (Ed.). (1990). *The concise Oxford dictionary of art and artists.* Oxford: Oxford University Press.

Costa, Jr., P. T., & McCrae, R. R. (1992*). NEO PI-R professional manual.* Odessa, FL: Psychological Assessment Resources, Inc.

Crean, S. (2001). *The laughing one: A journey to Emily Carr.* Toronto, ON: Harpercollins Canada.

Csikszentmihalyi, M. (1990). *Flow.* New York: Cambridge

Csikszentmihalyi, M. (1995). *Creativity.* New York: HarperCollins.

deMille, A. (1991). *Martha: The life and work of Martha Graham.* New York: Random House.

Dyer, W. (2006). *Inspiration: Your ultimate calling.* Carlsbad, CA: Hay House.

Eberle, B. (1996). *Scamper.* Waco, TX: Prufrock Press.

Edwards, B. (1979). *Drawing on the right side of the brain.* Los Angeles, CA: Tarcher.

Ericsson, K. A. (1996). *The road to excellence: The acquisition of expert performance in the arts and sciences, sports, and games.* Mahwah, NJ: Erlbaum.

Florida, R. (2003). *Rise of the creative class.* New York: Basic Books.

Franck, F. (1983). *The Zen of seeing: Drawing as meditation.* New York: Random House.

Freud, S (1976 [1908]). Creative writers and daydreaming. In A. Rothenberg & C. Hausman (Eds.), *The creativity question* (pp. 48–52). Durham, NC: Duke University Press.

Fromm, E. (1941). *Escape from freedom.* New York: Farrar & Rinehart, Inc.

Ghiselin, B. (Ed.). (1952). *The creative process.* New York: Mentor.

Goldberg, N. (1986). *Writing down the bones.* New York: Quality Paperbacks.

Goleman, D., Kaufman, P., & Ray, M. (1992). *The creative spirit.* New York: Dutton.

Guilford, J. P. (1950). Creativity. *American Psychologist,* **5**, 444–454.

Guilford, J. P. (1967). *The nature of human intelligence.* New York: McGraw-Hill.

Harris, L. (1964). *The story of the Group of Seven.* Toronto, ON: Rous & Mann Press Limited.

Harrison, J. (1991). *Just before dark: Collected nonfiction*. New York: Houghton Mifflin.

Hillman, J. (1975). *Re-visioning psychology*. New York: HarperColophon Books.

Hoffman, P. (1998). *The man who loved only numbers: The story of Paul Erdös and the search for mathematical truth*. New York: Hyperion.

Hogan, J. (2001). *The woman who watches over the world: A native memoir*. New York: W.W. Norton.

Hosmer, R. (1993). The art of poetry: Interview with Amy Clampitt. *The Paris Review*, **126**, 76–109.

Houtz, J. C., & Patricola, C. (1999). Imagery. In M. Runco and S. Pritzer (Eds.), *The encyclopedia of creativity*, Vol. II (pp. 1–11). San Diego, CA: Academic Press.

Isaacson, W. (2007). *Einstein*. New York: Simon and Schuster.

Johnson, K., & Paulenich, C. (Eds.). (1991). *Beneath a single moon: Buddhism in contemporary American poetry*. Boston, MA: Shambhala.

Jung, C. G. (1971). *Psychological types*. Trans. by R. F. C. Hull. Bollingen Series XX. Princeton, NJ: Princeton University Press.

Jung, C. G. (1976 [1923]). On the relation of analytical psychology to poetic art. In A. Rothenberg & C. Hausman (Eds.), *The creativity question* (pp. 120–126). Durham, NC: Duke University Press.

Kaufman, J., & Baer, J. (Eds.). (2004). *Creativity in domains: Faces of the muse*. Parsippany, NJ: Lawrence Erlbaum.

Kerr, B., & McKay, R. (2013). Searching for tomorrow's innovators: Profiling creative adolescents. *Creativity Research Journal*, **25**(1), 21–32.

Kuh, K. (1990). *The artist's voice: Talks with seventeen modern artists*. Cambridge, MA: DaCapo Press.

MacKinnon, D. (1978). *In search of human effectiveness: Identifying and developing creativity*. Buffalo, NY: Bearly Limited.

Maslow, A. (1968). *Creativity in self-actualizing people: Toward a psychology of being*. New York: Van Nostrand Reinhold Company.

Maritain, J. (1953). Creative intuition in art and poetry. Trustees of the National Gallery of Art, Washington, D.C. *The A.W. Mellon Lectures in the Fine Arts. Bollingen Series XXXV*. Princeton, NJ: Princeton University Press.

Marland, S. (1971). *Education of the gifted and talented: Report to the Congress of the United States by the U.S. Commissioner of Education*. Washington, DC: U.S. Government Printing Office.

May, R. (1975). *The courage to create*. New York: Bantam.

Meeker, M. (1977). *The structure of intellect*. Columbus, OH: Merrill.

Miles, B. (1989). *Ginsberg*. New York: Simon and Schuster.

Moyers, B. (1982). *Creativity*. Television series. Public Broadcasting Service.

Moyers, B. (1995). *The language of life: A festival of poets*. New York: Doubleday.

Mullis, K. (1997). The screwdriver. In F. Barron, A. Montuori & A. Barron (Eds.), *Creators on creating* (pp. 68–73). Los Angeles, CA: Jeremy P. Tarcher/Putnam.

Murphy, S. M., & Martin, K. A. (2002). The use of imagery in sport. In T. S. Horn (Ed.), *Advances in sport psychology* (2nd ed., p. 405–439). Champaign, IL: Human Kinetics.

Murray, J. (1984). *The best of the Group of Seven*. Toronto, ON: McClelland and Stewart, Ltd.

Murray, J. (2003). *Lawren Harris: An introduction to his life and art*. Toronto, ON: Firefly Books.

Myers, I. B., & McCaulley, M. H. (1985). *Manual: A guide to the development and use of the Myers-Briggs Type Indicator*. Palo Alto, CA: Consulting Psychologists Press.

Navarre, J. P. (1979). Incubation as fostering the creative process. *Gifted Child Quarterly*, **23**, 792–800.

Newton, B. (1998). *Improvisation: Use what you know – make up what you don't*. Scottsdale, AZ: Great Potential Press.

Oreck, B., & Piirto, J. (2014). Through the eyes of an artist: Engaging teaching artists in educational assessment. In D. Risner & M. E. Anderson (Eds.), *Hybrid lives of teaching artists in dance and theatre arts: A critical reader* (pp. 231–253). Amherst, NY: Cambria Press.

Perkins, D. (1981). *The mind's best work*. Boston, MA: Harvard University Press.

Piirto, J. (1985). *The three-week trance diet: A novel*. Columbus, OH: Carpenter Press.

Piirto, J. (1992). *Understanding those who create*. Dayton: Ohio Psychology Press.

Piirto, J. (1994). *Talented children and adults: Their development and education*. New York: Macmillan.

Piirto, J. (1995a). Deeper and broader: The Pyramid of Talent Development in the context of the giftedness construct. *Educational Forum*, **59**(4), 363–371.

Piirto, J. (1995b). The Pyramid of Talent Development in the context of the giftedness construct: Talent Development. *Proceedings of the European Council for High Ability Conference*. University of Nijmegen, The Netherlands.

Piirto, J. (1995c). *A location in the Upper Peninsula: Collected poems, stories, and essays*. Minneapolis, MN: Sampo.

Piirto, J. (1998). *Understanding those who create* (2nd ed.). Tempe, AZ: Gifted Psychology Press.

Piirto, J. (1999). A different approach to creativity enhancement. *Tempo*, 19(3), 1,ff.

Piirto, J. (2000). How parents and teachers can enhance creativity in children. In M. D. Gold & C. R. Harris (Eds.), *Fostering creativity in children, K–8: Theory and practice* (pp. 49–68). Needham Heights, MA: Allyn & Bacon.

Piirto, J. (2001). The Piirto Pyramid of Talent Development: A conceptual framework. *Gifted Children Today*, **23**(6), 22–29.

Piirto, J. (2002). *"My teeming brain": Understanding creative writers*. Cresskill, NJ: Hampton Press.

Piirto, J. (2004). *Understanding creativity*. Scottsdale, AZ: Great Potential Press.

Piirto, J. (2005). Rethinking the creativity curriculum. *Gifted Education Communicator*, **36**(2), 12–19.

Piirto, J. (2007a). A postmodern view of the creative process. In J. Kincheloe & R. Horn (Eds.), *Educational psychology: An encyclopedia* (Vol. 1). Westport, CT: Greenwood Press.

Piirto, J. (2007b). *Talented children and adults: Their development and education* (3rd ed.). Waco, TX: Prufrock Press.

Piirto, J. (2008a). Rethinking the creativity curriculum: An organic approach to creativity enhancement. *Mensa Research Journal*, **39**(1), 85–94.

Piirto, J. (2008b). *Saunas: Selected poems*. Woodstock, NY: Mayapple Press.

Piirto, J. (2009). The creative process as creators practice it: A view of creativity with emphasis on what creators really do. *Perspective in gifted education: Creativity*, Vol. 5 (pp. 42–67). Institute for the Development of Gifted Children. Ricks Center for Gifted Children, University of Denver.

Piirto, J. (2011). *Creativity for 21st Century Skills: How to embed creativity into the curriculum*. Rotterdam, The Netherlands: Sense.

Piirto, J. (Ed.). (2014). *Organic creativity in the classroom: Teaching to intuition in academics and in the arts*. Waco, TX: Prufrock Press.

Piirto, J., & Keller-Mathers, S. (2014). Mary M. Meeker: A deep commitment to individual differences (1921–2003). In A. Robinson and J. Jolly (Eds.), *Illuminating lives: A century of contributions to gifted education* (pp. 277–288). New York: Routledge.

Piirto, J., & Johnson, G. (2004). Personality attributes of talented adolescents. Paper presented at the National Association for Gifted Children conference, Salt Lake City, UT; at the Wallace Research Symposium, in Iowa City, IA; and at the European Council for High Ability conference, Pamplona, Spain.

Pink, D. (2006). *A whole new mind: Why right-brainers will rule the future*. New York: Riverhead Books.

Plato. The republic. In R. Ulrich (Ed.). (1954). *Three thousand years of educational wisdom: Selections from great documents* (pp. 31–62). Trans. by P. Shorey. Cambridge, MA: Harvard Univ. Press.

Plato. The ion. In *Great Books of the Western World*, Vol. 7 (1952). Chicago: Encyclopedia Britannica.

Progoff, I. (1980). *The practice of process meditation: The intensive journal way to spiritual experience*. New York: Dialogue House Library.

Reed, H. (1988). *Getting help from your dreams*. New York: Ballantine.

Reynolds, F. C. (1990). Mentoring artistic adolescents through expressive therapy. *Clearing House*, **64**, 83–86.

Reynolds, F. C., & Piirto J. (2005). Depth psychology and giftedness: Bringing soul to the field of talent development education. *Roeper Review*, **27**, 164–171.

Reynolds, F. C., & Piirto, J. (2007). Honoring and suffering the Thorn: Marking, naming, and eldering: Depth psychology, II. *Roeper Review*, **29**, 48–53.

Rogers, C. (1976). Toward a theory of creativity. In A. Rothenberg & C. Hausman (Eds.), *The creativity question* (pp. 296–305). Durham, NC: Duke University Press.

Roth, G. (1992). *The wave*. Videotape. Boston, MA: Shambhala.

Rothenberg, A. (1979). *The emerging goddess: The creative process in art, science, and other fields*. Chicago: University of Chicago Press.

Sawyer, K. (2007). *Group genius: The creative power of collaboration*. New York: Basic Books.

Simonton, D. (1995). *Greatness: Who makes history and why?* New York: Guilford.

Smith, S. M., & Dodds, R. A. (1999). Incubation. In M. Runco & S. Pritzker (Eds.), *Encyclopedia of creativity*, Vol. 2 (pp. 39–43). San Diego, CA: Academic Press.

Spender, M. (1999). *From a high place: A life of Arshile Gorky*. Berkeley: University of California Press.

Sternberg, R., & Lubart, T. (1999). The concept of creativity: Prospects and paradigms. In R. Sternberg (Ed.), *Handbook of creativity* (pp. 3–15). London: Oxford University Press.

Stravinsky, I. (1990). On conductors and conducting. *Journal of the Conductors' Guild*, **11** (1–2), 9–18.

Van Gogh, V. (1937). *Dear Theo*. I. Stone (Ed.). New York: Doubleday.

Walker, D. (Ed.). (1990). *Dear Nan: Letters of Emily Carr, Nan Chency, and Humphrey Toms*. Vancouver: University of British Columbia Press.

Wallas, G. (1926). *The art of thought*. New York: Harcourt Brace Jovanovich.

CHAPTER 11

Creativity Embedded into K–12 Teacher Preparation and Beyond

Fredricka K. Reisman

Drexel University School of Education

Creativity Dilemma

Given that creativity characteristics are appreciated, why is there so much bias against and resistance to incorporating, enhancing, championing, teaching and learning, and applying creativity in the real world, including in teacher education? Why is there "no room" for creativity (and innovation) in the preparation of teachers, based on the argument that there is no room in the teacher education curriculum due to the many state requirements for certification? Why are not parents crying out for creative pedagogies when research shows that creativity-enhanced learning results in more student engagement, better attendance, critical thinkers, and happy learners (Klawans, Aghayere, Katz-Buonincontro, & F. Reisman, 2015; Torrance, 1975a, 1975b, 1993; Reisman et al, 2002)? Today, we are in the midst of a global focus on creativity (IBM, 2010; Jeffrey, 2006; Kaufman & Sternberg, 2006; Piirto, 2011) with evidence that teaching to enhance student creativity produces active rather than passive learners, better problem solvers and communicators, and students more engaged in learning.

Why are the-powers-that-be stuck on teaching to the test and restricting state funding to standardized test results? Administrative bureaucracy, politics at the highest levels gone awry, the way it is always been done, lack of awareness of personal creative strengths and hidden student creativity, or just taking the easy way out – even if the easy way results in undereducated K–12 and beyond graduates?

Our future depends on changing this landscape. In fact, in a 2010 global study, IBM provides evidence for the importance of creativity:

> According to a major 2010 IBM survey of more than 1,500 Chief Executive Officers from 60 countries and 33 industries worldwide, chief executives believe that – more than rigor, management discipline, integrity or even vision – successfully navigating an increasing complex world will require creativity. (IBM, 2010, p. 1)

In-person interviews with senior leaders and consultants from IBM's Global Business Services division showed less than half of global CEOs believe their enterprises are adequately prepared to handle a highly volatile, increasingly complex business environment. CEOs are confronted with massive shifts – new government regulations, changes in global economic power centers, accelerated industry transformation, growing volumes of data, rapidly evolving customer preferences – that, according to the study, can be overcome by instilling "creativity" throughout an organization. Furthermore, a subsequent IBM study shows implications for teachers, demonstrating the importance of caring for their students as well as being technologically and socially savvy:

> 95 percent of top performing organizations identified getting closer to customers as their most important strategic initiative over the next five years – using Web, interactive, and social media channels to rethink how they engage with customers and citizens. They view the historic explosion of information and global information flows as opportunities, rather than threats. (IBM, 2010, p. 1)

Mueller, Melwani, and Goncalo (2012, p. 13) "suggest that if people have difficulty gaining acceptance for creative ideas especially when more practical and unoriginal options are readily available, the field of creativity may need to shift its current focus from identifying how to generate more creative ideas to identifying how to help innovative institutions recognize and accept creativity. Future research should identify factors, which mitigate or reverse the bias against creativity." But that is for another day.

Until teacher education programs realize the importance of infusing creativity into their curriculum, teachers need to move ahead to understand their creative students and to integrate tools and techniques designed to enhance creativity. This chapter deals with directly helping teachers become aware of their own creative strengths so they can identify and nourish the creativity of their students. Higher education instructors also may benefit from acquiring content knowledge involving important creativity theories and applications for enhancing creativity. Thus, this chapter strives to place control within the purview of the individual teacher/professor for creating awareness of one's creative strengths and integrating creativity into their students' educational experience.

Teacher Misperceptions of Creative Students

Torrance (1965), from a study of more than 1,000 teachers in five countries, concluded that teachers may be unduly punishing students who are good at guessing/estimating, those courageous in their convictions, emotionally sensitive, intuitive thinkers, and those who are unwilling to accept assertions without evidence. On the other hand, instructors may be unduly rewarding students for being courteous, doing work on time, being obedient, popular, and willing to accept the judgment of authorities.

Creative students may display challenging behaviors including dislike of routine-type learning, being self-directed learners, daydreamers, and persistent in tasks that interest them, and are often pinpointed by instructors as troublemakers and poor students (Guilford, 1950; Plucker & Runco, 1999; Michalko, 2006; Piirto, 2011; Reisman, 2011; Reisman & Hartz, 2011). Making teachers aware of possible challenging behaviors of creative students will give them the potential to view such student behavior in a different light and adjust their pedagogy, resulting in win-win student-instructor relations and increased opportunities for the student to achieve in the classroom. The key is patience and understanding, founded on the knowledge that such traits are common among people who are naturally independent, unconventional, and bored by trivialities (Davis, 1993). Because rigid enforcement of rules will alienate creative students and squelch their creativeness, flexibility and understanding are necessary; creativity needs a facilitative environment, not an authoritarian one (Mann, 2009).

Creative Characteristics

Over 60 years of research (Carson, Peterson, & Higgins, 2005; Gladwell, 2008; Guilford, 1950; Silvia, Wigert, Reiter-Palmon, & Kaufman, 2012; Torrance, 1967) has yielded a constellation of factors that indicate creative thinking, interacting, and attitude. The Reisman Diagnostic Creativity Assessment (RDCA) (Reisman, Keiser, & Otti, 2011, 2014), validated over several administrations, is a free self-report mobile app available for the iPad, iPhone, and iTouch that taps eleven of these factors that are the most prominent: *originality* (produce unique and novel ideas), *fluency* (generate many ideas), *flexibility* (generate many categories of ideas), *elaboration* (add either textual, verbal, or drawing detail), *tolerance of ambiguity* (comfortable with the unknown), *resistance to premature closure* (keep an open mind), *divergent thinking* (generate many solutions – related to fluency), *convergent thinking* (analyzes, evaluates, comes to closure), smart *risk-taking* (venturesome, adventurous, exploratory), *intrinsic motivation* (inner satisfaction), and *extrinsic motivation* (needs reward, incentive, reinforcement). The RDCA provides immediate feedback to the user and is diagnostic rather than predictive, with the focus on making the user aware of creative strengths and weaknesses.

Heuristic Diagnostic Creative Intervention

A pedagogy related to using the RDCA is *Heuristic Diagnostic Creative Intervention* (Reisman, 1982, 2010; Tanner & Reisman, 2014) that integrates three foci: (1) heuristic diagnostic teaching (HDT), (2) creativity, and (3) in-depth knowledge of a specific discipline. Heuristic diagnostic teaching is a creative problem solving (CPS) instructional/learning model that is framed on generic or core influences on learning (Reisman, 1977, 1981; Reisman & Kauffman, 1980). Core or generic influences on learning are categorized by cognitive, emotional, social, physical and sensory, and psychomotor factors. Each of these has an observable subset that is helpful in designing instruction. Selected cognitive, emotional, and social generic influences and their related RDCA creativity characteristics are presented in Table 11.1.

Creativity Factors

Figure 11.1 shows the circularity and feedback function of Heuristic Diagnostic Teaching and its relation to creative problem solving. First, we must diagnose the *real* problem, next hypothesize possible reasons for the problem, then formulate learning outcomes that will drive instruction, which will then result in problem solved – or if the problem is not solved, we come back to the cycle again; perhaps the *real* problem was not diagnosed, or maybe the hypotheses were faulty, or some other factors prevented the successful solution.

Figure 11.2 shows the strong similarities between heuristic diagnostic teaching and creative problem solving. Both involve identifying the "real" problem, generating hypotheses for existence of the problem(s) that in turn serve as guides for solutions (e.g., change in pedagogy to accommodate learning styles or physical/sensory needs; attention to attitudes, emotions, and social skills; enabling learners to fill in content gaps, etc.), and finally ongoing evaluation throughout the entire process.

Theorists Important for Teachers to Know

Creativity theories and how their applications complement heuristic diagnostic teaching must begin with an awareness of key theoretical models most closely associated with the development and application of creativity

Table 11.1 *Selected Generic Influences Cross-Listed with Creativity Factors*

Category	Generic Influence	Definition	Related RDCA Creativity Factor
Cognitive	Rate and Amount of Learning	Compared to Age Peers refers to the length of time taken to learn a given amount of material as well as the rapidity of making connections across concepts.	Fluency – generates many ideas
	Size of Vocabulary	Compared to Peers refers to the number of words a student understands and uses as well as the number of different meanings and nuances for a given word.	Elaboration – adds detail
	Ability to Form Relationships, Concepts, and Generalizations	Refers to the psychological nature of the content that is being learned. For example, constructing one-to-one correspondence is forming a relationship; abstracting the number property (three from a set of three objects) forms a concept; and putting two or more concepts together into some kind of relationship forms a generalization (e.g., combine the concepts two and three into an addition relationship).	Divergent thinking – generates many solutions (related to fluency)
	Ability to Make Decisions and Judgments	Involves recognizing salient aspects of a situation, using important information given, being aware of missing information, abstracting essential from nonessential details, evaluating relationships embedded in a situation, and choosing among alternatives.	Convergent Thinking – comes to closure
	Ability to Draw Inferences and Conclusions and to Hypothesize	Involves generating a set of possible alternatives, dealing with future ideas, and making judgments according to a set of criteria.	Flexibility – generates many categories of ideas

Table 11.1 *(cont.)*

Category	Generic Influence	Definition	Related RDCA Creativity Factor
	Ability in General to Abstract and to Cope with Complexity	Includes classifying objects or ideas, finding new relationships or analogies, performing simple operations of logical deductions, and using similes and metaphors.	Originality – involves generating unique and novel ideas
Emotional	Feeling Afraid, Anxious, Frustrated, Joyous, Angry, Surprised	Involves conscious experience that can be communicated to another person.	Tolerance of Ambiguity – comfortable with the unknown
Social	Modeling Other's Behavior	Can be positive if acceptable behavior is modeled.	Intrinsic Motivation – inner drive
	Being Aware of Cues in the Environment	Involves knowing when to quiet down, when to speak up, responding appropriately to others behavior.	Risk-Taking – adventuresome
	Relating to and Interacting with other people	Includes cooperation and consideration.	Extrinsic Motivation – needs reward or reinforcement
	Understanding another's point of view and empathizing	Includes having an emotional as well as a cognitive view of another's needs.	Resistance to Premature Closure – keeps an open mind

in real-world classrooms. These theories form the intellectual foundation of creativity – the body of knowledge that underlies creative thinking and transforms creativity into innovation.

This is not a chicken-and-egg issue; the knowledge base comes first. For one to deal with a changing environment infused with creativity, what is needed is an in-depth knowledge of the decades of relevant creativity research based on theories such as those presented below. This section summarizes the contributions of bedrock creativity theorists and the relevance of their main ideas to teaching.

Ellis Paul Torrance, building on Guilford's (1950, 1967, 1987) work, developed the Torrance Tests of Creative Thinking (Torrance, 1966) that

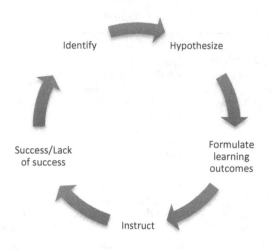

Identify
Hypothesize
Formulate learning outcomes
Instruct
Success/Lack of success
Ongoing Evaluation across every phase

Figure 11.1 Heuristic Diagnostic Teaching Cycle

represent a psychometric approach to measuring creativity. It is the most widely used creativity assessment worldwide and assesses *original thinking, fluency and flexibility of ideas, elaboration, and divergent thinking*. Torrance also created the *Future Problem Solving Program* (Crabbe et al., 1988) that includes the six steps: (1) find challenges/problems; (2) select an underlying

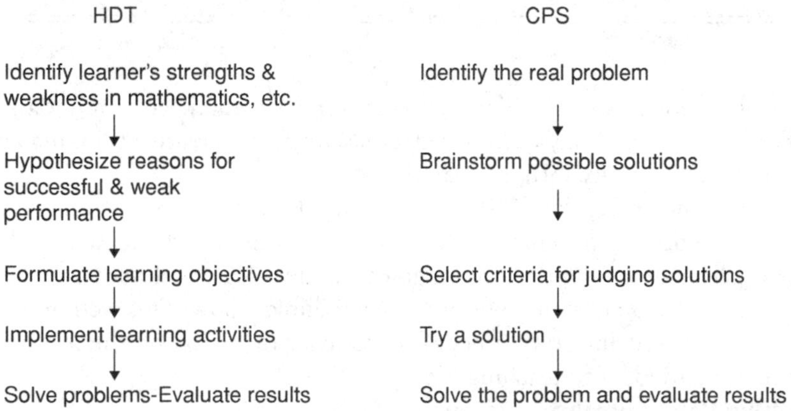

HDT
Identify learner's strengths & weakness in mathematics, etc.
Hypothesize reasons for successful & weak performance
Formulate learning objectives
Implement learning activities
Solve problems-Evaluate results
CPS
Identify the real problem
Brainstorm possible solutions
Select criteria for judging solutions
Try a solution
Solve the problem and evaluate results

Figure 11.2 Heuristic Diagnostic Teaching and Creative Problem Solving Compared

problem; (3) brainstorm solutions to solve the underlying problem; (4) generate/select criteria by which to judge the solutions; (5) apply criteria to solutions – judge the solutions with the criteria, and determine which solution is the best overall; and (6) action plan based upon the highest-scoring (best) solution, as judged by the criteria (see Creative Problem Solving Grid below.) Torrance also developed the *Incubation Model of Teaching and Learning* (TIM) (Torrance & Safter, 1990) that can be applied to a lesson, unit, or project. The application of TIM and the identification of a specific creativity skill is an effective way to teach creativity. TIM has three stages: (1) Heighten Anticipation during a warming up period; (2) Deepen Expectations, at which the problem is defined and applied and the creativity is nurtured; and (3) Extend the Learning through metaphors apply the project in a real context.

Alex Osborn recognized the need for a group problem-solving technique in which all members of the group could then participate. He collaborated with a professor at Buffalo State College, Sid Parnes, and their approach emerged as a four-step creative problem-solving model. Component stages include both divergent and convergent processes (Parnes and Meadow, 1959): (1) understanding the problem, (2) generating ideas, (3) planning for action, and (4) accepting the findings. An integral component of their creative problem-solving model is *brainstorming* (Osborn, 1953), which includes deferring judgment or criticism of ideas, attaining quantity of ideas, embracing unusual ideas, and combining and improving ideas.

Edward de Bono recognized the need to develop creative thinking tools to help people step outside their normal thinking patterns in dealing with difficult problems and searching for new opportunities (de Bono, 1969). He developed *lateral thinking* (see the Divergent Thinking subsection later in the chapter for description of lateral thinking) and many other creative thinking tools (de Bono, 1985). Each hat has a different color and represents a different dimension in thinking about the subject being addressed. The *White Hat* deals with information, the *Red Hat* with feelings, the *Yellow Hat* with benefits, the *Black Hat* with caution, the *Green Hat* with creative ideas, and the *Blue Hat* with thinking about managing the thinking. Everyone may wear the same hat at the same time or a different hat may be worn by members of the creative problem-solving team to indicate their role (e.g., the fact giver, the emotional reactor, the positive thinker, the squelcher, the creative one, the facilitator).

Graham Wallas's theory provides a structured approach to creative problem solving and contains five stages for creative thinking (Wallas, 1926): (1) *preparation* – focuses on the problem and explores the problem's dimensions; (2) *incubation* – subconscious mulling of the problem; (3) *intimation* – inkling that a solution is on its way; (4) *illumination* – discovery, a "Eureka!" moment; and (5) *verification* – focus on practicality, effectiveness, and appropriateness.

Mihaly Csikszentmihalyi's theory regards the interplay among the creative person (the individual), the domain (the discipline), and the field (the experts/gatekeepers). The individual might refer to the creative teacher and the students, the domain is the discipline (e.g., mathematics, science, social study, language arts, creativity, etc.), and the field is comprised of the gatekeepers, such as administrators, teachers, and parents, whose decisions either allow or inhibit creative teaching. Csikszentmihalyi (1996) also introduced "flow" experiences that involve energy that focuses attention and motivates action.

Motivation is central to **Teresa Amabile's** research, finding that intrinsic motivation (the joy within) is more apt to generate creativity than extrinsic motivation (requiring reward or recognition) (Amabile, 1983).

Robert J. Sternberg presented two ideas. His *Triarchic Theory of Human Intelligence* (Sternberg, 1986, 1998) proposes that creativity is a balance among three forms of thinking: analytical, creative, and practical. Teachers often deal with training on *analytical* thinking that includes having to analyze, critique, judge, compare/contrast, evaluate, and assess – all of which represent convergent thinking. *Creative* tasks deal with the ability to invent, discover, imagine, suppose, and predict – which exemplify divergent thinking. Finally, *practical* intelligence is involved in everyday problem solving. Sternberg further compared creativity to investment activities of *buying low and selling high*. Investment theory highlights perseverance in selling one's creative idea(s). Teachers and administrators need to do this both within their discipline and also in the context of the field (see Csikszentmihalyi previously).

Abraham Maslow's *Hierarchy of Human Needs* (Maslow, 1974) presents a ladder of human needs beginning with the most basic physiological needs (e.g., food, water, shelter, clothing), the security needs, both physiological and safety, the need for love and belonging, the esteem level that deals with self-confidence (self-assurance), and self-efficacy (believing in your abilities). To persevere and champion one's ideas, all of the phases of Maslow's theory are important for nurturing creativity in one's classroom and school. Success results in confidence, and those lacking confidence may not be able to produce creative ideas. Thus, it is important for the teacher to communicate to students that making mistakes is an opportunity for learning and thus encourage sensible risk taking. Finally, there is the self-actualization level, which involves peak experiences realizing all inner potential.

Carl Rogers believed that significant learning takes place when the task is perceived by the student as having relevance for his or her own purposes (Rogers 1995). A role of a creative teacher is to facilitate innovation by setting a positive climate for creative thinking, clarifying the purposes of student roles, organizing and making available creativity resources, balancing intellectual and emotional components of creative endeavors, and sharing feelings and thoughts with students while not dominating.

Howard Gardner developed a *theory of multiple intelligence (MI)*, which states that individuals have creative strength(s) that are domain specific (Gardner 1983). When teachers become aware of Gardner's theory, they can reflect on where they fall within the MI theory and then coach others to become aware of their creative strengths. Gardner proposed eight intelligences: bodily/kinesthetic, interpersonal, intrapersonal. linguistic, logic-mathematical, musical, naturalist, and spatial. Naturalist intelligence involves observing, understanding, and organizing patterns in the natural environment, such as recognizing and classifying plants and animals.

In summation, different perspectives of investigating creativity include a psychometric approach, which focuses on assessing one's creative strengths (Torrance); a systems approach to understanding creativity (Csikszentmihalyi), which focuses on the individual, the domain (discipline), and the field (gatekeepers); the role of intrinsic and extrinsic motivation (Amabile), which states that intrinsic motivation yields more creative products; comparison with intelligence (Guilford, Sternberg), multiple intelligences (Gardner); humanistic psychology (Rogers, Maslow); and creative problem-solving models (Wallas, Osborn, and Parnes).

Creativity-Enhancing Activities

Several tools and techniques for enhancing the creative factors identified by the RDCA are provided below as *creative pedagogies*. Each RDCA creativity factor is keyed to an online manual of enhancement strategies (under development, which should be available through the Drexel School of Education by the summer of 2017) that comprise both school- and corporate-related activities. Depending on how an assessment taker scores on the RDCA, the individual may wish to engage in activities to improve in a creativity area in which she or he obtains a low score, or an area they wish to strengthen or enhance. Following are sample activities for selected RDCA factors.

Originality

The Excursion Technique. This is a useful technique for forcing a group to have new thought patterns to formulate strategies. The process involves five steps (Higgins, 1996, pp. 370–380):

Step 1–the teacher asks students to take an imaginary excursion to a physical location (a museum, a jungle, a city, another planet, etc.) that has nothing to do with a real problem. After the excursion each student writes down 8–10 images that he/she saw during the journey (things, people, places, or items) in the first of three columns.

Step 2 – the teacher asks students to draw analogies or express relationships between what they saw on the excursion and the problem as defined, and to write them in the second column next to each of the items identified in the first column.

Step 3 – students are asked to determine what solutions to their problems are suggested by the analogies or the relationships in the second column, and write them in the third column beside the items and analogies identified in the other columns.

Step 4 – students share their experiences from the excursion: what they saw, their analogies, and their solutions.

Step 5 – as with brainstorming, students may discuss each other's ideas. Eventually the teacher helps the group come to a common solution or a set of solutions to the problem.

New Assessments. You may involve the class in discovering a new way to check spelling – for example, spelling bees, write a paragraph incorporating the weekly words, rewrite dictionary definitions in student's own words, and so forth. This approach may be applied across subjects.

Originality Activities may be found via the Internet. The following examples are from www.sanchezclass.com/creativity-activities.htm# originality:

Invent a machine to help you clean your room. Be sure to write down details on how the machine works, what it uses, and what it is made of. Draw a picture of your new invention and give it a creative title.

Design a t-shirt in honor of a family member of your choice. Be sure to include details on how the t-shirt looks and explain why you are honoring your family member. Draw a picture of your honorable t-shirt and give it a creative title.

The Statue of Liberty is a great American symbol for liberty. Design your own monument representing liberty. Be sure to write down details on how it looks and what it is made of. Draw a picture of your monument of liberty and give it a creative title.

Pretend you could have the perfect student desk at school. What would your desk have? Design your perfect student desk. Write down details on how it looks and what special features it has. Draw a picture of your perfect desk and give it a creative title.

Flexibility

Changing Categories. How are they alike? Using the list – orange, apple, banana, potato, rock, water, air – ask how an orange and an apple alike? They are both fruit (nominal category). They both grow on trees (intrinsic functional category – what they do). They are round (perceptible category). You can eat them (extrinsic functional category – what you do to them). How are an orange, apple, and banana alike? Keep adding an object. Commonalities change as you add more objects and the commonality becomes more abstract. (This is adapted from Jerome Bruner et al., 1966).

The Good Bad Interesting (GBI) exercise gets you looking at ideas from multiple perspectives. It encourages mental flexibility – a very important skill if you want to be creative. This exercise originates from Edward de Bono's concept of "lateral thinking" to describe the process of coming up with solutions to problems through playing with data or employing unorthodox methods to arrive at your end ideas. Compare this to traditional "vertical thinking" that employs a logical step-by-step approach to seeking solutions. GBI creative thinking involves considering your central theme, idea, or challenge and thinking about what is good about it, what is bad about it, and what is interesting about it. Generate as many examples of each as you can think of, but try to be fairly equal about it. Too much of one or another demonstrates bias in your thinking. This is not about finding the "right" answer; it is about looking at all the possible interpretations of an idea. Most people react to a new idea by either liking or disliking it. The GBI exercise forces creative thinking to generate multiple perspectives on an idea. It shows that ideas can be seen as good, bad, or interesting, depending on a particular frame of mind. Any idea can be looked at in a different way by reframing it. The idea changes in the mind of a person depending on how they are looking at it. The GBI creative thinking exercise enables you to understand other people's viewpoints and enhances flexible thinking.

Risk-Taking

What is a risk? One should be clear about the term "risk" and what an actual risk is – namely, trying something without clearly knowing the final outcome. Following are key questions regarding risk-taking.

- What is a risk?
- Are risks a good or a bad thing?
- Give examples where taking a risk has been a good thing to do.
- Give examples where taking a risk has been a bad thing to do.
- Describe when you have been forced to take a risk when you did not want to.
- Has anyone been forced to take a risk to help yourself or someone else?
- Determine whether your own actions are breaking rules or whether you are taking risks. (A rule is a principle or condition that customarily governs behavior. Taking a risk involves doing something with the hope of a favorable outcome.[1])
- Weigh the consequences of risk-taking. Write your own scenario in which risk-taking is a common theme.

Role-play may be used as a creative pedagogy to familiarize students with risky concrete situations they can write about (Katz-Buonincontro, 2006, 2008, 2011). Role-play helps make abstract problems more concrete and real, allows for immediate feedback, facilitates expression of attitudes and feelings, provides opportunities to speculate on uncertainties, and involves applying knowledge to solving problems.

Reflect. Have students draw or write about two risks that they have taken in their lives. What were the consequences? Would they take them again?

Self-Assessment. Have students avoid labeling themselves permanently as a risk-taker or risk-avoider. Instead, use the following exercise to celebrate risk-taking assets and risk-taking deficits.

Divergent Thinking

Lateral Thinking. Lateral thinking is perhaps the most productive tool to help break away from traditional thinking. It is described by the concept creator, Edward de Bono (1999a, 1999b). Lateral thinking is defined in the *Oxford English Dictionary as* "Seeking ways to solve problems by apparently illogical means." de Bono posited that the mind is a self-organizing

---

[1] Adapted from East Renfrewshire Council, Scottish Executive Education Department.

Table 11.2 *Risk-Taking Assessment*

Risk-Taking Statement	Agree	Disagree
1. Taking management risks makes good sense only in the absence of acceptable alternatives.		
2. I generally prefer stimulation over security.		
3. I have confidence in my ability to recover from my mistakes, no matter how big.		
4. I would promote someone with unlimited potential but limited experience to a key position over someone with limited potential but more experience.		
5. Anything worth doing is worth doing less than perfectly		
6. I believe opportunity generally knocks only once		
7. It is better to ask for permission than to beg for forgiveness.		
8. Success in management is as much a matter of luck as ability		
9. Given a choice, I would choose a $3,000 annual raise over a $10,000 bonus that I had about a one-in-three chance of winning.		
10. I can handle big losses and disappointments with little difficulty.		
11. If forced to choose between safety and achievement, I would choose safety.		
12. Failure is the long way to management success.		
13. I tolerate ambiguity and unpredictability well.		
14. I would rather feel intense disappointment than intense regret.		
15. When facing a decision with uncertain consequences, my potential losses are my greatest concern.		

Note: Scoring: Give yourself one point for each of the following statements with which you agree: 2, 3, 4, 5, 10, 13, 14. Give yourself one point for each of the following statements with which you disagree: 1, 6, 7, 8, 9, 11, 12, 15. Calculate your total. The higher your score, the more your risk-taking attitudes resemble those of risk-takers studied by social scientists. A score of about 11 or higher indicates strong to very strong pro-risk attitudes; about 6 to 10, medium-strength pro-risk attitudes; and 5 or less, low-strength pro-risk attitudes.

information system. As our mind absorbs information and digests experiences, our thinking organizes itself into patterns based on these inputs.

Pattern thinking is essential. Otherwise, for example, we would have to rethink each morning whether we put our shoes on before our socks or vice versa. We would have to relearn how to walk. In tackling problems or searching for new opportunities, it is sensible to start out with normal patterns of thinking. This generally provides many useful ideas. But to solve difficult problems or conceive radically new concepts that require a new direction in thinking, it is often necessary to step outside our normal patterns of thinking. Some refer to this as "thinking outside the box."

Provocations. Provocations are thoughts that are related to an identified problem, but that are illogical or unstable. They are bizarre, impractical, ridiculous, or provocative. They may take the form of exaggeration, distortion, reversal, or wishful thinking. For example, if there is a side road to your destination, you would likely speed past it, even though it might lead to a wider, faster highway and allows you to arrive at your destination more quickly. Using provocations is a way to test these side roads in problem solving or opportunity searching that might lead to better, more novel ideas. A productive approach is to create "provocations" that jar us outside our normal patterns of thinking. Instead of rejecting a provocation, we can learn to use it for its forward effect as a stepping-stone to shift laterally out of standard linear patterns of thinking. This process creates a new starting point to address the problem and always leads to a flow of new, useful ideas.

SCAMPER.[2] An activity called SCAMPER relies on divergent thinking proposed by Alex Osborn's (1964) brainstorming process, and later arranged by Bob Eberle (1997) as a mnemonic to increase interest in the perceptive, imaginative, and creative abilities. It involves looking at situations from new perspectives and incorporates rules of brainstorming. Osborn's ground rules for group brainstorming comprise the following: judicial judgment is ruled out; wildness is welcomed; quantity is wanted; and combination and improvement are sought. These four guidelines provide the power that underlies divergent thinking. The acronym, SCAMPER, refers to the skills of Substitute, Combine, Adapt, Modify, Put to another use, Eliminate or minify, and Rearrange or reverse.

Personal Qualities. Heather Sellers (2009), in her book *Page after Page: Discover the Confidence and Passion You Need to Start Writing and Keep Writing,* suggests to list your best qualities as someone who is trying to live with intensity and creativity. Do not limit the length of your list. Do not censor yourself. Resist the urge to think that writing something good about yourself means you are egotistical (that is so *not* what this is about). Do not be self-deprecating. You might write that you are open to new experiences, or well organized, or a lover of the arts. You might be willing to take emotional risks, or have a wonderful sense of humor. Write down *anything* positive about your personality as it is now and the choices you make and the person you are. Now build on your list and address the following:

---

[2] SCAMPER prompts suggested by kevin.byron@ntlworld.com

Table 11.3 *Scamper Prompts*

Category	Prompt
SUBSTITUTE	What can be substituted?
	Who else?
	Can the rules be changed?
	Other ingredients, material?
	Other processes or procedures?
	Other place?
	Other approach? What else instead?
COMBINE	What ideas can be combined?
	What about combining units or departments?
	What materials can be combined?
	What methods can be combined?
	What tasks can be combined?
	What procedures can be combined?
	What functions can be combined?
	What can be included with this idea?
	What about a blend, mixture, or assortment?
ADAPT	What else is like this?
	What other ideas does this suggest?
	Does the past offer a parallel?
	How do I adapt it for a different customer?
	How do I adapt it to a different market?
	What can be copied?
	Whom can I emulate?
	What else can be adapted?
	What different contexts can I put my concept in?
	What ideas outside my field can I incorporate?
MODIFY	What if I change the color, shape, form, scent, sound, movement?
	What if I scale up the idea/object?
	What if I scale down the idea/object?
	What if I multiply it?
	What changes can I make further up/down the system?
	What can be modified?
PUT TO OTHER USES	What else can this be used for?
	What else can be done with this?
ELIMINATE	What should I omit?
	Should I divide it?
	Should I separate it?
	Streamline? Miniaturize?
	Subtract? Delete? Remove?
	What's unnecessary?
REVERSE	What if I turn it inside out?
	What if I do the opposite?
	What if I reverse roles?
	What if I work backwards?
	What are the negatives?

How you were "weird" as a child (either in your or others' opinion):
>How you are definitely weird now
>How you try to hide your weirdness
>How your weirdness makes you happy or creative
>How you want to be weirder

Take a look at your previous two lists, then answer one or more of these questions:
>What is missing?
>What do you want to take away?
>Who do you want to be?
>What do you want to add to yourself?
>What if you were able to see all of your individuality traits as normal?
>How would that free you to move on?

Manifesto. Use E. Paul Torrance's Manifesto's (1983, p. 93) to generate ideas:
>Do not be afraid to fall in love with something and pursue it with intensity.
>Know, understand, take pride in, practice, develop, exploit, and enjoy your greatest strengths.
>Learn to free yourself from the expectations of others and walk away from the games they impose on you. Free yourself to play your own game.
>Find a great teacher or mentor who will help you.
>Do not waste energy trying to be well rounded.
>Do what you love and can do well.
>Learn the skills of interdependence.

Convergent Thinking

While divergent thinking involves separating topic components for purposes of expanding and exploring its various parts, convergent thinking involves combining or joining different ideas together based on common elements.

Closure may be interpreted as the resolution of tension. When we experience tension, there is movement toward its resolution. For example, resolution of a danger is closure in the form of protection. Reading an exciting novel results in closure of knowing "whodunnit." A long, thought-out purchase builds the tension of wanting and is resolved with the purchase, resulting in closure. Thus, anticipation of pleasure is finalized when closure occurs.

Role of the Incomplete. We remember better that which is unfinished or incomplete. Russian psychologist Bluma Zeigarnik (2012) identified the Zeigarnik effect, which states that people remember uncompleted or interrupted tasks better than they do completed tasks. Thus, give students a problem at the end of the day. By the next day they will have thought about it. To remember things, do something that is incomplete, such that the ongoing thinking helps keep important facts in mind. Zeigarnik theorized that an incomplete task creates "psychic tension" within us. This tension acts as a motivator to drive us toward completing the task. In Gestalt terms, we are motivated to seek "closure." However, creative thinkers resist *premature* closure.

Principles of Outlining.[3] Convergent thinking is an essential part of the outlining and organizing process. Research on the way the brain processes information demonstrates that people are able to efficiently absorb and retain up to seven main ideas. In term of communication, this suggests that a writer create an outline that follows a clear-cut pattern comprised of two to seven main sections or categories. In practice, creating an outline with three to five main categories or sections is ideal. This will help readers more easily comprehend and remember the information. Thus, have students strive for two to seven main sections or categories of information that underlie a writing project, a social studies paper, a research assignment, or the like. Make the sections or categories mutually exclusive. Deal with one topic at a time by grouping specific ideas within larger categories that do not overlap with one another.

Strive for balance between the main sections. An outline's main sections should be approximately equal in terms of the amount of information they contain. The principle of balance suggests that a document is weighted such that no one part is given substantially more space and importance than the others. Another outlining technique is to label each main section that will later become headings, which are inserted into the final document, to help the reader see how the paper is designed and organized.

Example: *Categorize Ideas on Television.* Below is a list of different aspects of television.[4] The task is to practice convergent thinking by grouping similar ideas together. Look for thoughts or ideas that appear to fit together,

[3] Source: http://faculty.washington.edu/ezent/imct.htm
[4] Source: http://faculty.washington.edu/ezent/aact.htm

then identify the category or group these ideas represent. Give a label or "heading" to each of the categories you identify. You should identify three to five categories such as the following:

Almost everyone has a TV today
Cartoons for children
Entertainment
Informs people with news
Violence
Unrealistic programs
Millions of people watch TV
Waste of time
Baseball
Advertising
Educational
Football
Most families have more than one TV
Romantic stories
Record shows with VCR
Makes me lazy
Average person spends three hours a day watching TV
Golf
Insults viewers' intelligence

Elaboration

Detail. Encourage students to add detail to their drawings, compositions, and verbal expressions. Questioning is a good tactic for enhancing elaboration: What do you mean? Where can you show the design of the boy's coat? I don't understand – can you give me an example?

Fluency

Brainstorming is appropriate for a group of four to seven. Generate ideas with no evaluation. Accept all ideas. A facilitator runs the session and a recorder writes the ideas for later categorization and evaluation.

Generate Many Ideas. This creative technique involves applying a series of words, verbs, adjectives, or phrases to an existing situation. Osborn's Checklist shown in Table 11.2 includes the verbs: *put to other uses, adapt, modify,*

Table 11.4 *Osborn's Trigger Words*

Question	Description
Put to other uses?	New ways to use as is? Other uses if modified?
Adapt?	What else is like this? What other idea does this suggest? Does past offer parallel? What could I copy? Whom could I emulate?
Modify?	New twist? Change meaning, color, motion, sound, odor, form, shape? Other changes?
Magnify?	What to add? More time? Greater frequency? Stronger? Higher? Longer? Thicker? Extra value? Plus ingredient? Duplicate? Multiply? Exaggerate?
Minimize?	Make it smaller/shorter/lower/lighter/thinner? Leave something out? Concentrate? Divide? Create miniature?
Substitute?	Who else instead? What else instead? Other ingredient? Other material? Other process? Other power? Other place? Other approach? Other tone of voice?
Rearrange?	Interchange components? Other pattern? Other layout? Other sequence? Transpose cause and effect? Change pace? Change schedule? Opposite/backward/inverted? Deconstruct and reconstruct? Change positive and negative?
Reverse?	Transpose positive and negative? How about opposites? Turn it backward? Turn it upside down? Reverse role? Change shoes? Turn tables? Turn other cheek?
Combine?	How about a blend, an alloy, an assortment, an ensemble? Combine units? Purposes? Appeals? Ideas? Benefits?

Source: http://manualthinking.com/tag/osborn-checklist/ and www.mycoted.com/Osborn%27s_Checklist

magnify, minify, substitute, rearrange, reverse and combine. In addition, triggers to expand discussion for a verb; for example, *substitute* might be: *Who else instead? What else instead? Other ingredient? Other material? Other process? Other power? Other place? Other approach? Other tone of voice?* (Osborn 1963). This activity done over an extended period of time can increase students' skills in generating many ideas – in other words, improve fluency.

Mindstorming.[5] Generate ideas or answers to your problem. Keep going until you have at least 20 answers or ideas. Your first answers will come easily. Keep pushing until you have reached at least 20. Just let the answers and ideas flow. While solo brainstorming or mindstorming, you set the judgmental mind aside. That means tell that inner critical voice to be quiet! You are just working with the creative mind. Once you have your

[5] Reference for mindstorming on Brian Tracy's audio program: Thinking Big: The Keys To Personal Power and Maximum Performance. www.amazon.com/Thinking-Big-Personal-Maximum-Performance/dp/0743562151

Table 11.5 *Activities to Enhance Tolerating Ambiguity*

- List the elements that would bring on success.
- List the elements that we visualize as failure.
- Visualize success seen from the viewpoint of 50 years from now.
- Visualize success seen from the perspective of 100 years ago.
- Look for impossible and desirable ideas.
- Create analogies with other things that have been successful.
- Imagine and write down ideas that are wild, illegal, crazy, etc.
- Insert the problem from its present scenario to a totally different scenario.
- Return from the fantasy scenario to the present scenario and try to associate the ideas generated in the fantasy scenario with ideas that might apply to the real problem.
- Imagine what people we admire would say.
- Search for pairs of ideas that are apparently unconnected and that can be associated by a third.
- Imagine that everything exists and all we have to do is find it.
- Change the level on which the problem is approached.

Source: European Commission, *Innovation Management Techniques in Operation*, European Commission, DG XIII, Luxembourg, 1998.

20 ideas, go back over them and choose the one that feels right to you. Trust your instincts with this. When you have chosen your idea, you can put that at the top of another page, and do mindstorming to generate 20 ideas on how you could implement that idea. This activity is relevant to both group and individual creative pedagogy to arrive at a solution.

Dreamstorming involves mindstorming while asleep. Have a notebook ready to record thoughts either during the night or first thing when you awaken. These notes become the fodder for creative thinking and a methodology to share with students.

Tolerate Ambiguity

OK with Uncertainty. This involves being comfortable with the unknown and is related to avoiding premature closure. Table 11.5 presents activities that enhance tolerating ambiguity.

Resist Premature Closure

Keep an Open Mind. The key to this creative thinking characteristic is to withhold judgment and closing on what you think you heard. For example, being in a conversation with someone and they complete your sentence – and that is *not* what you were going to say. This situation

Table 11.6 *Brainstorming Phases*

Phase	Application
Orientation Preparation Warm-up	Define the problem to be studied for the participants, clarify the rules of the game.
Production of ideas	Gather data and information necessary to approach the problem in an efficient manner. Carry out the exercise: redefine a problem different from the one to be studied, experiment with it for a few minutes.
Incubation	Generate the maximum of ideas without prior judgment – always ask "what else" – quantity of ideas is quality – no limits – no criticism – modify other's ideas to produce new ones.
Synthesis	Let the subconscious work.
Evaluation	Gather the ideas generated – analyze them – work with logical thinking. Evaluate the ideas gathered and analyzed – develop and combine them before proceeding to put them in practice.

Source: European Commission, *Innovation Management Techniques in Operation*, European Commission, DG XIII, Luxembourg, 1998.

involves coming to premature closure, which is not creative. Table 11.6 shows how proper use of brainstorming can enhance resisting premature closure.

Intrinsic Motivation

Intrinsic motivation involves doing something because it is enjoyable. For example, just coming to school is enjoyable for no obvious reason; you doing something that you desire to do for yourself without pay, an award, or a grade. Teachers who focus on the excitement of learning rather than on grades are fostering intrinsic motivation in their students. Teachers also may help their students develop intrinsic motivation by having students work on projects that allow them to see how the information is relevant to their lives and by allowing students to have greater autonomy, making the classroom fun and encouraging creativity.

Extrinsic Motivation

Extrinsic motivation reflects the desire to do something because of external rewards such as awards, money, grades, and praise. People who are

Table 11.7 *Creative Problem-Solving Grid to Help Prioritize Your Activities*

Issue: Possible Future Initiative	Evaluation Criteria							
	Enhance Other Grants	Creative	Unique	Visionary	Attainable	Funding Source	Current Expertise	Totals
1. NSF proposal								
2. Create new course								
3. Write paper								
4. Implement new pedagogy								
5. Present at a professional conference								

extrinsically motivated may only wish to engage in certain activities because they wish to receive some external reward.

There is a place for both intrinsic and extrinsic motivation. Sometimes a reward or recognition such as praise is necessary to get the student engaged. Then, after some success experiences, they become intrinsically motivated.

Creative Problem-Solving Grid

Reisman and Torrance often used the following quantitative approach, shown in Table 11.7, to find the "real problem." This approach may also be followed by finding the *best* solution. Directions follow:

1. Rank each Possible Future Initiative vertically within each Evaluation Criteria (In this case, 5 = most important/desirable/effective; 1 = least. The ranking scale depends on the number of possible problems or solutions generated – usually no more than 10.).
2. Add across Evaluation Criteria by row and enter sum in Totals column.
3. Consider the Possible Future Initiative with the highest score as your first activity to engage in.
4. If you are not comfortable with the Possible Future Initiative with the highest score, then consider the next highest. Remember, this grid is merely a heuristic (tool) for making a decision.

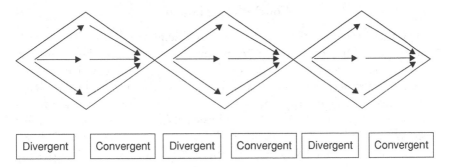

| Divergent | Convergent | Divergent | Convergent | Divergent | Convergent |

Figure 11.3 Creative thinking process

Critical Thinking and Logic as Essentials of Creative Thinking

Usually, creative thinking is associated with brainstorming (generating many ideas), novelty, and uniqueness of ideas. Critical thinking is analytical, judgmental, and involves evaluating choices before making a decision. When you are thinking critically, you are using logic, reason, and convergent-type thinking. However, creative thinking involves both divergent and convergent thinking as a sequential interaction of these two types of thinking – divergence and convergence as depicted in Figure 11.3. Divergent thinking is the ability to elaborate and think of diverse and original ideas with fluency and speed (e.g., brainstorming). Convergent thinking involves narrowing ideas by evaluating the previously generated ideas that emerged in the divergent portion of the sequence (e.g., settling on an idea from a selection of ideas).

Modeling Creativity

The most powerful way to develop creativity in your students is to be a role model. Students develop creativity not when you tell them to, but when you show them. Teachers who balance an emphasis on the discipline or content knowledge with emphasis on investigating and applying the content are opening up a new world of learning. As in many situations (e.g., honesty vs. cheating, helping another vs. self-promotion, being truthful vs. telling white lies, etc.), students observe and respond to adult behaviors more than to their teacher's or parent's words. When teaching for creative thinking and doing, modeling creative behavior is what counts.

Concluding Thoughts

My fondest memory of engaging with the discipline of creativity were the times when Dr. Torrance would visit my small office at the University of Georgia to come up with a title for one of our collaborative research presentations at a conference, and I would watch him as he implicitly generated possible topics. I could actually "see" his mind working. I previously would have jumped to closure; I learned from his mentoring to resist premature closure and to tolerate ambiguity. As a mathematics educator, I became aware that I was not a strong elaborator. I was used to dealing with equations and to thinking parsimoniously. However. I did become aware of my creative thinking strengths. For example, I came up with an original/novel approach to teaching place value (Reisman and Torrance, 2002); I noticed that I generated many ideas within alternate categories when in a brainstorming session with colleagues. I used both divergent and convergent thinking. I loved a challenge in identifying ways to help my undergraduate preservice education students, as well as my teachers in the field who were pursuing their master's degree, to engage their students who were experiencing learning problems. I shared with my education majors the strategies presented in this chapter, especially those that made them aware of their own and their students' creative strengths and activities that enabled them to teach creatively.

REFERENCES

Amabile, T. M. (1983). The social psychology of creativity: A componential conceptualization. *Journal of Personality and Social Psychology*, **45**(2), 357–376.

Buner, J. S., Olver, R. R., Greenfield, P. M., et al. (1966). *Studies in cognitive growth*. New York: Wiley.

Carson, S. H., Peterson, J. B., & Higgins, D. M. (2005). Reliability, validity, and factor structure of the creative achievement questionnaire. *Creativity Research Journal*, **17**, 37–50.

Crabbe, A. B., Torrance, E. P., Torrance, J. P., Shewach, D. L., & Shewach, G. J. (1988). *Fourteen years of fuzzies*. Laurinburg, NC: Future Problem Solving Program.

Csikszentmihalyi, M. (1996). *Creativity: Flow and the psychology of discovery and invention*. New York: HarperCollins Publishers.

Davis, B. (1993). *Tools for teaching*. Indianapolis, IN: Jossey-Bass.

de Bono, E. (1969). *Mechanism of mind*. Des Moines, IA: de Bono Thinking Systems, Inc.

de Bono, E. (1985). *Six thinking hats*. Boston, MA: Little, Brown & Company.

de Bono, E. (1999a). *Serious creativity*. Des Moines, IA: de Bono Thinking Systems, Inc.

de Bono, E. (1999b). *Six thinking hats*. Boston, MA: Little, Brown & Company.

Eberle, R. F. (1997). *Scamper: Creative games and activities for imagination*. East Aurora, NY: Games for Imagination Development.

Gardner, H. (1983). *Frames of mind: The theory of multiple intelligences*. New York: Basic Books.

Gladwell, M. (2008). *Outliers: The story of success*. New York: Little, Brown.

Guilford, J. P. (1950). Creativity. *American Psychologist*, **5**(**9**), 444–454.

Guilford, J. P. (1967). *The nature of human intelligence*. New York: McGraw-Hill.

Guilford, J. P. (1987). The 1950 Presidential Address to the American Psychological Association. In S. G. Isaksen (Ed.), *Frontiers of creativity research*. Buffalo, NY: Bearly Limited.

Higgins, J. M. (1996). Innovate or evaporate: Creative techniques for strategists. *Long Range Planning*, **29**(3), 370–380.

IBM. (2010). Global CEO Study. Retrieved June 6, 2014 from www.ibm.com/ceostudy.

Jeffrey, B. (2006). Creative teaching and learning: Towards a common discourse and practice. *Cambridge Journal of Education*, **36**(3), 399–414.

Katz-Buonincontro, J. (2006). Using the arts to promote creativity in leaders: A multiple case study of three executive institutes. *Journal of Research on Leadership Education*. www.ucea.org/JRLE/issue.php

Katz-Buonincontro, J. (2008). Can the arts assist in developing the creativity of educational leaders? *The International Journal of Creativity and Problem Solving*. Special Issue on Creativity in Schools and Classrooms, 18, 69–79.

Katz-Buonincontro, J. (2011). How might aesthetic knowing relate to leadership? A review of the literature. *International Journal of Education & the Arts*, 12 (SI 1.3). Retrieved from www.ijea.org/v12si1/.

Kaufman, J. C., & Sternberg, R. J. (Eds.). (2006). *The international handbook of creativity*. New York: Cambridge University Press.

Klawans, M., Aghayere, A., Katz-Buonincontro, J., & Reisman, F. (2015) Creativity assessment of senior design projects using an engineering expert panel. *Proceedings of the 2015 Conference for Industry and Education Collaboration*. American Society for Engineering Education.

Mann, E. (2009). The search for mathematical creativity: Identifying creative potential in middle school students. *Creativity Research Journal*, 338–348.

Maslow, A. H. (1974). *Toward a psychology of being*. New York: Van Nostrand Reinhold Company.

Michalko, M. (2006). *Tinkertoys: A handbook of creative-thinking techniques* (2nd ed.). Berkeley, CA: Ten Speed Press.

Mueller, J. S., Melwani, S., & Goncalo, J. A. (2012). The bias against creativity: Why people desire but reject creative ideas. *Psychological Science January*, **23**(1), 13–17.

Osborn, A. F. (1953). *Applied imagination*. New York: Charles Scribner's Sons.

Osborn, A. F. (1963). *Applied imagination: Principles and procedures of creative thinking*. New York: Charles Scribner's Sons.

Osborn, A. F. (1964). *How to become more creative.* New York: Charles Scribner's Sons.

Parnes, S. J., & Meadow, A. (1959). Effects of brainstorming instruction on creative problem solving by trained and untrained subjects. *Journal of Educational Psychology*, **50**, 171–176.

Piirto, J. (2011). *Creativity for 21st century skills: How to embed creativity into the curriculum.* Rotterdam, The Netherlands: Sense Publishers.

Plucker J., & Runco, M. A. (1999). Deviance. In M. A. Runco & S. Pritzker (Eds.), *Encyclopedia of creativity.* San Diego, CA: Academic.

Reisman, F. (1977). *Diagnostic teaching of elementary school mathematics: Methods and content.* Chicago: Rand McNally College Publishing Co.

Reisman, F. (1981). *Teaching mathematics: Methods and content for grades K–8.* Boston, MA: Houghton Mifflin.

Reisman, F. K. (1982). *A Guide to the diagnostic teaching of arithmetic* (3rd ed.). Columbus, OH: Charles E. Merrill.

Reisman, F. K. (2010). Creative and Critical Thinking in Biomedical Research. In Y. K. Gupta, G. Jagadeesh, S. Murthy, & A. Prakash (Eds.). *From Getting Started in Research to Presenting Data in a Scientific Paper.* Auckland, New Zealand: Wolters Kluwer Health.

Reisman, F. K. (2011). Creative, critical thinking and logic in research. *Journal of Pharmaceutical Sciences*, **1**(2), 96–175.

Reisman, F. K., Bach, C. N., Auth, P. C., Batastini, S., Clark, S., Gigli, R. W., Keiser, L. J., Nessler, C., & Whitelaw, L. (2002). Creativity stems from divergent chaotic crisis. In A. G. Aleinikov (Ed.), *The future of creativity* (pp. 91–112). Bensonville, IL: Scholastic Testing Services.

Reisman, F. K., & Hartz, T. A. (2011). *Generating a culture for creativity and innovation.* Talent Management Handbook, 2nd ed. Edited by Lance A. Berger & Dorothy R. Berger. New York: McGraw Hill.

Reisman, F. K., & Kauffman, S. (1980). *Teaching mathematics to children with special needs.* Columbus, OH: Merrill.

Reisman, F. K., Keiser, L., & Otti, O. (2011). Reisman Diagnostic Creativity Assessment Lite (RDCA) [Mobile application software]. Retrieved June 3, 2011 from https://itunes.apple.com/us/app/reisman-diagnostic-creativity/id416033397?mt=8.

Reisman, F. K., Keiser, L., & Otti, O. (2014). Development, use and implications of diagnostic creativity assessment app: Reisman Diagnostic Creativity Assessment (RDCA) –Update. Paper presented at the 2014 University of Georgia Torrance Center Conference.

Reisman, F. K., & Torrance, E. P. (2002). *Learning mathematics creatively: Place value.* Bensenville, IL: Scholastic Testing Service.

Reisman, F., & Kauffman, S. (1980). *Teaching mathematics to children with special needs.* Columbus, OH: Charles E. Merrill Publishing Co.

Rogers, C. R. (1995). *On becoming a person: A therapist's view of psychotherapy*: New York: Houghton Mifflin.

Sellers, H. (2009). *Page after page: Discover the confidence and passion you need to start writing and keep writing.* Blue Ash, OH: Writer's Digest Books.

Silvia, P. J., Wigert, B., Reiter-Palmon, R., & Kaufman, J. C. (2012). Assessing creativity with self-report scales: A review and empirical evaluation. *The Psychology of Aesthetics, Creativity, and the Arts,* **6**, 19–34.

Sternberg, R. J. (1986). *Beyond IQ: Triarchic theory of human intelligence.* New York: Cambridge University Press.

Sternberg, R. J. (1998). *Handbook of creativity.* Cambridge: Cambridge University Press.

Tanner, D., & Reisman, F. K. (2014). *Creativity as a bridge between education and industry: Fostering new innovations.* North Charleston, SC: CreateSpace.

Torrance, E. P. (1965). *Rewarding creative behavior.* Englewood Cliffs, NJ: Prentice-Hall.

Torrance, E. P. (1966). *The Torrance Tests of Creative Thinking-Norms-Technical Manual Research Edition-Verbal Tests, Forms A and B.* Princeton, NJ: Personnel Press.

Torrance, E. P. (1967). *Understanding the fourth grade slump in creative thinking: Final Report.* Athens, GA: The University of Georgia.

Torrance, E. P. (1975a). *Preliminary manual: Ideal child checklist.* Athens, GA: Georgia Studies of Creative Behavior.

Torrance, E. P. (1975b). Creativity research in education: Still alive. In I. A. Taylor & J. W. Getzels (Eds.), *Perspectives in creativity* (pp. 278–296). Chicago: Aldine.

Torrance, E. P. (1983). *The manifesto: A guide to developing a creative career.* Westport, CT: Ablex.

Torrance, E. P. (1993). Understanding creativity: Where to start? *Psychological Inquiry,* 4(3), 232–234.

Torrance, E. P., & Safter, H. T. (1990). *The incubation model of teaching.* Buffalo, NY: Bearly Limited.

Wallas, G. (1926). *Art of thought.* New York: Harcourt, Brace and Company.

Zeigarnik, B. (2012). The Zeigarnik Effect Session ETD 351. Proceedings of the 2012 Conference for Industry and Education Collaboration. *American Society for Engineering Education.* (1), 23.

CHAPTER 12

Attitude Change as the Precursor to Creativity Enhancement

Jonathan A. Plucker and Gayle T. Dow

Educational theorists such Dewey, Piaget, and Vygotsky have all high-lighted the importance of using experiential learning, active hands-on learning, and problem-solving activities to promote learners' creative development. More recently, research has provided evidence that these engaging instructional strategies can be used to enhance creativity. For example, inquiry-based laboratory activities appear to increase creative thinking levels and attitudes among pre-service science teachers (Yakar & Baykara, 2014).

Although many of these techniques have a well-established track record of success in motivating students and improving critical and creative think-ing (Dow & Wagner, 2015), not all teachers embrace these techniques in their own classrooms. Policy and environmental factors, such as test-based accountability systems and diminishing teacher autonomy (Olivant, 2015), can be in direct conflict with creativity-fostering classrooms. And teach-ers' negative attitudes toward creativity may be a potential source of bias when promoting creative behavior (Geake & Gross, 2008). The goal of this chapter is to propose a practical approach to enhancing creativity in today's schools and classrooms, primarily by modifying learner attitudes toward and beliefs about creativity.

Attitudes toward creativity are influenced by prior experiences (e.g., teacher education programs) and experiences in the classroom. These atti-tudes develop and grow into complex, organized mental frameworks of knowledge (Anderson, 1977; Piaget, 1926) that then influence curriculum planning, lesson plan development, and classroom activities. Although atti-tudes may be flexible, it is very difficult to completely change them, even in light of contradictory evidence (see Palmer, 1981; Wheatley & Wegner, 2001). This causes particular concern among educational psychologists, because some attitudes may be inaccurate or based on partially incorrect information.

Creativity is not immune from inaccurate attitudes or myths. *Creativity,* defined in this chapter as "the interaction among *aptitude, process, and environment* by which an individual or group produces a *perceptible product* that is both *novel and useful* as defined within a *social context*" (Plucker, Beghetto, & Dow, 2004, p. 90, emphasis in original), is plagued by implicit myths that, in our view, have led to widespread, inaccurate schemata.

These myths about creativity are problematic because there appears to be no shortage of areas in which creativity can be applied constructively to improve people's lives and, perhaps more important, areas in which people can use creativity to improve their own lives. However, few educators address divergent thinking, creativity, and innovation in primary, secondary, or postsecondary education, areas that are generally considered to be ripe for helping students develop schema. We strongly believe that these problems are primarily due to myths and stereotypes about creativity and innovation that are, at best, loosely related to research in this field.

Examples of Some Unhelpful Myths

Plucker et al. (2004) identified four myths that lead to inaccurate attitudes toward creativity. Many, if not all, are widespread both in practice and in the research literature (Isaksen, 1987; Treffinger, Isaksen, & Dorval, 1996). Common themes that run throughout the myths are their pervasiveness, even among creativity scholars, and their exclusionary undertones (i.e., their role in reinforcing who is *not* creative). The myth that *people are born creative or uncreative* yields an inaccurate conclusion that creativity is an innate quality resilient to improvement (Burkus, 2013; Treffinger et al., 1996). If this myth were adopted, any attempt to increase one's creative output would be abandoned as a fruitless task. This myth continues to flourish in light of ample evidence to refute it. For example, research has long established that creativity training and environmental techniques can foster creative thinking (e.g., Amabile, 1983, 1996; Dow & Mayer, 2004; Dow & Wagner, 2015; Fontenot, 1993; Hennessey & Amabile, 1988; Osborn, 1963; Parnes, 1962; Pyryt, 1999; Sternberg & Lubart, 1992; Torrance, 1962, 1972a, 1987; Westberg, 1996).

The myth that *creativity is a negative attribute* evokes the image of a mad genius with neurotic tendencies (Isaksen, 1987). Such stereotypes are fostered by media portrayals of crazy scientists (e.g., Dr. Frankenstein) and exocentric artists and poets such as Edgar Allen Poe (2005).

However, deviant behavior is not a necessary condition for creativity; instead, it is possible that openness to experience, which is found in both creativity and deviate behavior (Beaty et al., 2014; Benedek et al., 2014; Isaksen, 1987; Nusbaum & Silvia, 2011; Plucker, Runco, & Long, 2011), or latent inhibition, the capacity to filter irrelevant information, is the underlying connection between creativity and deviance (Carson, Peterson, & Higgins, 2003). In other words, correlation does not necessarily imply causation.

Another myth is that *creativity is a fuzzy, soft construct* limited to shamans, crystal ball mystics, and tea-leaf readers (an exaggeration, but only a small one). This stereotype leads people to believe that creative behavior resides in the world of pop psychology and is not worthy of scientific scrutiny or empirically supported interventions that enhance creativity. However, a large quantity of creativity research is conceptually and empirically rigorous, with a large body of work focused on cutting-edge topics such as complex cognition and neuropsychology (e.g., Dow & Mayer, 2004; Fink & Benedeck, 2014; Runco, 2014; Smith, Ward, & Finke, 1995; Ward, Smith, & Vaid, 1997).

The myth that *creativity is enhanced within a group* stems from the business community. This myth has grown from the belief that quantity of ideas equates to greater creativity – thus, the more people working together, the more ideas will be produced, and the greater will be the creativity. However, this myth does not take into account group dynamics that can hinder creative potential (Michinov, Jamet, Métayer, & Le Hénaff, 2015). For example, fear of negative evaluation from other group members can reduce idea production, certain group members may dominate the discussion, or the group may fall prey to group-think and agree, wholeheartedly, without giving each idea careful consideration and thought (Dacey & Lennon, 1998; Kurtzberg, 1998; Williams & Yang, 1999). Diehl and Strobe (1986), Finke, Ward, and Smith (1992), and Thornburg (1991), among many others, have found that brainstorming, or generating lists of ideas for a given problem or situation, will result in more ideas if completed in solitude followed by pooling ideas (see Rickards, 1999).

These myths are detrimental to both personal (e.g., the development on one's unique talents) (Silvia et al., 2014) and external (e.g., the enhancement of creativity in education and business) processes. Since attitudes begin to develop in schools, it is logical to target preventing the development of these attitudes and myths at the source.

Unfortunately, the environments in primary and secondary classrooms often do not support or encourage creativity; rather, they tend to opt for traditional structured curriculum with standardized testing and accountability (Fusarelli, 2008; Maisuria, 2005; Olivant, 2015; Paige, Hickok, &

Neuman, 2002) or with creativity restricted to the arts and music (Diakidoy & Phtiaka, 2001; Hass, 2014; Olton & Johnson, 1976).

A New Model of Innovation Enhancement

Our team has been working for more than 15 years on the development of a new model of creativity enhancement. The goal of this work is not to generate a model of creativity per se, but rather to design a model that seeks to explain how creativity, as defined earlier, can be effectively and efficiently enhanced. We believe that a model of creativity enhancement needs to (1) focus on attitude change, (2) help people identify their strengths, and (3) emphasize both personal and external factors related to creativity.

Based on the prevalence of the previously stated myths, attitude adjustment forms the foundation of the model. The roots of these myths have grown very deep, to the point that many of them are still widely held despite recent theoretical and empirical advances in the field and the often overwhelming evidence of the misperceptions' fallibility (Plucker et al., 2004; Treffinger et al., 1996). To address these myths at the source, a three-prong approach was adopted based on affective changes through direct experiences with creativity, on behavioral changes through altering the students' actions regarding creativity, and on cognitive changes through highlighting inconsistencies in current beliefs (Olson & Zanna, 1993; Weber & Crocker, 1983). Without a personal analysis of these myths, most creativity enhancement efforts are short-term patches. Throughout the course, changing the students' attitude was addressed by focusing explicitly on identifying the students' affect (e.g., "I *feel* that a person is more often born with creativity"), behavior (e.g., "Creativity is *doing* something in a way that is not the standard"), and cognitive processing ("I *believe* that creativity would be impaired by mental disorders"). This approach was used with the hope that incorrect attitudes can be brought to the surface and then adjusted or eliminated.

The next component of the model is to help people determine which creativity strategies work best for them. These strategies can be conceptualized in a variety of ways: We have used the traditional Five P approach (i.e., process, product, person, press, and persuasion; Albert & Runco, 1990), and we have alsoused an approach we call CPSEE (i.e., identifying Cognitive, Political, Social, Environmental, and Emotional strengths and preferences). Regardless of the approach, the emphasis is on respecting individual differences in abilities, interests, and preferences.

The third component of the model is the balance in emphasis on external and personal factors in creativity. Influential research encourages practitioners to be aware of external or environmental factors when fostering creativity (e.g., Amabile, 1983; Baer, 1997, 1998), but we believe the cautions have often been oversold. When we focus exclusively on external factors (which is how we often see this research applied to education), we remove the responsibility for creativity from the individual. Rather, practitioners should promote a more balanced perspective, one in which students learn to interact successfully with their environment when attempting to solve problems creatively.

Undergraduate Coursework Based on the Model

Several undergraduate courses based on this model have been developed and taught at Indiana University and Christopher Newport University, and an undergraduate minor based on the model is being implemented at the University of Connecticut. The goal of this coursework is to help undergraduates enhance their long-term creativity using methods based on this model. To this end, we created a two-stage set of courses: entry-level courses (e.g., "Debunking Myths and Enhancing Innovation," "Creativity in You and the World Around You," and "The Pinnacle of Human Thinking") and senior-level capstone (e.g., "Applied Creativity Seminar" and "Creativity and Critical Thinking").

Many of the students who begin a class on creativity bring with them several of the aforementioned myths and stereotypes about creativity. The purpose of the entry-level courses in creativity is to identify those myths and debunk them. The course sequence is based on the model – specifically, the premise that creativity cannot be enhanced in the long term until myths and stereotypes are examined on a personal level.

In the introductory courses, students actively explore contemporary thought and research by investigating the numerous myths about creativity. The major goal of this course is to provide students with the necessary tools for enhancing creatively in other courses. Students are required to participate in discussions, individual and group projects, and class presentations in an effort to obtain a better understanding of creativity; learn techniques for stimulating creativity; discover ways to stimulate the creativity of others; learn to avoid common blocks to creativity; and explore the campus and its numerous resources. The basic approach to the course is depicted in Figure 12.1. The majority of class activities revolve

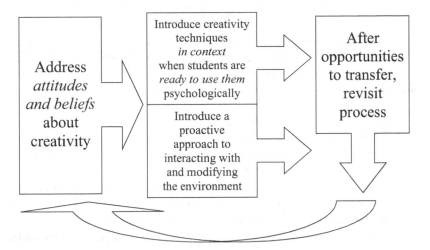

Figure 12.1 Proposed Model of Creativity Enhancement (© 2008 Jonathan Plucker).

around experiential learning, inquiry-based activities, and problem-based learning.[1]

Participants consisted of undergraduate students enrolled in the entry-level creativity courses at Indiana University and Christopher Newport University. Students came from a wide range of majors, including business, biology, chemistry, education, political science, psychology, sociology, interior design, premed, and prelaw, among many others. Most students took the course during their first and second years of college, but juniors and seniors also participated. Instructors included the authors of this chapter and an advanced doctoral student with two years of college teaching experience and multiple teaching awards.

Evaluating the Application of the Model

Data were collected via a precourse and postcourse version of a demographic worksheet, the Creativity Questionnaire, an Observational Note List, group and individual interviews, and document analysis of the textbook and syllabus used for coursework.

---

[1] Space limitations do not permit a more detailed description of course activities. Interested readers should contact the authors for this information.

Data Sources

Creativity questionnaire. Participants completed copies of a creativity questionnaire to assess precourse and postcourse beliefs about creativity. The questionnaire contained the following ten questions regarding the nature of creativity and its implications on the participants' lives:

1. How do you define "creativity"?
2. Can we increase creativity, or are you just born with or without it?
3. How is creativity related to mental illness, drug abuse, and other disorders and negative behaviors?
4. Are individuals or groups more creative when working on a project?
5. Are people creative in many areas or only in a few specific content areas or tasks? In other words, does creativity generalize?
6. How does evaluation influence creativity? For example, how do grades influence your creativity?
7. What is the relationship between constraints and creativity?
8. Is it important to market your creativity? In other words, is it important to get others to accept your creativity? Why or why not?
9. What is the relationship between age and creativity? Consider "age" to represent the entire life span, birth through death.
10. How effective are creativity techniques, such as brainstorming, SCAMPER, etc.?

Observations. Throughout the course, naturalistic recording methods were used to review (1) participants' experiences engaging in creativity coursework and (2) participants' experiences engaging in experiential learning, inquiry-based activities, and problem-based curricular experiences. The Observational Note List was designed in accordance with assessment methods defined by Bechtel (1977) and Krasner (1980). It consisted of notes of participants engaging in activities during coursework.

Group and individual interviews. Some participants at Indiana University were randomly selected to participate in group and individual interviews. Interviews were of a semistructured nature and lasted approximately 15 to 20 minutes. Group interviews occurred following individual interviews. Specific questions were asked regarding (1) their perspectives on the course under study, (2) their beliefs regarding creativity curriculums, and (3) their perspectives on students' and teachers' roles during class activities.

Document analysis. Document analysis was performed to gain information about the curriculum used during the course. Document analysis was performed on the following items: (1) the textbooks used for coursework, (2) the products created during course activities, (3) the course syllabi, and (4) the lesson plans and other documents used by the course instructors. Information taken from the textbook was used in confirming statements that participants made regarding their coursework and their perceptions of creativity.

Triangulation of data sources. Triangulation of data sources was critical in gaining a holistic picture as to the efficacy of creativity coursework in improving student innovation. Triangulation included triangulation by observer, with two observers performing field observations. Triangulation of interpretation also was important as information on the course was reviewed.

Two-Step Member Checking Process

Forty-four students from Indiana University who participated in the study were consulted as to the accuracy of field observations, interview information, and the completed paper. These consultations were performed to assess the validity of records and the accuracy of the results in describing how problem-based learning projects affected creativity-related beliefs and behaviors.

Procedure

All initial data collection took place during the creativity class experience. Participants were observed as they completed a number of hands-on, in-class activities that required both individual and group work.

The creativity questionnaire was administered to the participants in a group by the researcher following one day of coursework. Participants completed the same questionnaire at the end of the last session of the course. Group and individual interviews occurred throughout the course – but in balance primarily toward the end of each semester.

Some Preliminary Evidence

Seventy-seven participants at Indiana University and 18 at Christopher Newport University completed both the precourse and postcourse versions of the creativity questionnaire. Initial data analysis suggests that the myths and stereotypes that plague creativity also inhibit the opportunities of undergraduate students to increase their innovation. Students' responses to the course followed three patterns: (1) deconstructing the myths surrounding creativity takes hands-on work to help students experiment with alternatives; (2) the coursework is difficult for students but "not because it is hard"; and (3) improvements in students' creativity and innovation are not necessarily immediate.

Findings Related to Belief and Attitude Change

The stereotypes that were commonly identified by both practitioners and researchers were also pervasive in the beliefs of students. Their exclusionary undertones dominated the first weeks of the class with such statements as "I am not a creative individual," "You have to be born creative," "You can't increase creativity through experience," "You only are creative if you are an artist or a musician," and so forth (course observations, multiple students).

Myth 1: People are born creative or uncreative. By asking students, "Can we increase creativity, or are you just born with or without it," we are able to tap into the strongest-held myth – that creativity is an innate characteristic and that you will never be creative if you are not "born with creativity." For example, Anne, a junior psychology major, was frustrated by the idea that everyone could be taught to be creative:

> Beauty is in the eye of the beholder they say. With this statement comes the implication that beauty is a subjective unit that only can be identified by the people looking at it; there is no objective definition of it. In class we came up with many examples of people that one person thought was creative and another did not. I finally had to move beyond the objective and just admit that a creative person was one who used common elements in an uncommon way. I [realized] that we can increase creativity by allowing ourselves to think outside of the lines. By trying to see another's point of view or not letting limitations defeat you, an individual's creativity will always be able to be increased. (Amy, creativity postcourse questionnaire)

Although the majority at both Indiana University and Christopher Newport University (69% and 73%, respectively) of students began to believe that creativity can be increased, 52% and 73% of those who believed you were born with it changed their minds by the end of the semester to say that you could increase creativity, whereas only 9% and 2% of students from the respective universities changed their minds in the opposite direction.

Of those students who continued to hold the myth that creativity is an innate characteristic, their views tended to soften over the semester. For example, at the beginning of the course, Samantha wrote that, "I think that you either have [creativity] or you don't. You can't force a person to be creative." At the time of the postcourse questionnaire, although she still held onto the myth that creativity is innate, she was beginning to recognize that creativity can be enhanced: "I still believe you are born with or without [creativity], although I think some activities may enhance creativity." Similarly, Carrie noted at the beginning of the course that, "A person is more often born with creativity rather than taught it." Yet by the end of the course, she, too, had softened her view: "I believe that some are born very creative and others are not. But I also feel that if one is born with it, then it can be increased and built upon."

We noted that, at the end of the course, many students claimed to have changed their view of creativity *in others* but not necessarily *in themselves*. For example, Kim shared that:

> Throughout the course of this class, my own personal creativity has not changed as much as my perceptions of other people's creativity have. I am definitely more appreciative of a good movie or an amazing song or a fantastic book. In short, I can now contemplate how creative someone has become through experience instead of just saying "Wow, that's cool" and moving on. I have witnessed how others, through thinking and practicing and challenging themselves, have moved beyond what might be innate or what might have been an earlier socializing agent... parents, school, television... which is especially damaging to creativity.

In a similar vein, when asked at the end of the course about the effectiveness of creativity techniques such as brainstorming, Catherine wrote that, "For me they aren't effective because I see them as restrictions and criteria I have to meet. For others they provide ideas to build upon."

These results suggest that the goal of completely removing this particular myth may be unrealistic. A more reasonable goal may be to moderate the extreme you-have-to-be-born-with-it perspective.

Myth 2: There is a limited time to be creative. By asking students, "What is the relationship between age and creativity?" we were able to assess a myth that paralleled the idea that creativity was an innate gift – that creativity was a gift of the young. Those holding this belief tend to think that if you have reached age 30 without a major creative contribution, you will never achieve one. This belief, outlined in the peak-and-decline model, claims that creativity reaches its peak in young adulthood and begins to decline with dramatic losses in older adulthood. Although there is evidence to suggest that creativity does decline with age (Alpaugh, Parham, Cole, & Birren, 1982; Dennis, 1966; Hui, et al, 2014; Lehman, 1953; Lindauer, 1993; Simonton, 1999), there is also evidence to suggest that the accumulated knowledge that comes with advancing age can be a positive contribution to one's creativity.

In our questionnaire, students' beliefs regarding the influence of age on creativity fell into four categories. The first category of belief was that children are more creative due to their lack of pressure to adapt to social norms. The perspective is exemplified by Beth, who noted at the beginning of the course that, "As people get older they become less creative, as they are inhibited by what others might think of them. Kids could care less, so they try many more options." And John, who stated, "When you get older you have more pressure from school, deadlines, and work. You focus more on the task and getting the work done. Creativity is just sacrificed."

The second category of beliefs was that adults are more creative and that creativity increases with age due to the building of experiences. The third belief was that creativity peaks twice, once in children and again during retirement. The drop during adulthood was explained as caused by social constraints that are rare in childhood, surge in adulthood, and are again absent in retirement. This category is represented by Beth's postcourse comments, in which she said that, "Children, being less inhibited, tend to be more creative. . . . As one matures, your personal environment and past experiences with sharing innovation can make or break your creativity for life."

The fourth category of beliefs was that all ages are creative, but the manner of expression changes form. Although there was movement across categories, in general there was little change in beliefs about the relationship between age and creativity over the course of the semester.

Myth 3: Creativity does not generalize. By asking students, "Are people creative in many areas or only in a few specific content areas or tasks? In other words, does creativity generalize?" we were able to determine if they believed that creativity is limited to one area (e.g., art) or is a general thinking pattern that can be applied to many areas. In reality, there is both general ability and specific content areas of creativity (Blicbau & Steiner, 1998; Dow & Mayer, 2004; Innamorato, 1998; Kaufman & Baer, 2005; Plucker & Beghetto, 2004; Reiter-Palmon, Illies, Cross, Buboltz, & Nimps, 2009).

At the onset of the course, the majority of students believed that creativity is a general rather than specific or combined trait. At the end of the semester, the students' beliefs were more balanced. A typical belief transformation was that of Jenna, who stated at the start of the course that, "People can be creative in many areas. Some are more interested in specific things and may

Table 12.1 *Precourse, Postcourse, and Change Questionnaire Results for "How do you define creativity?"*

Components	Precourse	Postcourse	Change
Problem solving/finding solutions	10%	30%	20%
Product/thing	45%	51%	6%
Innovative/invention	11%	14%	3%
Risk taking	1%	3%	2%
New/novel/unique	41%	43%	2%
Looking at things differently	8%	9%	1%
Thinking outside the box/going beyond the norm	10%	9%	−1%
Happy/humor	2%	1%	−1%
Original	24%	22%	−2%
Create/creation	16%	14%	−2%
Imagination	10%	5%	−4%
Thought/idea/process	37%	31%	−5%
Self-expression	12%	4%	−8%
Intelligence	8%	0%	−8%
Art/writing	14%	0%	−14%

Note: Indiana University N = 75; Christopher Newport University N = 18

put more time and ability in that area. But I don't think it's generalized." Four months later, however, she expressed a more balanced conception: "I think people have a specific area they are very creative with. But I think it can go further than that. That area may be their strong point, but that creative ability can spill over to other areas." Similarly, Victoria stated at the end of the course, "I think there is a general cognitive ability that helps you be creative but you can have a specific talent, or lack of talent, in specific areas."

Myth 4: Creativity is a fuzzy, soft construct. Often, creativity is viewed as a "fuzzy, soft" construct rather than a coherent topic warranting empirical investigations. This stereotype is not limited to undergraduate students; often psychologists and researchers tend to be biased in their thinking that creativity is "soft psychology," even though intelligence, problem solving, and other related topics are not prone to this bias.

Fifteen main components emerged when students were asked, "How do you define creativity?" (Table 12.1). The main difference between precourse and postcourse responses was that problem solving was rarely identified as a component in the precourse questionnaire responses (10%), whereas it was a reoccurring theme in the postcourse questionnaire responses (30%).

Additionally, although several students, at the start of the course, identified the need to have a self-expression product (12%), this was reduced (4%) by the end of the course. Similarly, both intelligence (8%) and art/writing (14%) exhibited extreme declines (both 0%) by postcourse questionnaire.

Myth 5: Creativity is enhanced within a group. By asking, "Are individuals or groups more creative when working on a project?" we were able to assess the degree that students support the myth that creativity is enhanced within a group. The majority of students believed that working in a group as opposed to individually enhances creative productivity. However, although this myth was still supported at the end of the semester, there was a decrease in the number of students stating that groups enhance creativity and an increase in the view that both individual and group contexts can foster creativity.

A few students elaborated on this idea, suggesting that they are more creative when they are able to work alone initially and then interact with others after a period of time. Still others disliked group work and challenged that their college careers had been plagued by courses where "the quality of the class suffers because not every student invests a sufficient amount of effort in it." Students believed that the group experiences only worked when a substantial number of those participating were invested in the experience, as highlighted by Jacob: "Groups foster creativity if everyone is on board and has a specific role to play and contributes to the groups."

The students who held onto the myth that creativity is enhanced when working in a group tended to modify this stance slightly and began to accept alternative views. For example, Chris, on the precourse questionnaire, believed that creativity is enhanced in a group: "Groups are more creative than individuals because they possess the energy, experience, and unique perceptive of an individual multiplied several times over." At the time of the postcourse questionnaire, although he still held onto the myth that the creativity is enhanced in a group, he was recognizing the possibility of alternative views: "Generally speaking, a group will be more creative because there are more minds to contribute information, energy, and perspective; however, individuals in complete control of a project have free reign and are not inhibited at all by any close-working group members. It can go either way."

Myth 6: Constraints hinder creativity. One goal of the course is to help students understand that constraints can both help and hinder creativity, depending on one's approach to the constraints they face in a given context. On the precourse questionnaire, more than half of the students believed that constraints hinder creativity: Nathan noted that, "Constraints put limits on creativity, which should never have them." Fewer than 10% of the students believed that constraints helped creativity or both helped and inhibited creativity.

However, we observed substantial shifts in attitudes about constraints by the end of the course. Of the 43 students interviewed at Indiana University who believed that constraints hinder creativity, 37% maintained that belief at the end of the semester, 23% changed their belief to state that creativity is helped by constraints, and 33% changed their belief to say that constraints can both help and hinder. This resulted in an almost even division in beliefs between constraints inhibiting creativity (n = 25), helping creativity (n = 23), or both helping and hurting (n = 24). Nathan exemplified this somewhat dramatic change in beliefs by observing that "Constraints to a point are positive guidelines to get you on the right track," a very different sentiment from the one he shared at the start of the semester. Similar thoughts were shared by Tara when she wrote that, "Some constraints are useful to most people, just in putting some sort of framework to a task that needs to be accomplished. Too many guidelines/rules, however, can be stifling to some."

Several students who held onto the belief that creativity is always hindered by evaluation or constraints tended to modify this belief slightly. For example, Amy wrote on the precourse questionnaire that, "When constraints are applied, creativity diminished. People no longer have limitless directions, in which they can go off in any direction. They now have limitations." However, by the end of the course, she recognized the validity of different perspectives on this issue: "Constraints make people less creative, although sometimes it gives people a starting point because it points people away from things that are restricted." This idea was also observed by Carly who stated on a postcourse questionnaire, "Constraints and rules provide guidelines. If you bend those rules you are more apt to be creative."

Additional Observations: Creativity Coursework Is Difficult for Students, But "Not Because It Is Hard"

In both precourse and postcourse questionnaires, students indicated that being creative is a difficult enterprise. An overwhelming majority of students shared that the coursework gave them greater insight into themselves and their abilities to tap into unappreciated and underutilized aspects of self. They rarely described their struggles in the class as being "hard," yet many clearly struggled to confront their misconceptions. Interviews provided evidence that the students considered a course to be hard if there was a lot of reading and writing – yet they did not see a course that made them think a lot as being "hard!" The students reported that this newfound growth carried over into other classes, into the workplace, and into their personal relationships (also see Anderson, 1977; King & Pope, 1999; Livingston, 1999; Reiter-Palmon, 2011; Torrance, 1972b, 1987; Zelinger, 1990).

Even more interesting, students suggested that involvement in the class improved their leadership abilities (also see Tierney, Farmer, & Graen, 1999). Being at a large, midwestern university, Indiana University students also shared that it was the only class they had taken in college where they knew everyone, were able to learn from each other, and were given the opportunity to form cohesive groups and a sense of community (see Bowman & Boone, 1998; Malekoff, 1987).

Improving Students' Creativity and Innovation

Improvements in students' creativity and innovation are not necessarily immediately obvious. Challenging one's beliefs and worldviews to inact change can be a slow and dutiful process. A few students were not ready to challenge their beliefs and instead experienced frustration with the experience, as Kelly stated:

> Reflecting back, I definitely believe my views on creativity and my own innovation have changed for the better. There are more things about myself that I recognize as creative which never would have struck me as such before this class. My worldview is certainly creative. The way I live my life is also. Probably the least creative thing about me is my job, which is pretty routine and simple. But there is a lot of down time for me at work, so I am trying to devise something creative to do besides just twiddling my thumbs.

Students who had initially perceived themselves to be creative later reflected on their classmates creativity, causing them to reevaluate their own creative strengths. In an interview, Martina, an elementary art preservice teacher, asserted,

> I feel that I am more creative . . . because I am now able to come up with ideas that I would not have seen without this class. I think that changing my definition of what creativity is altered my ideas of my own strengths. When I go places now, I look for creative things. I see creativity much more easily than I had previously, and I appreciate it more. I have a much broader definition of what creativity is.

Other students had been told by teachers and family members that they were not creative, and they had to overcome the myths surrounding their own ineptitude at being original and innovative. However, by the end of the semester, most of these students appeared to benefit from the course, showing greater self-efficacy and improved ability to identify and express the creativity within themselves.

Changing Misconceptions about Creativity

To reduce or eliminate students' misconceptions regarding creativity, not only must the misconception be identified but also further components such as affective (Van Kleef, van den Berg, & Heerdink, 2014) behavioral, and cognitive aspects that underlie this misconception must be targeted for elimination (Halloran, 1967). The result is a three-pronged approach that, once put in place, can aid in the identification and modification of their incorrect attitude (Olson & Zanna, 1993). The first step entails correctly identifying any affectively based misconceptions that are often in direct conflict with logical reasoning or scientific evidence; the second step involves targeting any active behaviors that are propagating the misconception (Albarracín & Handley, 2011); and the third step requires the modification of thoughts regarding the misconception. Targeting all three components, we believe, makes changing an incorrect creativity attitude possible.

Furthermore, explicitly providing students with information from scientifically based creativity research makes them more likely to begin to identify and relinquish any of their incorrect views and to slowly begin to change their attitudes toward creativity. Through creativity courses, such as the one outlined here, we hope to begin a course of action in misconception identification and a movement toward schema correction regarding creativity.

Conclusion

The experiences in the undergraduate courses presented here suggest that the proposed model has potential and should be explored further. The activities do seem to change student attitude – more effectively in some areas (e.g., nature vs. nurture, defining creativity, the role of constraints) than in others (e.g., the impact of age, generality vs. specificity, group vs. individual work). However, we did observe change in the beliefs and behaviors of individual students regarding all of the targeted myths and stereotypes, suggesting that the model allowed students to create significant change at the individual level. A lack of observed creativity among

K–12 students is believed to be largely cultural, stemming from task commitment and attitudes (Kim, Shim, & Hull, 2009). Therefore, teachers are encouraged to actively work at identifying any misconceptions, engage in active behaviors to correct misconceptions, and finally adjust their thoughts regarding the misconceptions. Attitudes are not fixed attributes but are constantly under modification based on educational and social influences.

Acknowledgments

The authors wish to thank the many students who took the courses described in this chapter for their participation and forthrightness. We also appreciate the assistance of the staff of the Indiana University Human Subjects Committee and the Institutional Review Board for the Protection of Human at Christopher Newport University, who worked with us to find ways to evaluate and improve the course in a way that met all ethical standards and guidelines.

REFERENCES

Albarracín, D., & Handley, I. M. (2011). The time for doing is not the time for change: Effects of general action and inaction goals on attitude retrieval and attitude change. *Journal of Personality and Social Psychology*, 100, 983–998.

Albert, M. A., & Runco, R. S. (1990). *Theories of creativity*. London: Sage.

Alpaugh, P. K., Parham, I. A., Cole, K. D., & Birren J. E. (1982). Creativity in adulthood and old age: An exploratory study. *Educational Gerontology*, **8**, 101–116.

Amabile, T. M. (1983). *The social psychology of creativity*. New York: Springer Verlag.

Amabile, T. M. (1996). *Creativity in context*. Boulder, CO: Westview Press

Anderson, R. (1977). The notion of schemata and the educational enterprise: General discussion of the conference. In R. C. Anderson, R. J. Spiro, & W. E. Montague (Eds.), *Schooling and the acquisition of knowledge*. Hillsdale, NJ: Erlbaum.

Baer, J. (1997). Gender differences in the effects of anticipated evaluation on creativity. *Creativity Research Journal*, **10**, 25–31.

Baer, J. (1998). Gender differences in the effects of extrinsic motivation on creativity. *Journal of Creative Behavior*, **32**, 18–37.

Barron, F. (1969). *Creative person and creative process*. New York: Holt.

Beaty, R. E., Benedek, R. W., Jaukb, E. Finkb, A. Silvia, P. J., Hodges, D. A., Koschutnigb, K., & Neubauerb, A. C. (2014). Creativity and the default network: A functional connectivity analysis of the creative brain at rest. *Neuropsychologia*, **64**, 92–98.

Bechtel, R. B. (1977). *Enclosing behavior*. Stroudsburg, PA: Dowden, Hutchinson, & Ross.

Benedek, M., Jauk, E., Sommer, M., Arendasy, M., & Neubauer, A. C. (2014). Intelligence, creativity, and cognitive control: The common and differential involvement of executive functions in intelligence and creativity. *Intelligence*, **46**, 73–83.

Blicbau, A. S., & Steiner, J. M. (1998). Fostering creativity through engineering projects. *European Journal of Engineering Education*, **23**, 55–65.

Bowman, V. E., & Boone, R. K. (1998). Enhancing the experience of community: Creativity in group work. *Journal for Specialists in Group Work*, **23**, 388–410.

Burkus D. (2013). *The myths of creativity: The truth about how innovative companies and people generate great ideas*. San Francisco, CA: Jossey-Bass.

Carson, S., Peterson, J. B., & Higgins, D. M. (2003). Latent inhibition and creative achievement in a high-achieving normative population. *Journal of Personality and Social Psychology*, **89**, 499–506.

Chan, S., & Yuen, M. (2014). Personal and environmental factors affecting teachers' creativity-fostering practices in Hong Kong. *Thinking Skills and Creativity*, **12**, 69–77.

Dacey, J. S., & Lennon, K. H. (1998). *Understanding creativity: The interplay of biological psychological and social factors*. San Francisco, CA: Jossey-Bass.

Davis, G. A. (1999). *Creativity is forever* (4th ed., revised). Dubuque, IA: Kendall-Hunt.

Davis, G. A., & Subkoviak, M. J. (1978). Multidimensional analysis of a personality-based test of creative potential. *Journal of Educational Measurement*, **12**, 37–43.

Dennis, W. (1966). Creative productivity between the ages of 20 and 80 years. *Journal of Gerontology*, **21**, 1–8.

Diakidoy, I. N., & Phtiaka, H. (2001). Teachers' beliefs about creativity. In S. Nagel (Ed.), *The handbook of policy creativity: Creativity from diverse perspectives* (Vol. 3, pp. 12–32). Huntington, NY: Nova Science Publishers.

Diehle, M., & Stroebe, W. (1986). Productivity loss in brainstorming. Toward the solution of a riddle. *Journal of Personality and Social Psychology*, **53**, 497–509.

Domino, G. (1970). Identification of potentially creative persons from the Adjective Check List. *Journal of Consulting and Clinical Psychology*, **35**, 48–51.

Dow, G. T., & Mayer, R. E. (2004). Teaching students to solve insight problems: Evidence for domain specificity in training. *Creativity Research Journal*, **16**, 389–402.

Dow, G. T., & Wagner, S. (2015). Promoting integrative STEM in the classroom. Virginia Journal of Education.

Finke, R. A., Ward, T. B., & Smith, S. M. (1992). *Creative cognition: Theory, research and applications*. Cambridge, MA: Bradford MIT Press.

Fontenot, N. A. (1993). Effects of training in creativity and creative problem finding upon business people. *The Journal of Social Psychology*, **133**, 11–22.

Fusarilli, L. (2008). Flying (partially) blind: School leaders' use of research in decisionmaking. In F. M. Hess (Ed.), *When research matters: How scholarship influences education policy* (pp. 177–196). Cambridge, MA: Harvard University Press.

Gardner, H. (1993). *Creating minds.* New York: Basic Books.

Geake, J., & Gross, M. (2008). Teachers' negative affect toward academically gifted students: An evolutionary psychologic study. *Gifted Child Quarterly*, **52**(1), 40–54.

Halloran, J. D. (1967). *Attitude formation and change.* London: Leicester University Press.

Halpern, D. F. (1996). *Thought and knowledge: An introduction to critical thinking* (3rd ed.). Mahwah, NJ: Lawrence Erlbaum Associates.

Hass, R. W. (2014). Domain-specific exemplars affect implicit theories of creativity. *Psychology of Aesthetics, Creativity, and the Arts*, **8**, 44–52.

Hennessey, B. A., & Amabile, T. M. (1988). The conditions of creativity. In R. J. Sternberg (Ed.), *The nature of creativity: Contemporary psychological perspectives* (pp. 11–38). New York: Cambridge University Press.

Hui, N. N., Yeung, D. Y., Sue-Chan, C., Chan, K., Hui, D. C. K., & Cheng, S. (2014). Gains and losses in creative personality as perceived by adults across the life span. *Developmental Psychology*, **50**, 709–713.

Innamorato, G. (1998). Creativity in the development of scientific giftedness: Educational implications. *Roeper Review*, **21**, 54–59.

Isaksen, S. G. (1987). Introduction: An orientation to the frontiers of creativity research. In S. G. Isaksen (Ed.), *Frontiers of creativity research* (pp. 1–26). Buffalo, NY: Bearly Limited.

Fink, A., & Benedek, M. (2014). EEG alpha power and creative ideation. *Neuroscience and Biobehavioral Reviews*, **44**, 111–123.

Kaufman, J. C. (2001). The Sylvia Plath effect: Mental illness in eminent creative writers. *The Journal of Creative Behavior*, **35**(1), 37–50.

Kaufman, J. C., & Baer, J. (2005). The amusement park theory of creativity. In J. C. Kaufman & J. Baer (Eds.), *Creativity across domains: Faces of the muse* (pp. 321–328). Hillsdale, NJ: Lawrence Erlbaum Associates.

Kim, K. H., Shim, J., & Hull, M. (2009). Korean concepts of giftedness and the self-perceived characteristics of students selected for gifted programs. *Psychology of Aesthetics, Creativity, and the Arts*, 3, 104–111.

King, B. J., & Pope, B. (1999). Creativity as a factor in psychological assessment and healthy psychological functioning. *Journal of Personality Assessment*, **72**, 200–207.

Krasner, L. (1980). *Enviromental design and human behavior.* London: Pergamon.

Kurtzberg, T. R. (1998). Creative thinking cognitive aptitude and integrative joint gain: A study of negotiator creativity. *Creativity Research Journal*, **11**, 283–293.

Lehman, H. C. (1953). *Age and achievement.* Princeton, NJ: Princeton University Press.

Lindauer, M. S. (1993). The old-age style and its artists. *Empirical Studies of the Arts*, **11**, 135–114.

Livingston, J. A. (1999). Something old and something new: Love, creativity and the enduring relationship. *Bulletin of the Menniger Clinic*, **63**, 40–52.

Maisuria, A. (2005). The turbulent times of creativity in the National Curriculum. *Policy Futures in Education*, **3**(2), 141–152.

Malekoff, A. (1987). The preadolescent prerogative: Creative blends of discussion and activity in group treatment. *Social Work with Groups*, **10**(4), 61–81.

Michinov, N., Jamet, E., Métayer, N., & Le Hénaff, B. (2015).The eyes of creativity: Impact of social comparison and individual creativity on performance and attention to others' ideas during electronic brainstorming. *Computers in Human Behavior*, **42**, 57–67.

Nusbaum, E. C., & Silvia, P. J. (2011). Are openness and intellect distinct aspects of openness to experience? A test of the O/I model. *Personality and Individual Differences*, **51**, 571–574.

Olivant, K. F. (2015). "I am not a format": teachers' experiences with fostering creativity in the era of accountability. *Journal of Research in Childhood Education*, **29**(1), 115–129.

Olson, J. M., & Zanna, M. P. (1993). Attitudes and attitude change. *Annual Review of Psychology*, **44**, 117–154.

Olton, R. M., & Johnson, D. M. (1976). Mechanisms of incubation in creative problem. *American Journal of Psychology*, **89**, 617–630.

Osborn, A. (1963). *Applied imagination: Principles and procedures of creative problem-solving* (3rd ed.). New York: Charles Scribner and Sons.

Paige, R., Hickok, E., & Neuman, S. (2002). *No child left behind: A desktop reference*. Jessup, MD. Education Publications Center, U.S. Department of Education.

Palmer, W. S. (1981). Research: Reading theories and research: A search for similarities. *The English Journal*, **70**(8), 63–66.

Parnes, S. J. (1962). Can creativity be increased? In S. J. Parnes & H. F. Harding (Eds.), *A source book for creative thinking* (pp. 185–191). New York: Scribner's Publishing.

Piaget, J. (1926). *The language and thought of the child*. New York: Harcourt, Brace.

Plucker, J. A., & Beghetto, R. A. (2003). Why not be creative when we enhance creativity? In J. H. Borland (Ed.), *Rethinking gifted education* (pp. 215–226). New York: Teachers College Press.

Plucker, J. A., & Beghetto, R. A. (2004). Why creativity is domain general, why it looks domain specific, and why the distinction does not matter. In R. J. Sternberg, E. L. Grigorenko, & J. L. Singer (Eds.), *Creativity: From potential to realization* (pp. 153–167). Washington, DC: American Psychological Association.

Plucker, J. A., Beghetto, R. A., & Dow, G. T. (2004). Why isn't creativity more important to educational psychologists? Potential, pitfalls, and future directions in creativity research. *Educational Psychologist*, **39**, 83–97.

Plucker, J. A., & Dana, R. Q. (1999). Drugs and creativity. In M. A. Runco & S. Pritzker (Eds.), *Encyclopedia of creativity* (Vol. 1, pp. 607–611). San Diego, CA: Academic Press.

Plucker, J. A., Runco, M. A., & Long, H. (2011). Deviance. In M. A. Runco & S. R. Pritzker (Eds.), *Encyclopedia of creativity: Vol. 1* (2nd ed., pp. 379–382). San Diego, CA: Academic Press/Elsevier.

210   JONATHAN A. PLUCKER AND GAYLE T. DOW

Poe, E. A. (1996). *Tales of mystery and imagination.* Consett, UK: Wordsworth Classics.

Poe, E. A. (2005). *Tales of mystery and imagination.* Whitefish, MT: Kessinger Publishing.

Pyryt, M. C. (1999). Effectiveness of training children's divergent thinking: A meta-analytic review. In A. S. Fishkin, B. Cramond, & P. Olszewski-Kubilius (Eds.), *Investigating creativity in youth: Research and methods* (pp. 351–365). Cresskill, NJ: Hampton Press.

Reiter-Palmon, R. (2011). Introduction to special issue: The psychology of creativity and innovation in he workplace. *Psychology of Aesthetics, Creativity, and the Arts,* **5**, 1–2.

Reiter-Palmon, R., Illies, M. Y., Cross, L. K., Bubolz, C., & Nimps, T. (2009). Creativity and domain specificity: The effect of task type on multiple indexes of creative prooblem solving. *Psychology of Aesthetics, Creativity, and the Arts,* **3**, 73–80.

Rickards, T. (1999). Brainstorming. In M. A. Runco & S. Pritzker (Eds.), *Encyclopedia of creativity* (pp. 219–227). San Diego, CA: Academic Press.

Runco M. A. (2014). *Creativity: Theories and themes: Research, development, and practice.* Waltham, MA: Elsevier.

Russ, S. (1993). *Affect and creativity: The role of affect and play in the creative process.* Hillsdale, NJ: Lawrence Erlbaum Associates.

Schoen, L., & Fusarelli, L. (2008). Innovation, NCLB, and the fear factor: The challenge of leading 21st century schools in an era of accountability. *Educational Policy,* **22**, 181–203.

Silvia, P. J., Beaty, R. E., Nusbaum, E. C., Eddington, K. M., Levin-Aspenson, H., & Kwapil, T. R. (2014). Everyday creativity in daily life: An experience-sampling study of "little c" creativity. *Psychology of Aesthetics, Creativity, and the Arts,* **8**, 183–188.

Simonton, D. K. (1999). Creativity from a historiometric perspective. In R. J. Sternberg (Ed.), *Handbook of creativity* (pp. 116–133). New York: Cambridge University Press.

Smith, S. M., Ward, T. B., & Finke, R. A. (Eds.). (1995). *The creative cognition approach.* Cambridge, MA: MIT Press.

Stein, M. I. (1974). *Stimulating creativity: Individual procedures.* New York: Academic Press.

Sternberg, R. J., & Lubart, T. I. (1992). Buy low and sell high: An investment approach to creativity. *Current Directions in Psychological Science,* **1**, 1–5.

Sternberg, R. J., & Lubart, T. I. (1999). The concept of creativity: Prospects and paradigms. In R. J. Sternberg (Ed.), *Handbook of creativity* (pp. 3–15). New York: Cambridge University Press.

Thornburg, T. (1991). Group size and member diversity influence on creative performance. *Journal of Creative Behavior,* **25**, 324–333.

Tierney, P., Farmer, S. M., & Graen, G. B. (1999). An examination of leadership and employee creativity: The relevance of traits and relationships. *Personnel Psychology,* **52**, 591–620.

Torrance, E. P. (1962). *Guiding creative talent.* Englewood Cliffs, NJ: Prentice-Hall.

Torrance, E. P. (1972a). Can we teach children to think creatively? *The Journal of Creative Behavior,* **6**, 114–143.

Torrance, E. P. (1972b). Career patterns and peak creative achievements of creative high school students 12 years later. *Gifted Child Quarterly,* **16**, 75–88.

Torrance, E. P. (1987). Recent trends in teaching children and adults to think creatively. In S. G. Isaksen (Ed.), *Frontiers of creativity research: Beyond the basics* (pp. 204–215). Buffalo, NY: Bearly Limited.

Treffinger, D. J., Isaksen, S. G., & Dorval, B. K. (1996). Creative problem solving: An overview. In M. A. Runco (Ed.), *Problem finding, problem solving, and creativity* (pp. 223–235). Norwood, NJ: Ablex.

Van Kleef, G. A., van den Berg, H., & Heerdink, M. W. (2014). The persuasive power of emotions: Effects of emotional expressions on attitude formation and change. *Journal of Applied Psychology,* doi: http://o-dx.doi.org.read.cnu .edu/10.1037/apl0000003

Ward, T. B., Smith, S. M., & Vaid, J. (1997). *Creative thought: An investigation of conceptual structures and processes.* Washington, DC: American Psychological Association.

Weber, R., & Crocker, J. (1983). Cognitive processes in the revision of stereotypic beliefs. *Journal of Personality and Social Psychology,* **45**, 961–977.

Westberg, K. L. (1996). The effects of teaching students how to invent. *Journal of Creative Behavior,* **30**, 249–267.

Wheatley, T., & Wegner, D. M. (2001). Psychology of automaticity of action. In N. J. Smelser & P. B. Baltes (Eds.), *International encyclopedia of the social and behavioral sciences* (pp. 991–993). Oxford: Elsevier Science Limited.

Williams, W. M., & Yang, L. T. (1999). Organizational creativity. In R. J. Sternberg (Ed.), *Handbook of creativity* (pp. 373–391). New York: Cambridge University Press.

Yakar, Z., Baykara, H. (2014). Inquiry based laboratory practices in a science teacher training program. *Eurasia Journal of Mathematics, Science & Technology Education,* **10**, 173–183.

Zelinger, J. (1990). Charting the creative process. *British Journal of Projective Psychology* **35**: 78–96.

CHAPTER 13

Nurturing Creativity in the Engineering Classroom

David H. Cropley

School of Engineering University of South Australia

Creativity Is Vital to Engineering

Throughout history, a key factor in human development has been our ability to solve problems. Those problems take a variety of forms, but many of the most critical ones have been problems that are highly amenable to the application of engineering in the sense defined by the U.S. Accreditation Board for Engineering and Technology (ABET) – that is, solutions that, at their core, make use of the "materials and forces of nature for the benefit of mankind". Thus, the problem of warmth and shelter was solved by mankind's ability to create structures from stone, wood and other materials. The problem of feeding large numbers of people was tackled by the development of the plough and irrigation. Problems of health were solved by the creation of systems for removing and processing waste. Our success at solving these problems through the application of engineering has resulted in rapid growth and development.

It is important to note, however, that this process of problem solving for human development is highly dynamic in nature. We are all too familiar with the fact that each solution that is developed contains the seeds of new problems. The solutions developed and applied since the industrial revolution – for example, steam engines, the use of coal as a fuel, the development of internal combustion engines, the exploitation of oil – have provided many benefits, but they also have given rise to new problems that themselves must be addressed. Pollution and climate change, for example, are by-products of earlier solutions that now stimulate both a drive to replace those older technologies with better and more efficient solutions, as well as a push to mitigate the undesirable effects of earlier systems.

Where does creativity come into play in this process of engineering solutions for the needs of mankind? The cycle of *problem–solution–problem– solution* has one distinct characteristic that explains why creativity is so vital to engineering, and therefore to society. Every time a *new* problem emerges – one that is *unprecedented* or *has never been seen before* – it is axiomatic that previous solutions will not be suitable. The solution, for instance, to the problem of diesel engines polluting the environment is not to build more diesel engines! Something has to change! If we keep applying the same old solution but hope for a different result, then we are, as Einstein suggested, flirting with insanity. The key ingredient is the addition of novelty – something new. The diesel engine problem may be solved, therefore, by the addition of novelty in the form of *new* components that reduce the emissions of the engine (i.e., incremental change), or it may be solved by a completely *new* paradigm – electric motors instead of diesel engines (i.e., radical, or disruptive, change). Whichever approach is taken, the key ingredient is novelty, and novelty is a defining characteristic of creativity.

Our ability to harness the materials and forces of nature for the benefit of mankind – engineering problem solving – therefore cannot look past the role of creativity. With the exception of routine *replication* – solving old problems with old technologies – engineering is a forward-looking, optimistic pursuit that seeks to develop new technological solutions to the stream of new and challenging problems that we face as the world continues to develop. It follows that engineers themselves must have, as a core competency, the ability to find and develop these novel solutions.

It might be tempting to lay the blame for any deficiency in creativity in engineering education at the feet of the primary and secondary education systems; surely engineering departments can only work with what they are given by the K–12 pipeline? However, this would be both unfair and irresponsible. While there is no doubt that engineering education will benefit from an influx of more creative students, as schools address their own question of nurturing creativity in the classroom, any failure to reform the tertiary system with respect to creativity will quickly undo any gains made elsewhere. For this reason, creativity must be deliberately and carefully nurtured in the engineering classroom.

The Need for Creativity in Engineering Education

Both Buhl (1960) and Cropley (2015) have underlined the case that creativity is a vital, integral and valuable part of engineering, and the preceding discussion touches on the key reasons. Creativity needs to be nurtured in engineering education because without it, engineers are not fully equipped for their role as technological problem solvers. This is supported by empirical evidence from one of the key stakeholders in the development of technological solutions – the employers who hire engineers. In fact, not only do these stakeholders echo the importance of creativity in engineers; they highlight an alarming concern – that the engineers emerging from the educational pipeline are not equipped with this core competency to the degree required to be fully effective. In fact, the problem is not unique to engineering, as evidence shows.

A 1999 survey of employers in Australia suggested that 75% of new university graduates in that country show "skill deficiencies" in creativity, problem solving, and independent and critical thinking. The importance of creativity and related skills was again confirmed by the 2013 annual *Graduate Outlook Survey* conducted by Graduate Careers Australia[1], which indicated that "Problem solving/Lateral thinking" is third on the list of top selection criteria for employers. However, of greater significance, and an indicator that all is not well in the educational process with respect to creativity, was the fact that employers indicated that only 57.3% of graduates hired exceeded average expectations in problem solving – a figure that has been declining in recent years! If further evidence of both the importance of creativity in engineering and the apparent failure of engineering education to produce creative engineers is needed, Tilbury, Reid and Podger (2003) also reported on an employer survey in Australia which concluded, quite simply, that graduates *lack creativity*.

A similar state of affairs is apparent in other developed nations. In the United Kingdom, Cooper, Altman, and Garner (2002) concluded that the education system, in general, discourages innovation. More specifically, the British General Medical Council noted that medical education is overloaded with factual material that discourages higher-order cognitive functions such as evaluation, synthesis and problem solving, and engenders an attitude of passivity – criticisms that could be levelled also at engineering curricula. Closer to the discipline of engineering, Bateman (2013) reports on results of UK employment survey data in the area of computer science and IT, suggesting that graduates in this technological domain miss out on employment opportunities due to a lack of creativity.

The same picture is also reported in the United States in various sources. Articles in *Newsweek* (2010), *Time* (2013a, 2013b), and *Forbes* Magazine (2014), for example, reiterate the fact that not only is creativity vital to economic growth and general societal well-being, but that employers continue to be frustrated by the fact that new graduates are emerging from universities lacking skills in creativity and problem solving.

---

[1] www.graduatecareers.com.au/wp-content/uploads/2014/03/Graduate_Outlook_2013.pdf

Turning to engineering education more specifically, the circumstances seem to be no different. The Royal Academy of Engineering (RAE) in the United Kingdom provides a good example. In 2007, the RAE published the report, *Creating Systems That Work: Principles of Engineering Systems for the 21st Century* (Elliott & Deasley, 2007), and among six principles that the report sets out as critical for "understanding the challenges of a system design problem and for educating engineers to rise to those challenges" (p. 11) was an ability to "be creative". The report also connected creativity firmly to the engineering process defining it as the ability "to devise novel and . . . effective solutions to the real problem" (p. 4)! Baillie (2002) echoes the same points, noting an "increasing perception of the need for graduates of engineering to be creative thinkers" (p. 185).

Of particular concern is the fact that this conversation has been taking place for decades, with little to show for it. The same concerns that we see raised currently about a lack of creativity in school and university education are not new. From the very beginning of the modern creativity era (e.g., Guilford, 1950) researchers have been troubled by the neglect of the study of creativity in educational contexts, as well as its inherent value and accessibility as a "learning advantage" (e.g., Cropley, 1992). More specifically, in relation to engineering, Cropley and Cropley (2005) reviewed findings on fostering creativity in engineering education in the United States, concluding that there was little support for creative students in the curriculum.

Even efforts to address the identified deficiencies – for example, the 1990 National Science Foundation (NSF) Engineering Coalition of Schools for Excellence and Leadership (ECSEL) – have had little success, if the views of stakeholders are correct. ECSEL had the goal of transforming undergraduate engineering education, but a subsequent review of practice throughout higher education in the United States (Fasko, 2001) found that the deliberate training in creativity was rare. Cropley (2015) has summarized many of these arguments, and also noted an unflattering view amongst engineering students; engineering curricula continue to focus on traditional topics, taught in traditional ways, and these make little room for the creativity that almost everyone agrees is critical to engineering education.

The Problem: i-Shaped Engineering Graduates

There are many ways to look at this problem, but if we are to find ways to address it, so that creativity is properly nurtured in the [engineering] classroom, then it is helpful if two things can be achieved. One is to move beyond simply restating the problem. There seems to be no dispute: creativity, with rare exceptions, is not being adequately or appropriately nurtured in engineering education. The second is to understand the problem in a holistic sense – put another way, if we define the problem in a piecemeal way, then it is no surprise if the solutions are similarly piecemeal. In other words, we need to treat the disease and not merely mask the symptoms. A helpful starting point along this path is to understand the nature of the graduates that we are producing in the engineering education pipeline.

A good way to characterize the ideal engineering graduate is through the construct of *T-shaped* professionals. The concept has been attributed to different sources – for example, Karjalainen, Koria and Salimaki (2009) give credit to Iansiti (1993), while Oskam (2009) links it to Kelley and Littman's (2005) work at IDEO. Regardless of the source, the T-shaped concept describes an ideal professional, such as an engineer, with a *blend* of domain-specific, specialist knowledge and skills (the vertical arm of the T) and complementary, extra-disciplinary knowledge and skills that facilitate collaboration, communication and creativity (the horizontal bar of the T). More simply, the ideal T-shaped professional combines breadth of knowledge with depth of expertise.

Putting the problem that has been articulated – engineering graduates lack creativity – in these terms, it is as though engineering programs are producing, not T-shaped professionals, but *i-shaped* professionals! The vertical component of the "T" – the domain-specific knowledge and skills – is *partly* filled, mainly with declarative (*what*) and procedural (*how*) knowledge, and isolated "dots" of complementary skills and abilities – creativity, for example – may be developed, forming the beginnings of the horizontal component, but lacking integration with the technical (vertical) knowledge (see Figure 13.1). The domain knowledge frequently fails to address higher-order conditional (*when* and *why*) aspects of the discipline, and the "dots" often float free from the domain knowledge, added on almost as an afterthought.

The real problem that must be addressed is *not* "where do we add in some creativity to an engineering program?" or "how to we develop more conditional knowledge in engineering courses?" – both Band-Aid solutions – but "why are engineering programs failing to produce T-shaped graduates?", who, among other things have the necessary skills and abilities in creativity that complement their domain-specific knowledge, so that they are able to solve, efficiently and effectively, the problems that we face in society today.

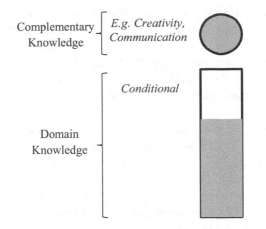

Figure 13.1 "i-Shaped" Professionals

Why Are Programs Producing i-Shaped Graduates?

The evidence at the end of the education pipeline – that is, the opinions of employers – suggests that engineering educators are not providing what the customer needs, that is, T-shaped engineering graduates. In Cropley (2015) I suggested that there are three problems that are contributing to a general misalignment of engineering education and creativity: (a) over-specialization; (b) pseudo-expertise; (c) lack of knowledge. Briefly, those are as follows:

- Over-specialization – in what seems to have been a reaction to a paradigm of breadth at the expense of depth, described by Buhl (1960), the modern paradigm of engineering education seems to have swung to a focus on depth of knowledge in narrow specializations (the vertical arm of the "T"). The negative impact of this has been to focus attention only on the technical content of the specialization, leaving little or no room in the curriculum for students to "learn to solve problems in a creative way" (Buhl, 1960, p. 11), as illustrated by Figure 13.1.
- Pseudo-expertise – in essence, an excessive focus on declarative (*what*) and procedural (*how*) knowledge, not balanced by the development conditional (*when* and *why*) knowledge. In addition, a focus is on developing only intermediate levels of understanding in these forms of knowledge. The particular deficiency here is not so much in creativity itself, but in a failure to develop fully the domain expertise which then serves as a pre-requisite for domain creativity (Figure 13.1).

- Lack of Knowledge – this pervasive problem is simply the fact that, across many disciplines, a significant block to creativity is the fact that educators frequently have a poor understanding of what creativity is, why it is important, how to develop it and how to embed it in their curricula. As a result, the best that can be expected is something approaching an i-shaped professional.

I now believe that these problems are, in fact, symptoms of a deeper issue. Kazerounian and Foley (2007) touched on this when they asked why creativity is "not an obvious part of the engineering curriculum at every university?" (p. 762). The real problem that is preventing creativity from being properly nurtured in the engineering classroom – and preventing the development of T-shaped engineers – is *structural* in nature. In fact, the structure of engineering programs may be reinforcing the three problems described earlier in the chapter, and making any transition difficult to achieve, even where the will to do so exists.

The Real Problem

The deeper problem blocking a change to a curriculum that is inclusive of creativity in engineering is complex, but stems from a reductionist tradition in science. This approach seeks to understand objects, phenomena or theories in terms of their constituent parts. *Analysis* is the process by which we apply reductionism, taking apart an object, for example, to find out how it works. Classical mechanics is a case in point. While it is certainly true that analysis is a valuable tool and means for gaining knowledge, especially in an engineering context, it cannot shed any light on the properties of a more complex entity that *emerge* only at the level of interacting components – that is, a system. To illustrate, we cannot find the music emitted by a piano simply by disassembling it.

Engineering, both as a discipline and in terms of the education of engineers, nevertheless is frequently tackled in a reductionist, analytical fashion. The mechanistic, reductionist mindset, ingrained in our thinking through hundreds of years of influence from the scientific method, des Cartes and the like, still dominates engineering education.

Why is reductionism an issue? First, the reductionist, analytical mindset, when applied to engineering education, steers us into a curriculum structure that is *bottom-up* in nature. The "i" is populated from the bottom, focusing first on declarative knowledge. Both an "i" and a "T" look the same from this perspective, so that it is difficult to see beyond the declarative component of knowledge. In the same way that a reductionist thinker breaks apart an object and studies the pieces in order to gain knowledge, the reductionist educator breaks the end product – the engineer – into his or her pedagogical parts, seeking to gain knowledge about what needs to be taught. To the detriment of creativity, those building blocks look predominantly declarative in nature.

Like the piano, the pieces that remain after taking the engineer apart – the equivalent of the frame, the strings, the hammers, the keys – are then taken as the building blocks of engineering education. In engineering these building blocks become: calculus and Laplace transforms; classical mechanics and Ohm's law; Boolean algebra and thermodynamics. While they are not unimportant, the bottom-up approach emphasizes these components at the expense of higher-order components of knowledge.

The second reason that reductionism is an issue is that the reductionist mindset, by definition, excludes one important element of creative work. Sternberg and colleagues (Sternberg, 1985; Sternberg & Lubart, 1995; Sternberg & Williams, 1996) described creative work and three abilities that are amenable to training and education. They noted the importance of not only analytical and practical ability – of obvious relevance to engineering – but also of a *synthetic ability* relating to the generation of novel and effective ideas. By definition, a reductionist and analytical mindset shuts out this vital synthetic ability that is a key building block of creativity.

The third issue arising from reductionism can be understood by considering the opposite mindset. The converse of reductionist, bottom-up thinking is a *top-down*, systems approach. If reductionism is analytical in nature, a systems mindset is synthetic in nature. Not only is this a vital element of creative work, as indicated earlier, but in reductionism we also lose the emergent properties that are inherent in complex systems.

Like the piano, a complex system exhibits properties – for example, the ability to produce music – that only appear when all the components of the system are working together; they *emerge* only at the level of the system. By reducing engineering education to its component parts, we succeed in identifying the building blocks such as those mentioned, but we risk losing sight of the emergent aspects – those aspects that are only apparent in the integrated, functioning system – that is, the working engineer. For engineering, these emergent properties seem to include not only communication skills and teamwork but also the creativity that results from the interaction of all of the building blocks (both analytical and synthetic).

The real problem facing engineering education – the impediment to nurturing creativity in the engineering classroom – is a faulty program structure driven by three reductionist parameters:

- A bottom-up focus that is oriented towards filling the vertical bar of the "i" with the lowest level building blocks of engineering knowledge;
- An analytical emphasis that keeps the attention focused away from synthetic elements of knowledge and ability – the cross-piece of a "T";
- A mindset that excludes the importance of the integration of the building blocks of knowledge and leaves no room for properties which emerge only at the top of the "T".

Under these conditions, the development of an i-shaped professional seems almost inevitable. At best, this leaves employers with the job of turning the "i" into a "T", and at worst, it leaves the engineering graduate without the full set of knowledge and skills needed not only for effective engineering problem solving but also for effective professional practice.

How the Problem Is Manifested in Practice

How does the real problem – the reductionist paradigm – affect engineering education in practical terms? What are the visible signs of reductionism in the engineering curriculum?

First, we see the impact in the structure of typical engineering degrees. A bottom-up, analytical focus dictates that we begin with the smallest, analytical, declarative and procedural building blocks, which in engineering typically includes:

- Introductory computer programing:
  - learning about (i.e., *what* and *how*) data types, variables, constants, Boolean operators, arrays and strings.
- Basic engineering mathematics:
  - learning about (i.e., *what* and *how*) vectors, complex numbers, types of functions, rates of change and calculus.
- Basic electricity and electronics:
  - learning about (i.e., *what* and *how*) the analysis of resistive networks, learning about capacitors and inductors, learning how to analyse alternating current circuits.

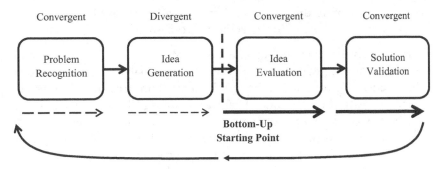

Figure 13.2 The development of the "i-Shaped" engineer

- Introductory mechanics:
  - learning about (i.e., *what* and *how*) statics and dynamics, forces, moments and equilibrium, rigid bodies and structural members.

Second, the analytical focus means that these building blocks tend to congregate in what can be characterized as the *convergent* phases of the engineering process. If a simplified representation of the process is captured in four phases – (1) problem recognition; (2) idea generation; (3) idea evaluation, and; (4) solution validation (see Figure 13.2) – then the bottom-up focus locates the engineering education process more specifically at beginning of idea evaluation – that is, engineering education begins *in the middle* of the engineering process.

The latter two stages – idea evaluation and solution validation – are the business of the vertical bar of the T-shaped concept. The education process therefore begins with the idea evaluation stage, filling the vertical bar from the bottom-up. This is followed by further convergent knowledge associated with solution validation (Figure 13.2). The higher-order, emergent and conditional (i.e., *when* and *why*) knowledge of the *problem recognition* stage may follow unless blocked by the dominant focus on lower-level building blocks. Finally, although it may follow sequentially, the key *divergent* stage of *idea generation* is impeded, both by the fact that it is synthetic in nature and therefore does not fit into an analytical framework, and simply because it is left until last, and often is excluded simply through a perceived lack of time and space. I have seen this occur, in practice, with statements like "you can put in as much of that creativity stuff as you like, as long as you don't take out any existing material". This reductionist mindset is saying, in effect, "We don't want any *synthetic* content in this program".

Fixing the Problem: Nurturing Creativity in
Engineering Education

The three issues surrounding the dominance of a reductionist mind-set in engineering education – the bottom-up, analytical, non-emergent characteristics – drive, and are driven by, a program structure that tends to act to maintain the status quo. That status quo is little or no creativity.

There is a risk that we can spend all our time debating the cause and effect, and see no progress made towards the obvious goal of nurturing creativity in engineering education. Is the program structure that tends to develop i-shaped engineers caused by a reductionist mindset, or is the mindset the way that we rationalize a long-standing structure? Are both the mindset and the structure the result of a lack of understanding of what creativity is and how it is fostered in people, or do the mindset and structure of programs make it impossible for engineering educators to incorporate creativity into their programs?

What seems clear is that something has to change, because the key stakeholders – employers and students – seem to be unanimous in their view that creativity is both a vital component of engineering education and poorly addressed by current programs. Students want to be T-shaped, and employers want T-shaped graduates, but the education process is manufacturing i-shaped engineers who lack key competencies, in particular with respect to creativity.

If part of the problem is the impact of a reductionist mindset – manifest as a bottom-up, analytical and non-emergent approach and structure – then what would the opposite to this look like? How would an engineering education process achieve the T-shaped result if we had a free hand to design the structure to achieve this end?

Driven by a top-down, holistic approach to engineering education that values a balance of analysis, practice and synthesis, and seeks to develop both the basic building blocks of knowledge, as well as higher-order, emergent elements, we can speculate that engineering education would do the following:

1. We would need to begin with a realistic, high-level model of the engineering process:
    a. This would probably look rather like the core stages depicted in Figure 13.2, but would also recognize that the development of an engineered system itself proceeds from a more abstract, conceptual level to a more concrete, detailed level.

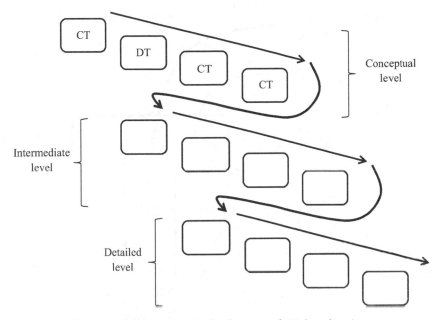

Figure 13.3 Stages driving the development of a T-shaped engineer

   b. This would also highlight the fact that there are two core processes that need to be taught – Divergent Thinking (DT) and Convergent Thinking (CT) – and that these recur as engineering design moves from a higher, conceptual level to a lower, detailed level (Figure 13.3).
2. We would probably *begin at the beginning*. Engineering problem solving, as depicted in Figure 13.2, first requires us to recognize and define the problem, before generating solution ideas, and then evaluating these and finally validating the solution.
   a. This would push engineering education to start with Problem Recognition (Figure 13.2) and *not* Idea Evaluation.
3. We would recognize that engineered systems are progressively refined from a higher, conceptual level down to a lower, detailed level (i.e., Figure 13.3), and this would permeate the way that engineering is taught, breaking a reductionist, bottom-up mindset and focusing as much attention on synthetic ability and emergent, conditional knowledge as it would on lower-level declarative and procedural knowledge.
4. This would almost certainly mean that some elements currently taught in Year 1 – for example, the declarative building blocks mentioned

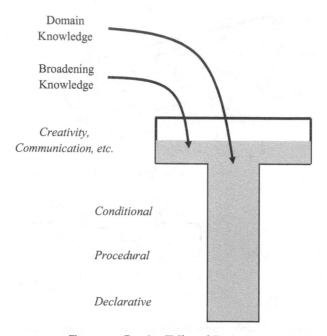

Domain
Knowledge

Broadening
Knowledge

Creativity,
Communication, etc.

Conditional

Procedural

Declarative

Figure 13.4 Creating T-Shaped Engineers

previously – might, in the future, not be taught until Year 4, and vice versa. This would also ensure that the higher-order knowledge, both in the vertical component of the T as well as in the horizontal bar, could not be left out of the curriculum.

Nurturing creativity in the engineering classroom would flow out of this structure, as a result of the shift *away from* the reductionist mindset that cannot help but develop i-shaped engineers and *towards* a systems mindset that leads to the development of T-shaped individuals. Viewed from the top down, a "T" looks very different from an "i", and this change in perspective would radically alter what is taught and how it is taught (Figure 13.4).

Concluding Thoughts

In writing about nurturing creativity in the engineering classroom, it is tempting, and seems obvious, to focus on proximate issues. What can an instructor do, here and now, to help his or her students generate some novel ideas? Let's teach them how to brainstorm, or introduce mind-mapping as a technique, and nobody can claim that we are ignoring creativity!

However, this seems too short-sighted and simplistic, and avoids the more fundamental question of whether or not the students are being taught the right things, in the right order, and at the right depth. In more simple terms, there may be little value in knowing how to execute a process like brainstorming if you do not know when or why this is of value. Indeed, treating idea generation itself as another declarative or procedural building block – here is what it is, and here is how to do it – seems doomed to failure. Buhl (1960) probably captured this notion best when he stated that "schools must educate the student for change. Students must not only learn the fundamental ideas upon which the various subjects are based [the *vertical* components], but they must learn how to solve problems in a creative way" (p. 11). It seems clear that if engineering programs tackle the process of learning how to solve problems in a creative way by jumping into the mid-point of the process (Figure 13.2), and if the guiding philosophy excludes the key synthetic piece of the process, then engineering graduates will only emerge as i-shaped individuals, knowing, as Gandhi warned, more and more about less and less and unable to actually solve the problems that society needs them to be able to solve to ensure continued development and prosperity.

REFERENCES

Baillie, C. (2002). Enhancing creativity in engineering students. *Engineering Science & Education Journal*, **11**(5), 185–192.

Bateman, K. (2013, 18 April). IT students miss out on roles due to lack of creativity. *ComputerWeekly.com*.

Buhl, H. R. (1960). *Creative engineering design*. Iowa City: Iowa State University Press.

Cooper, C., Altman, W., & Garner, A. (2002). *Inventing for business success*. New York: Texere.

Cropley, A. J. (1992). *More ways than one: Fostering creativity*. Norwood, NJ: Ablex Publishing.

Cropley, D. H. (2015). *Creativity in engineering: Novel solutions to complex problems*. San Diego, CA: Academic Press.

Cropley, D. H., & Cropley, A. J. (2005). Engineering creativity: A systems concept of functional creativity. In J. C. Kaufman & J. Baer (Eds.), *Faces of the muse: How people think, work and act creatively in diverse domains* (pp. 169–185). Hillsdale: NJ: Lawrence Erlbaum.

Elliott, C., & Deasley, P. (Eds.). (2007). *Creating systems that work: Principles of engineering systems for the 21st century*. London: The Royal Academy of Engineering.

Fasko, D. (2001). Education and creativity. *Creativity Research Journal,* **13**(3–4), 317–327.

Guilford, J. P. (1950). Creativity. *American Psychologist,* **5**, 444–454.

Iansiti, M. (1993). Real-world R&D: Jumping the product generation gap. *Harvard Business Review,* **71**(3), 138–147.

Karjalainen, T.-M., Koria, M., & Salimaki, M. (2009). *Educating T-shaped design, business and engineering professionals.* Paper presented at the 19th CIRP Design Conference, Cranfield University.

Kazerounian, K., & Foley, S. (2007). Barriers to creativity in engineering education: A study of instructors and students perceptions. *Journal of Mechanical Design,* **129**, 761–768.

Kelley, T., & Littman, J. (2005). *The ten faces of innovation: IDEO's strategies for defeating the devil's advocate and driving creativity throughout your organization.* New York: Doubleday.

Oskam, I. F. (2009). *T-shaped engineers for interdisciplinary innovation: an attractive perspective for young people as well as a must for innovative organisations.* Paper presented at the 37th Annual Conference – Attracting students in Engineering, Rotterdam, The Netherlands.

Sternberg, R. J. (1985). *Beyond IQ: A triarchic theory of human intelligence.* New York: Cambridge University Press.

Sternberg, R. J., & Lubart, T. I. (1995). *Defying the crowd: Cultivating creativity in a culture of conformity.* New York: Free Press.

Sternberg, R. J., & Williams, W. M. (1996). *How to develop student creativity.* Alexandria, VA: Association for Supervision and Curriculum Development.

Tilbury, D., Reid, A., & Podger, D. (2003). *Action research for university staff: Changing curricula and graduate skills towards sustainability, Stage 1 Report.* Canberra: Environment Australia.

CHAPTER 14

Intrinsic Motivation and Creativity in the Classroom
Have We Come Full Circle?

Beth A. Hennessey

Wellesley College

As I organized my ideas in preparation for the writing of the original version of this chapter, I came to realize that my thinking and my research efforts had almost come full circle. Now, half a decade later, that circle is closer than ever before to becoming closed. Almost 35 years ago, I moved to Denver, Colorado, to begin my career as a fledgling teacher. My experiences in my mixed-age classroom filled with five-, six-, and seven-year-olds kindled within me a deep interest in motivation and creativity of performance. My concerns about what our educational system was *not* doing to promote student growth in these areas became so great that I eventually left my elementary classroom to return to school myself. I was convinced that it was the field of psychology, and more specifically the study of the social psychology of creativity, that could best provide the answers I was looking for. As a graduate student and later as a professor of psychology, I have been almost single-minded in my attempts to answer empirically the question of how best to structure classrooms so that they are most conducive to student motivation and creativity. Over the past 40 years, researchers in this area have contributed literally hundreds of investigations to the psychological and educational psychology literatures; for my own part, in the last few years, I have even been bold enough to end a few chapters or monographs with a "laundry list" of what teachers and school administrators should and should not do if student intrinsic motivation and creativity are the goal.

Our research has lead to the establishment of a number of models of the intersection between intrinsic motivation and creativity of performance (Amabile, 1996; Hennessey, 2003; Hennessey & Amabile, 1988), rubrics that are now widely accepted by investigators in the areas of social psychology and related specialties. The so-called Intrinsic Motivation Principle of Creativity (Amabile 1996; Hennessey, 2003) on which much of our work is based has even been the subject of heated professional debate (Eisenberger, 2003; Eisenberger, Armeli, & Pretz, 1998; Eisenberger & Cameron, 1996, 1998; Eisenberger, Pierce, & Cameron, 1999; Hennessey &

Amabile, 1998). While initially disconcerting, I have come to see this argument as the sincerest form of flattery, as only established theories garner sufficient criticism and ire to be considered controversial. In other words, the academic community has sat up and taken notice. We now understand a great deal about the impact of the environment (classroom and workplace) on creative performance. Yet that question that so haunted me as a young teacher – that question as to how our schools may be undermining the creativity and motivation of students – for me looms larger than ever. Our world community faces seemingly intractable crises that can only be met with groundbreaking, yet to be imagined creative solutions. Global warming; AIDS, ebola and the threat of other equally devastating pandemics; poverty; starvation; water shortages; food shortages; tribal, cultural and nationalistic strife – the task of finding answers to these and other equally pressing problems rests on the shoulders of young scientists, researchers, and policy makers – and on the next generation of professionals who will be entering the workforce in the years to come. The promotion of creativity in our schools is now much more than an idealistic nicety or frill. It is essential for our very survival.

But can our laboratory and field study demonstrations as to how to promote creativity be translated into practical educational reforms? What are the applied implications of our work? Over the years, a number of teachers have e-mailed me or approached me at professional conferences or after a presentation I have made to groups of educators or parents to say that our research findings have directly affected the way they think about their own instructional process or the classroom experiences of their children. And practicing teachers continue to contact me to inquire about how they might get a copy of the intrinsic motivation training tapes I used in a series of "immunization" studies published in 1989 and 1993 (Hennessey, Amabile, & Martinage, 1989; Hennessey & Zbikowski, 1993). But for me, the most important question is: What would an entire school filled with classrooms modeled after our research findings look like? Would students' intrinsic motivation and creativity be anywhere near the levels our laboratory-based and field studies would lead us to predict? Especially in this age of accountability and high-stakes testing, would it be possible and practical for teachers to implement our recommendations on a daily basis? If given the freedom to make significant changes in the school day, would faculty, students, and staff be able to sustain an excitement for learning and an atmosphere that promotes creative exploration and performance?

A few researchers focusing on related areas of psychology have, in fact, been able to explore directly similar questions in conjunction with their own scholarship. Howard Gardner's seminal work on Multiple Intelligences (Chen & Gardner, 2005; Gardner, 1983, 1989, 1991, 1993, 1999; Koenhaber & Gardner, 2006), for example, has had a profound impact on educational practice worldwide. Teachers are now almost routinely asking, "*How* are my students smart?" And entire schools have been named for and constructed according to Gardner's now eight-part model of Multiple Intelligences (see, for example, http://howardgardnerschool.com/). Similarly, Fischer and colleagues involved in the so-called Brain and Education Movement (Fischer & Immordino-Yang, 2008; Hanna, 2005; Posner & Rothbart, 2006) have had the opportunity to investigate the real-world implications of their own pioneering studies connecting biology and cognitive science to education in an ever-growing number of what have come to be called "brain-based" schools (see, for example, www.ross.org/about/ philosophy?rc=0 and www.thecountryschool.org/page.cfm?p=961). These schools and other examples like them have been purposefully patterned after the work of investigators in the fields of psychology, neuroscience, and related areas. To the best of my knowledge, my own research and the work of other researchers in the area of the social psychology of creativity has not directly led to the construction of specific curricula or educational approaches. But what has happened is that a small but growing number of schools have independently arrived at virtually the same conclusions we have. Apparently, at least in many cases, without the benefit of our research findings and theorizing, they have come to structure their classrooms and teaching in precisely the ways that our investigations would recommend.

In short, we have available a valuable naturalistic experiment: individual classroom teachers and in some cases entire schools implementing our research recommendations without any risk of experimenter bias or related pitfalls. Before describing a few of these educational programs and their outcomes, it is first important to set the stage with an explanation of the social psychology of creativity – its roots and major contributions to the field.

The Social Psychology of Creativity

Explorations of what has come to be termed the social psychology of creativity were begun in the mid-1970s. Before this time, theoretical and empirical investigations of creativity were almost entirely restricted to questions of the "creative personality" and the individual difference variables that distinguish highly creative persons from the rest of their peers. Gradually, a small group of social psychologists began to focus their research attention on the impact of situational factors on creative performance, and over time, there emerged the dual understanding that our motivational orientation directly affects the creativity of our behavior and that motivation is largely determined by the social environment in which we find ourselves.

Pioneering this new investigative direction were Lepper, Greene, and Nisbett, who in 1973 explored the effect of expected reward on young children's motivation and artistic performance. These researchers selected into their study only preschoolers who displayed an especially high level of intrinsic interest in drawing with magic markers. Children met individually with the experimenter and were randomly assigned to either a constraint or no-constraint condition. Children in the expected reward group were told that if they made a drawing, they would be awarded a "Good Player Certificate." Children in the control/no-reward and unexpected reward groups made their drawings without any expectation of reward. The quality of these products was later assessed, as was the motivational orientation of the preschoolers.

Results revealed that working for an expected "Good Player Award" significantly decreased these preschoolers' interest in and enjoyment of the marker task. When compared with the unexpected reward group and the control (no reward) group, the children who had made drawings for the experimenters in order to receive a Good Player Award spent significantly less time using the markers during subsequent free-play periods than did their nonrewarded peers. Moreover, this undermining of interest persisted for at least a week beyond the initial experimental session. Because Lepper and colleagues had set out to examine the impact of expected reward on task motivation, they had not originally planned to code or systematically examine the overall quality of the pictures produced. But a casual examination of the products made by preschoolers in the two experimental conditions showed what these researchers believed were important between-group differences. A subsequent systematic assessment of the globally assessed "quality" of the drawings confirmed this view. Products produced under expected reward conditions were found to be of significantly lower quality than products made by the unexpected reward or control groups. How was it that this simple, one-time offer of a Good Player Award could serve to undermine the motivation and performance of preschoolers who were passionate about using magic markers? This published paper and research question captured my attention as I wrestled with questions of student motivation and creativity in my own elementary school classroom.

It was 1980, and I was in my second year of what I had thought would be a lengthy teaching career. My classroom served a mixed-age group of five-, six-, and seven-year-olds. The idea was that children would stay with me for three years. I would get to know them very well; they would get to know me; older students would help to "teach" and serve as an example for younger students; and the entire learning experience would be enhanced. My first few years of teaching, although supremely challenging, went fairly smoothly. My students were learning to read and write and manipulate numbers, and parents and administrators were pleased with my accomplishments. But after some time, I found that the same nagging problem kept coming back to worry me. While the children may have been gaining essential skills, what was not developing the way I had hoped was their motivation and creativity. Because I had kindergartners and first and second graders in this one classroom, it was all too apparent that, over time, my kids were actually losing their excitement about learning as well as their willingness to experiment, take risks, and exercise their creativity. Kindergartners arrived at the start of the school year bursting with enthusiasm. They were ready and willing to tackle almost any challenge, and their energy and excitement knew no bounds. They were eager to share wild and fanciful ideas, and their artwork and stories were fantastic. But by the time these same children reached second grade, many had lost their excitement about learning and were reticent to take a chance or try something new. Fairly quickly my worries as a teacher began to shift from issues of neat handwriting or the mastery of multiplication tables and reading fluency to the realization that my students' motivation and creativity were dying right before my eyes. Was it something I was doing? Or was this progression inevitable?[1] I decided that I would not be satisfied until I found the answer to one fundamental question: How can teachers structure their classroom routines and curriculum so as to keep students' motivation and creativity alive?

Initially at least, I was confident that I would find the answers I was looking for. I assumed that there were a number of experts working on this problem. But the more I talked with other teachers and administrators and the more I read, the more discouraged I became. I began to realize

---

[1] My familiarity with the research literature now tells me that I was not the only teacher who observed my students losing motivation and excitement about learning. Working in a variety of settings and using a wide range of measures, a number of investigators have found children's reported intrinsic motivation in school to decrease steadily over time (e.g., Anderman & Maehr, 1994; Harter, 1981; Lepper, Sethi, Dialdin, & Drake, 1997).

that while virtually everyone seemed to think that the promotion of student motivation and creativity was extremely important, no one appeared to have any concrete suggestions as to how teachers could accomplish this goal. Eventually I came across research spearheaded by McGraw and colleagues (McGraw, 1978; McGraw & McCullers, 1979) suggesting that in the classroom, intrinsic motivation is almost always preferable to an extrinsic motivational orientation. I found research evidence showing that intrinsic motivation leads to better problem solving and a deeper level of conceptual understanding and learned that, in the classroom, extrinsic motivation will consistently lead to better performance only on tasks requiring rote recitation, precise performance under strong time pressure, and the completion of familiar, repetitive procedures. Research psychologists and educational experts speculated that school environments fraught with rewards, competition, and frequent evaluation do not offer the best situations for students' overall learning. And the studies I found also suggested that classrooms incorporating these extrinsic constraints might not be the best environments for promoting students' creativity.

Researching further, I soon learned that there were at least a handful of investigators and theorists who were actively pursuing work on the link between motivation and creativity of performance. Unlike the majority of creativity researchers, this group had chosen not to concentrate their efforts on issues of creative personality or process. Instead, they were attempting to take a social psychological approach that focused on the impact of various environmental constraints and motivators placed on students. The same question that I was asking as an elementary school teacher also guided their work: What kind of classroom setting is most conducive to student motivation and creative performance? This research direction was new and exciting, and I was hooked. I left the elementary school classroom and returned to graduate school.

The Picture-Taking Study

A few years later, in 1986, I coauthored a paper (Amabile, Hennessey, Grossman, 1986, Study 1) that outlined what was to become a prototypical paradigm for my own research program. Unlike the Lepper, Green, and Nisbett's (1973) "Magic Marker Study," in this investigation, the reward offered to elementary school children was not a tangible gift to be delivered afterward. Instead, it was an activity – the chance to play with a camera – that was to be completed before engaging in the target experimental task. Importantly, this opportunity to play with a camera had been found in pretesting to be especially exciting and attractive to this group of children. Study participants assigned to the reward condition signed a contract and promised to tell a story later in order to first have a chance to use the camera. Children in the no-reward condition were simply allowed to use the camera and then were presented with the storytelling instructions; there was no contingency established between the two tasks.

To examine the impact of reward contingency on children's verbal creativity, the students in this study were asked to tell a story into a tape recorder to accompany a set of illustrations in a book with no words (see Hennessey & Amabile, 1988). Elementary school teachers familiar with writing done by children in this age group later rated the stories relative to one another on creativity and a variety of other dimensions. A high level of interrater reliability was reached, and results indicated that, overall, stories produced by children in the no-reward condition were judged to be more creative than were stories produced by children in the reward condition. This main effect of reward was, in fact, statistically significant. Importantly, all children taking part in this investigation took pictures with the camera. The only difference in the experience of the rewarded and nonrewarded students in this paradigm was their *perception* of the picture-taking reward as contingent or not contingent on the target storytelling activity.

A Focus on Real-World, Everyday Creativity

In the investigation just described, the creativity of elementary school students was assessed based on their performance on a storytelling task not all that different from other language art activities being carried out in their classroom. Rather than concentrate on creative genius and persons at the forefront of their respective fields, our investigations have always been driven by the belief that every individual has some degree of creative potential, and it is our goal to find ways to help them reach that potential. Toward this end, we do not administer a paper-and-pencil creativity assessment, such as the Torrance Tests of Creative Thinking (Torrance, 1974). Instead, we ask participants in our studies to produce some sort of real-world product. While the Torrance tests and related measures may, in fact, accurately tap one or more creative abilities or predispositions, we believe that a test that captures the full range of creativity components is yet to be developed. Investigators like ourselves have come to rely on the consensual assessment of experts as we set out to determine whether products produced under one set of circumstances are more or less creative than products produced under other, very different conditions.

This Consensual Assessment Technique (CAT) (Amabile, 1982b; Hennessey & Amabile, 1999; Hennessey, Amabile, & Mueller, 2011) is based on the assumption that a panel of independent expert raters, persons who have not had the opportunity to talk with one another or with the researcher about possible hallmarks of product creativity, are best able to make such judgments. Research conducted over the past 30 years has, in fact, clearly established that product creativity can be reliably and validly assessed based on the consensus of experts. Moreover, this approach has proved to be especially well suited to investigations of classroom environmental influences on creativity. Researchers such as myself, who take a social-psychological approach, must control for and, as much as possible, eliminate within-group variability in their dependent measures so that they might detect more global between-group differences produced by their direct experimental manipulations of social and environmental factors. This is clearly a different approach from research into personality variables in which individual differences, not experimental condition differences, are the main focus.

In our investigations, in other words, individual differences constitute error variance. We are not interested in whether a particular child is likely to consistently evidence greater levels of creativity than the majority of her peers. We are interested in creativity not as a relatively enduring and stable *trait*, but as the result of a fleeting and delicate motivational *state,* a state very much influenced by environmental factors such as the presence or absence of reward. What we need is a measurement tool that deemphasizes individual differences between study participants, and this measure must also allow for considerable flexibility and novelty of response without depending heavily on the level of a child's skills or the range of her experience. The CAT fills each of these criteria.

Our elementary school teacher-raters in the 1986 (Amabile, Hennessey, & Grossman, 1986, Study 1) investigation did not know one another, and they were not permitted to confer with one another before or during the rating process. Using 7-point scales and guided only by their own, subjective definitions of creativity, these judges were asked to rate the transcripts of the stories relative to one another rather than against some abstract norm. As has almost always been the case in our research program, in this investigation, interrater reliability for story creativity was high, and a sum of the ratings made by our three judges was computed for each product. Finally, these calculations were then used as the dependent measure of product creativity in the remainder of the analyses.

"Killers" of Creativity

Like the investigation just described, the majority of early studies designed to explore the impact of environmental constraints on motivation and performance were focused on the effects of expected reward (e.g., Deci, 1971, 1972; Garbarino, 1975; Greene & Lepper, 1974; Kernoodle-Loveland & Olley, 1979; Kruglanski, Friedman, & Zeevi, 1971; Lepper, Greene, & Nisbett, 1973; McGraw & McCullers, 1979; Pittman, Emery, & Boggiano, 1982; Shapira, 1976). In more recent years, experimental approaches have become increasingly complex, but the basic findings have remained the same. Hundreds of published investigations reveal that the promise of a reward made contingent on task engagement often serves to undermine intrinsic task motivation and qualitative aspects of performance, including creativity (for a more complete review of the literature, see Amabile, 1996; Hennessey, 2000; Hennessey & Amabile, 1988). This effect is so robust that it has been found to occur across the entire life span, with preschoolers and seasoned professionals experiencing the same negative consequences.

Investigators have also expanded their scope to uncover the deleterious impact of a variety of other environmental constraints, such as deadlines, surveillance, and competition (e.g., Amabile, 1982a; Amabile, Goldfarb, & Brackfield, 1990). And there is a good deal of research evidence to show that the expectation that one's work will be judged by others may well be the most deleterious extrinsic constraint of all. Perhaps because situations of evaluation often combine aspects of each of the other "killers" of motivation and creativity, the promise of an evaluation has been shown to undermine severely the task interest and performance of individuals from all walks of life, from preschoolers to professionals whose very livelihood depends on the creativity of their work.

As is the case with the reward literature, studies of the impact of expected evaluation have also become increasingly fine-tuned over the years. Researchers now have a much more sophisticated understanding of evaluation effects and are quick to point out that not all evaluative contingencies can be expected to have the same deleterious consequences. Theorists now understand that the type of task presented to study participants can, in large part, drive their experimental results; and recent studies reveal that under certain specific conditions, both the delivery of a competence-affirming evaluation and the expectation of an impending evaluation can sometimes increase levels of extrinsic motivation without having any negative impact on intrinsic motivation or performance. In fact, some forms of evaluation expectation can actually enhance creativity of performance. These complex effects of expected evaluation are reviewed in several comprehensive publications (e.g., Harackiewicz, Abrahams, & Wageman, 1987; Jussim, Soffin, & Brown, 1992).

The Intrinsic Motivation Principle of Creativity

Studies from this research tradition as just outlined distinguish between two types of motivation. Intrinsic motivation is the motivation to do something for its own sake, for the sheer pleasure and enjoyment of the task itself. Extrinsic motivation, on the other hand, is the motivation to do something for some external goal. More than 30 years of exploration into the role played by motivational orientation in the creative process have led my colleagues and me to the Intrinsic Motivation Principle of Creativity – intrinsic motivation is conducive to creativity, and extrinsic motivation is usually detrimental (Amabile, 1983, 1996). In its earlier incarnations, this proposed relation between motivational orientation and creativity of performance was advanced as a tentative research hypothesis. But investigators working within this tradition have now gathered so much unequivocal research evidence, that this proposition has been elevated to the status of an undisputed principle. Importantly, while the work of Eisenberger (1996), Cameron and Pierce (1994) and a handful of other behaviorally trained psychologists (e.g., Eisenberger, 2003; Eisenberger, Armeli, & Prezt, 1998; Eisenberger & Cameron, 1998; Eisenberger, Pierce, & Cameron, 1999) appears to demonstrate that the promise of a reward can, under very specific conditions, have either no impact or even a positive impact on task interest and qualitative aspects of performance, the fact remains that for the majority of persons in the majority of circumstances, intrinsic motivation and creativity are bound to suffer in the face of an expected reward (see Hennessey, 2000, 2002, 2003; Hennessey & Amabile, 1998).

The Rest of the Story – The Creative Intersection

The Intrinsic Motivation Principle of Creativity and investigations like the Magic Marker and Picture-Taking studies described earlier focus on the individual's motivational orientation and its impact on creative performance. But intrinsic motivation is not the only essential ingredient for creative behavior. Amabile and colleagues, myself included, have long argued that it is a mistake to stop at the individual level of analysis – the person doing the creating (see Amabile, 1996; Hennessey, 2003; Hennessey & Amabile, 1988). And, in fact, even the additional attention paid

The individual brings to an
open-ended task or problem
three essential elements ...

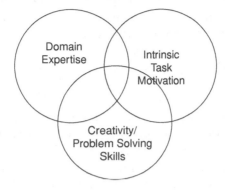

Figure 14.1 The Creative Intersection

by social psychologists to aspects of the environment that may impact motivational orientation does not tell the whole story. In our work, we emphasize the fact that the confluence of a variety of environmental and person variables is necessary for creativity. More formally, our research is built on a three-part conceptualization of creative performance. For a creative solution to be found or a creative idea or product to be generated, an individual must approach a problem with the appropriate *domain skills* (background knowledge and expertise in a given discipline or area), *creativity skills* (willingness to take risks, experiment, play with idea), and *task motivation*. Under ideal circumstances, the coming together of these three factors forms what Amabile (1997) terms the "creative intersection."

From the perspective of a teacher hoping to promote her students' creativity, the motivational component of this componential model can prove to be the most problematic. It is certainly possible to provide students with domain skills such as facility with a paintbrush or knowledge of chemistry, physics, or engineering. In fact, most educators would argue that this is what school is all about. And even creativity skills, such as the ability to "think outside the box," brainstorm ideas, or temporarily suspend judgment, are taught in some schools and corporate environments. Motivational orientation, on the other hand, is much more ephemeral. In other words, while creativity skills or domain skills may be fairly stable, motivational state is highly variable and largely situation dependent. Each of us finds some activities more interesting or enjoyable than we do others.

No one approaches every task with the same degree of excitement; to a large degree, our level of enthusiasm and task commitment is determined by the specific circumstances in which we find ourselves. If the classroom environment or the overall atmosphere of a school is not conducive to intrinsic motivation, then all the domain knowledge and creativity skills in the world will not make up for this detriment.

Recipe for the Typical American Classroom

Expected reward, expected evaluation, competition, deadlines, surveillance – this list of killers of intrinsic motivation reads very much like the blueprint for the typical American school. I know that when I was setting up my own elementary-level classroom, I built into the school day a wide variety of rewards and incentives, some subtle and some not so subtle. Charts bearing gold, silver, and blue stars next to children's names lined my classroom walls. Students who completed high-quality work before the deadline were rewarded with extra recess time, and everyone hoped that their short story, poem, or most recent artwork would be chosen as one of the "best" to be displayed on the bulletin board in the hall. My intentions were good. I was trying my best to boost the children's motivation by loading on the incentives. But now, more than three decades later, I know better.

What I and other researchers have come to learn is that most of us are not all that in touch with our own motivations. We do not always know why it is that we do the things we do. Almost as if we were outside observers of our own actions, we seem to use essentially the same rubrics for explaining our own behaviors as we do for explaining why others behave in the ways that they do. In situations where both a plausible internal and a plausible external (intrinsic and extrinsic) cause of behavior are present, we tend to *discount* the internal cause in favor of the external cause. For example, a preschooler in the Magic Marker study (Lepper et al., 1973) thinks to herself: "I must be making this picture not because it's fun and I love using markers but because this man has told me that I will get a Good Player Award."

When multiple explanations for their behavior are available, young and old alike have been found to discount their own intrinsic interest in favor of a purely external explanation for task engagement. Researching motivation in the 1970s, one group of social psychologists came to refer to this process as the "discounting principle" (e.g., Kelley, 1973). Other theorists proposed a related explanation termed the "overjustification" hypothesis, a formulation derived from the attribution theories of Bem (1972), Kelley (1967, 1973), and deCharms (1968). According to this model, when a behavior is overjustified (when there exists both a possible internal and external cause for one's own or another's behavior), each of us will tend to overlook the internal cause (the presence of intrinsic task motivation) in favor of the external cause (a reward or evaluation was at stake). In effect, we discount the excess justification for explaining why we did something.

Offering a similar but more contemporary and nuanced view, Deci and Ryan (1985a, 1985b) have attempted to expand on these formulations with a consideration of individual differences. The focus of their theorizing is on causality orientations, or characteristic ways that each of us develops for understanding and orienting to inputs. More specifically, they hypothesize that individuals vary in the degree to which they exhibit three such orientations ("autonomy," "control," and "impersonal"), and they argue that these individual differences have important implications for a variety of motivationally involved processes, including creativity. At the core of what they term their Self-Determination Theory (SDT) (Ryan & Deci, 2000a, 2000b) is the consideration of innate psychological needs and the degree to which persons are able to satisfy these basic needs as they pursue and attain their valued goals. Within this SDT framework, extrinsic motivation is not seen as the simple absence of intrinsic motivation. Instead, motivational orientation is viewed as a highly complicated and multilayered continuum.

In short, when teachers promise their students a reward or impose some other form of extrinsic constraint in the classroom, they set into motion a complex sequence of events that run the risk of doing far more harm than good. It is easy to understand why teachers (as well as parents and managers in the workplace) are drawn to rewards and other controlling systems of evaluation and behavioral control. Extrinsic incentives really do help ensure that work will get done and that it will be completed on time. If every task required of students were straightforward and algorithmic – with one "right" answer and one best, most straightforward path to solution – extrinsic incentives would make sense. The difficulty, of course, is that much of the work that teachers assign calls for open-ended approaches to problems, far-reaching thinking, a willingness to take risks, and deep stores of intrinsic motivation and excitement about learning that will allow students to persist with challenging tasks.

The impact of expected reward, expected evaluation, and competition on task interest and creativity of performance is significant and complicated. And research shows that teachers would be advised to avoid the use of these constraints as they set out to motivate their students and help them work to their full potential. But what are educators to do? Most teachers, no matter how committed they might be to promoting their students' intrinsic motivation, creativity, and excitement about learning, find themselves stewards of a system that makes this goal of reducing, and maybe even eliminating, extrinsic constraints virtually impossible to reach. For a wide variety of reasons, some intentional and other accidents of history, we have somehow managed to structure educational environments in such a way that intrinsic motivation and creativity are bound to suffer, if not be completely destroyed. The all-important question that needs to be addressed is how this situation can be turned around. One solution would be for educators at all levels, preschool through university, to eliminate from their classrooms all task-contingent rewards, competitive elements, and controlling systems of evaluation. But old habits die hard, and it is clear these fundamental changes in the way that students are taught will not come easily. In fact, in this age of high-stakes testing, teacher accountability, and national "one size fits all" educational mandates like No Child Left Behind and the more recent Common Core, such reforms may literally be impossible.

The work of Seymour Sarason speaks eloquently to this problem of effecting change within the schools; in fact, Sarason's seminal book on this subject is titled *The Culture of School and the Problem of Change* (Sarason 1971, revised 1996). In his research and theorizing, Sarason demonstrates how long-standing educational structures and practices, both at the institutional level and within individual classrooms, stifle reform efforts. The notion that students must be *controlled* via grades, rewards, and other extrinsic constraints is endemic to the school culture. Moreover, Sarason points out that reasoned arguments for the abandonment of these control systems have been met in the past and will continue to be met with strong protests from various groups (classroom teachers, administrators, unions) who believe they must defend their power.

Sarason (1996) doubts whether the unilateral definition and exercise of power are desirable for the development of children, and he argues that the sense of powerlessness that schools engender in students frequently breeds reductions in task interest and excitement about learning. Apparently, one need not be a researcher interested in creativity to be struck by the fact that our schools are fraught with killers of motivation. Yet in his research, Sarason repeatedly found that it had never occurred to the majority of teachers (or administrators) to question the rules and practices that govern this country's classrooms. Were he to poll teachers in 2016, he might well find that the situation has changed. There is a growing movement in this country among teachers and administrators to question and fight against what many professionals have come to believe is the abuse of standardized testing (and children). National organizations like FairTest (see www.fairtest.org/arn/caseagainst.html) are partnering with teachers' associations as well as parent and student groups to call for a broad reexamination of state and federal educational policies. Organizers in Seattle, Chicago, Toledo, New York City, Long Island, New Mexico, and beyond have staged massive boycotts of high-stakes tests, and teachers have refused to administer particularly flawed and punitive exams.

Fortunately for our nation's children, Sarason's concerns are now being echoed by others. Committed visionaries like Jesse Hagopian (see http://iamaneducator.com/2015/05/05/resistance-to-high-stakes-tests -serves-the-cause-of-equity-in-education-a-reply-to-we-oppose-anti -testing-efforts/) work tirelessly to make their message heard: Schools should and must exist to serve students, not bureaucrats and politicians. Yet the external pressure on students (and teachers) to perform according to standards is immense. The gulf between what students are interested in and the ways they best learn and what their teachers are told they must teach and how they must teach is growing ever wider, and it must be bridged. Perhaps the time will come when curricular reforms imposed from afar, "teaching to the test," and high-stakes evaluations are things of the past. Until that day, a less desirable but certainly more feasible alternative to transforming classroom practice would be to change the way students react to situations of competition or to the promise of an upcoming reward or evaluation.

The Immunization Studies

In a series of three related investigations, my colleagues and I set out to study whether creativity and motivation might be maintained even in the face of competition or expected reward. In our design of these experiments we were guided by a medical metaphor. We decided to look at extrinsic constraints as a kind of germ or virus and wondered whether it might be possible to "immunize" children against their usually negative effects on intrinsic motivation and creativity. Again drawing on a biological analogy, our goal was twofold: (1) to strengthen intrinsic motivation and (2) to provide antibodies (techniques) for fighting the negative effects of extrinsic motivation.

In the first of these research attempts (Hennessey, Amabile, & Martinage, 1989, Study 1), elementary school students (ages 7 to 11 years) were randomly assigned to intrinsic motivation focus or control groups and met with an experimenter over two consecutive days for the purpose of viewing videos and engaging in directed discussion. The tapes shown to students in the intrinsic motivation focus condition depicted two 11-year-olds talking with an adult about various aspects of their schoolwork. Scripts for this condition were constructed so as to help children focus on the intrinsically interesting, fun, and playful aspects of a task. Ways to make even the most routine assignment exciting were suggested, and participants were helped to distance themselves from socially imposed extrinsic constraints such as rewards or situations of competition. Tapes shown to students in the control condition featured the same two young actors talking about some of their favorite things, including foods, music groups, movies, and seasons.

Following this training procedure, all students met individually with a second adult for testing. As in the previous study described earlier in the chapter, half the children in each of the training conditions were told that they could take two pictures with an instant camera only if they promised to tell a story later for the experimenter. For children in the no-reward conditions, this picture-taking was presented simply as the first in a series of "things to do." In this 2 × 2 factorial design, presentation of reward was crossed with type of training received. It was expected that only those participants who had been specifically instructed in ways to overcome the usual deleterious effects of extrinsic constraints would maintain baseline levels of intrinsic motivation and creativity in situations of expected reward (i.e., they would be immunized against the negative effects of extrinsic constraints). The data from this initial investigation not only confirmed these expectations but gave us reason to believe that our intervention had much more of an impact than we had expected. Intrinsic motivation-trained children tended to report higher levels of intrinsic motivation on a paper-and-pencil assessment than did children in the control (no-training) condition; in addition, we found that the offer of reward actually augmented the creativity of the trained group. This additive effect of intrinsic and extrinsic motivation was quite robust. In fact, the creativity of children who received intrinsic motivation training and expected a reward was significantly higher than that of any other design group.

In our initial discussion of these immunization study results, we conjectured that children who entered the creativity testing situation after having undergone intrinsic motivation training would have a much more acute awareness of their own intrinsic interest in school-type tasks. Thus, the reward may have served to heighten their already positive feelings about the tasks they were doing. In an effort to test these hypotheses, two follow-up investigations of our intrinsic motivation focus techniques (Hennessey, Amabile, & Martinage, 1989, Study 2; Hennessey & Zbikowski, 1993) were subsequently carried out. Each was designed as a conceptual replication of Study 1. Essentially the same experimental design was used, and it was again the children who had received immunization training and who were expecting a reward who produced the most creative products. Yet, in these subsequent two studies, the effect of training was far less dramatic. Taken together, the results of Studies 2 and 3 indicate that we cannot expect that children exposed to our intrinsic motivation training and offered a reward for their performance will demonstrate unusually high levels of creativity. Nevertheless, we can expect that these children will be able to maintain baseline levels of intrinsic motivation and creativity under reward conditions.

What is it about our immunization procedures that allow students to maintain their creativity even when they expect a reward? It appears that our efforts to help them learn to deemphasize the importance of extrinsic incentives and concentrate instead on their own intrinsic interest and task enjoyment paid off. Even in the face of reward, the children were able to maintain a positive, intrinsically motivated approach. They brought to our experimental tasks a playfulness and a willingness to take risks that many researchers believe are crucial to creativity (Amabile, 1983, 1996; Barron, 1968; Campbell, 1960; Crutchfield, 1962; Dansky & Silverman 1975; Lieberman, 1965; Stein, 1974).

Evidence from nonexperimental studies coupled with observations of and interviews with artists and other persons who rely on their creativity for their life's work echo our "immunization" results. While all of the "killers" of motivation and creativity that have been isolated experimentally have also been found to be detrimental in the "real world" of work, these negative effects have not proved to be universal. For some people, certain extrinsic motivators have been shown to have either no effects or even a positive effect on task interest and creativity of performance. For example, in a study of commissioned and noncommissioned works done by professional artists, the extrinsic incentive of a commission was seen by some artists as a highly controlling constraint, and the creativity of their work plummeted. Yet for those who looked at the commission as an opportunity to achieve recognition or a confirmation of their competence by respected others, creativity was enhanced (Amabile, Phillips, & Collins, 1994).

How can these individual differences be explained? Our data on these professional artists and the children taking part in our immunization studies parallel nicely earlier work exploring the relevance of self-perception processes to the overjustification effect. In a 1981 investigation carried out by Fazio, the negative impact of expected reward was also mitigated in young children for whom initial intrinsic interest in the target activity had been made salient. In other words, it may not be the expectation of reward per se that undermines intrinsic motivation; rather, it may be the individual's interpretation of that reward and his or her role in the reward process that in large part determines whether task motivation will be undermined, enhanced, or remain unchanged.

Trickle Down

In the 35 years that I have been engaged in the research process, I have spoken with thousands of parents, classroom teachers, and school administrators about the undeniable link between intrinsic motivation and creativity of performance and the killers of motivation that are intentionally and routinely built into the school day. My audiences, most especially the teachers, nod their heads in agreement as I outline the seriously negative impact of reward systems and a variety of other extrinsic constraints. They know in their heart of hearts that the research findings I present make sense, but they feel overwhelmed by the prospect of trying to fight an educational system entrenched in tradition and driven by the notion that "if it was good enough for me and my peers, it's good enough for this next generation."

The major impetus behind the immunization studies was, in fact, the overwhelming and paralyzing sense of hopelessness that so many classroom teachers have expressed to me over the years. In my experience as a researcher, it has always been far easier to demonstrate how to kill intrinsic motivation and creativity than it has been to show how motivation and creative behavior might be maintained or even promoted. Intrinsic motivation is an especially delicate and fleeting entity. But I was tired of presenting such a negative message, tired of telling teachers and administrators what they were doing wrong. The immunization research allowed me to offer a concrete list of changes that did not necessitate sweeping curricular or policy reform – changes that teachers interested in preserving the intrinsic motivation and creativity of students could implement in their own classrooms. It has now been more than two decades since the first intrinsic motivation training study results were published. In the past 20 years, I have spoken to numerous educational groups and have heard from a number of teachers about their successful implementation of immunization techniques in their own classrooms. The effectiveness of our admittedly amateurish research videotapes and follow-up scripted conversations conducted by an unfamiliar adult cannot begin to compare to the positive impact of naturalistic teacher-driven discussions built into the school day, conversations about ways students might put grades or test scores into perspective and think less about competing with peers and more about what really interests and excites them.

Recipe for Classroom Reform

In consideration of our research findings, what exactly would a classroom designed to promote student motivation and creativity look like? In my talks with educators and my more recent publications, I have offered a number of practical suggestions for change. For example, a monograph written as part of the NAEG Senior Scholar Series (Hennessey, 2004) concludes with the following suggested steps:

- Teachers must work diligently to create an interpersonal atmosphere that allows students to feel in control of their learning process.
- Students should be helped to feel like "origins" rather than "pawns." In other words, the classroom should be a place in which student behavior is self-determined. There is no room in the classroom for intimidation or coercion.
- Teachers and administrators must step back and critically review the incentive systems that are currently in place.
- When presenting lessons and subject matter that are inherently interesting to students, teachers should work to use tangible rewards as little as possible; they also must avoid setting up situations that encourage students to compare their progress to that of others in the classroom. Performance on in-class and statewide "high stakes" tests must not be driven by a sense of competition, and teachers must work to deemphasize the extrinsic incentives built into the myriad of citywide, statewide, or nationwide competitions available to students.
- In situations where extrinsic incentives are in place, students must be helped to distance themselves from those constraints as much as possible.
- We must remember that each of us will be most creative when we enjoy what we are doing. Every effort should be made to encourage

students to take risks, to experiment, and to have fun with projects and assignments. Students must be given the opportunity to take pride in what they have already accomplished and to dream of what lies ahead. And at all times, teacher evaluation and surveillance of student work must be kept to a minimum.

• Students must be helped to become more proficient at recognizing their own strengths and weaknesses.

All students, including the most gifted and talented children, must be helped to identify the subject areas that give them the most pleasure and ignite their passion. Since the publication of the results of our own three attempts at immunization, intrinsic motivation training (Hennessey, Amabile, & Martinage, 1989; Hennessey & Zbikowski, 1993), a small number of research psychologists as well as practicing classroom teachers have experimented with our immunization techniques and replicated our results (e.g., Gerrard, Poteat, & Ironsmith, 1996). These investigators have consistently underscored the unexpected benefits accrued to students who are explicitly asked to consider and talk about their favorite subjects and activities in school.

Intrinsic motivation must be made a regular focus of class discussion because when left to their own devices, students engage in such conversations far too infrequently. Students must be helped to recognize their own excitement for learning. Rather than relying on the feedback of teachers, they must be taught to monitor their own progress; and, whenever possible, they must be given choices about what they will do and how they will accomplish their goals. They must be encouraged to become active, independent learners, confident in their ability to take control of their own learning process.

Real-World Applications

These are the data-driven recommendations coming from academe. But what exactly would an actual classroom (or an entire school) that has been built on this rubric look like? In many respects, our research findings call for a return to the open classroom model. The "open" terminology has traditionally been used to describe a student-centered classroom design made popular in the United States in the 1970s. This educational innovation originated in the British public elementary ("infant") schools after World War II and spread slowly to the United States. American educators visiting Great Britain's primary schools during the late 1960s encountered classrooms where informal, unstructured approaches dominated both the teaching and learning process. They were struck by what they saw and came away convinced that open classrooms were the answer to our own nation's education ills. For more than a decade, U.S. schools had been attacked from all sides and blamed for producing only unimaginative and unmotivated students who lacked the scientific and other skills necessary to win the Cold War or tackle the growing challenges posed by the civil rights movement and other sweeping societal changes.

The fundamental building block of the American open classroom of the 1970s was individualized, hands-on learning, and this approach gave new hope to critics who had long argued that America's formal, teacher-dominated classrooms were crushing students' creativity. Rather than present one-size-fits-all lessons, teachers trained in open classroom techniques were encouraged to abandon detailed, preestablished whole-class lesson plans in favor of an ever-changing and entirely flexible curriculum tailor-made to build on the strengths and interests of each individual child. In the classic open classroom environment, students moved freely and at their own pace from "station" to "station" – exploring reading skills, hands-on science experiments, mathematical manipulatives, and art materials.

My own teacher training took place at the Shady Hill School in Cambridge, Massachusetts. Shady Hill was, in fact, the first U.S. school to adopt the British Infant model. I was well versed, or so I thought, in every aspect of the open classroom approach, and the "Integrated Day" environment (another buzzword of the 1970s) that I constructed when I took my first teaching position in Denver certainly *looked* like the classrooms portrayed in C. E. Silberman's extremely influential and powerful 1973 book, *The Open Classroom Reader*. What I did not understand at that time was that a classroom, not to mention an entire educational philosophy, is much, much more than its physical layout or daily routines.

Unfortunately, like many other American teachers and administrators who set out to duplicate the highly successful British educational innovation, I concentrated almost entirely on the *visible* hallmarks of the open classroom approach. Instead of individual desks for students and teacher, my classroom was populated by a series of workstations offering a wide variety of materials with which children were invited to engage. In a constant flow of activity, my kindergarten and first- and second-grade students traveled either alone or in small, often multi-age groups from space to space – enlisting, when necessary, my help or the help of my co-teacher. I was taught to view my role as more similar to that of a coach or a facilitator than a traditional teacher. Like many other schools across the country, over time, my own school's quest for openness was even extended to the physical layout of the building itself. An architectural firm was brought in to design "a school without walls," with the idea that children and their teachers needed freedom from the constraints of an arbitrarily restrictive and isolating age-graded system.

Ironically, it was in this open environment, this classroom that I had created for the express purpose of boosting children's confidence, building on their interests and promoting their creativity, that my concerns about what teachers, myself included, were doing to kill student motivation and creativity took root. Like many other "open" educators across the country, I had failed to see the forest for the trees. I had become almost entirely caught up in the physical trappings and other unique aspects of the open classroom approach. I rightfully took pride in the fact that even my youngest students had become masters at making a contract about how they would spend their time and following through with their plan. They learned how to work together, teach one another, negotiate disagreements, and solve interpersonal problems. They learned how to read, write, and manipulate numbers, and along the way they also built some amazing marble chutes and gained some sophisticated understandings about the development of a chick embryo, the ecology of a sea-island farm, and how the rotation of our planet impacts the change of seasons.

According to the yardsticks of standardized testing, administrative approval, or parental satisfaction, my open classroom was a resounding success. What I came to realize over time, however, is that I failed to drive home the most fundamental lessons of all – lessons about the importance of finding joy in learning, of taking intellectual risks, of identifying and then following one's passions, and of being driven by genuine curiosity rather than the promise of reward, the threat of evaluation, or the fear of making mistakes in front of one's peers. And I was not alone in these failings. As more and more districts moved toward the schools-without-walls approach, a growing number of educational theorists began to worry that America's attempt at open education had missed the mark. As Silberman warned as early as 1973,

> Creating large open spaces does not, by itself, constitute open education. Replacing desks and chairs with "interest areas" does not, by itself constitute open education. Filling the interest areas with concrete materials that children can manipulate and use does not, by itself, constitute open education. Individualizing instruction does not, by itself, constitute open education. All these techniques, it should be emphasized, can be useful, and some may be essential, in creating and running an open classroom. Technique

is important; without a mastery of technique, all the understanding in the world can leave a teacher helpless when he or she comes face to face with thirty or forty children. But method alone, without serious, sustained, and systematic thought about education, will turn a teacher into a mere technician with a bag of sterile tricks. No technique should be used unless a teacher has thought about why it is being used, what he or she hopes to accomplish with it, and how it will affect the children in question. (Silberman, 1973, p. xxi)

For my own part, I left elementary education in 1981 to pursue graduate study, in an attempt to figure out once and for all how to construct classrooms that would boost student motivation and creativity. Over time, many other educators and entire school systems also came to question and eventually move away from the open classroom approach, with the result that today in the United States, open classrooms are fairly unusual. Classrooms that are physically open have become a rarity, as the majority of schools "without walls" have long ago constructed permanent partitions in an attempt to control noise and reduce distractions. This return to a more traditional school space, this architectural backlash, has been accompanied by a nationwide call for the abandonment of student-centered learning and a return to more traditional teacher-centered approaches, standards-based curricula, and test-based accountability.

A review of the development of American public education across the last 200 years reveals that sweeping changes in educational policy and theorizing, such as the open classroom movement, have taken hold on a number of occasions. Throughout U.S. history, educational decision making has tended to mirror the social and political trends of the time. But was the open education movement in the United States just another misguided and fleeting fancy – a by-product of the "flower child" generation or dissatisfaction with the Vietnam War? To discount open classrooms as merely another ideological fad would negate the deeper message of the Open Education Movement. Children really do learn best when they are genuinely interested in and see the importance of what they are doing, and their creativity is dependent on this intrinsic interest as well. Educators did not get things exactly right in the 1970s. But their message rings as true today as it did some three or four decades ago.

The Importance of Intrinsic Motivation for Long-Lasting Learning

As outlined earlier, intrinsic motivation is described in the literature as the motivation to do something for its own sake – for the sheer pleasure and enjoyment of the task itself rather than for some external goal. Malone and Lepper (1987) define *intrinsic motivation* simply as "what people will do without external inducement." While almost every educator (and student) would prefer that their classroom be filled with engaged and happy learners, the importance of intrinsic motivation for learning and creativity reaches far beyond affective considerations. Researchers have demonstrated that an intrinsically motivated state is characterized by deeply focused attention, enhanced cognitive functioning, and increased and persistent activity (Alexander & Murphy, 1994; Maehr & Meyer, 1997). Simply stated, intrinsic motivation leads to deeper, longer-lasting learning.

Empirical data supporting this contention come from a variety of sources. As early as 1913, Dewey identified the link between student interest or curiosity and effort expended in the classroom, and in 1967, Simon empirically demonstrated that learners driven by intrinsic motivation and curiosity try harder and exert consistent effort to reach their learning goals. Several studies found in the reading literature demonstrate that personally interesting text segments and passages written on high-interest topics facilitate children's, as well as college students', comprehension, inferencing, and retention. For example, Guthrie, Wigfield, Metsala, and Cox (1999) reported that intrinsically motivated young readers read more and showed significantly higher levels of reading comprehension and recall than did students who were not excited by or engaged in the reading process. In addition to increasing the amount of recall, student interest also seems to have a substantial effect on the quality of learning. In a variety of investigations, interest has also been reported to lead to more elaborate and deeper processing of texts. In 2000, McDaniel, Waddill, Finstad, and Bourg found that readers asked to engage with uninteresting narratives focused on individual text elements, such as extracting proposition-specific content, whereas readers of interesting texts tended to engage in organizational processing of information. This research suggests that student interest (or lack of interest) in the text being read may affect the degree to which processing strategies benefit memory performance.

Corroborating these findings, Conti, Amabile, and Pollak (1995) reported that college students who approached a learning task with intrinsic motivation demonstrated superior long-term retention of information compared to their extrinsically motivated peers. A large number of related investigations also demonstrate that when students approach new concepts with high levels of curiosity and interest, information is better learned and remembered (e.g., Flink, Boggiano, & Main, 1992; Gottfried, 1985, 1990; Harter & Jackson, 1992; Hidi, 1990; Lepper & Cordova, 1992;

Malone, 1981; Malone & Lepper, 1987; Renninger, Hidi, & Krapp, 1992; Schank, 1979; Tobias, 1994). Moreover, when students are given a choice of problems to be solved or learning and performance goals to be reached, intrinsically motivated learners are likely to take risks and explore solutions to problems that represent for them a moderate level of difficulty and challenge. Extrinsically motivated students, on the other hand, will tend to choose the easiest possible problems (Condry & Chambers, 1978; Harter, 1978; Pittman, Emery, & Boggiano, 1982).

A variety of explanations have been offered for this well-documented link between intrinsic motivation and deep, long-lasting learning. Students who are intrinsically motivated have been found to put more effort into studying and use deeper, more logical, efficient, and effective strategies (Condry & Chambers, 1978; Nolen, 1988). Some theorists argue that the harnessing of student interest and curiosity serves to activate learners' prior knowledge, which in turn allows them to make better connections with new material (Alexander, Kulikowich, & Jetton, 1994; Brophy, 1999; Deci, 1992; Thomas & Oldfather, 1997). And another prominent cognitively based view (Malone & Lepper, 1987) explains the link between intrinsic motivation and learning with a "spreading interest" model of curiosity. According to this formulation, people will be interested in new material to the extent that it relates to other topics that are already of interest to them. In other words, intrinsic task motivation may fan out along links between nodes of differing interest values, much like the process suggested by "spreading activation" theories of memory (Collins & Loftus, 1975).

Others point to the intensity and prolonged duration of intrinsically motivated learning activities (Pintrich, Roeser, & de Groot, 1994; Vollmeyer & Rheinberg, 2000). Csikzentmihalyi's (1993, 1997) studies of the phenomenon he calls "flow" echo this emphasis. Csikzentmihalyi used the term "flow" because in his earliest investigations, several persons described their experience as being carried along by a current. Since that time, research reveals that nearly all individuals occasionally reach an intensely intrinsically motivated and pleasurable state of "optimal experience." While in flow, one's sense of time becomes distorted and all feelings of self-consciousness slip away. For the majority of persons, flow is not an everyday occurrence, and some persons experience it more than others. But when flow does come, it is characterized by feelings of intense concentration and enjoyment... feelings that transport the individual into a new reality to "previously undreamed-of states of consciousness" (Csikszentmihalyi, 1990, p. 74).

What's a Teacher to Do?

Clearly, intrinsic motivation is a crucial ingredient both for students' deep, long-lasting learning and for the creativity of their performance. In terms of the practical, classroom-based implications of the intrinsic motivation research just reviewed, teachers would do well to capitalize on students' existing interests as they construct lesson plans and present new material. In addition, as outlined earlier, there is a great deal of empirical data to suggest that extrinsic constraints such as expected reward, expected evaluation, and restricted choice should be avoided whenever possible.

Combining these two investigative areas, research conducted by Cordova and Lepper (1996) argues for the construction of classroom situations that allow for the provision of student choice coupled with the contextualization and personalization of lessons. Individualized or small-group instruction tailored to build on students' existing areas of interest and incorporating elements of choice in terms of what to learn and how to learn lead not only to increased levels of intrinsic motivation in students but also to deeper levels of engagement in learning and increased amounts of material learned in a fixed time period. Does this mean that schools wishing to promote students' intrinsic motivation and creativity of performance must return to the open classroom approach? And would such a return even be possible in this age of budget cuts, high-stakes testing, Common Core legislation, and accountability? All across this country, decision making in schools is now dominated by the political rhetoric of corporate-based, standards-based changes. While the intentions of many policy makers and the wealthy philanthropists funding their reforms may be good, their mandates are based on the unproved and arguably faulty assumption that "stack ranking" of teachers, standardized instruction, and standardized tests will serve to raise intellectual standards and student achievement. More than any other time in our nation's history, teachers and administrators find that both their own job security and their schools' very survival are dependent on student test scores. Deep-seated, meaningful educational reform would appear to be an impossibility in this climate. And yet a small but growing number of schools at the elementary and secondary levels have set out to do just that – to rethink the teaching/learning process and devise what appears to be a workable and highly successful solution to the dilemma faced by educators wishing to combine individualized and personalized instruction with increasing assessment and other requirements mandated at the state and national levels.

Spearheading this movement is a core group of educators and theorists committed to integrated curricula, performance-based assessments (as opposed to standardized tests), and smaller schools. One of the more vocal and visible leaders in this initiative is teacher, activist, and noted educational reformer Deborah Meier, who helped orchestrate groundbreaking changes first at New York's Central Park East (CPE) Schools and later in Boston at the Mission Hill School. The founding of the first CPE school came in 1974, just as the open classroom movement was falling into disfavor and being blamed for the failings of the nation's teachers to educate our children. For more than 35 years, educational reforms at Meier's schools in Harlem and Boston have taken shape to construct a learning environment designed to explore specific reproducible ways of redesigning classroom life and curricula so as to promote individualized instruction and student excitement about learning. Although I doubt that they are aware of research carried out by myself and my colleagues, teachers, and students at CPE and Mission Hill have, in fact, incorporated many of the recommendations we make in our monographs, chapters, and empirical journal articles.

In the city of Boston, right in my own backyard, there is a full-scale naturalistic experiment being carried out. Unbiased by the literature or expectations that classroom data will support university laboratory findings, Mission Hill teachers, children, and parents are testing the conclusions made by psychologists like myself as to how teachers can promote student intrinsic motivation and creativity in the classroom. In sharp contrast to my own lament that "old habits die hard," teachers and parents at Mission Hill demonstrate a true optimism about the possibility of making fundamental and dramatic changes in the ways schools operate, teachers teach, and children learn. One of 27 pilot schools in the Boston Public School System, Mission Hill serves approximately 250 urban students in grades K through 8. This intentionally small school employs one principal, twelve lead teachers, and a variety of support staff. Children learn in multi-age groups of no more than 20 students and typically spend two years with the same lead teacher. Mission Hill classrooms are a combination of art gallery, museum, library, and scientific laboratory. Activities at all grade levels reflect the current school-wide curriculum theme, which changes each trimester. One trimester is dedicated to life or physical sciences and technology. A second trimester focuses on the study of an ancient civilization, how people lived long ago and the legacies we owe to the past. The third trimester explores U.S. history and the struggle for justice in America. Themes are presented over a four-year rotation, with children in kindergarten through third grade getting initial exposure to these topics and then revisiting them again in fourth grade through seventh grade. Eighth-grade students study the effects of media in society and prepare for their portfolio requirements necessary for graduation.

The majority of classrooms at all levels start and end each day with student-led meetings designed to set the classroom agenda and evaluate progress. Most work is done either individually or in small groups, and about half the day is devoted to thematic work, which can incorporate reading, writing, research, mathematical computation, art, or the engineering of constructions. Mission Hill teachers use a variety of methods to gage student progress in acquiring knowledge, skills, and the habits of work and mind. Every day, they make written observations about children's progress. They observe and carefully document both evidence of growth and sticking points and use these notes to guide their plans for the type of individualized instruction that will come next. Students too have many opportunities to voice their own ideas about and evaluations of themselves as learners. These include journal entries, conversations with peers and teachers, and more formal interviews. Tests and quizzes are also a part of the assessment process, but they are heavily supplemented by portfolios and other methods (e.g., research papers, school-wide presentations, and "on demand" essays) devised to give children an opportunity to showcase their accomplishments. The portfolio approach long championed by the late Theodore Sizer and others affiliated with the Coalition of Essential Schools rests on the belief that less is more. Depth is emphasized over coverage, as students learn to probe deeply and stretch their capabilities. Seventh and eighth graders present portfolios of their work to committees composed of teachers and community experts in their area of study; and in their final eighth-grade year, as part of Mission Hill's competency-based graduation requirements, students are expected to prepare and present tangible demonstrations of their knowledge and skills in literature, science, art, and mathematics.

Because it is a public school in the city of Boston, Mission Hill has for a few years now been required to administer the Massachusetts Comprehensive Assessment System (MCAS) to all students in grade three and above. As described by Knoester in his 2012 book, *Democratic Education in Practice: Inside the Mission Hill School,* when under the direction of founder Deborah Meier, fewer than 40% of Mission Hill families opted for their children to take standardized tests (Knoestner, 2012). But when No Child Left Behind legislation came on the scene, the Boston Public School system threatened serious repercussions for schools that did not make so-called Adequate Yearly Progress (AYP). That AYP measure necessitated that at least 95% of Mission Hill's students be tested. Testing at Mission Hill is now the norm rather than the exception. In school year 2014–15, the English language arts and mathematics portions of the MCAS were replaced by the computer-based PARCC testing system aligned to the Common Core.

While it is clear that the "Mission Hill School staff believes that these test scores are given too much legitimacy and carry far too much weight" (Knoester, 2012, p. 109), teachers now include test preparation in the curriculum, explicitly instructing students how to interpret testing language, how to budget test-taking time, and how to "think like a testmaker" (Knoester, 2012, p. 118). Mission Hill teachers work hard to ensure that students are gaining the skills and knowledge necessary to perform well on these assessments, but at the same time they are diligent about maintaining a range of alternative, authentic objective measures such as biannual tape-recorded reading interviews, scored samples of student writing, and one-on-one math interviews.

The challenges faced by educators at Mission Hill, and any school serving an especially diverse, low-income student body, are many. Generally speaking, standardized test scores earned by Mission Hill students are uneven, although at times higher than BPS averages (Knoester, 2012). What these numbers fail to reveal is the important, deep learning that is taking place at the school and the toll that high-stakes testing has taken on teachers and students. Knoester (2012) describes how, once test scores began to be publically reported, they became an inevitable focal point for parents and staff. Teachers continue to struggle with the question of how to help students improve their scores without changing all the things that Mission Hill already does so well. Mission Hill is adamant about not giving up its core values or compromising those values. As one parent recently explained, Mission Hill exists within a context that, in large part, is hostile to the school's core mission. "The whole culture is about hierarchy and Mission Hill is all about antihierarchy" (Knoester, 2012, p. 118).

At issue is whether Mission Hill and other progressive schools committed to challenging students' curiosity and promoting their creativity can stay true to their core beliefs with the current emphasis on standards-based assessments. As the school's founder Deborah Meir (1995) explains, high-stakes testing mandates that material be broken down into a series of discrete skills (to be tested) and makes it unlikely, if not impossible, that teachers will spend their time and effort introducing strong conceptual subject matter which will challenge students to become fully engaged. In the view of noted learning theorist Eleanor Duckworth, our schools are preventing students from the "having of wonderful ideas" (Duckworth, 1996). Multiple-choice tests are no substitute for authentic and meaningful performance.

Everything Old Is New Again

In many respects, the concerns that drove me out of my Integrated Day classroom are the same concerns that prompted Meier to establish her groundbreaking schools in Harlem and Boston. As I watched my students lose their creativity and intrinsic motivation as they moved from kindergarten through second grade, I wrestled with the question of how to keep alive children's playfulness, willingness to take intellectual risks, and excitement about learning. Meier (1995) also talks about the importance of keeping the spirit of kindergarten alive – of constructing school environments that allow students of all ages to become as deeply involved and absorbed in their "work" as kindergarteners are in their "play." Under the present U.S. public education system, teachers are expected to work diligently to wean students *away* from their natural tendency to play with objects and ideas. In the eyes of mainstream contemporary educators, books and standardized exams must replace the student-driven learning approach offered to kindergarteners if older students are to excel and reap maximal benefits from the teaching and learning process. As they move through the grades, students are given less and less control over their own learning. Open-ended curricula and opportunities for discovery are replaced with artificial 45-minute periods offering one-size-fits-all lessons driving home the messages that learning is a passive activity and that knowledge really can and should be divided into neatly packaged units. Courses in science, mathematics, language arts, social studies, and history are presented in isolation, and rarely, if ever, are attempts made to meld these disciplines. Yet it does not have to be this way. Even middle school and high school students can benefit enormously from the discovery-based integrated learning techniques we have come to reserve only for the kindergarten classroom.

A large body of recent research shows, in fact, that hands-on, open-ended learning that allows for true engagement with the curriculum significantly boosts both the interest and performance of older students (Marks, 2000; Mitchell, 1993; Shernoff, Csikszentmihalyi, Schneider, & Shernoff, 2003; Shernoff & Hoogstra, 2001; Shernoff, Knauth, & Makris, 2000; Shernoff, Schneider, & Csikszentmihalyi, 2001; Stipek, 1996; Yair, 2000). As

Meier (1995) rightly points out, "expertise in early childhood development is a good foundation for starting a school for adolescents" (p. 47).

So what has changed? How is it that I abandoned my own attempts at teaching in an environment dedicated to students' hands-on exploration and the integration of subject matter only to come back years later to a research program that calls for a revival of the "open" education approach? What I, along with a growing group of other researchers and teachers at schools like Mission Hill, now realize is that a classroom is much more than its physical trappings. The substitution of learning stations for desks is all well and good, but what is fundamentally important is that attention be paid to students' motivational orientation. Teachers and their students must remain mindful of the fundamental purpose behind education and of what it means to be an active, engaged, and self-determined learner. And schools and the curricula they offer must be constructed in such a way that the development and maintenance of this mindfulness is possible. Students and teachers at all grade levels must engage in frequent directed and explicit discussion about issues of motivation and the pressures that come with testing and other evaluative or competitive educational trappings. While it would be wrong to assume that there is only one right way, one single path that must be taken to accomplish this goal, it would also be a mistake to assume that the habits of mind practiced at Mission Hill and a handful of other sites across the country are out of the reach of most schools in this nation.

Yes, intrinsic motivation and creativity have been driven out of the majority of U.S. classrooms with the imposition of ever-increasing curricular standards, high-stakes testing, Common Core legislation, and other accountability mandates. But careful experimental investigation coupled with real-world application of research findings in classroom settings demonstrate that it *is* still possible for teachers who value creativity to nurture students' creative development and expression without drifting into curricular and assessment chaos. In short, the myriad constraints faced by today's teachers need not lead to choosing conformity over creativity or extrinsic motivation over intrinsic motivation. Educational reform has never been and never will be easy. But reform *is* possible. Reform *is* happening. And reform *is* essential. One recent iteration of the small school, individualized education approach comes in the form of AltSchool, a growing consortium of schools in the San Francisco area that has recently expanded to Palo Alto, CA, Brooklyn, NY and the East Village. AltSchool, the brainchild of a team of entrepreneurs, educators, and technologists, bills itself as "a technology-driven network of micro-schools that offers a new, radically personalized experience" (www.altschool.com/). Is the AltSchool approach, in fact, all that new or radical? Perhaps not. Instead, like Mission Hill, AltSchool is working to recapture the atmosphere of the 1960s' open class-room. Like Mission Hill, AltSchool works with partners in the community to offer students a holistic educational experience that takes advantage of the knowledge and talents of professionals and experts. Everything old is new again. Yet AltSchool is unique in that it is based on a for-profit model and its founders are working to develop and market a variety of techno-logical innovations, including "Playlist" – a tablet-driven, personalized set of weekly activities for each student to complete.

Will profit motives and a strong emphasis on technology prove compat-ible with the visions of Meier, Duckworth, Dewey, Piaget, and those who came before? Only time will tell. The future of AltSchool and other sim-ilar initiatives is uncertain. What is certain, however, is that our children deserve far more than the instruction mandated by Common Core. The time is now to harness the growing discontent of teachers, parents, and students from around the country to effect change.

REFERENCES

Alexander, P. A., Kulikowich, J. M., & Jetton, T. L. (1994). The role of subject matter knowledge and interest in the processing of linear and non-linear texts. *Review of Educational Research*, **64**, 201–252.

Alexander, P. A., & Murphy, P. K. (1994, April). The research base for APA's learner-centered principles. Presented at the annual meeting of the American Educational Research Association, New Orleans, LA.

Amabile, T. M. (1982a). Children's artistic creativity: Detrimental effects of compe-tition in a field setting. *Personality and Social Psychology Bulletin*, **8**, 573–578.

Amabile, T. M. (1982b). Social psychology of creativity: A consensual assessment technique. *Journal of Personality and Social Psychology*, **43**, 997–1013.

Amabile, T. M. (1983). *The social psychology of creativity*. New York: Springer-Verlag.

Amabile, T. M. (1996). *Creativity in context*. Boulder, CO: Westview.

Amabile, T. M. (1997). Motivating creativity in organizations: On doing what you love and loving what you do. *California Management Review*, **40**, 39–58.

Amabile, T. M., Goldfarb, P., & Brackfield, S. C. (1990). Social influences on creativity: Evaluation, coaction and surveillance. *Creativity Research Journal*, **3**, 6–21.

Amabile, T. M., Hennessey, B. A., & Grossman, B. (1986). Social influences on creativity: The effects of contracted-for reward. *Journal of Personality and Social Psychology*, **50**, 14–23.

Amabile, T. M., Phillips, E. D., & Collins, M. A. (1994). *Creativity by con-tract: Social influences on the creativity of professional artists*. Unpublished manuscript, Brandeis University.

Anderman, E. M., & Maehr, M. L. (1994). Motivation and schooling in the middle grades. *Review of Educational Research,* **64**, 287–309.

Barron, F. (1968). *Creativity and personal freedom.* New York: Van Nostrand.

Bem, D. (1972). Self-perception theory. In L. Berkowitz (Ed.), *Advances in experimental social psychology* (Vol. 6, pp. 1–62). New York: Academic Press.

Brophy, J. (1999). Toward a model of the value aspects of motivation in education: Developing appreciation for particular learning domains and activities. *Educational Psychologist,* 34, 75–85.

Cameron, J., & Pierce, W. D. (1994). Reinforcement, reward, and intrinsic motivation: A meta-analysis. *Review of Educational Research,* **64**, 363–423.

Campbell, D. (1960). Blind variation and selective retention in creative thought as in other knowledge processes. *Psychological Review,* **67**, 380–400.

Chen, J.-O., & Gardner, H. (2005). Assessment based on Multiple-Intelligences Theory. In D. P. Flanagan & P. L. Harrison (Eds.), *Contemporary intellectual assessment: Theories, tests, and issues* (pp. 77–102). New York: Guilford.

Collins, A. M., & Loftus, E. F. (1975). A spreading-activation theory of semantic processing. *Psychological Review,* **82**, 407–428.

Condry, J., & Chambers, J. (1978). Intrinsic motivation and the process of learning. In M. R. Lepper & D. Greene (Eds.), *The hidden costs of reward* (pp. 61–84). Hillsdale, NJ: Lawrence Erlbaum.

Conti, R., Amabile, T. M., & Pollak, S. (1995). The positive impact of creative activity: Effects of creative task engagement and motivational focus on college students' learning. *Personality and Social Psychology Bulletin,* **21**, 1107–1116.

Cordova, D. L., & Lepper, M. R. (1996). Intrinsic motivation and the process of learning: Beneficial effects of contextualization, personalization and choice. *Journal of Educational Psychology,* **88**, 715–730.

Crutchfield, R. (1962). Conformity and creative thinking. In H. Gruber, G. Terrell, & M. Wertheimer (Eds.), *Contemporary approaches to creative thinking* (pp. 120–140). New York: Atherton Press.

Csikszentmihalyi, M. (1990). The domain of creativity. In M. Runco & A. S. Robert (Eds.), *Theories of creativity* (pp. 190–212). Thousand Oaks, CA: Sage.

Csikszentmihalyi, M. (1993). *Flow.* New York: Harper Collins.

Csikszentmihalyi, M. (1997). *Creativity: Flow and the psychology of discovery and invention.* New York: HarperCollins.

Dansky, J., & Silverman, I. (1975). Play: A general facilitator of fluency. *Developmental Psychology,* **11**, 104.

deCharms, R. (1968). *Personal causation.* New York: Academic Press.

Deci, E. L. (1971). Effects of externally mediated rewards on intrinsic motivation. *Journal of Personality and Social Psychology,* **18**, 105–115.

Deci, E. L. (1972). The effects of contingent and noncontingent rewards and controls on intrinsic motivation. *Organizational Behavior and Human Performance,* **8**, 217–229.

Deci, E. L. (1992). The relation of interest to the motivation of behavior: A self-determination theory perspective. In K. A. Renninger, S. Hidi, & A. Krapp

(Eds.), *The role of interest in learning and development* (pp. 43–70). Hillsdale, NJ: Lawrence Erlbaum.

Deci, E. L., & Ryan, R. M. (1985a). The general causality orientations scale: Self-determination in personality. *Journal of Personality and Social Psychology*, **19**, 109–134.

Deci, E. L., & Ryan, R. M. (1985b). *Intrinsic motivation and self-determination in human behavior*. New York: Plenum.

Dewey, J. (1913). *Interest and effort in education*. Boston: Houghton Mifflin.

Duckworth, E. (1996). *"The having of wonderful ideas" and other essays on teaching and learning*. New York: Teachers College Press.

Eisenberger, R. (1996). Reward, intrinsic interest and creativity: New findings. *American Psychologist*, **53**, 676–679.

Eisenberger, R. (2003). Rewards, intrinsic motivation and creativity: A case study of conceptual and methodological isolation. *Creativity Research Journal*, **15**, 121–130.

Eisenberger, R., Armeli, S., & Pretz, J. (1998). Can the promise of reward increase creativity? *Journal of Personality and Social Psychology*, **74**, 704–714.

Eisenberger, R., & Cameron, J. (1996). Detrimental effects of reward: Reality or myth? *American Psychologist*, **51**, 1153–1166.

Eisenberger, R., & Cameron, J. (1998). Reward, intrinsic interest, and creativity: New findings. *American Psychologist*, **53**, 676–679.

Eisenberger, R., Pierce, W. D., & Cameron, J. (1999). Effects of reward on intrinsic motivation – Negative, neutral, and positive: Comment on Deci, Koestner, and Ryan. *Psychological Bulletin*, **125**, 677–691.

Fazio, R. H. (1981). On the self-perception explanation of the overjustification effect: The role of salience of initial attitude. *Journal of Experimental Social Psychology*, **17**, 417–426.

Fischer, K. W., & Immordino-Yang, M. H. (2008). The fundamental importance of the brain and learning for education. In *The Jossey-Bass reader on the brain and learning* (pp. xvii–xi). San Francisco: Jossey-Bass.

Flink, C., Boggiano, A. K., & Main, D. S. (1992). Children's achievement-related behaviors: The role of extrinsic and intrinsic motivational orientations. In A. K. Boggiano, & T. S. Pittman (Eds.), *Achievement and motivation: A social-developmental perspective* (pp. 189–214). New York: Cambridge University Press.

Garbarino, J. (1975). The impact of anticipated reward upon cross-age tutoring. *Journal of Personality and Social Psychology*, **32**, 421–428.

Gardner, H. (1989). *To open minds: Chinese clues to the dilemma of contemporary education*. New York: Basic Books.

Gardner, H. (1991). *The unschooled mind: How children think and how schools should teach*. New York: Basic Books.

Gardner, H. (1993 [1983]). *Frames of mind: The theory of multiple intelligences*. New York: Basic Books.

Gardner, H. (1999). *Intelligence reframed: Multiple intelligences for the 21st century*. New York: Basic Books.

Gerrard, L. E., Poteat, G. M., & Ironsmith, M. (1996). Promoting children's creativity: Effects of competition, self-esteem, and immunization. *Creativity Research Journal*, **9**, 339–346.

Gottfried, A. E. (1985). Academic intrinsic motivation in elementary and junior high school children. *Journal of Educational Psychology*, **77**, 631–645.

Gottfried, A. E. (1990). Academic intrinsic motivation in young elementary children. *Journal of Educational Psychology*, **82**, 525–538.

Greene, D., & Lepper, M. R. (1974). Intrinsic motivation: How to turn play into work. *Psychology Today*, **8**, 49–54.

Guthrie, J. T., Wigfield, A., Metsala, J. L., & Cox, K. E. (1999). Motivational and cognitive predictors of text comprehension and reading amount. *Scientific Studies of Reading*, **3**, 231–256.

Hanna, J. (2005). Mind, brain, & education: Linking biology, neuroscience, & educational practice. *Harvard Graduate School of Education News* (June 1). Retrieved May 12, 2008 from www.gse.harvard.edunewsfeaturesmbe06012005.html.

Harackiewic, J. M., Abrahams, S., & Wageman, R. (1987). Performance evaluation and intrinsic motivation: The effects of evaluative focus, rewards, and achievement orientation. *Journal of Personality and Social Psychology*, **53**, 1015–1023.

Harter, S. (1978). Effectance motivation reconsidered: Toward a developmental model. *Human Development*, 1, 34–64.

Harter, S. (1981). A new self-report scale of intrinsic versus extrinsic orientation in the classroom: Motivational and informational components. *Developmental Psychology*, **17**, 300–312.

Harter, S., & Jackson, B. K. (1992). Trait vs. nontrait conceptualizations of intrinsic-extrinsic motivational orientation. *Motivation and Emotion*, **16**, 209–230.

Hennessey, B. A. (2000). Rewards and creativity. In C. Sansone & J. Harackiewicz (Eds.), *Intrinsic and extrinsic motivation: The search for optimal motivation and performance* (pp. 55–78). New York: Academic Press.

Hennessey, B. A. (2002). The social psychology of creativity in the schools. *Research in the Schools*, **9**, 23–33.

Hennessey, B. A. (2003). The social psychology of creativity. *Scandinavian Journal of Educational Psychology*, **47**, 253–271.

Hennessey, B. A. (2004). *Developing creativity in gifted children: The central importance of motivation and classroom climate (RM04202)*. The National Research Center on the Gifted and Talented Senior Scholar Series. Storrs, CT: NRCGT, University of Connecticut.

Hennessey, B. A., & Amabile, T. M. (1988). The conditions of creativity. In R. Sternberg (Ed.), *The nature of creativity* (pp. 11–38). New York: Cambridge University Press.

Hennessey, B. A., & Amabile, T. M. (1998). Reward, intrinsic motivation, and creativity. *American Psychologist*, **53**, 674–675.

Hennessey, B. A., & Amabile, T. M. (1999). Consensual assessment. In M. Runco & S. Pritzker (Eds.), *Encyclopedia of creativity* (pp. 347–359). New York: Academic Press.

Hennessey, B. A., Amabile, T. M., & Martinage, M. (1989). Immunizing children against the negative effects of reward. *Contemporary Educational Psychology*, **14**, 212–227.

Hennessey, B. A., Amabile, T. M., & Mueller J. S. (2011). Consensual assessment. In M. A. Runco & S. R. Pritzker (Eds.), *Encyclopedia of creativity* (2nd ed., Vol. 1, pp. 253–260). San Diego, CA: Academic Press.

Hennessey, B. A., & Zbikowski, S. M. (1993). Immunizing children against the negative effects of reward: A further examination of intrinsic motivation training techniques. *Creativity Research Journal*, **6**, 297–307.

Hidi, S. (1990). Interest and its contribution as a mental resource for learning. *Review of Educational Research*, **60**, 549–571.

Jussim, L., Soffin, S., & Brown, R. (1992). Understanding reactions to feedback by integrating ideas from symbolic interactionism and cognitive evaluation theory. *Journal of Personality and Social Psychology*, **62**, 402–421.

Kelley, H. (1967). Attribution theory in social psychology. In D. Levine (Ed.), *Nebraska symposium on motivation*, Vol. 15. Lincoln: University of Nebraska Press.

Kelley, H. (1973). The processes of causal attribution. *American Psychologist*, **28**, 107–128.

Kernoodle-Loveland, K., & Olley, J. G. (1979). The effect of external reward on interest and quality of task performance in children of high and low intrinsic motivation. *Child Development*, **50**, 1207–1210.

Knoestner, M. (2012). *Democratic education in practice: Inside the Mission Hill School.* New York: Teachers College Press.

Kornhaber, M. L., & Gardner, H. (2006). Multiple intelligences: Developments in implementation and theory. In M. A. Constas & R. J. Sternberg (Eds.), *Translating theory and research into educational practice: Developments in content domains, large-scale reform, and intellectual capacity* (pp. 255–276). Mahwah, NJ: Erlbaum.

Kruglanski, A. W., Friedman, I., & Zeevi, G. (1971). The effects of extrinsic incentive on some qualitative aspects of task performance. *Journal of Personality*, **39**, 606–617.

Lepper, M. R., & Cordova, D. I. (1992). A desire to be taught: Instructional consequences of intrinsic motivation. *Motivation and Emotion*, **16**, 187–208.

Lepper, M. R., Greene, D., & Nisbett, R. E. (1973). Undermining children's intrinsic interest with extrinsic rewards: A test of the overjustification hypothesis. *Journal of Personality and Social Psychology*, **28**, 129–137.

Lepper, M. R., Sethi, S., Dialdin, D., & Drake, M. (1997). Intrinsic and extrinsic motivation: A developmental perspective. In S. S. Luthar, J. Burack, D. Cicchetti, & J. R. Weisz (Eds.), *Developmental psychopathology: Perspectives on adjustment, risk and disorder* (pp. 23–50). New York: Cambridge University Press.

Lieberman, J. N. (1965). Playfulness and divergent thinking: An investigation of their relationship at the kindergarten level. *Journal of Genetic Psychology,* **107**, 219–224.

Maehr, M. L., & Meyer, H. A. (1997). Understanding motivation and schooling: Where we've been, where we are, and where we need to go. *Educational Psychology Review,* **9**, 371–409.

Malone, T. W. (1981). Toward a theory of intrinsically motivating instruction. *Cognitive Science,* **4**, 333–369.

Malone, T. W., & Lepper, M. R. (1987). Making learning fun: A taxonomy of intrinsic motivations for learning. In R. E. Snow & M. J. Farr (Eds.), *Aptitude, learning and instruction: III. Cognitive and affective process analyses* (pp. 223–253). Hillsdale, NJ: Erlbaum.

Marks, H. M. (2000). Student engagement in instructional activity: Patterns in the elementary, middle and high school years. *American Educational Research Journal,* **37**, 153–184.

McDaniel, M. A., Finstad, K., Waddill, P. J., & Bourg, T. (2000). The effects of text-based interest on attention and recall. *Journal of Educational Psychology,* **92**, 492–502.

McGraw, K. O. (1978). The detrimental effects of reward on performance: A literature review and a prediction model. In M. Lepper & D. Greene (Eds.), *The hidden costs of reward* (pp. 33–60). Hillsdale, NJ: Erlbaum.

McGraw, K. O., & McCullers, J. (1979). Evidence of a detrimental effect of extrinsic incentives on breaking a mental set. *Journal of Experimental Social Psychology,* **15**, 285–294.

Meier, D. (1995). *The power of their ideas: Lessons for America from a small school in Harlem.* Boston: Beacon Press.

Meier, D. (2002). *In schools we trust: Creating communities of learning in an era of testing and standardization.* Boston: Beacon Press.

Mitchell, M. (1993). Situational interest: Its multifaceted structure in the secondary school mathematics classroom. *Journal of Educational Psychology,* **85**, 424–436.

Nolen, S. B. (1988). Reasons for studying: Motivational orientations and study strategies. *Cognition and Instruction,* **5**, 269–287.

Pintrich, P. R., Roeser, R., & de Groot, E. (1994). Classroom and individual differences in early adolescents' motivation and self-regulated learning. *Journal of Early Adolescence,* **14**, 139–161.

Pittman, T. S., Emery, J., & Boggiano, A. K. (1982). Intrinsic and extrinsic motivational orientations: Reward-induced changes in preference for complexity. *Journal of Personality and Social Psychology,* **42**, 789–797.

Posner, M., & Rothbart, M. K. (2006). *Educating the human brain.* Washington, DC: American Psychological Association.

Renninger, K. A., Hidi, S., & Krapp, A. (1992). *The role of interest in learning and development.* Hillsdale, NJ: Erlbaum.

Ryan, R. M., & Deci, E. L. (2000a). Self-determination theory and the facilitation of intrinsic motivation, social development, and well-being. *American-Psychologist,* **55**, 68–78.

Ryan, R. M., & Deci, E. L. (2000b). When rewards compete with nature: The undermining of intrinsic motivation and self-regulation. In C. Sansone & J. M. Harackiewicz (Eds), *Intrinsic and extrinsic motivation: The search for optimal motivation and performance* (pp. 13–54). San Diego, CA: Academic.

Sarason, S. (1971, revised 1996). *Revisiting "The Culture of School and the Problem of Change."* New York: Teachers College Press.

Sarason, S. (1996). Power relationships in the classroom. In R. L. Fried (Ed.), *The skeptical visionary: A Seymour Sarason education reader* (pp. 46–57). Philadelphia: Temple University Press.

Schank, R. C. (1979). Interestingness: Controlling inferences. *Artificial Intelligence,* **12,** 273–297.

Shapira, Z. (1976). Expectancy determinants of intrinsically motivated behavior. *Journal of Personality and Social Psychology,* **34,** 1235–1244.

Shernoff, D. J., Csikszentmihalyi, M., Schneider, B., & Shernoff, E. S. (2003). Student engagement in high school classrooms from the perspective of flow theory. *School Psychology Quarterly,* **18,** 158–176.

Shernoff, D. J., & Hoogstra, L. (2001). Continuing motivation beyond the high school classroom. *New Directions in Child and Adolescent Development,* **93,** 73–87.

Shernoff, D. J., Knauth, S., & Makris, E. (2000). The quality of classroom experiences. In M. Csikszentmihalyi & B. Schneider (Eds.), *Becoming adult* (pp. 122–145). New York: Basic Books.

Shernoff, D. J., Schneider, B., & Csikszentmihalyi, M. (2001). Assessing multiple influences on student engagement in high school classrooms. Presented at the Annual Meeting of the American Educational Research Association, Seattle, WA.

Silberman, C. E. (Ed.). (1973). *The open classroom reader.* New York: Vintage.

Simon, H. A. (1967). Motivational and emotional controls of cognition. *Psychological Review,* **74,** 29–39.

Stein, M. I. (1974). *Stimulating creativity* (Vols. 1 and 2). New York: Academic Press.

Stipek, D. J. (1996). Motivation and instruction. In D. C. Berliner & R. Calfee (Eds.), *Handbook of educational psychology* (pp. 85–113). New York: Simon & Schuster Macmillan.

Thomas, S., & Oldfather, P. (1997). Intrinsic motivations, literacy, and assessment practices: "That's my grade. That's me." *Educational Psychologist,* **32,** 107–123.

Tobias, S. (1994). Interest, prior knowledge and learning. *Review of Educational Research,* **64,** 37–54.

Torrance, E. P. (1974). *Torrance Tests of Creative Thinking.* Bensenville, IL: Scholastic Testing Service.

Vollmeyer, R., & Rheinberg, F. (2000). Does motivation affect performance via persistence? *Learning and Instruction,* **10,** 293–309.

Yair, G. (2000). Educational battlefields in America: The tug-of-war over students' engagement with instruction. *Sociology of Education,* **73,** 247–269.

CHAPTER 15

Learning for Creativity

R. Keith Sawyer

Most educators believe that creativity and the arts should be an important part of the school day. But the arts have been struggling to hold their place in the curriculum. The No Child Left Behind Act, with its mandatory annual testing on math and reading, has increased pressure on schools to demonstrate that their students are proficient in math and reading. Low math and reading scores in some school districts have led to an increasing emphasis on teaching these basic skills. When these pressures are combined with tight budgets, as is often the case in districts with high percentages of underprivileged students, administrators often choose to dedicate a larger percentage of the budget to math and literacy instruction. In exchange, the amount invested in arts education is reduced or removed completely.

It is ironic that the arts are losing their place in school curricula at the same time that creativity is increasingly in demand around the globe. In the last several decades many of the world's most developed countries have shifted from an industrial economy to a knowledge economy (e.g., Bell, 1973; Drucker, 1993). Scholars of the knowledge age have argued that creativity, innovation, and ingenuity are today more important than ever before. Florida (2002) argued that "we now have an economy powered by human creativity" (pp. 5–6) and that human creativity is "the defining feature of economic life" (p. 21). Several best-selling books have extended Florida's argument to the international arena. Dan Pink, in *A Whole New Mind* (2005), argued that any activity that does not involve creativity will someday be automated; ultimately, the only jobs remaining will be those requiring creativity. Tom Friedman, in *The World is Flat* (2005), argued that creativity is becoming increasingly important due to increasing global competitiveness. And Tony Wagner, in *Creating Innovators* (2012), argued that schools need to change to better educate young people to become innovators.

Early in this new century, educators began to realize that if the economy was no longer an industrial-age factory economy, then our schools were designed for a quickly vanishing world (Bereiter, 2002; Hargreaves, 2003; Sawyer, 2006b). To determine how schools should respond, many major governmental and international bodies commissioned research efforts that resulted in reports containing policy recommendations; these reports include the OECD's *Innovation in the Knowledge Economy: Implications for Education and Learning* (2004), and two high-profile 2005 reports in the United States (Business Roundtable, 2005; Council on Competitiveness, 2005). These reports, and many others, recommended transforming education to emphasize innovation. (The Council on Competitiveness report led directly to the America Competes Act of 2007, with bills introduced into both houses of Congress; the bill never became law.)

Why are schools reducing their investments in arts education, at the same time that creativity and innovation are more important than ever? In conversations with colleagues, I have discovered that there are two widespread explanations for this paradox – one is depressing and one is hopeful. I think the depressing explanation is incorrect, and I side with the hopeful explanation.

The Depressing Explanation: Schools as Bureaucratic Institutions

The depressing explanation is that schools as institutions are fundamentally incapable of incorporating innovation. There is a long tradition in the sociology of education of arguing that schools function as institutions that reproduce the social order; the social order does not really want innovative graduates, because they might use their innovation to challenge the social order. Creative thinking might be desirable within the ruling elites, but not among the working classes. This neo-Marxist critique, common in the sociology of education in the 1960s and 1970s, emphasizes institutional structures such as tracking – arguing that the ultimate function of tracking is to reproduce social class. This critique has also emphasized the unwritten or informal curriculum – the subconscious and often unexamined actions taken by teachers, and the interaction patterns that become established in classrooms – and has concluded that these aspects of schools function to reproduce power structures. The logic of these largely leftist scholars is that knowledge is power; thus, those in power would attempt to preserve their knowledge advantage and deliver no more education to the masses than is absolutely necessary for them to fulfill their role at the bottom of the economic order.

I don't think the depressing explanation is tenable anymore, given the rising chorus of business and government leaders calling for more creativity and innovation. The Marxist arguments increasingly sound dated, like a distant echo from an earlier time – a time when we were still an industrial economy. The chorus of high-profile reports emanating from business leaders and government leaders makes it clear that they genuinely believe that the pressures of global competitiveness require all U.S. citizens to realize their full potential, and that no country can be successful if substantial segments of the population are poorly educated and thereby incapable of playing a role in the creative age.

I accept one component of the depressing explanation: I believe that schools as institutions are organizationally structured in ways that block the spread of innovation. In most sectors of the economy, organizations have transformed away from a Weberian bureaucracy toward flatter organizational structures, with looser relationships among organizational units; the terms used by management scholars are "organic" or "loosely coupled" or "agile." Apart from government agencies, schools are the only large human institutions that still have an industrial-era structure. This structure blocks innovation, and I believe that schools will have to be redesigned organizationally before education will become more creative (see Sawyer, 2006b).

Although assessment has always been a central component of schools as modern institutions, one effect of No Child Left Behind has been an increasing use of assessments to measure student, teacher, and institutional performance. I support accountability in general, but the tests in use today are largely focused on the assessment of superficial knowledge rather than the deeper conceptual understanding that supports innovative performance. As long as schools and teachers are held accountable to industrial-age tests, they will find it difficult to shift away from industrial-age teaching methods and begin to educate for innovation. The common core state standards are a step in the right direction, because they place greater emphasis on deeper conceptual understanding and 21st-century skills. But I believe we can do better: here I argue that we need to develop new and fundamentally different assessments before creativity will be fully integrated into the curriculum.

The Hopeful Explanation: Transforming Schools Based on Learning Sciences Research

Just because the arts are disappearing from the curriculum does not mean that creativity is disappearing too. What schools ultimately need is for creativity to be spread throughout the curriculum. Math, science, literacy – the learning sciences are providing research showing how all subjects could be taught to foster innovation. If creativity were introduced throughout the curriculum, the arts would no longer stand out as the one time during the school day when creativity were welcomed and fostered. Our schools are not there yet, but learning sciences research is pointing the way toward a new type of learning environment, one that helps learners master deeper conceptual understanding, problem solving, and critical thinking.

Many advocates of arts education implicitly assume that classroom instruction in other subjects follows a traditional model that I call *instructionism* (following Papert, 1993). Creativity is rarely found in instructionist classrooms, and as a result, arts educators have been able to argue that only in arts classes do students have an opportunity to be creative. This model of classroom instruction, which emerged late in the 19th century, is based on commonsense assumptions:

- Knowledge is a collection of *facts* about the world and *procedures* for how to solve problems. Facts are statements like "The earth is tilted on its axis by 23.45 degrees," and procedures are step-by-step instructions like how to do multi-digit addition by carrying to the next column.
- The goal of schooling is to get these facts and procedures into the student's head. People are considered to be educated when they possess a large collection of these facts and procedures.
- Teachers know these facts and procedures, and their job is to transmit them to students.
- Simpler facts and procedures should be learned first, followed by progressively more complex facts and procedures. The definitions of "simplicity" and "complexity" and the proper sequencing of material were determined either by teachers, by textbook authors, or by asking expert adults like mathematicians, scientists, or historians – not by studying how children actually learn.
- The way to determine the success of schooling is to test students to see how many of these facts and procedures they have acquired.

Because this traditional vision of schooling has been taken for granted for so long, it has not been explicitly named until recently. Within the OECD/CERI program "Alternative Models of Learning" project, this traditional model is referred to as *the standard model*. Along with other learning scientists, I refer to the traditional model as instructionism, because it assumes that the core activity of the classroom is instruction by the teacher.

Other education researchers have called this a *transmission and acquisition* model of schooling (e.g., Rogoff, 1990), because it emphasizes that a knowledgeable teacher transmits knowledge, and a learner then acquires that knowledge.

Instructionist schools were designed to prepare students for the industrialized economy of the early 20th century; schools based on this model have been effective at transmitting a standard body of facts and procedures to students. The goals of instructionist classrooms were to ensure standardization – all students were to memorize and master the same core curriculum – and instructionism has been reasonably effective at accomplishing these goals. Traditional schools were structured, scheduled, and regimented in a fashion that was explicitly designed by analogy with the industrial-age factory (Callahan, 1962), and this structural alignment facilitated the ease of transition from school student to factory worker.

It is extremely difficult to incorporate creativity into instructionist classrooms. Consequently, as long as instructionism continues to be the dominant form of schooling, arts educators can argue that arts classes are the only time during the school day when students can engage in creative thinking and practice. But we are now at the beginning of a historic transformation in schools – a shift away from the commonsense but unscientific instructionism of industrial-age schooling toward a more creative form of instruction that is based in learning sciences research. In the future, in new schools based on learning sciences research, creativity will be suffused throughout the curriculum. As a result, arts classes will no longer have a monopoly on creativity.

The learning sciences is grounded in cognitive science research of the 1970s and 1980s. By the 1980s, cognitive scientists had discovered that children retain material better, and are able to generalize it to a broader range of contexts, when they learn deep knowledge rather than surface knowledge, and when they learn how to use that knowledge in real-world social and practical settings. Studies of creative workers show that they almost always apply their expertise in complex social settings, with a wide array of technologically advanced tools along with old-fashioned pencil, paper, chalk, and blackboards. These observations have led learning sciences researchers to a *situated* view of knowledge (Greeno, 2006). "Situated" means that knowledge is not just a static mental structure inside the learner's head; instead, knowing is a process that involves the person, the tools and other people in the environment, and the activities in which that knowledge is being applied. This perspective moves beyond instructionism; in addition to acquiring content, what happens during learning is that patterns of participation in collaborative activity change over time (Rogoff, 1990, 1998).

In the creative age, memorization of facts and procedures is not enough for success. Educated graduates need a deep conceptual understanding of complex concepts, and the ability to work with them creatively to generate new ideas, new theories, new products, and new knowledge. They need to be able to critically evaluate what they read, to express themselves clearly both verbally and in writing, and to understand scientific and mathematical thinking. They need to learn integrated and usable knowledge rather than the sets of compartmentalized and decontextualized facts emphasized by instructionism. They need to be able to take responsibility for their own continuing, life-long learning. These abilities are important to the economy, to the continued success of participatory democracy, and to living a fulfilling, meaningful life. Instructionism is particularly ill suited to the education of creative professionals who can develop new knowledge and continually further their own understanding.

Many of today's schools are not teaching the deep knowledge that underlies innovative activity. But it is not just a matter of asking teachers to teach different curricula, because the structural configurations of instructionist classrooms make it very hard to create learning environments that result in deeper understanding. One of the central underlying themes of the learning sciences is that students learn deeper knowledge when they engage in activities that are similar to the everyday activities of professionals who work in a discipline. This focus on authentic practice is based on a new conception of the expert knowledge that underlies knowledge work in today's economy. In the 1980s and 1990s, scientists began to study science itself, and they began to discover that newcomers become members of a discipline by learning how to participate in all of the practices that are central to professional life in that discipline. And increasingly, cutting-edge work in the sciences is done at the boundaries of disciplines; for this reason, students need to learn the underlying models, mechanisms, and practices that apply across many scientific disciplines, rather than learning in the disconnected and isolated six-week units that are found in many instructionist classrooms – moving from studying the solar system to studying photosynthesis to studying force and motion, without ever learning about connections among these units.

The implication of learning sciences research is that instruction in all subjects must undergo a dramatic transformation – a shift from instructionist delivery of facts and procedures to the creation of learning environments that scaffold active learning and creative knowledge building. This changes the debate about how best to introduce creativity into schools. No longer is the argument about the number of arts classes, or whether or not the arts should be integrated into other content areas; no longer is the argument about whether to add a weekly class on creativity techniques. It is now a much more profound argument about how to transform classrooms across content areas. As we engage in this argument moving forward, we will benefit from the perspective provided by the history of attempts to introduce the arts and creativity into the curriculum.

The next two sections consider, in turn, the arts and education, and creativity and education, before I turn to my recommendation: schools should use ensemble performance to foster collaborative creative learning.

Arts and Education

The first scholars arguing for creativity in the classroom were arts educators, because in instructionist schools, creativity is rarely found outside of arts, music, and drama classes. There are three basic arguments in support of arts education. The first argument is that the arts are important in and of themselves, and that all educated citizens should have a solid grounding in the arts as a part of our shared cultural heritage. This argument is open to various criticisms, from the instrumental (critics argue that schools should focus on learning that is useful to graduates in the economy) to the political (Whose cultural heritage should be emphasized? What arts traditions are worthy of being taught to all students?). The argument of "art for art's sake" tends to lose in the face of tight budgets and hard choices.

When financial pressures first began to impact arts programs in schools, in the 1970s and increasingly in the 1980s, arts education researchers developed a second and a third argument in defense of arts education, both based on the argument that arts education provided unique cognitive benefits to the learner, and that these benefits would transfer to other content areas (including math, science, and literacy) and would result in enhanced learning across the curriculum.

The second argument is that education in the arts results in enhanced cognitive skills that would then transfer to other content areas, resulting in enhanced learning of all content areas. One of the hypothesized benefits of arts education was enhanced creativity. These new arguments emerged at the same time that the cognitive revolution spread through psychology and education research more generally (Eisner, 1982, 2002a; Gardner, 1973). Perhaps the most influential cognition and arts research was that done at Harvard's Project Zero, and the several books about arts, education, and development by Howard Gardner during the 1970s (e.g., Gardner, 1973). The primary impact of Gardner's 1983 book, *Frames of Mind*, was to provide academic support for educators who wanted to prevent schools from being narrowly focused on the "rationalist" content areas of math, science, and literacy. (Ironically, *Frames of Mind* was published in the same year as the "Nation at Risk" report; the latter publication contributed to a subsequent emphasis on math and science education and increased cuts in arts education.) Gardner's 2007 book, *Five Minds for the Future*, argues even more explicitly that schools should provide a broad education that incorporates not only disciplinary knowledge but also creativity, ethics, and integrative knowledge.

Many general cognitive skills have been hypothesized to result from arts education. For example, it has been hypothesized that music listening enhances spatial reasoning, that classroom drama enhances verbal achievement, and that music enhances mathematic ability. Elliot Eisner (2002b) proposed six distinctive "artistically rooted forms of intelligence": (1) experiencing qualitative relationships and making judgments; (2) working with flexible goals that emerge from the work; (3) form and content are inseparable; (4) some forms of knowledge cannot be represented propositionally; (5) thinking with a medium that has unique constraints and affordances; (6) thinking and work that results in satisfaction and flow that are inherently engaging. The question of whether or not the arts provide unique cognitive benefits that transfer to other content areas is controversial, with education researchers divided (see Burnaford, 2007 in support, and Hetland & Winner, 2004, and Moga, Burger, Hetland, & Winner, 2000, for a critique). Yet even the strongest critics of transferable cognitive benefits nonetheless argue that arts education results in unique "habits of mind" or dispositions that are valuable in learning other content areas (Hetland, Winner, Veenema, & Sheridan, 2007): the dispositions to observe, envision, express, reflect, stretch and explore, engage and persist, develop craft, and understand the art world.

The third argument in defense of arts education is that when the arts are integrated with instruction in another content area, such as math or science, that knowledge is learned more effectively. Arguments to integrate the arts throughout the curriculum began in the progressivist era of the 1930s (Efland, 2002, p. 104); the arts as a mode of experience was a central component of John Dewey's framework (Dewey, 1934). This line of thought led to the founding of the Waldorf schools in Germany and Switzerland in the 1920s, based on the ideas of Rudolf Steiner. During this era, perhaps the strongest advocate of arts integration was Leon Winslow (1939). Winslow argued that art teachers should relate the arts to the full range of content areas.

In recent decades, arts educators use the term "interdisciplinary" or "arts integration" to refer to curricula that integrate the arts with other subjects (e.g., Burnaford, 2007; Cornett, 1999; Schramm, 2002; Strokrocki, 2005). Eisner (2002a) identified four possible curricular structures for arts integration: (1) a unit focusing on a particular historical period or culture; (2) a unit that focuses on similarities and differences among art forms; (3) a unit that is centered on a major theme or idea that can be explored through the arts and other fields too; and (4) a unit in which students are asked to solve a problem that has roots in both the arts and another content area. The claim is that when the arts are integrated with instruction in other content areas, learners achieve a deeper understanding, acquire an ability to think more flexibly using content knowledge, and develop enhanced critical thinking and creativity; the arts helps teachers engage students more deeply, and reach a broader range of learning styles (Burnaford, 2007).

It has proven to be exceedingly difficult to design studies that support these second and third arguments. The most exhaustive survey of research in support of transfer (argument 2) and arts integration (argument 3) is found in a 2007 report from the Arts Education Partnership (Burnaford, 2007). The most extensive critique of research in support of transfer is a meta-analysis by Lois Hetland, Ellen Winner, and colleagues (Moga et al., 2000; Hetland & Winner, 2004). My reading of this debate is that the jury is still out on whether arts education enhances creativity in general. In fact, the general consensus among creativity researchers is that creativity is domain specific – that the ability to be creative in any given domain, whether physics, painting, or musical performance, is based on long years of study and mastery of a domain-specific set of cognitive structures (Sawyer, 2012). If so, then learning how to be creative in one of the arts would not transfer to being creative in other content areas.

In the final section that follows, I argue that a unique benefit of arts education, one that has been neglected in this research tradition, is in the enhancement of social interaction and collaboration: collective benefits that improve the learning environment by helping create a community of learners.

Creativity Education

The modern era of creativity research in psychology can be dated to 1949, when J. P. Guilford gave his legendary Presidential Address to the American

Psychological Association (Guilford, 1950). In this address, Guilford noted that psychologists had neglected creativity, and he advocated increased funding and effort. After Guilford's stamp of approval at the national psychology conference, studies of creativity blossomed. During the years that followed Guilford's address, there were almost as many studies of creativity published in each year as there were for the entire 23 years prior to his address (Getzels, 1987; Sternberg & Dess, 2001).

During the 1950s, creativity became associated with *divergent thinking* – the ability to come up with many potential answers or solutions. During the 1960s, many researchers developed tests of divergent thinking. One of the most widely used measures of divergent thinking was developed by Paul Torrance and is known as the Torrance Tests of Creative Thinking, or TTCT (Torrance, 1974). Torrance's tests were designed to satisfy one of the key goals of 1960s creativity research: to identify children with high creative potential so that they could be steered into careers requiring creativity, and to transform education to fully realize the creative potential of every student. The TTCT is still widely used, particularly for admission to gifted programs in schools.

Educational programs to teach creative thinking first emerged during the 1960s; Torrance (1965) developed one of the most influential programs. A series of studies has shown that participation in Torrance's creativity curriculum results in increased scores on the TTCT. But these studies have a weakness: because the students were told the course would enhance their creativity, and because the students knew their divergent thinking was supposed to go up, they might have provided more answers on the post-test in a desire to conform to teacher expectations (Wallach, 1988). An even bigger problem with measures of divergent thinking is that high scores on these tests do not correlate highly with real-life creative output (Guilford, 1970, 1971; also see Baer, 1993; Cattell, 1971; Wallach, 1971). Barron and Harrington (1981) reviewed hundreds of studies; in some, divergent thinking was correlated with other measures of creative achievement, but in others they were not. Most psychologists now agree that divergent thinking tests do not predict creative ability, and that divergent thinking is not the same thing as creativity. Creative achievement requires a complex combination of both divergent and convergent thinking, and creative people are good at switching back and forth at different points in the creative process.

Torrance's work is the model for what any advocate of creativity in schools will have to do in the future: to propose both a curriculum and an outcome assessment (because standardized assessments in use today do not reflect creative potential or ability). If divergent thinking tests are not an adequate measure of creative potential (or of "creative thinking" or "creativity"), then a high priority for researchers should be the development of a new assessment, one that is correlated with real-world creative achievement, and one that could be used to demonstrate the desired outcomes of a more creative curriculum.

Learning How to Create in Groups

Ensemble performances – musical groups like jazz ensembles and European orchestras, or stage performances like traditional Western theater or the performative rituals found in cultures throughout the world – require collaborative ability and interactional skill. But the form of ensemble performance that enhances collaborative ability most greatly is improvisational group performance. In improvisational theater, a group of actors creates a performance without using a script. Some groups specialize in short skits only a few minutes long, and others specialize in fully improvised one- or two-act plays of an hour or more. These performances emerge from unpredictable and unscripted dialogue, on stage and in front of an audience. In a similar way, an effective classroom discussion emerges from classroom discourse, and is not scripted by the lesson plan or by the teacher's predetermined agenda. In a study of improvised theater dialogues, Sawyer (2003b) referred to this type of discourse as *collaborative emergence*. Both classroom discussion and theater improvisations are *emergent* because the outcome cannot be predicted in advance, and they are *collaborative* because no single participant can control what emerges; the outcome is collectively determined by all participants.

Unfortunately, arts education has neglected the performing arts. For example, Arthur Efland's 2002 book *Art and Cognition* is about visual arts only. Ellen Winner's book *Invented Worlds: The Psychology of the Arts* (1982) has chapters on writing, music, and painting, but omits performance. Scholars on both sides of the debate about whether or not arts education transfers to other content areas have almost completely omitted the performing arts (including the "pro" camp, Burnaford, 2007, and the "con" camp, Hetland et al., 2007). Instead, arts educators have emphasized solitary activities like painting and creative writing, activities that are consistent with a "lone genius" myth that creativity research has dispelled long ago. This tendency is reinforced by the desire of many arts educators to teach creative traditions that have been historically important in European cultures: fine art painting, literature and poetry, and music composition or playwrighting. Unfortunately, all of these "high art" activities can be engaged in as solo endeavors.

Psychologists who study creativity have reinforced this tendency in arts education with their focus on activities that result in objective, ostensible products, which remain after the creative act is complete. In scientific disciplines, these creative products include theories, experimental results, and journal articles; in the arts, products include paintings, sculptures, and musical scores. While focusing on creative products, and the psychological processes that generate them, creativity researchers have tended to neglect the creativity of performance (Sawyer, 1998). In Western cultures, creative individuals often choose to enter the sciences or the arts, where they will generate creative products such as journal articles, books, paintings, and orchestral scores.

In my 2012 book *Explaining Creativity (second edition)*, I described a historical debate about the creative process as a debate between *idealist theories* and *action theories* of creativity. Idealist theorists argue that once you have the creative idea, your creative process is done. Creativity does not involve execution of the idea, and it does not require an audience. The creative work is done when the idea is fully formed in one's head. This idea is often called the Croce-Collingwood theory, after two philosophers who promoted it in the 20th century (see Sawyer, 2000). Those who associate creativity with divergent thought – the having of lots of ideas – implicitly accept the idealist theory.

Action theorists, in contrast, argue that the execution of the creative work is essential to the creative process. Action theorists point out that in real life, creative ideas often happen while the creator is working with discipline-specific materials. Once the creator begins to execute an idea, he or she often realizes that it is not working out as expected, and he or she often changes the original idea. Sometimes the final product that results is nothing like the beginning idea. Perhaps the purest example of action creativity is jazz improvisation. Because it is improvised, musicians do not know what they will play in advance; the notes emerge in the moment, from the complex give-and-take among the members of the ensemble. In improvisation, performers start playing with essentially no ideas at all.

As I argue in *Explaining Creativity*, scientific studies of creativity have shown that the idealist theory is false. Creativity takes place over time, and most of the creativity occurs while doing the work. The medium of the artwork is an essential part of the creative process, and creators often get ideas while working with their materials. However, our creativity myths align better with idealist theory than with action theory. We tend to think that ideas emerge spontaneously, fully formed, from the unconscious mind of a solitary creator. And we tend to think that executing the idea – generating the finished work – does not involve creativity. Craft, yes; talent, yes; but creativity, we associate with the moment of inspiration.

Although product creativity dominates in Western cultures, cross-cultural study indicates that performance genres may be a much more common form of creativity worldwide. Unlike product creativity, which involves a long period of creative work leading up to the creative product, in performance creativity, the creative process and the resulting product are co-occurring. This is particularly true of improvisational performance. Although most Western performance genres are scripted or composed, most non-Western performances incorporate improvisational elements.

Even though performance has rarely been a subject for creativity research, it may actually represent a more common, more accessible form of creativity than do privileged domains such as the arts and sciences. If one recognizes that all social interactions display improvisational elements, then everyday activities such as conversation also become relevant to creativity theory. Creativity in interactional domains, including teaching, parenting, leadership, and mentoring, is recognized to be important to our lives and our culture (Sawyer, 2001).

Psychological studies of performance creativity are rare. Partly this is because acting is an ensemble art form, and it is hard to isolate the creative contribution of any one actor (Sawyer, 2003b). But it is also due to an implication of idealist theory: that performance is not creative, but is just execution and interpretation (Kogan, 2002). For example, creativity researchers have usually separated ideation, divergent thought, and insight on the one hand and execution, implementation, and performance on the other. But with performance creativity, it is particularly difficult to separate individual creativity from social and contextual factors. Perhaps this partially explains why creativity researchers have almost completely neglected performance. It is fundamentally public, interactional, and social, making it problematic for psychology's focus on the individual.

Even with solitary product creativity, the creativity does not happen all in the head, as idealist theory would have it; it happens during the hard work of execution. Thus, explaining creativity requires a focus on the creative process. No creative process is ever completely predictable; there is always some improvisation. A painter constantly responds to his canvas and oils as he is painting. Each step of the painting changes the artist's conception of what he is doing – the first part of a painting often leads to a new insight about what to do next. Fiction writers constantly interact with the story as they write. A character or a plot line frequently emerges from the pen unexpectedly, and an experienced writer will respond and follow that new thread, in an essentially improvisational fashion. Improvisation is most essential in stage performance, because unlike the painter or the writer, performers have no opportunity to revise their work. The improvisations of the painter can be painted over or discarded, and the writer has the power of a word processor to generate the next draft. But the improvisations that occur on stage are exposed to the audience. Even the most famous artists often destroy or paint over a significant number of their canvases, and these aborted attempts are generally lost to history. But actors can never take back a bad night.

I believe that ensemble performing arts can teach creativity better than solitary product-focused art forms, and I believe that ensemble performance is more likely to result in transferable skills that are useful in learning other content areas. I base this belief, first of all, on the previous observations that ensemble performance is more similar to real-world creativity than our mythical belief in the solitary genius artist. But to provide additional support for my claim, there is a large body of research showing that collaborative learning is more likely to result in deeper conceptual understanding and greater creative potential in math and science (Sawyer, 2006a). Much learning sciences research recommends that groups of students work together: a recommendation grounded in social constructivist findings that clashes of views and argumentation result in greater learning, and in sociocultural findings that social interaction is often a "zone of proximal development."

However, research also shows that many students do not know how to collaborate effectively (e.g., Azmitia, 1996). Participation in a group musical performance or in theater could result in transferable improvements in collaborative ability. The basic insight of constructivism is that learning is a creative improvisational process (Sawyer, 2003a). Recent work that extends constructivist theory to classroom collaboration conceives of learning as co-construction. Both neo-Piagetian social constructivists and Vygotskian-inspired socioculturalists focus on how knowledge is learned in and by groups (see Sawyer, 2006a). Sociocultural studies have demonstrated the importance of social interaction in groups, and have shown that a microgenetic focus on improvised interactional process can reveal many insights into how learning takes place. A central theme in the sociocultural tradition is the focus on the group rather than the individual. Socioculturalists analyze the entire group as their unit of analysis; cognition is "an aspect of human sociocultural activity" rather than "a property of individuals"

(Rogoff, 1998, p. 68). As a result of this emphasis, these scholars examine how groups collectively learn and develop; in Rogoff's (1998) terms, learning is reconceptualized as a "transformation of participation in sociocultural activity" (p. 687). Socioculturalists hold that groups can be said to "learn" as collectives, and that knowledge can be a possession or property of a group, not only of the individual participants in the group (Rogoff, 1998).

In sociocultural and social constructivist theory, effective teaching must be improvisational, because if the classroom is scripted and directed by the teacher, the students cannot co-construct their own knowledge (Sawyer, 2004). Such talk is open-ended, is not structured in advance, and is an interaction among peers, where any participant can contribute equally to the flow of the interaction.

The sociocultural perspective implies that the entire classroom is improvising together, and it holds that the most effective learning results when the classroom proceeds in an open, improvisational fashion, as children are allowed to experiment, interact, and actively participate in the collaborative construction of their own knowledge. In improvisational teaching, learning is a shared social activity, and is collectively managed by all participants, not only the teacher. In improvising, the teacher creates a dialogue with the students, giving them freedom to creatively construct their own knowledge, while providing the elements of structure that effectively scaffold that co-constructive process.

Collaboration is increasingly important in professions that require creativity (Sawyer, 2007). Creative products in today's economy are not the result of isolated work; they result from collaborative teams and geographically dispersed social networks (as in open-source communities). Ask any older scientist today and you will hear that science has become dramatically more collaborative in recent decades. When Dan Pink or Tom Freidman argue that the United States is losing ground because our graduates are not capable of creative work, they are not talking about isolated individuals. They are talking about the need for creative teams. Creative teaching and learning must be fundamentally collaborative and improvisational.

Recommendations

Conceiving of creative teaching and learning as an improvisational performance emphasizes the interactional and responsive creativity of a teacher working together with a unique group of students. In particular, effective classroom discussion is improvisational, because the flow of the class is unpredictable and emerges from the actions of all participants, both teachers and students (Sawyer, 2011). Several studies have found that as teachers become more experienced, they improvise more (Berliner & Tikunoff, 1976; Borko & Livingston, 1989; Moore, 1993). Creative teaching is *disciplined* improvisation because it always occurs within broad structures and frameworks. Expert teachers use routines and activity structures more than novice teachers, but they are able to invoke and apply these routines in a creative, improvisational fashion (Berliner, 1987; Leinhardt & Greeno, 1986). Several researchers have noted that the most effective classroom interaction balances structure and script with flexibility and improvisation (Borko & Livingston, 1989; Brown & Edelson, 2001; Erickson, 1982).

There is a national consensus developing that we need math and science curricula that results in cognitive outcomes that support creative performance. Our economy needs workers who can use math and science creatively, not workers who have simply memorized decontextualized facts and procedures. If math and science continue to be taught in the instructionist style, then no amount of creativity training or arts education can help redress the problem. The problem is deeper and more foundational than that, and this is why learning sciences research can be invaluable. Learning scientists emphasize the importance of deeper conceptual understanding, problem solving, and thinking – the cognitive structures that support innovative work. And learning scientists are developing innovative new curricula that are aimed at transforming classrooms, particularly in math and science.

In today's climate of accountability, what isn't assessed doesn't count. Any benefits we claim accrue from creativity in the classroom must be demonstrated using a standardized test. No good tests for creative learning exist right now. Existing tests are inadequate, because students in many of the new learning sciences-based classrooms perform at comparable levels on existing tests to students in traditional, instructionist classrooms. However, on newer experimental tests that assess deeper conceptual understanding, students in learning sciences–based classrooms score substantially higher than do students in traditional classrooms.

The most widely used test of creativity, the TTCT, is inadequate in its focus on divergent thinking. It is also inadequate because it does not assess for creative learning in specific content areas; we need new tests in both math and the sciences. The first step in developing an assessment is to identify the claimed cognitive benefits of educating for creativity. They must be those for which there is a consensus that they are essential to graduates, to the workforce, and to the economy.

Thus, the way for schools to generate more creative graduates is not to add a new course to the curriculum called "being creative." And not necessarily to add more arts courses. No amount of such instruction can help if the cognitive outcomes of math and science instruction are not the deeper conceptual understanding that underlies creative work. If we want creative scientists and engineers, we have to start by reforming math and science education.

To some extent, arts educators have been able to argue that the arts are essential for creative learning simply because math and science education has been so bereft of teaching for creativity. A line of reasoning that was common in the past was that the arts are creative, therefore the best way to make students more creative is to give them more arts classes. But when the discussion about school reform is reframed as a discussion about which learning environments result in the deeper conceptual understanding that supports innovative work, it changes the discussion about creativity and arts education, because in this future school all content areas would be taught in a creative manner. My argument is that all content area classrooms need to educate for innovation; when math and science education are reformed, and creativity is embedded throughout the curriculum and in all content areas, then what place is left for the arts? We can no longer easily argue that arts education is the best way to help students develop creativity-linked outcomes, whether personal expression, creativity, or flexible thinking.

Conclusion

Historically, discussions about creativity in school have been compartmentalized. Advocates of creativity have either argued for more arts (or for arts integration), or have argued for dedicated creativity training. Consequently, math educators and science educators have, for the most part, ignored research on creativity. But in this volume, we are concerned with creativity throughout the curriculum. Although much of the volume focuses on the creativity of teachers, I have focused on fostering creativity in learners. I have claimed that the latest findings in learning sciences research argue for a fundamental transformation of schooling, a shift to a form of teaching and learning, in all content areas, that would result in creative learners. If so, then creativity in the classroom becomes central to all content areas – not just the arts, but also math, science, language arts, and social studies.

As schools transform in this direction, research on creativity and learning will become diverse. One key finding to emerge from learning sciences research is that learning trajectories are discipline specific. Designing a learning environment that leads to creative learning of one body of knowledge requires deep understanding of that body of knowledge. Research on the best ways to teach math in a creative fashion will not necessarily apply to teaching other content areas. Consequently, creativity research per se will not be the academic home of this research. It will be conducted by math educators, science educators, and other content area experts.

If the depressing explanation is correct, then schools will never change along the lines suggested by learning sciences research. Or perhaps a few elite schools will change, so that the children of the rich and powerful acquire creative understanding. But this is not a very satisfying future for arts education – to be a tool to reproduce social inequities.

If my hopeful explanation turns out to be the right one, it will be a happier situation for arts education, but also a challenging one. Once all content areas are transformed along learning sciences principles, the arts can no longer claim to be unique among all school subjects. The cognitive benefits claimed to accrue from arts education would now be acquired across the curriculum. Advocates for arts education will need to become experts in learning sciences research, and will need to craft increasingly sophisticated arguments about what unique educational benefits are provided by the arts. I am impressed with the work done in the United Kingdom in connection with their current national curriculum; researchers there have shifted from talking about "arts education" to talking about "creative learning" and "possibility thinking" (Craft, Cremin, & Burnard, 2008; Craft, Jeffrey, & Leibling, 2001).

The jury is still out on whether the solitary product arts contribute to cognitive development. However, we have not concentrated enough on the performing arts, and on the ensemble arts. There are almost no studies of the transferable benefits of participating in ensemble performance. I recommend future studies along these lines. I predict that participation in group improvisational arts will be shown to lead to a form of sociocultural learning – learning at a group level of analysis, not only at an individual level of analysis. Learning that can result in collective knowledge building. Learning that can contribute to the formation of a community of learners.

REFERENCES

Azmitia, M. (1996). Peer interactive minds: Developmental, theoretical, and methodological issues. In P. B. Baltes & U. M. Staudinger (Eds.), *Interactive minds: Life-span perspectives on the social foundation of cognition* (pp. 133–162). New York: Cambridge University Press.

Baer, J. (1993). *Creativity and divergent thinking: A task-specific approach.* Hillsdale, NJ: Erlbaum.

Barron, F., & Harrington, D. M. (1981). Creativity, intelligence, and personality. *Annual Review of Psychology,* **32**, 439–476.

Bell, D. (1973). *The coming of the post-industrial society: A venture in social forecasting.* New York: Basic Books.

Bereiter, C. (2002). *Education and mind in the knowledge age.* Mahwah, NJ: Erlbaum.

Berliner, D. C. (1987). Ways of thinking about students and classrooms by more and less experienced teachers. In J. Calderhead (Ed.), *Exploring teachers' thinking* (pp. 60–83). London: Cassell Education Limited.

Berliner, D. C., & Tikunoff, W. J. (1976). The California beginning teacher study. *Journal of Teacher Education,* **27**(1), 24–30.

Borko, H., & Livingston, C. (1989). Cognition and improvisation: Differences in mathematics instruction by expert and novice teachers. *American Educational Research Journal,* **26**(4), 473–498.

Brown, M., & Edelson, D. C. (2001, April). Teaching by design: Curriculum design as a lens on instructional practice. Paper presented at the Annual meeting of the American Educational Research Association, Seattle, WA.

Burnaford, G. (2007). *Arts integration frameworks, research, & practice: A literature review.* Washington, DC: Arts Education Partnership.

Business Roundtable. (2005). *Tapping America's potential: The education for innovation initiative.* Washington, DC: Business Roundtable.

Callahan, R. E. (1962). *Education and the cult of efficiency: A study of the social forces that have shaped the administration of the public schools.* Chicago: University of Chicago Press.

Cattell, R. B. (1971). *Abilities: Their structure, growth, and action.* Boston, MA: Houghton Mifflin.

Cornett, C. E. (1999). *The arts as meaning makers: Integrating literature and the arts throughout the curriculum.* Upper Saddle River, NJ: Merrill.

Council on Competitiveness. (2005). *Innovate America: National innovation initiative summit and report.* Washington, DC: Council on Competitiveness.

Craft, A., Jeffrey, B., & Leibling, M. (Eds.). (2001). *Creativity in education.* London: Continuum.

Craft, A., Cremin, T., & Burnard, P. (Eds.). (2008). *Creative learning 3–11: And how we document it.* Stoke on Trent, UK: Trentham Books.

Dewey, J. (1934). *Art as experience.* New York: Perigree Books.

Drucker, P. F. (1993). *Post-capitalist society.* New York: HarperBusiness.

Efland, A. D. (2002). *Art and cognition: Integrating the visual arts in the curriculum.* New York: Teachers College Press.

Eisner, E. W. (1982). *Cognition and curriculum: A basis for deciding what to teach.* New York: Longman.

Eisner, E. W. (2002a). *The arts and the creation of mind.* New Haven, CT: Yale University Press.

Eisner, E. W. (2002b). What can eduction learn from the arts about the practice of education? In *The encyclopedia of informal education*. Retrieved June 3, 2016 from www.infed.org/biblio/eisner_arts_and_the_practice_of_education.htm.

Erickson, F. (1982). Classroom discourse as improvisation: Relationships between academic task structure and social participation structure in lessons. In L. C. Wilkinson (Ed.), *Communicating in the classroom* (pp. 153–181). New York: Academic Press.

Florida, R. (2002). *The rise of the creative class and how it's transforming work, life, community and everyday life*. New York: Basic Books.

Friedman, T. L. (2005). *The world is flat: A brief history of the twenty-first century*. New York: Farrar, Straus, and Giroux.

Gardner, H. (1973). *The arts and human development: A psychological study of the artistic process*. New York: Wiley.

Gardner, H. (1983). *Frames of mind: The theory of multiple intelligences*. New York: Basic Books.

Gardner, H. (2007). *Five minds for the future*. Boston, MA: Harvard Business School Press.

Getzels, J. W. (1987). Creativity, intelligence, and problem finding: Retrospect and prospect. In S. G. Isaksen (Ed.), *Frontiers of creativity research* (pp. 88–102). Buffalo, NY: Bearly Limited.

Greeno, J. G. (2006). Learning in activity. In R. K. Sawyer (Ed.), *Cambridge handbook of the learning sciences* (pp. 79–96). New York: Cambridge.

Guilford, J. P. (1950). Creativity. *The American Psychologist*, 5(9), 444–454.

Guilford, J. P. (1970). Creativity: Retrospect and prospect. *The Journal of Creative Behavior*, 4(3), 149–168.

Guilford, J. P. (1971). Some misconceptions regarding measurement of creative talents. *The Journal of Creative Behavior*, 5, 77–87.

Hargreaves, A. (2003). *Teaching in the knowledge society: Education in the age of insecurity*. New York: Teacher's College Press.

Hetland, L., & Winner, E. (2004). Cognitive transfer from arts education to non-arts outcomes: Research evidence and policy implications. In E. W. Eisner & M. D. Day (Eds.), *Handbook of research and policy in art education* (pp. 135–162). Mahwah, NJ: Erlbaum.

Hetland, L., Winner, E., Veenema, S., & Sheridan, K. M. (2007). *Studio thinking: The real benefits of visual arts education*. New York: Teachers College Press.

Kogan, N. (2002). Careers in the performing arts: A psychological perspective. *Creativity Research Journal*, 14(1), 1–16.

Leinhardt, G., & Greeno, J. G. (1986). The cognitive skill of teaching. *Journal of Educational Psychology*, 78(2), 75–95.

Moga, E., Burger, K., Hetland, L., & Winner, E. (2000). Does studying the arts engender creative thinking? Evidence for near but not far transfer. *Journal of Aesthetic Education*, 34(3/4), 91–104.

Moore, M. T. (1993). Implications of problem finding on teaching and learning. In S. G. Isaksen, M. C. Murdock, R. L. Firestien & D. J. Treffinger (Eds.),

Nurturing and developing creativity: The emergence of a discipline (pp. 51–69). Norwood, NJ: Ablex.

Organisation for Economic Co-operation and Development (OECD). (2004). *Innovation in the knowledge economy: Implications for education and learning.* Paris: OECD Publications.

Papert, S. (1993). *The children's machine: Rethinking school in the age of the computer.* New York: Basic Books.

Pink, D. H. (2005). *A whole new mind: Why right-brainers will rule the future.* New York: Riverhead Books.

Rogoff, B. (1990). *Apprenticeship in thinking: Cognitive development in social context.* New York: Oxford University Press.

Rogoff, B. (1998). Cognition as a collaborative process. In D. Kuhn & R. S. Siegler (Eds.), *Handbook of child psychology, 5th edition, Volume 2: Cognition, perception, and language* (pp. 679–744). New York: Wiley.

Sawyer, R. K. (1998). The interdisciplinary study of creativity in performance. *Creativity Research Journal,* **11**(1), 11–19.

Sawyer, R. K. (2000). Improvisation and the creative process: Dewey, Collingwood, and the aesthetics of spontaneity. *Journal of Aesthetics and Art Criticism,* **58**(2), 149–161.

Sawyer, R. K. (2001). *Creating conversations: Improvisation in everyday discourse.* Cresskill, NJ: Hampton Press.

Sawyer, R. K. (2003a). Emergence in creativity and development. In R. K. Sawyer, V. John-Steiner, S. Moran, R. Sternberg, D. H. Feldman, M. Csikszentmihalyi & J. Nakamura (Eds.), *Creativity and development* (pp. 12–60). New York: Oxford.

Sawyer, R. K. (2003b). *Improvised dialogues: Emergence and creativity in conversation.* Westport, CT: Greenwood.

Sawyer, R. K. (2004). Creative teaching: Collaborative discussion as disciplined improvisation. *Educational Researcher,* **33**(2), 12–20.

Sawyer, R. K. (2006a). Analyzing collaborative discourse. In R. K. Sawyer (Ed.), *Cambridge handbook of the learning sciences* (pp. 187–204). New York: Cambridge.

Sawyer, R. K. (2006b). The schools of the future. In R. K. Sawyer (Ed.), *Cambridge handbook of the learning sciences* (pp. 567–580). New York: Cambridge.

Sawyer, R. K. (2007). *Group genius: The creative power of collaboration.* New York: Basic Books.

Sawyer, R. K. (2011). What makes good teachers great? The artful balance of structure and improvisation. In R. K. Sawyer (Ed.), *Structure and improvisation in creative teaching* (pp. 1–24). New York: Cambridge University Press.

Sawyer, R. K. (2012). *Explaining creativity: The science of human innovation.* New York: Oxford.

Schramm, S. L. (2002). *Transforming the curriculum: Thinking outside the box.* Lanham, MD: Scarecrow Education.

Sternberg, R. J., & Dess, N. K. (2001). Creativity for the new millennium. *American Psychologist,* **56**(4), 332.

Strokrocki, M. (Ed.). (2005). *Interdisciplinary art education: Building bridges to connect disciplines and cultures.* Reston, VA: National Art Education Association.

Torrance, E. P. (1965). *Rewarding creative behavior: Experiments in classroom creativity.* Englewood Cliffs, NJ: Prentice-Hall.

Torrance, E. P. (1974). *Torrance tests of creative thinking: Norms-technical manual.* Princeton, NJ: Personnel Press/Ginn.

Wallach, M. A. (1971). *The intelligence/creativity distinction.* New York: General Learning Press.

Wallach, M. A. (1988). Creativity and talent. In K. Gronhaug & G. Kaufmann (Eds.), *Innovation: A cross-disciplinary perspective* (pp. 13–27). Oslo: Norwegian University Press.

Winner, E. (1982). *Invented worlds: The psychology of the arts.* Cambridge, MA: Harvard University Press.

Winslow, L. (1939). *The integrated school art program.* New York: McGraw-Hill.

CHAPTER 16

Creativity and Prosocial Values
Nurturing Cooperation within the Classroom

Vlad Petre Glăveanu

Aalborg University, Denmark

Angela Branco and Monica Souza Neves-Pereira

University of Brasília, Brazil

This chapter focuses on the relationship between creativity and prosocial values, in particular those associated with cooperation and collaborative activities. Despite the fact that, in developmental studies and the literature on education, creativity and values are often treated separately, our premise here is that both psychological theory and educational practice would greatly benefit from reuniting them within an integrative framework. In this chapter, we consider creativity and prosocial values as they develop within the Self–Other dynamic specific for communal living and sociability (see Simmel, 1949; Jovchelovitch, 2015). We start by outlining the theoretical foundation for our argument and reflect on schools as socio-cultural contexts that socialize children to become creative *and* moral agents. We then unpack the relation between creativity, cooperation and prosocial values with particular reference to studies done in Brazilian schools. Following this, we propose a tentative set of guidelines for nurturing creativity and cooperation in the classroom. We conclude with a few reflections on the role of dialogue and reflexivity for enhancing moral creative behavior. However, before developing these ideas, a more basic question needs to be addressed first.

Why Creativity and Values?

In engaging with this question it is important, from the start, to stress the fact that the axiological dimension is typically included in the very definition of creativity. This makes it one of the few scientific concepts in psychology that are assumed to always contribute (by definition) to the well-being of individuals and the welfare of groups and communities. If creativity is characterized by novelty and *value*, as most researchers tend to think (Gruber & Wallace, 1999; Gruys, Munshi & Dewett, 2011; for an extension of this definition, see Kharkhurin, 2014), this value cannot be understood exclusively in terms of appropriate, fitting responses to the task at hand. Creative value ultimately derives from society's appreciation of what is an "appropriate" task, worthy of creative investment. This is what systemic models emphasize (Csikszentmihalyi, 1988): that is, that the meaning and value of a creative act, for it to be actually called creative, are related to socially and culturally instituted domains, safeguarded by gatekeepers and historically constituted within society.

Moreover, we live in a day and age where creativity *is* a value in itself, the very marker of the modern era (Mason, 2003; Neelands & Choe, 2010), a construct easily detected in most social discourses, especially those associated with political, educational and entrepreneurial activities. The present-day rhythm of technological and social change demands new ways of solving more and more complex problems. The mere reproduction of old formulas and strategies cannot adequately respond to the avalanche of complex and challenging puzzles of contemporary life. Hence the substantial cultural demand for new ideas and new solutions that ultimately entails the ever-growing value of creativity and its encouragement by educational institutions in charge of promoting human development. It is true that, in recent years, this all-positive meaning of creativity has been challenged, and the "dark side" of creative acts became a topic on the agenda of creativity researchers (see Cropley, Cropley, Kaufman & Runco, 2010). But, of course, even in such cases, the value component is still central. The issue is that what appears as valuable or moral from the perspective of an individual or group, at one point in time, can change if we consider other groups and/or another historical times. Value judgments of creative work are ever-present, while socially and historically situated.

A second reason encouraging us to elaborate on the articulation of creativity and prosocial values derives from the complexity of the relationships between these phenomena, revealed by recent work on the ethics of creativity. This was, in fact, the topic of a recent book edited by Moran, Cropley and Kaufman (2014). Their volume addresses a multitude of issues, from the development of morality and creativity to the role of ethics in supporting or limiting creative expression. It also shows the difficulties inherent to this kind of inquiry. First and foremost, are ethics and creativity personal, social, or both? If scholarly work on ethics often portrayed it in terms of a society's prescribed code of conduct, creativity enjoyed a long tradition of being individualized as a mental function and form of expression, particularly in psychology. This division is, however, artificial. Not only, as many of the contributors to the volume mentioned above demonstrate, are ethics and creativity two faces of the same coin, but we cannot fully appreciate one without the other. Questions of ethics, moral behavior and values should be placed at the core of creativity research.

Finally, the third, and more pragmatic reason to address these topics together resides in the likelihood that cooperative practices, stemming from prosocial values within educational settings, may facilitate the emergence of creativity among students (see, for example, the special issue edited by Littleton, Rojas-Drummond and Miell in 2008 for Thinking Skills and Creativity on the topic of "Collaborative Creativity: Socio-cultural Perspectives"). In the second part of our chapter we take a few preliminary steps, from a socio-cultural and developmental perspective (Branco & Valsiner, 2012; Glăveanu, 2010a, 2010b), towards the rapprochement between creativity and values. From this theoretical standpoint, the child appears as an emerging social actor, both shaped and shaping his/her social environment through bi-directional interactions with adults and peers (Branco, 2003; Kuczynski, Marshall & Schell, 1997). In discussing these kinds of interactions, our focus here will be on creativity and prosocial values, in particular the meaning and role of cooperation for the development of children within educational contexts. In opening up this topic, and considering the fact that, out of our two key terms, creativity is extensively discussed in the present volume, we shall start with a few general reflections on values and their relation to practice.

The Co-Constructive Nature of Values and Practices

From a cultural psychology perspective, values are deep-rooted, affect-laden beliefs that are especially powerful in guiding our actions and interactions. These beliefs however cannot be separated from social practices and the cultural contexts to which individuals belong. Branco (2012), while elaborating on the sociogenesis of values, emphasized the mutual construction of social practices/activities and the internalized semiotic dimension of what we designate as cultural values within a given society. The latter, according to Valsiner (2007, 2014) and to Branco (2012), should be conceived as referring to the individual (*personal* cultural values) or to the group (*collective* cultural values): in both cases, however, their origin lies within the context of lived-through practices and experiences.

Consequently, the reciprocal construction of practices and semiotic processes highlights the bidirectional dynamics that explains why a certain kind of experience may bring forward a certain kind of belief orientation, and, simultaneously, why specific motivations favor the occurrence of corresponding practices and social interactions. For example, competitively structured settings favor competitive interactions that facilitate the internalization of competitive values and motivation; in turn, these will lead to new competitive activities. Conversely, the same happens with prosocial values, which are engendered within prosocial contexts that give rise to renewed semiotic processes compatible with prosociability. These types of processes can be easily noticed in classroom contexts, where designing educational activities and guiding student participation reveals the close interplay between student's motivation and beliefs and the nature of the tasks they engage in. Therefore, when we use terms such as the promotion of cooperation in the classroom, we mean the encouragement of both observable social interactions as well as of the cooperative motivation that may favor – or result from – such activities.

At this point, it is also useful to clarify the meaning of *cooperation*. As discussed in the literature, prosocial behavior and motivation encompass numerous types of social interactions, from altruism to cooperation (Branco, 2003; Staub, 2003). In the present chapter, however, we focus on cooperation in particular, since this specific pattern of sociability – due to the presence of reciprocity, mutual help and respect, and its co-constructive characteristics – received a lot of attention and theorizing within the realms of developmental psychology (Branco, 2003; Piaget, 1990).

Bridging Creativity and Prosocial Values through Sociability

Simmel's (1949) notion of sociability is in many ways idealistic. He referred to the "impulse to sociability" in man, leading to togetherness and union with others and, ultimately, to the creation of human society. Pure sociability has "no ulterior end, no content, and no result outside itself" since it is associated with "an emancipating and saving exhilaration" (p. 261). Supporting this outlook, Simmel places playful associations between people at the heart of sociability, a notion that brings to the fore its creative dimension (see also Jovchelovitch, 2015). According to him, it is the free-playing, interacting interdependence between individuals that brings about unity and a sense of conviviality and togetherness. From his sociological standpoint, Simmel thus presents us with a larger perspective on what makes society, and his answer points our attention to playful, prosocial impulses to associate with others. Along a similar vein, Maturana (1998) argues for the prosocial nature of humans by presenting the notion of conversation – which we can interpret from his work as dialogical social interactions – and so highlights the central role of *pro*-sociability for the development of our human condition.

From a psychodynamic paradigm, Donald Winnicott (1971) adds interesting ideas regarding the dynamics between sociability, creativity, and human development. For Winnicott (1971), creativity and cultural experience are twinborn in a potential or transitional space made possible by creative playing in early childhood (see also Glăveanu, 2009). Being trained in the psychoanalytic tradition, Winnicott emphasized the traumatic separation between child and caregiver as a fundamental event, leading to the constitution of the "me" and "not-me" world. When the caregiver is not available, the child experiences anxiety caused by this separation and earns for recovering unity. This unity, however, can only be recovered by symbolic means, when the child invests objects like a toy or blanket with meaning and they can "stand in" for the Other. This is what Winnicott referred to as transitional objects. The interesting point from his theory for our discussion here has to do with the importance of the Self–Other relation (initially, child–caregiver) for early forms of creative expression in play. For Winnicott, psychological health is associated with the child's capacity to recover unity with the Other through the creative, playful use of symbolic means.

In summary, in the case of Simmel, Maturana and Winnicott, coming from different disciplinary backgrounds and answering different questions, sociability offered the frame for understanding the *prosocial* orientation of human beings, the *value* we place on togetherness and association, and the role *creativity* plays in building sociability itself. Reversely, creative action itself would be unimaginable outside Self–Other cooperative relations. Just like any other form of activity, creative expression is constantly being scaffolded by interactions with adults or more capable peers (see Vygotsky, 1978; also Wood, Bruner & Ross, 1976). These processes start in the family, but schools certainly play a major part in how they unfold in the life of the child.

The School as a Socio-Cultural System

The school has a much broader role in human developmental processes than existing pedagogical models commonly assume. It is the role of the school to insert the individual in the universe of culture by passing on the legacy of knowledge left by previous generations. By organizing the curriculum and educational activities, teachers struggle to shape the learning and developmental processes children and youth experience at school;

this process extends over a long period of time and its dynamic continues also outside the classroom (Rogoff, 2003). Experiencing different social situations by means of educational activities and games is essential for the internalization of culture to take place, starting from daily, systematic practices. The school is also, or at least should be, the place where human potentialities are nurtured. From learning curricular content to forming the self, the classroom context plays a key role in the development of values and the development of creativity. As a socio-cultural system, the school is, by definition, a space where individuals and culture meet in mutual, concomitant, constitutive actions (Bodrova & Leong, 2007; Corsaro, 2011; Fleer, Hedegaard & Tudge, 2009; Kozulin, Gindis, Ageyev & Miller, 2011).

When we think of the school as a privileged space for human development, we realize that important developmental aspects will be directly shaped by the cultural practices and everyday exchanges between teachers, students, and other members of the educational system. The school mediates the cognitive, affective, moral, and ethical development of those who attend it (Branco, 2009; Rogoff, 2003; Vygotsky, 1999). Last but not least, schools guide their students' creative activities, and because of this, they are primary arenas for their development.

Unfortunately, the educational system can also resist assuming its role as a promoter of students' creativity (Lubart, 2007) and a source of role models for moral development (Branco, Barreto & Barrios, forthcoming). In relation to the former, Lubart (2007) discussed the impact of education on the development of creativity and identified several issues that hinder creative expression in the classroom, namely: (a) teacher's misconceptions of what creativity is (see also Neves-Pereira, 2004); (b) teacher's urge to work with idealized, obedient, rule-abiding students; (c) strict educational practices that favor compliance with fixed rules (tests, grades, attendance, etc.); (d) school assignments that focus on memorization, copying and reproduction instead of focusing on new answers and creative problem solving; and (e) efforts to avoid mistakes, among others. In response, particularly in developed countries, various initiatives are aimed at offering educators strategies to assist them in the double task of fostering creative abilities among students and developing innovative forms of teaching (Craft, 2005; Cropley, 1997; Starko, 1995).

When values are concerned, the school's role in contributing to the creation of moral citizens is often taken for granted. While creativity as a topic received a lot of attention from psychologists and educators for more than half a century (see Guilford's 1950 call addressed to fellow members of the American Psychological Association), issues related to morality are not as prominent (Branco, 2006, 2009). Moreover, when it comes to prosocial values, in particular cooperation, we can often notice a discrepancy between what most teachers would like to see (i.e., collaborative students) and what educational practices tend to produce (i.e., individually oriented, competitive students). Although there are surely cross-cultural differences in this regard, competition has traditionally been, and continues to be, favored over cooperation (Johnson & Johnson, 1989; Palmieri & Branco, 2015). In relation to the promotion of ethics and moral development at school, Branco, Barreto and Barrios (forthcoming) brought new evidence recently regarding the prevalence of discipline and obedience – clear examples of heteronomy – over autonomy, moral actions and reflexivity.

The ideal school, if such a thing actually existed, would not only promote creative teaching and learning (Starko, 1995) but also invest in the construction of prosocial values. In fact, as we argue here, it would consider these two aims *inter-related* and supporting each other in the construction of future citizens immersed in various political, economic and social contexts, and capable of democratic, ethical, engaged social action. The articulation between the development of creativity and the construction of prosocial values at school represents a key nexus for curricular enrichment, in addition to being an important political objective for educational systems worldwide. However, despite declarative support, everyday school practices often fail to recognize or foster either prosocial values or creativity.

Cooperation and creativity in a school context

Educational contexts promoting cooperation among students facilitate the development of autonomy, empathy and collaborative efforts that make creative use of group resources. Within cooperative contexts, students' goal orientations are not diverted into outperforming each other in terms of achievements or popularity – what many teachers, more or less explicitly, encourage pupils to do. Therefore, students can fully, and freely, employ a wide range of material and psychological resources often in ways that lead to creative outcomes. Research on cooperative learning and school experiences has provided significant empirical evidence suggesting that cooperative practices among students, and between teachers and their students, represent the best approach to promote students' academic performance and social development (see, for instance, Johnson & Johnson, 1989). Research data from our studies in Brazil have also revealed the power of cooperation in promoting prosocial interactions among young children (Branco, 2003, 2009; Branco & Valsiner, 1997).

In a study carried out to analyze what sort of child-child interactions preschool teachers promoted within the classroom, and *how* they did that (Branco & Mettel, 1995), we found that the promotion of cooperation was closely associated with stimulating autonomy and with the social negotiation of conflicts. Among other results, we found that the teacher considered by the school staff as excellent was particularly talented in organizing creative activities cooperatively, as well as stimulating self-reflection and conflict negotiation practices among her four- to five-years-old students (Branco & Mettel, 1995). Children in her classroom were very active, verbally expressive and often came up with innovative ideas for subjects to work with the group and with fresh suggestions for specific activities. What was especially interesting, however, was the way they interacted with each other: they mostly collaborated and did things together, only rarely engaging in aggressive behavior for the whole time (about six months) we observed the group.

In subsequent studies with preschoolers, however, teachers used to promote mostly competition and individualism among children (Barrios & Branco, 2010; Palmieri & Branco, 2008, 2015; Salomao & Branco, 2001). Palmieri and Branco (2008, 2015), for instance, investigated the actual concept of cooperation held by two preschool teachers, from different schools in Londrina, a major city in the south of Brazil. We asked teachers to think, organize and carry out what they conceived as a cooperative activity with their students. The results were particularly striking: one teacher proposed, and enthusiastically developed, a typically competitive activity in which children had to be the first to blow up balloons tied to their ankles. The other teacher did not encourage competition; instead, she promoted strictly individual performances, even though the task – a collective drawing – could have been a perfect activity for sharing and cooperation. Both teachers, in different ways, were very effective along their interactions with children, but their effectiveness worked to inhibit, rather than encourage, collaboration.

Such results come as no surprise when we take into account the nature of the cultural values and practices widespread in Western culture. Researchers and theorists from diverse scientific fields agree on the power of individualism and competition as deeply rooted values that pervade many of our practices and life experiences (Dumont, 1985; Lash, 1982; Sennett, 2004). Consequently, when teachers translate cooperation into individualistic or competitive activities, they are simply – and unintentionally – revealing the fact that issues concerning social and moral development are indeed poorly addressed in their professional experiences, as well as in their specific training. After all, the topics of socio-moral cultural values are superficially, or rarely – if ever – discussed within the socio-cultural contexts to which they belong, such as family, school, church or club, as well as within larger contexts that include the Internet and other media.

In two other research projects developed by our group, we found similar results regarding moral development (Barrios & Branco, 2010) and creativity (Neves-Pereira & Branco, 2015). In both cases, when we asked teachers to translate into practice their underlying concepts of moral development, or creativity, they clearly showed a clear misconception of these psychological constructs. Barrios and Branco (2010) investigated teachers' practices within a public preschool, located in Brasilia, using both naturalist observations – filmed along a couple of months – and the aforementioned technique: the researcher asked the teachers to propose and carry out specific activities meant to foster moral development among young children. Interviews also took place in order to explore and make sense of teachers' concepts, ideas and beliefs. As a result, we detected a clear mismatch between observable practices within the classrooms, teachers' verbal conceptualizations, and the definition of moral development, either according to a cognitivist-constructivist perspective (Blasi, 2004; Kohlberg, 1981; Piaget, 1965, 1990) or a cultural psychological approach (Branco, 2012; Paolichi, 2007; Ratner, 2002).

For example, at a discursive level, teachers emphasized the need to guide children to be obedient and follow the rules. Concepts such as autonomy or reflexivity were totally absent from teachers' discourses. Sometimes they referred to the importance of promoting empathy, sharing and mutual respect among their students. However, when we observed their practices within the classroom context, they mostly inhibited children's interactions and provided no opportunity for sharing or social exchange. They would systematically censure children whenever they tried to talk, cooperate or negotiate with one another. One of the most interesting results of this study was the particular nature of the activity one teacher selected and executed with her students after being asked by the researcher to carry out a "special activity to foster moral development." She chose to read aloud, for her five-year-old students, a book meant for three-years-olds (according to the author). The book was entitled *What We Can and What We Cannot Do*. The book showed pictures of different situations illustrating what is allowed and what is forbidden that would apply to young children, such as "we can color a picture but cannot color the walls" or "we can play with friends but cannot take a medicine by ourselves," and so on. Nothing in this book concerned social interactions, empathy or any sort of moral suggestions, nor during the activity did the teacher make any move to elicit discussion over social or moral issues.

We conducted another study on moral and values development with nine- to ten-year-old children in the context of a public school, also situated in Brasilia (Branco & Barrios, 2014). Once again, we observed a mismatch between psychological theories of moral development and the teacher's practices and conceptualizations. In this case, the teacher was coherent to his own convictions concerning morality: moral subjects are those who "follow the rules," so the students who struggle to learn the proper rules (according to him there are "rules for all kinds of situations") and behave accordingly should be considered morally developed. As in the studies mentioned earlier, students had neither incentive nor opportunities to discuss, reflect upon or negotiate their ideas – in other words, no room to develop autonomy or creativity. The major goal of the teacher – considered the best in school, according the other staff – was to convey academic knowledge efficiently and to shape his students into disciplined, well-behaved and obedient adults.

The last study worth mentioning here is a research carried out on the sociogenesis of creativity within two different preschool settings in Brasilia (Neves-Pereira & Branco, 2015). Both preschools had a reputation for promoting creativity among young children. The study was designed to identify and analyze practices and interactions supposedly meant to pro-mote creativity (Neves-Pereira, 2004; Neves-Pereira & Branco, 2015) and, once more, the findings revealed a substantial difference between theo-retical knowledge and teachers' conceptualizations and understanding of relevant psychological constructs. One of the teachers developed an activ-ity where children had to strictly, and individually, follow a model: using pre-prepared pieces of paper, the students' task was to assemble a little dog whose parts (including its tongue) were supposed to be positioned exactly at the same place! The other teacher came a bit closer to the notion of a creative activity: She asked her students to draw whatever they wanted on a black sheet of paper marked with a white circle. According to the first teacher's account during the interviews, promoting creativity meant asking children to produce any sort of artistic work. The second teacher, however, was able to identify some important characteristics of the construct – such as initiative and originality – but she was unable in her proposed activity to interact with the students, to accept their own suggestions and to encourage originality. In other words, they both were unable to provide incentives for children to be autonomous or creative, and their strong belief in individualistic practices unveiled their firm conviction that human development is a purely individualistic enterprise. This became clear through their selection of classroom activities and their social/pedagogical interactions with children.

The aforementioned studies invite us to reflect on teacher's conceptions and everyday school activities: How is it possible to break with old beliefs and practices, and to innovate our schools in order to really promote creativity? Based on the arguments presented here, we claim that cooperation and prosociability are excellent grounds for the development of creativity in the classroom. In order to fruitfully exploit this potential in school we would need, however: (1) to acknowledge, first of all, the relation between cooperation and prosociability, on the one hand, and creativity, on the other; and (2) to facilitate teachers' access to professional training and educational resources that can help them cultivate both. In the following section, we focus on a set of guidelines moving us in this direction.

Nurturing Creativity and Cooperation in Classroom Settings

What can be part of an agenda oriented towards the development of creativity and values at school? There are certainly several actions that should be implemented in the classroom, actions that are better aligned with the ideals of most educational contexts. It has been argued that creativity is best understood when perceived in its *distributed* dimension (Glăveanu, 2014). When we think of creative action as something distributed among agents, creations, places, historical time and cultural artifacts, we notice also the complexity and challenge of developing creativity in school. A proactive agenda, such as the one discussed here, should include planning several actions spanning different levels and contexts. It is essential to act on all levels, from the macrosystemic ones – here represented by the values and beliefs of the social groups that guide school practices – to the meso and microsystemic ones, such as the classroom, for instance. It is not possible to offer an exhaustive list of suggestions for accomplishing this in a single book chapter. However, there are some general recommendations that can help schools to foster creativity based on mutual respect and cooperative values.

Promoting creativity and cooperation in the classroom is a complex task that demands effective participation from the whole school community. In terms of encouraging cooperation among students, it is *not* sufficient for teachers to learn about the importance and meaning of cooperation.

Teachers and those ultimately in charge of school administration and policies need to develop a deep belief – or value – concerning the reason
why actually promoting cooperation and prosocial practices and values
among students is a fundamental part of their pedagogical mission. If they
are not convinced about the role of cooperation and dialogue to foster
moral development and social responsibility, they will not invest their time
and efforts into introducing changes in their traditional everyday practices
within schools. Concerning the promotion of creativity as well, the mere
presence of teachers capable of fostering their students' creative abilities
is not enough when they cannot count on a physical and socio-cultural
space rich in stimuli, knowledge and props useful for creativity development. Innovative pedagogical models are not enough if educators cannot
build and maintain an environment favorable to the emergence of novelty
(Beghetto & Kaufman, 2010). A scenario conducive to the development of
creativity includes the following: (a) properly prepared human resources;
(b) physical resources availability; (c) favorable environmental conditions;
(d) social and cultural atmosphere favorable to the promotion of creativity;
and (e) joint efforts made so that all these elements can operate smoothly
and be directed towards achieving the same goals (Neves-Pereira, 2007).

Those who investigate the relationship between creativity and education
are aware that, in general, teachers do not know how to engage in creative forms of teaching or how exactly to stimulate collaboration between
students. Creativity tends to be perceived by teachers and students in a
distorted way, permeated by myths and beliefs that do not allow a deeper
understanding of its nature, development, dynamics and the strategies
to promote it. Equally, as previously argued, competition is preferred to
cooperation in the classroom due to the pervasive belief that it encourages
motivation (Kohn, 1986) and even creativity (primarily in the case of boys;
see Conti, Collins & Picariello, 2001), and partially also because it is easier
to "set up" and assess. In addition to this lack of knowledge or expertise, there is also considerable confusion regarding the different nuances of
creativity within teaching.

Starko (1995; see also Gregerson, Snyder & Kaufman, 2013) made a
significant contribution when she differentiated teaching for creativity and
creative teaching. How good is it to bring the circus to the classroom if
students do not have the opportunity to use their creative abilities? Also, it
is not enough to focus on the development of students' creativity if teaching
does not provide opportunities for new challenges, bringing in elements
that stimulate creativity. Overall, the school has traditionally emphasized
the reproduction and memorization of knowledge, with little incentive to

research and problem solving (Alencar, 2001, 2003). Almost all the time spent at school is dedicated to acquiring knowledge individually. Teaching strategies reinforce conservatism and stimulate obedience. Children often miss the opportunity, at school, to develop their creative thinking as well as their ability to collaborate with others.

In summary, promoting creativity and prosocial values – including the motivation to cooperate – is a complex task which demands, on the part of the educator, not only knowledge regarding creative phenomena and cooperation but also sustained efforts aimed at developing *his or her own* collaborative abilities and creative competencies. On the other hand, being a creative teacher does not help when you do not know how to nurture students' creative collaborations. The reverse is also true: Knowing strategies for promoting individual creativity is not enough when teaching remains bound to a non-creative standard in the classroom and a focuses only on individual students. In order to endorse creative collaborations in an effective way, it is essential to promote teacher's knowledge, motivation, training and expertise, on the one hand, as well as the use of appropriate strategies, on the other.

Concerted efforts are necessary to form a creative and collaborative teacher who is not only able to organize a school environment that stimulates creativity and prosocial values, but who also prioritizes such goals. Moreover, this teacher needs to master different strategies to promote creative collaboration. Based on Neves-Pereira's (2004, 2007) ideas concerning creativity in the school context, we can summarize some general guidelines for such promotion concerning teachers' orientations, expertise and abilities:

1. It is fundamental for teachers to develop deep-rooted values and beliefs concerning the importance of fostering creativity and prosocial motivation among students, associated with conceptual, theoretical and practical knowledge about the dynamics of creativity and cooperation in a classroom context.

When teachers do believe in, or are intrinsically motivated to encourage creativity and prosocial values among their students, they are more likely to notice or to create educational contexts favorable for both. A clear understanding of the theoretical and practical aspects of both topics also plays an essential role. It is worth noting, however, that pure intellectual knowledge in the area of creativity or cooperation is important, but this knowledge alone does not determine whether coherent teaching practices will be developed in this regard. Knowledge is important, but ultimately it is not enough.

2.   For a teacher to be able to effectively encourage students' creative collaboration, he or she must have specific practical experience in this area.

In order for teachers to construct and deliver educational activities that favor the development of creativity and prosocial values in the classroom, they must master the practice of nurturing creative collaborations in a school context. This kind of mastering is associated with continuous training, either self-directed or directed by others (in particular more experienced teachers or professionals in this area of expertise). It is essential that teachers study, read, investigate, research and, most of all, practice different ways of stimulating creativity and cooperation focused on individuals and the group as a whole.

3.   Teachers may inadvertently inhibit rather than promote creativity or collaboration, even in tasks meant to have the opposite effect; this is why the teacher's capacity to step back and reflect on his or her own actions and educational practices is vital in an educational context.

This point draws attention to the importance of preparing teachers to be aware of and reflect on their own actions and teaching strategies. Even those teachers who have lots of experience need to be open to the possibility that new students (or students at different moments) understand and respond differently to similar tasks and guidance. To be aware of messages conveyed by paralinguistic (tone of voice, etc.) and nonverbal messages (facial expressions, looks and gestures) is central to make sense of how students might be interpreting one's actions and discourse.

4.   It is important for teachers to be able to analyze in detail the nature of each activity they propose to their students, paying close attention to expected results, instructions and social rules. By doing this, they will be able to construct activities that, both explicitly and implicitly, require creativity and cooperation in order to be accomplished.

What often happens in class is that teachers are not fully aware of the range of expected results their tasks can lead to. This is especially true concerning the social rules embedded in the activities themselves. For instance, some teachers think that any artistic activity necessarily promotes creativity; however, depending on how she/he guides the student through this activity, creative expression might actually be inhibited. The same can happen when an activity that supposedly should lead to cooperation ends up stimulating competition among students.

5. Teachers should acquire up-to-date knowledge regarding the latest conceptual and methodological developments within their area of expertise.

When teachers have a solid preparation and extensive knowledge in their area of expertise, there is a high probability that they will understand the meaning of creativity and cooperation as significant contributors to the students' development. Competent teachers are more likely to structure creative lessons than less competent ones, who tend to ignore creative processes and demand less collaboration and critical thinking from their students. Therefore, quality training for teachers is extremely important.

6. Teachers are more capable of developing creative collaboration in the classroom when this concept truly becomes part of their personal and cultural history.

When teachers perceive themselves as creative, value creativity, are interested in several activities and have multiple hobbies and interests, they end up promoting their own creativity, which will sensitize them to promote their students' creativity. The same happens with the development of a prosocial orientation: to experience mutual help and collaboration in one's own lives may indeed facilitate such development. We need to consider, thus, the relevance of teachers' life experiences. A person who actively searches to create contexts that values creativity and collaboration will probably be "contaminated" by these same contexts. Environments that value creativity facilitate the construction of a holistic and flexible view of the world, which helps the person to cope better with all sorts of everyday situations. Being a role model for cooperative and creative actions might be one of the best venues to promote such actions and interactions among students.

7. Multi- and transdisciplinary approaches are very welcome, as well as cooperation with other teachers, parents and, of course, the students themselves. Such collaborations are significantly useful for nurturing cooperation and creativity in the classroom and in life outside school walls.

Preparing a teacher to promote creativity and cooperation in the classroom is a highly complex task, but multiplying perspectives and opening up new

ways of thinking about one's topic and one's teaching experiences is fundamental for providing the necessary personal and professional development.
In the end, it is not only student cooperation that we should be concerned
with but also the active collaboration between teachers and students, as
well as among teachers and the wider world outside of the classroom.

Final Thoughts on Dialogue and Reflexivity

The practical suggestions presented in the preceding section aim at stimulating creativity and prosocial values, in particular the active cooperation
between students, and between students and teachers, within the classroom. Moreover, a key part of our argument here has been that one cannot
foster one without the other, or in other words, that creativity is *necessarily*
fostered by collaborative activities and, in turn, prosocial values are upheld
when engaging in distributed creative action. This should be good news
for teachers and parents who wonder about what to prioritize of the two.
However, it can also leave them with the question of where to start.

This question invites us to consider, once more, the Self-Other processes
that underpin creative and moral behavior and thus, ultimately, foster
sociability. A key process that has been directly or implicitly mentioned
throughout the chapter, in particular in our last practical suggestions, is
represented by reflexivity. Being reflexive is essential for the development
of self and society according to Mead (1934). In his social theory, reflexivity
is not a simple act of thinking about oneself. It refers instead to our
capacity to take the perspective of others and understand our own position
through the eyes of other people. Mead was particularly interested about
how this capacity emerges in human development and, just like Winnicott,
pointed to the importance of play and games in early development. Along
the same line as Piaget (1990), who stressed the value of decentration,
perspective taking and cooperation to promote cognitive development,
Mead gave perspective taking a fundamental role in the development of
cooperative action (first expressed as a conversation of gestures between
child and caregiver). It is because we are capable of understanding the
situation as an Other would that human communication is made possible,
and this requires both recognizing and being open to other perspectives on
the world. Needless to say, this openness to different perspectives is also
essential for creative expression (see Glăveanu, 2015).

Reflexivity and perspective taking are involved in *dialogical encounters*
between people (Jovchelovitch, 2007), both within and outside school
contexts. These kinds of encounters are marked by respect for Otherness

and by valuing the perspective and knowledge of others. Fruitful forms of cooperation, in the spirit of Simmel's notion of sociability, are rooted in dialogical, reflexive encounters. Without this engagement with the Other, cooperation would be simply a juxtaposition of people and their ideas. The truly creative or emergent quality of cooperation resides in our willingness to learn from others, to take their perspective in concrete situations and to reflect on what this perspective brings to us and to our actions. Nurturing the development of creativity and prosocial values would be unimaginable in the absence of dialogical and reflective relations between Self and Other.

The most serious difficulties to implement changes in education practices come from traditional pedagogical beliefs in purely individual development through individualized practices and competitive motivation. From a socio-cultural perspective, it is evident how strongly those traditional practices are rooted in our individualist and competitive culture (Branco, 2012). Therefore, the significant transformation of school practices, guided by recent theoretical advances in developmental and socio-cultural psychology, is in great demand. This leaves us with a final, crucial question: How easy is it to facilitate such relations within the context of contemporary schools, burdened by constant demands, constrained by the curriculum – both documented and implicit – and often by a lack of resources, suffocated by an outcome-based approach that neglects process and the value of experience? Perhaps less difficult than we think. What it takes is a deeper understanding of *human interactions in their full expression as **both** creative and ethical*. Many small adjustments can be done to foster mutual respect, creative collaboration, and reflexivity in day-to-day educational practices, making them an integral part of the educational act. If our assumptions are correct, the consequences of these small changes can be truly monumental.

REFERENCES

Alencar, E. M. L. S. (2001). *Criatividade e educação de superdotados*. Petrópolis: Vozes.

Alencar, E. M. L. S. (2003). Barreiras à criatividade pessoal entre professores de distintos níveis de ensino. *Psicologia: Reflexão e Crítica*, **16**(1), 63–69.

Barrios, A., & Branco, A. U. (2010). Desenvolvimento moral: estudo das concepções de professores da Educação Infantil na perspectiva sociocultural construtivista. Paper presented at the XL Reunião Anual da Sociedade Brasileira de Psicologia, Curitiba, PR, Brazil, October.

Beghetto, R. A., & Kaufman, J. C. (Eds.). (2010). *Nurturing creativity in the classroom*. New York: Cambridge University Press.

Blasi, A. (2004). Moral functioning: Moral understanding and personality. In K. Daniel, D. K. Lapsey, & D. Narvaez (Eds.), *Moral development, self, and identity* (pp. 335–347). Mahwah, NJ: Lawrence Erlbaum Associates.

Bodrova, E., & Leong, D. J. (2007). *Tools of the mind: The Vygotskian approach to early childhood education*. Upper Saddle River, NJ: Pearson Education.

Branco, A. U. (2003). Social development in cultural context: Cooperative and competitive interaction patterns in peer relations. In J. Valsiner & K. Connolly (Eds.), *Handbook of developmental psychology* (pp. 238–256). London: Sage.

Branco, A. U. (2006). Crenças e práticas culturais: co-construção e ontogênese de valores sociais. [Cultural practices and beliefs; coconstruction and ontogenesis of social values]. *Revista Pro-Posições - UNICAMP*, 17, 139–155.

Branco, A. U. (2009). Cultural practices, social values, and childhood education. In M. Fleer, M. Hedegaard, & J. Tudge (Eds.), *Constructing childhood: Global–local policies and practices. World Yearbook 2009, Childhood studies and the impact of globalization* (pp. 44–66). London: Routledge.

Branco, A. U. (2012). Values and sociocultural practices: Pathways to moral development. In: J. Valsiner (Ed.), *The Oxford handbook of cultural psychology* (pp. 109–132) New York: Oxford University Press.

Branco, A. U., Barreto, A., & Barrios, A. (forthcoming). Educational practices and young children's socio-moral development: A cultural psychological approach. To appear in: M. Fleer & B. van Oers (Eds.), *International handbook on early childhood education*. Amsterdam: Springer.

Branco, A. U., & Barrios, A. (2014). Desarrollo moral y ontogenesis de los valores democráticos en la escuela. In: F. Gonzalez-Londra & A. R. Rivero (Eds.), *Hacer(se) ciudadan@s: una psicología para la democracia* (pp. 187–214). Buenos Aires: Mino y Davila.

Branco, A. U., & Mettel, T. P. L. (1995). O processo de canalização cultural das interações criança-criança na pré-escola. [Cultural canalization processes of child-child interactions in preschool]. *Psicologia: Teoria e Pesquisa*, 11, 13–22.

Branco, A. U., & Valsiner, J. (1997). Changing methodologies: A co-constructivist study of goal orientations in social interactions. *Psychology and Developing Societies*, **9**(1), 35–64.

Branco, A., & Valsiner, J. (Eds.). (2012). *Cultural psychology of human values*. Charlotte, NC: Information Age Publishing.

Conti, R., Collins, M., & Picariello, M. (2001). The impact of competition on intrinsic motivation and creativity: Considering gender, gender segregation, and gender-role identity. *Personality and Individual Differences*, **31**, 1273–1289.

Corsaro, W. (2011). *The sociology of childhood*. London: Sage.

Craft, A. (2005). *Creativity in schools: Tensions and dilemmas*. London: Routledge Taylor & Francis Group.

Cropley, A. J. (1997). Fostering creativity in the classroom: General principles. In M. A. Runco (Ed.), *The creativity research handbook* (pp. 83–114). Creskill, NJ: Hampton Press.

Cropley, D. H., Cropley, A. J., Kaufman, J. C., & Runco, M. A. (Eds.). (2010). *The dark side of creativity*. New York: Cambridge University Press.

Csikszentmihalyi, M. (1988). Society, culture, and person: A systems view of creativity. In R. Sternberg (Ed.), *The nature of creativity: Contemporary psychological perspectives* (pp. 325–339). Cambridge: Cambridge University Press.

Dumont, L. (1985). *O individualismo: uma perspectiva antropológica da ideologia moderna*. Rio de Janeiro: Rocco.

Fleer, M., Hedegaard, M., & Tudge, J. (2009). *Constructing childhood: Global–local policies and practices. World Yearbook 2009, Childhood studies and the impact of globalization*. New York: Routledge.

Glăveanu, V. P. (2009). The cultural genesis of creativity. *Revista de Psihologie Şcolară*, **2**(4), 50–63.

Glăveanu, V. P. (2010a). Paradigms in the study of creativity: Introducing the perspective of cultural psychology. *New Ideas in Psychology*, **28**(1), 79–93.

Glăveanu, V. P. (2010b). Principles for a cultural psychology of creativity. *Culture & Psychology*, **16**(2), 147–163.

Glăveanu, V. P. (2014). *Distributed creativity: Thinking outside the box of the creative individual*. Cham: Springer.

Glăveanu, V. P. (2015). Creativity as a sociocultural act. *Journal of Creative Behavior*, 49(3), 165–180.

Gregerson, M., Snyder, H., & Kaufman, J. C. (Eds.). (2013). *Teaching creatively and teaching creativity*. New York: Springer Science.

Gruber, H., & Wallace, D. (1999). The case study method and evolving systems approach for understanding unique creative people at work. In R. Sternberg (Ed.), *Handbook of creativity* (pp. 93–115). Cambridge: Cambridge University Press.

Gruys, M. L., Munshi, N. V, & Dewett, T. C. (2011). When antecedents diverge: Exploring novelty and value as dimensions of creativity. *Thinking Skills and Creativity*, **6**(2), 132–137.

Guilford, J. P. (1950). Creativity. *American Psychologist*, **5**, 444–454.

Johnson, D. W., & Johnson, R. T. (1989). *Cooperation and competition: Theory and research*. Minneapolis, MN: Interaction.

Jovchelovitch, S. (2007). *Knowledge in context: Representations, community and culture*. London: Routledge.

Jovchelovitch, S. (2015). The creativity of the social: Imagination, development and social change in Rio de Janeiro's favelas. In V. P. Glăveanu, A. Gillespie, & J. Valsiner (Eds.), *Rethinking creativity: Contributions from social and cultural psychology* (pp. 76–92). London: Routledge.

Kharkhurin, A. V. (2014). Creativity.4in1: Four-Criterion Construct of Creativity. *Creativity Research Journal*, **26**(3), 338–352.

Kohlberg, L. (1981). *Essays on moral development, Vol. I: The Philosophy of Moral Development*. San Francisco: Harper & Row.

Kohn, A. (1986). *No contest: The case against competition*. Boston, MA: Houghton Mifflin Company.

Kozulin, A., Gindis, B., Ageyev, V. S., & Miller, S. M. (Eds). (2011). *Vygotksy's educational theory in cultural context.* New York: Cambridge University Press.

Kuczynski, L., Marshall, S., & Schell, K. (1997). Value socialization in a bidirectional context. In J. E. Grusec & L. Kuczynski (Eds.), *Parenting and the internalization of values: A handbook of contemporary theory* (pp. 23–50). New York: Wiley.

Lash, C. (1982). *The minimal self: Psychic survival in troubled times.* New York: W.W. Norton & Company.

Lubart, T. (2007). *Psicologia da criatividade.* Porto Alegre: ARTMED Editora.

Mason, J. H. (2003). *The value of creativity: An essay on intellectual history, from Genesis to Nietzsche.* Hampshire, UK: Ashgate.

Maturana H. (1998). *Emoções e linguagem na educação e na política.* Belo Horizonte, Brazil: UFMG.

Mead, G. H. (1934). *Mind, self and society from the standpoint of a social behaviorist.* Chicago: University of Chicago Press.

Moran, S., Cropley, D., & Kaufman, J. C. (Eds.). (2014). *The ethics of creativity.* New York: Palgrave.

Neelands, J., & Choe, B. (2010). The English model of creativity: Cultural politics of an idea. *International Journal of Cultural Policy,* **16**(3), 287–304.

Neves-Pereira, M. S. (2004). *Criatividade na Educação Infantil: Um estudo sociocultural construtivista de concepções e práticas de educadores.* Tese de Doutorado: Universidade de Brasília, Brasília.

Neves-Pereira, M. S. (2007). *Estratégias de promoção da criatividade. Em A construção de práticas educacionais para alunos com altas habilidades/ superdotação.* Volume 2: Atividades de estimulação de alunos. MEC/Brasil.

Neves-Pereira, M. S., & Branco, A. U. (2015). Criatividade na educação infantil: Contribuições da psicologia cultural para a investigação de concepções e práticas de educadores. *Estudos de Psicologia (Natal),* 20, 161–172.

Palmieri, M., & Branco, A. U. (2008). Educação infantil, cooperação e competição: analise microgenética sob uma perspectiva sociocultural. [Early education, cooperation and competition: a sociocultural microgenetic analysis]. *Psicologia Escolar e Educacional,* **11**, 365–378.

Palmieri, M., & Branco, A. U. (2015). *Cooperação na educação infantil.* Londrina, Brazil: Editora da Universidade Estadual de Londrina.

Paolichi, P. (2007). The institutions inside: Self, morality, and culture. In J. Valsiner & A. Rosa (Eds.), *The Cambridge handbook of sociocultural psychology* (pp. 560–575). New York: Cambridge University Press.

Piaget, J. (1965 [1932]). *The moral judgement of the child.* New York: Free Press.

Piaget, J. (1990). *Seis estudos.* São Paulo: Martins Fontes.

Ratner, C. (2002). *Cultural psychology: Theory and method.* New York: Plenum.

Rogoff, B. (2003). *The cultural nature of human development.* New York: Oxford University Press.

Salomao, S. & Branco, A.U. (2001). Cooperação, competição e individualismo pesquisa e contemporaneidade. *Temas em Psicologia,* **9**(1), 11–18.

Sennett, R. (2004). *Respeito*. Rio de Janeiro: Editora Record.

Simmel, G. (1949). The sociology of sociability (Trans. E. C. Hughes). *American Journal of Sociology*, **55**(3), 254–261.

Starko, A. J. (1995). *Creativity in the classroom: Schools of curious delight*. New York: Longman Publishers.

Staub, E. (2003). *The psychology of good and evil: Why children, adults, and other groups help and harm others*. New York: Cambridge University Press.

Valsiner, J. (2007). *Culture in minds and societies: Foundations of cultural psychology*. New Delhi: Sage.

Valsiner, J. (2014). *An invitation to cultural psychology*. London: Sage.

Vygotsky, L. S. (1978). *Mind in society: The development of higher psychological processes*. Edited by M. Cole, V. John-Steiner, S. Scribner, & E. Souberman. Cambridge, MA: Harvard University Press.

Vygotsky, L. S. (1999). *O desenvolvimento psicológico na infância*. São Paulo: Editora Martins Fontes.

Winnicott, D. W. (1971). *Playing and reality*. London: Routledge.

Wood, D. J., Bruner, J. S., & Ross, G. (1976). The role of tutoring in problem solving. *Journal of Child Psychiatry and Psychology*, **17**(2), 89–100.

CHAPTER 17

How Social-Emotional Imagination Facilitates Deep Learning and Creativity in the Classroom

Rebecca Gotlieb, Erik Jahner, Mary Helen
Immordino-Yang and Scott Barry Kaufman

Imagination is not only the uniquely human capacity to envision that which is not, and therefore the fount of all invention and innovation. In its arguably most transformative and revelatory capacity, it is the power that enables us to empathise with humans whose experiences we have never shared.

J. K. Rowling, 2008

Developing creativity in students is not a luxury. Technology experts project that about 47% of current jobs in the United States will become obsolete because of computers within the next decade or two, and the jobs that will remain are those that require creative intelligence (Frey & Osborne, 2013). In this chapter we propose that supporting youths' capacities for *social-emotional imagination* – their abilities to creatively conjure alternative perspectives, emotional feelings, courses of action, and outcomes for oneself and others in the short- and long-term future – is a critical missing piece in many classrooms. This mental act of imagining precedes and translates into creative behaviors – behaviors that demonstrate divergent thinking or a novel approach to a problem and result in the formation of a useful idea or work.

Students' school success and lifelong creativity are facilitated not only by the cognitive skills measured by IQ tests but by other cognitive and social-emotional attributes. Critically, a capacity for imagination enables many of these cognitive and social-emotional skills, such as intellectual curiosity, openness to experience, passion, inspiration, love of work, envisioning future goals, persistence, sense of mission, courage, delight in deep thinking, tolerance of mistakes, and feeling comfortable as a "minority of one" (e.g., Cox, 1926; Duckworth & Seligman, 2005; Fredricks, Blumfeld & Paris, 2004; Furnham & Bachtair 2008; Kaufman, 2013a, 2013b; Kaufman et al., 2015; Nusbaum & Silvia, 2011; Oyserman & Destin, 2010; Runco, Millar, Acar, & Cramond, 2010; Torrance, 1993, 2003, 2004; von Stumm,

Hell, & Chamorro-Premuzic, 2011). Imagination is central because it allows students to reflect holistically about what they learn such that school-related tasks are more meaningful, personally relevant and rewarding, and more connected to the adulthood they hope to achieve one day. Imagination facilitates creative, critical dispositions toward new content and skills by helping students conjure new connections between ideas and invent new ways to represent and apply information.

Clearly, students who are able to find personally relevant meaning in the content and skills they are learning, who are able to envision the instrumental connections between their current work and their later success, and who can dream about a more accomplished life than they currently have are better able to persist and achieve (Oyserman, Bybee, & Terry, 2006; Oyserman & Destin, 2010). Yet, schools often singularly emphasize developing youths' task-related competencies in the near term. Some schools may not recognize that students' abilities to persist with the hard work of academic learning, and to use what they learn as groundwork for a satisfying life, are tied to something bigger. Students are rarely taught that their persistence is enhanced by their abilities to cultivate an imagined possible future and to connect what they are learning to the meaning that future holds (e.g., Oyserman & Destin, 2010; Torrance, 1993). Thus imaginativeness not only helps students persist in school, but it also helps them develop the creative skills that will be most critical for their employability when they leave school. Preparing students to undertake creative intelligence tasks means scaffolding them in the ability to focus intently on a task at hand and also in consciously, appropriately, and temporarily disengaging from the task to situate its broader purpose in a larger, personally meaningful goal.

Given the link between students' personal socio-emotional qualities, creativity, and long-term achievement in the face of obstacles, how might schools support young people in developing creative dispositions toward learning – the kinds of creative dispositions that will support persistence, well-being, meaning making, and hard work? To help answer this question, we first review recent research in the emerging field of social-affective neuroscience. We then discuss the roles of future-oriented cognition, constructive internal reflection, positive constructive daydreaming, mind wandering, social-emotional reasoning, and multiculturalism on learning and creativity. We conclude with practical recommendations to help learners and supportive adults harness students' social-emotional imagination, and hence their skills for thinking creatively, in the classroom.

A Tale of Two Brain Networks

Recent neuroscientific research suggests that two interdependent but distinct brain states support, on the one hand, attention to the current context, task-oriented focus, action-oriented mindset, and contextualized cognition, and on the other hand imagination, creativity, meaning making, personally relevant cognition, retrospection, and prospective thinking (Andrews-Hanna, Smallwood, & Spreng, 2014; Immordino-Yang, Christodoulou, & Singh, 2012). Both mindsets are clearly important for student achievement: attention to the current context and an action orientation are necessary to participate in class discussions, focus on challenging work, and learn new information. Imagination-oriented mindsets, by contrast, are important for connecting to the broader, longer-term purpose of the work, and for inferring the connections across domains and exemplars.

That the brain state that supports creativity and maintenance of long-term goals often requires a relative "tuning out" of the current physical context has critical implications for education. Building from what is known about the brain states that underlie these two modes of thought, here we argue that classrooms should be designed to scaffold *both* kinds of thinking, and to support students in mindfully maneuvering between these two states. We argue that by overly emphasizing task-oriented focus (e.g., stressing standardized test performance) while providing little support or opportunity for reflection or meaning making, standard educational environments, and practices may undermine both creativity and long-term goal attainment.

The Brain's Default Mode Network Is the Neural Engine of Imagination

For more than a decade neuroscientists have investigated a network within the brain that they refer to as the default mode network (DMN; Greicius, Krasnow, Reiss, & Menon, 2003; Raichle & Snyder, 2007). The DMN is composed of a distributed system of brain areas in frontal and parietal regions along the midline of the brain, as well as medial regions in the temporal lobe and lateral sections in the inferior part of the parietal lobe (see Figure 17.1). The DMN was so named because it is active when individuals are resting and it is generally not activated when individuals engage attentively in cognitive, task-oriented processing (e.g., in working memory tasks; Greicius et al., 2003). When one brain network is more active, the other tends to be less so (Esposito et al., 2006; Fox, Snyder, Vincent,

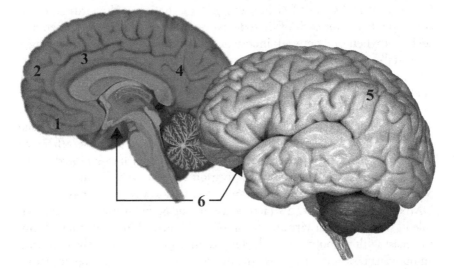

Figure 17.1 Overview of the main brain regions comprising the default mode (DM) network, with brief descriptions of associated socioemotional functions. The DM regions listed are relatively more active and show coordinated activity during wakeful "rest." The regions depicted are also involved in many other functions, including various cognitive association functions and aspects of homeostatic regulation and somatosensation, especially for the milieu of the internal body (i.e., the "guts"). The left side of the image shows the front of the brain: the right and left hemispheres are split apart to show the medial surface. Note that these brain areas cannot be said to "do" the functions listed. Instead, they are especially "associated" with these functions and as such are thought to play important roles within the complex networks of regions underlying the functions. 1. Ventromedial prefrontal cortex (vmPFC): induction of social emotions; nonconscious induction of somatic responses, such as skin sweating associated with a sense of risk; modulation of the parasympathetic branch of the autonomic nervous system (important for calming of heart rate). 2. Dorsomedial prefrontal cortex (dmPFC): representation of self in relation to others; predicting emotional outcomes of social interactions for self and close others; judging psychological and emotional qualities and traits; feeling emotions about others' mental situations. 3. Anterior middle cingulate cortex (ACC): a centrally connected "hub" of the cortex, also heavily interconnected with somatosensory regions that feel the guts and viscera; error monitoring, emotion, and empathy; feeling physical and social pain; modulation of the sympathetic branch of the autonomic nervous system (important for activation of heart rate, arousal). 4. Posteromedial cortices (PMC): the most centrally connected "hub" of the cortex; high-level integrative representation of the physiological condition of the visceral "gut" body; construction of a subjective sense of self-awareness; activated in social emotions, moral decision making, and episodic memory retrieval; contains dorsal posterior cingulate cortex (dPCC); involved in attention monitoring or switching and integration of information. 5. Inferior parietal lobule (IPL): involved in successful episodic memory retrieval; empathically simulating others' perspectives and the goals of others' actions. 6. Hippocampus: formation and recall of long-term memories (not visible in these views).

Corbetta, Van Essen, & Raichle, 2005). Also, the internal coordination of components within each of these networks appears to be complementary, such that when one network increases coordinated co-activation (stronger "cross-talk" between relevant brain regions), the other network's coordinated co-activation tends to attenuate (Greicius & Menon, 2004; Dwyer et al., 2014).

Because neural activity in the DMN tends to decrease when individuals engage in many typical academic and cognitive tasks, and because the mind-wandering activities that it undergirds tend to decrease efficiency and productivity in the moment, a body of research has explored problems associated with involuntary activation of the DMN (Mooneyham & Schooler, 2013; Smallwood & Schooler, 2015). However, emphasizing the DMN's role in academic distraction and disengagement misses its essential role in students' creativity and meaning making, and likely in their ability to persist with schooling over the long term. Indeed, exclusively activating an outward task focus may bias the mind away from integrating academic experiences into one's own personal understanding – a bias that could potentially undermine long-term learning, retention, and persistence.

In recent years, research has accumulated suggesting that the DMN (and its interaction with the networks that support attentional control) are critical to the healthy development of a variety of skills that facilitate deep learning, including cognitive control, self-regulation, emotion regulation, memory suppression, mindfulness, and meta-awareness (Cocchi, Zalesky, Fornito, & Mattingley, 2013; Depue, Curran, & Banich, 2007; Dwyer et al., 2014; Hare, Camerer, & Rengel, 2009; Kilpatrick et al., 2011; Ochsner, Silvers, & Buhle, 2012; Peters & Buchel, 2010; Smallwood, McSpadden, & Schooler, 2008; Spreng et al., 2014; Taylor et al., 2012). DMN connectivity is even positively correlated with IQ scores (Song et al., 2009) and supports processes for encoding and retrieving information from memory (Piccoli et al., 2015). There is a robust correlation between high scores on traditional cognitive tests (e.g., of divergent thinking, reading comprehension, and memory) and more efficient functioning in the DMN. Critically, these positive associations are not due to greater or more consistent activity over time. Instead, high scorers show greater decoupling of the DMN from the externally focused networks during situations that call for flexible engagement of attention, perception, and cognition (Li et al., 2009).

Evidence suggests that students need to increase DMN activation to optimally enable a global, personal type of academic engagement. The DMN seems to support mental states that are critically important for generating imaginative thoughts and facilitating creative action

(Beaty et al., 2014; Beaty, Benedek, Kaufman, & Silvia, 2015; Jung, Mead, Carrasco, & Flores, 2013). For example, the DMN is activated when we daydream, construct mental representations of ourselves and our future personal goal attainment, or think about autobiographical events (Addis, Wong, & Schacter, 2007; D'Armgembeau et al., 2010; Kucyi & Davis, 2014; Qin & Northoff, 2011). Similarly, individuals who spontaneously describe autobiographical memories when reacting to others' situations also show tighter connectivity of the DMN to memory-supporting brain regions during rest (Yang, Bossmann, Schiffhauer, Jordan, & Immordino-Yang, 2013). Simulating our social-emotional world, and feeling complex emotions such as compassion for social pain, admiration for virtue, or worry about our own anticipated pain also activate the DMN (Immordino-Yang, McColl, Damasio, & Damasio, 2009; Ochsner et al., 2006). Greater co-activation among DMN regions when at rest is associated with less self-doubt in a threatening academic testing condition and a more accurate impression of one's performance (Forbes et al., 2014). Thus, the DMN is thought to be critically involved in how we understand ourselves, how we learn about our emotional worlds, how we think abstractly about social situations, and how we construct and strategize to attain desireable possible futures (Immordino-Yang et al., 2012).

Though DMN activation supports the development of a personally relevant understanding of learned content, DMN activity must be reduced to engage in specific academic tasks that require external attentional control. For example, a study comparing high and low math anxiety students with similar mathematical proficiency found that students with high math anxiety showed greater activation in the DMN when attempting to stay on task in math problem solving, suggesting that they were completing the math tasks with less processing efficiency (Pletzer, Kronbichler, Nuerk, & Kerschbaum, 2015). Given these findings, next we focus on the skills that help students make meaning of academic content, connect to it personally, and relate it to their future goals.

Psychological Self and Creativity

Cultivating Creativity through Future-Oriented Thought and Imagined Possible Selves

The DMN underlies the process involved in imagining the steps one will take to achieve a goal or desired self (Gerlach, Spreng, Madore, & Schacter, 2014). One component of social-emotional imagination is the generation of future-oriented thoughts in which individuals forecast themselves or others into a temporally, spatially, and (sometimes) emotionally different context. This aspect of social-emotional imagination in itself involves creativity in the sense of creating a scenario that does not actually exist. Further, it is a skill that that has proven adaptive for helping students achieve and that positive psychologists suggest is key for psychological adjustment and happiness (Seligman & Csikszentmihalyi, 2000; Seligman, Railton, Baumeister, & Sripada, 2013). In turn, because positive emotion has been associated with expansive, divergent thinking (Fredrickson, 2004), future-oriented thinking could also indirectly promote some forms of creativity (e.g., Davis, 2009).

Future-oriented thinking, itself a creative endeavor, also impacts students' feelings and actions about their academic work in the present by lessening procrastination and promoting persistence. Whereas objective time can be measured predictably by the hours in a day and the days on a calendar, subjective time – the way one thinks about time or the feeling one has about the relative closeness of events across time – is dynamic and individually variable (Wilson, Gunn, & Ross, 2009) and impacts performance on academic tasks. For example, first-year college students who were made to feel as though their college graduation was near were more motivated to work hard now than students who were made to feel as though their graduation was in the distant future (Peetz, Wilson, & Strahan 2009). Similarly, students who thought they would perform poorly on a test reported feeling as though the test would occur further in the future than did their peers who believed they would perform well on the test (Peetz et al., 2009). Individuals who were asked to estimate time to future events in smaller units (e.g., days rather than months) also perceived that they should begin preparations sooner in order to be ready (Lewis & Oyserman, 2015). Together, these findings suggest that students' perception of time, and specifically their abilities to mentally imagine themselves at a future time, is tied to their ability to work hard now and to persist toward meaningful goals (Horstmanshof, & Zimitat, 2007; Oyserman & Destin, 2010; Gerlach et al., 2014). After all, it is easier to start down a productive path once we have imagined its existence.

The fact that individuals vary in the extent to which they spontaneously simulate distant or improbable future experiences (Tamir & Mitchell, 2011) suggests that we can teach them to engage these simulations. Oyserman and colleagues have shown that this variation can be productively translated into effective interventions that help middle and high school students, including students from low-income families and challenging backgrounds, to envision desired future selves and then to attain them. They found that students who had been taught to connect their goal with the steps necessary to achieve it were more positive in their interpretations of the inevitable difficulties they encountered up to two years later. Students' visions of their future self appeared to help them regulate their current behavior, leading to better academic grades, more time devoted to homework, and more frequent participation in class (Oyserman, Bybee, Terry, & Hart-Johnson, 2004). In short, skills for mentally simulating a future self helped students take steps toward that future self.

Though these interventions leverage adolescents' developing abilities to realistically imagine the longer-term future, interventions have also been designed that are effective at supporting young children in managing their behavior to attain a shorter term goal. For example, Goleman (2013) reports that Walter Mischel, the researcher who conducted the famous marshmallow experiment with nursery school students, has collaborated with Sesame Street around a story line to help children envision a future self. One character on the show helps Cookie Monster resist the urge to wolf down a plate of cookies by asking him, "What's more important: this cookie now, or getting into the club where you'll get all kinds of cookies?" With the thought of potential membership in the Cookie Connoisseur Club in mind, Cookie Monster is able to limit himself to only a nibble of a cookie now (Goleman, 2013). Young kids learn to hold their future goals online, in their working memory, as they weigh decisions about how to act now. They learn that present actions affect future, imagined outcomes. If we take creativity to mean thinking in a novel way and producing a new, useful idea, the aforementioned teenagers have acted creatively and the Sesame Street watchers have seen creativity modeled. They have created an imagined future in a way that supported their behavioral regulation in the present.

Future-oriented thoughts are a form of creative thinking that research has shown can support students in becoming their best, desired selves. Because simulating far-future events is challenging and important for persistence, parents and educators can scaffold students in imagining their future selves. They can also model creative behavior as this spurs students to act more creatively themselves (Yi, Plucker, & Guo, 2015). Asking questions about students' goals and the steps they are taking to achieve those goals or to avoid undesirable futures, as well as demonstrating steps to do so, can help students move along the path to their future self. In that spirit, we now turn our attention to the ways that reflection, daydreaming, mind wandering, and social-emotional reasoning engage and promote creative thinking.

Cultivating Creativity through Constructive Internal Reflection

In addition to future-oriented thinking, to cultivate creative, compassionate learners, the new information on DMN functioning suggests that students need downtime in which outward demands are not placed on their attentional resources and they are free to reflect (Immordino-Yang et al., 2012). Constructive internal reflection is a term we have defined previously to describe internally oriented thoughts that can range from free-form day-dreaming to focused, deliberate processing of information about abstract information, especially with socio-emotional relevance (Immordino-Yang et al., 2012). During constructive internal reflection an individual may build a complex representation of the self, envision possible futures, or engage in moral reasoning. Given that the DMN is thought to support multiple modes of constructive internal reflection, and given that the DMN does not readily co-activate with outwardly focused attention networks, Immordino-Yang and colleagues (2012) hypothesized that the opportunity for constructive internal reflection can be compromised by heavy environmental attention demands, such as may be produced by overbooked school schedules, the challenges of urban environments, or incessant texting and engagement with social media. Consistent exposure to such circumstances could conceivably undermine youths' ability to reflect and to think creatively, an idea that Immordino-Yang and her colleagues are currently testing (e.g., Rotenstein, Bansal, Yang, & Immordino-Yang, 2014).

Though the long-term effects of high environmental attention demands on inwardly directed thought are only now being tested, evidence already exists that productively engaging in constructive internal reflection can offer immediate benefits, such as improved academic performance. For example, the negative effects on academic performance of identity-based stereotypes can sometimes be reversed by priming activities involving constructive internal reflection. In one study, one group of women were encouraged to reflect about the full complexity of their identity and subsequently generated, on average, 38 self-descriptors; another group only thought of their most basic characteristics and subsequently generated about 7 self-descriptors. For those who reflected on the richness and complexity of their identity, but not for those who only thought about their basic identity characteristics, the typical gender-based performance decrement on a math task subsequently disappeared (Gresky, Ten Eyck, Lord, & McIntrye, 2005). Similarly, female physics students who wrote two 15-minute reflections over the course of the semester about values that were most important to them outperformed a control group of female physics students on both an objective physics knowledge measure and course grades (Miyake et al., 2010). Internal reflection has also been shown to boost high-stakes exam scores. For high school and college students, writing about their thoughts and feelings about an impending test (but not writing about unrelated content) improved test performance. Further, the largest improvements were seen for the most anxious testers (Ramirez & Beilock, 2011). Though the results have been attributed to resolved worries and subsequent decreased cognitive load and greater working memory capacity (Forbes & Schmader, 2010; Rydell, Beilock, & McConell, 2009), we argue that part of dealing with worries involves helping the student consider the broader social implications of the task – a mental process likely supported by constructive internal reflection.

In any learning environment, but especially when students are experiencing states of high emotional arousal, supportive adults can encourage students to reflect about their goals and values. Educators can help create protected periods of time for engagement in constructive internal thought that allows them to see the implications of their current decisions for their future outcomes, and to conjure an image of self as a person on the path to the goal. Not only is this reflection intrinsically rewarding for students, but it may open students to thinking more freely and performing at their potential by helping them be comfortable with intellectual risk and divergent thinking (Dweck, 2006). Constructive internal reflection allows students to process information in terms of emotion and self, which facilitates the transfer of knowledge from a lecture to life (Immordino-Yang & Damasio, 2007).

Cultivating Creativity through Positive Constructive Daydreaming

One important dimension of internally focused thought that is often neglected in educational environments despite its relation to creativity is free-form, task-independent thought, sometimes described as daydreaming. Jerome L. Singer and colleagues discovered three daydreaming styles: poor attentional control, guilty dysphoric daydreaming, and positive constructive daydreaming (Zhiyan & Singer, 1997). The first two styles have been the focus of much daydreaming research and have painted daydreaming as a maladaptive activity. Conversely, the third area – positive constructive daydreaming – is a pervasive, healthy, and beneficial human experience. We have previously defined positive constructive daydreaming as "characterized by playful, wishful imagery and planful, creative thought" (McMillan, Kaufman, & Singer, 2013). Similar to constructive internal reflection, positive constructive daydreaming can enable meaning making, idea integration, prospective thinking, metacognition, divergent thinking, creativity, and patience (McMillan et al., 2013). Strategic activation of the DMN enables positive constructive daydreaming (McMillan et al., 2013).

Positive constructive daydreaming is highly valued by Singer and his colleagues but relatively understudied and underappreciated more broadly (McMillan et al., 2013). Those who are more likely to engage in this kind of daydreaming also tend to score more highly on the big-five personality dimensions of openness to experience (Zhiyan & Singer, 1997). Early work by Singer (1961) suggests that daydreamers may also be more patient. He divided children into two groups – frequent daydreamers and infrequent daydreamers. When asked to wait quietly for as long as possible, the frequent daydreamers waited significantly longer. Having time to mind wander facilitated fortitude, delaying gratification and making adaptive choices for long-term rather than short-term benefits (Smallwood, 2013). Mind wandering, a critical component of positive constructive daydreaming, is also associated with strong personal and cognitive skills that produce creative students.

Cultivating Creativity through Encouraging Productive Mind Wandering

A cross-cultural investigation of mind wandering with participants from more than 80 countries suggests that mind wandering consumes nearly half of our waking hours (Killingsworth & Gilbert, 2010). Smallwood and Schooler (2015) posit from an evolutionary perspective that something to which individuals devote so much time must have had some adaptive features. Indeed, it enables creative behaviors that help people thrive in diverse and changing environments. One benefit of mind wandering is that it facilitates the reprocessing of long-term memories (Wang et al., 2009). Mind wandering also may help reduce boredom when engaging in certain types of tasks with low cognitive demand (Smallwood & Schooler, 2015). When students let their minds wander, they have a more enjoyable experience completing simple tasks (e.g., cutting out pictures for a concept collage or organizing a binder).

Mind wandering can be pleasurable and can help the thinker achieve a future goal or consider alternative courses of action (McMillan et al., 2013). In neuro-typical individuals, mind wandering is associated with thinking about one's future, planning for upcoming events, and contemplating plans to overcome potential obstacles (Baumeister & Masicampo, 2010; Oettingen & Schwörer, 2013; Smallwood, Nind, & O'Connor, 2009).

As such, students who allow their mind to wander may be better prepared to tackle future challenges.

What appears to be most critical, however, is that meta-awareness about one's mind wandering can promote mind wandering that is productive. Mind wandering is often an uncontrolled process – we "catch" ourselves doing it and must exert considerable effort to stop (Smallwood & Schooler, 2015). Like other automatic processes that can be cognitively controlled when we become aware of them (Flavell, 1979), so too can we develop mind wandering meta-awareness. One study found that when individuals were aware that they were mind wandering (i.e., "tuning out"), as opposed to when they were unaware that their mind had drifted from the task at hand (i.e., "zoning out"), there was no decrement in performance on a reading task (Smallwood et al., 2008).

Compared to individuals with smaller working memory capacity, individuals with larger working memory capacity mind wander *less* as tasks become increasingly demanding (Kane & McVay, 2012), but they mind wander *more* than individuals with smaller working memory capacity when engaging in simple tasks (Kane et al., 2007; Levinson, Smallwood, & Davidson, 2012). It is possible then that higher working memory capacity increases an individual's ability to regulate one's mind wandering – to tune out and not zone out. When cognitive resources are available, individuals with high working memory strategically engage in mind wandering, but when the task requires greater cognitive resources, the high working memory individuals prioritize engagement with the demanding task. Individuals with lower working memory capacity have greater difficulty determining whether the demands of a task allow for mind wandering, and their performance suffers as a result.

Metacognitive regulation not only improves the strategic use of mind wandering; mind wandering also increases metacognitive awareness when performing a task. Allen and colleagues (2013) argue that individuals who are better able to switch between the DMN and the network that supports decontextualized cognition may be better at monitoring and optimizing their performance on cognitive tasks. These individuals have greater metacognitive awareness of the errors they commit while completing the task. The researchers suggest that mind wandering and self-monitoring are intertwined (Allen et al., 2013). Similarly, turning attention inward to examine the components of one's thoughts facilitates making creative connections and imagining new solutions to problems. While outwardly focused attention and high working memory capacity facilitates analytic problem solving, too much of this type of attentional focus undermines creativity and one's ability to solve intractable problems with original solutions (Wiley & Jarosz, 2012).

This is consistent with lore across various disciplines that some of society's greatest discoveries have come to individuals in a flash of insight – Archimedes, the bath tub, and determining volume of irregular objects; Isaac Newton, the apple, and gravity; and Paul McCartney, a sleepy morning haze, and the song "Yesterday." What is often not described in the legend of tremendous breakthroughs, and what makes Allen and colleagues' (2013) finding so important, is that years of dedicated study and countless hours of outwardly focused learning about the topic of interest contributed to the ideas coming together in the moment of insight. Ericsson's theory of deliberate practice suggests that long-term focused and sustained engagement with a practice (across disciplines and domains) is necessary to develop expertise (e.g., Ericsson & Charness, 1994; Ericson, Krampe, & Tesch-Römer, 1993). A warm bath, a falling apple, or sleepiness alone would not have allowed these giants to come to their realizations without the years of study they already undertook. Research that we have just conducted suggests that creative thinking draws on both spontaneous thought, originating from the DMN, and on sustained cognitive control over those thoughts (originating from a separate brain network; Beaty et al., 2015).

Inspiring the next Archimedes, Newton, or McCartney involves scaffolding learners to mindfully oscillate between internally and externally focused thoughts. The creative individual gathers seeds of knowledge from explicit instruction and withdraws to plant those seeds in the soil of what is meaningful to her. In this view, educators should be less concerned with squelching lapses in attention and more concerned with ensuring that shifts between inwardly and outwardly focused attention are well timed and productive.

Social Processing and Creativity

Understanding Our Social World Requires Creative Thought

The ability to understand one's social world – to make meaning of socially complex scenarios, to reason empathically about others' circumstances, and to take the perspective of other individuals and cultures – is a form of imagination that leads to the reflective and motivated citizens our society would hope to create. Empathic and social reasoning enables individuals to act creatively in finding solutions to social problems and to strive to better themselves by adopting the values undergirding others' admirable acts. Students engage in constructive internal reflection (Immordino-Yang et al., 2012), which helps them build a nuanced understanding of another's perspective. In the process of coming to understand the other person's feelings, they may imagine how that person must have felt by imaging themselves in that person's situation. This, in turn, could inspire them to behave more like that person. For example, in responding to a story depicting a young woman who, after tragically losing her sight, goes on to invent a braille system for the Tibetan language and moves to Tibet to open a school for the blind, one young woman responds,

> It kind of makes me reflect upon my own life and realize that considering that I haven't had as extreme, like, uncontrollable circumstances as all these people, it makes me realize, well, if they can do that despite whatever hardships they have then I definitely should be making more of my resources in my life. (Quoted in Immordino-Yang, 2010, p. 218)

As this young woman has done, students who come to engage deeply with stories about another person's virtuous actions or admirable personal qualities like bravery, determination, and selflessness may undergo a shift in their thinking. They can move from thinking about the specifics of the stories and toward thinking about the possibility of how they might alter their own behavior and actions in the future. When students make meaning of others' virtue, they are often inspired to act more virtuously themselves (Immordino-Yang, 2011; Immordino-Yang et al., 2009). Young people who tended toward internal reflection in responding to similar stories (as evidenced by looking away and slowing their speech) also reported feeling more inspired, and later showed increased brain activation in the DMN regions when responding to narratives about others' virtue (Yang, Pavarini, Schnall, & Immordino-Yang, 2012).

Astute teachers sense that when students pause in response to complex questions, they should be allowed time to answer. The student may be synthesizing information and drawing connections to their own understanding during that pause (Immordino-Yang et al., 2012). In this way educators can protect mini-moments in which students productively engage the DMN.

Empathy and Perspective Taking

Researchers suggest that empathic reasoning, an element of social-emotional imagination, has a cognitive and affective component. In its cognitive form, empathy is the ability to assume another person's perspective and comprehend that person's state of being; in its affective form, empathy is the will and ability to experience that person's thoughts or feelings (Riggio, Tucker, & Coffaro, 1989; Singer & Lamm, 2009). The maxim, "I feel your pain" is neurobiologically accurate. A meta-analysis of fMRI studies about empathy suggests that the same regions of the brain that are recruited when an individual feels her own pain (e.g., the anterior insula and the medial/anterior cingulate cortex) are recruited when empathizing with another (Lamm, Decety, & Singer, 2011). Relatedly, an fMRI study with individuals high in psychopathy, known for having deficits in affective empathy, found that those individuals recruited different neural circuits when thinking about another's physical, bodily pain than controls (Decety, Chen, Harenski, & Kiehl, 2013). Batson (2009) proposes that empathy arises most consistently from taking another person's perspective and imagining what he thinks or feels.

Seeing someone else's point of view or sharing another person's feelings are important skills in the classroom. Understanding contextual considerations and taking the perspective of a historical figure might lead a student to a richer understanding (and better performance) in a social studies class, for instance (see, for example, the "Facing History and Ourselves" Curriculum; Schultz, Barr, & Selman, 2001). In addition, perspective taking and empathy can facilitate beneficial interactions among classmates, such as intervening to stop bullying (Gini, Albiero, Benelli, & Altoe, 2008). Some scholars have suggested that perhaps teaching empathic reasoning and perspective taking (two components of social-emotional imagination) could be one step toward curbing bullying for this reason (Nickerson, Mele, & Princiotta, 2008; van Noorden, Haselager, Cillessen, & Bukowski, 2014). Because feeling empathy results in students taking the perspective of another and can motivate students to imagine possible solutions to address a social problem (e.g., bullying) and then take action, empathy too can be thought of as generating creative social behavior and a deeper understanding.

Multiculturalism

Extending social behavior outside even further, exposure to other cultures, individuals from different backgrounds, and new languages promotes creative thinking. Polyculturalism, or being part of multiple interacting and interrelated cultures, primes creativity (Morris, Chiu, & Liu, 2015). College students who study abroad score higher on culturally specific and general tests of creativity than their peers who intend to study abroad but have not yet done so and peers who have not and do not intend to study abroad

(Lee, Therriault, & Linderholm, 2012). Similarly, actively participating in a novel and strange "diversifying" experience, even if simulated, has been shown to lead to more creative thinking (Ritter et al., 2012). Bilingualism in preschool-age children is associated with higher performance on measures of general creativity (Leikin, 2013), and across ages, people who have a greater degree of bilingualism score higher on a creativity test (Lee & Kim, 2011). Not only do these multicultural experiences promote creativity, but also one's acculturation and ability to reason based on different cultural norms impacts creativity.

Evidence from neurobiological studies suggests that an individual's cultural background and embodied experience processing emotions impact the way he constructs conscious experiences of his emotional reactions to the social world (Immordino-Yang, Yang, & Damasio, 2014). While cultures have traditionally been characterized dichotomously as individualistic or collectivist, culture-as-situated cognition argues that all human cultures are imbued with individualistic and collectivist primes and that all individuals can reason through either of these lenses (Oyserman, Novin, Flinkenflogel, & Krabbendam, 2014). Thinking about problems from the perspective of a different culture helps individuals come to understand that there may be a variety of possible solutions to a problem – an insight indicative of creativity. Thus, exposure to other cultures is valuable not only for cultivating global citizens but also for building more creative thinkers. Educators and parents should strive to provide opportunities for meaningful engagement with or at least exposure to diverse ways of thinking and living, as well as opportunities to take others' perspectives.

Harnessing the Power of Social-Emotional Imagination

The evidence presented in the preceding section can support and guide effective educational practices. To move in this direction, we developed the following recommendations for practice, based on our reasonable assumptions from the research. Many of these practices are frequently utilized in the classroom, but their importance is often overlooked as less important "soft skill" development. Thus, we emphasize appreciating these essential instructional practices and discourage their well-intentioned sacrifice in the name of academic evaluation and task-oriented classroom management strategies.

- **Schedule time for reflection, or capitalize on naturally occurring reflective moments.** By ensuring sufficient time for reflection schools, teachers, and parents can support social-emotional imagination and cultivate learners who are more mindful, more strategic, and ultimately more creative. Building reflection time and skills into educational activities while minimizing external distraction may facilitate students synthesizing information, building complex connections, and recognizing potential relevance to other domains and experiences. Allowing time for reflection may involve giving students quiet moments following an on-task academic activity in which students generate deeper questions, or in which instructors ask guiding questions to help students reflect on what they have learned. Because it helps students process worries and focus on goals, encouraging a few moments of reflection before high-stakes testing has also been demonstrated to actually boost performance (as reviewed earlier in this chapter). Further, writing about one's emotional response to personal events has been associated with improved mental and physical health (Pennebaker & Segal, 1999).

- **Scaffold and model mindfully moving between task-oriented focus and meaning making.** We encourage educators to offer cues to help students recognize times when they need to attend to a task versus times when reflection is appropriate. For example, a teacher might remind students of the environmental signals that task-oriented focus is necessary by saying something such as, "When your classmate speaks, please look at him." Similarly, a teacher might remind students of behaviors that aid reflection such as looking out the window, explaining to a friend, or encouraging them to write freely with minimal self-criticism. Not only can this help students recognize in the moment what they need to attend to, but it also can help students develop long-term strategies for focus on a task and alternately for imagining without inhibition.

- **Encourage strategic internal reflection.** Recognizing that momentary lapses in externally focused attention may be strategic or restful highlights their importance. By continually directing students to stay on task, and by providing entertainment or other distraction when students are resting, we may diminish students' problem-solving capacity by tiring them and by making it more difficult for them to connect their current work to future goals – in short, to make their academic efforts personally meaningful. Generating imagined possibilities to problem solutions and generalizing strategies toward other problem solving contexts may also have benefits in some contexts that extend beyond the benefits of rapid processing and action orientation. For example, a common strategy to help students read technical texts proficiently and actively is to encourage the student to pause periodically to synthesize, connect the information with personally meaningful content, and integrate new information into existing knowledge schemas. This can help students consolidate information, make new information more readily available for subsequent tasks, and bring technical discourse into a student's personal life narrative.

- **Scaffold meta-awareness.** Increasing mindfulness through meditative moments may increase metacognitive awareness and control over mind-wandering processes (Mrazek, Franklin, Phillips, Baird, & Schooler, 2013). By leading students in directed thought about the flow of their mental processes in age-appropriate ways and depending on the metacognitive abilities of the students, educators can help students begin to practice strategic switching between task focus and reflection.

- **Encourage actively imagining pathways to goals.** Activities that scaffold students' imagination as they construct pathways toward goal attainment can empower students to take better control of their academic and personal futures. Reflective writing or quiet contemplation in which students imagine themselves engaging in the process of studying or taking concrete steps toward achieving a desired academic goal can be more helpful in attaining academic success than focusing on achieving a higher test score or grade. Thinking of the future is not itself sufficient, nor is digging in to work hard now. The critical piece is connecting these two kinds of thinking together, such that students develop the habit of consciously reflecting on their hopes and dreams in both the near and farther future, and of translating those dreams into strategies for success and purposefulness in the current context.

- **Appropriate times for communicative technologies.** Parents and instructors can model and encourage context-appropriate disengagement from social media and communication technologies. While teenagers frequently switch between tackling a task and texting, for the reasons above we must preserve some "free" moments for internal reflection. Many middle and high school students have an overly involved relation with technology (Steinar-Adair & Barker, 2013), but adults can implement clear rules to allow for its appropriate use. For example, no texting at the dinner table, no cells phones during class discussion, or only searching for lecture-relevant content at appropriate times during class.

- **Effectively integrate social media and social imagination.** We should engage in productive discussions about technology use within social-emotional contexts. While social media, video conferencing, and other technologies connect us to each other in novel and productive ways, overuse can reduce attention to the multisensory content of social environments in which a student is physically embedded, thereby impacting social emotional imagination and development. During adolescence, when students' identities are fragile, teenagers are at risk for unhealthy obsessions with their online personas (Steinar-Adair & Baker, 2013). We encourage adults to assist students in understanding appropriate use of social and other media, and translating the subtleties found in face-to-face interactions into the complexities of social media interactions and relations. For example, adults can help students appreciate privacy concerns that exist in online relations that may not exist in face-to-face relations and help them recognize that emotion and intent may be perceived differently online than in person.

- **Use stories to help students build personal narratives**. Though technical academic content often feels disconnected from the people who invented or discovered it, in reality all human knowledge has humans behind it. It can be very motivating for students, as well as promoting of more complex and productive personal daydreams, to expose students to role models' accounts of struggles, interests, and accomplishments. Research into social emotional imagination suggests that these stories may have benefits to classroom instruction and students' long-term retention of course content. For one example, we all recognize that knowing that the sun is at the center of the solar system is critical to our understanding of Earth, but the importance of heliocentrism is amplified by the story of Galileo's willingness to endure the castigation of the Catholic Church to defend his scientific findings in support of that theory. A role model's narrative can be integrated into a student's imagined path to her future selves. By observing the process of discovery students learn about it, and gain skills for simulating their own possible future accomplishments.
- **Give students meaningful opportunities to make informed choices about curricular content**, for example in the form of projects, reports, or student-led initiatives. The best way to develop creative citizens is to give them supported practice at conceiving, developing, and following their interests, curiosity, and talents.

Overall, the research discussed in the earlier sections suggests strategically utilizing effective practices for encouraging imagination is beneficial for students both in the short and long terms, and in both "hard" and "soft" skills. Imagination is a lifeline that connects the student's inner, developing self with her exposure to the myriad of opportunities for formal and informal learning school and life experience provide.

Conclusion: Toward Fostering Creativity in Schools

Schools and teachers today are saddled with constraints to teach specific content and burdened by standardized testing pressures. In this climate of accountability, curricula scaffolding students' so-called "soft" skills are often among the first activities to be pruned. Recognizing that it is possible to foster students' academic achievement and their creativity can ease concerns about investing in students' imaginativeness. Ultimately, our country's future is in the hands of today's students, and a skilled, ethical, and creative body of students will hold the greatest promise for advancing our country.

In this vein, an integrative research approach that explores how to promote creativity is needed, including a deeper understanding of the biological, psychological, and cultural conditions that encourage productive reflection. Specifically, social and affective neuroscientists, cognitive psychologists, and educational psychologists can collaborate to improve our understanding of how to harness the benefits of the DMN and the psychological states that it produces, and how to teach deliberate, appropriate, and mindful switching between task-oriented attention and imagining. We echo our previous call for additional research about the way in which internal reflection and meaning making impact cognitive skills and social-emotional development (Immordino-Yang et al., 2012).

Social-emotional imagination and positive constructive daydreaming are two psychological processes that are undergirded by the brain's default mode network and that contribute to developing innovative, compassionate, and grounded learners. Social-emotional imagination is by its nature creative in its fullest form, but it also produces creativity in the more generic sense by enabling thinkers to apply emotional insights to their interpretation of technical material (Immordino-Yang, 2011). Renowned cognitive and educational psychologist Jerome Bruner (1986) argues that educators should foster in students "an appreciation of the fact that many worlds are possible, that meaning and reality are created and not discovered, that negotiation is the art of creating new meanings by which individuals can regulate their relations with each other" (p. 149).

Each of these ideas depends on social-emotional imagination. Learners must interpret new information, cull emotionally relevant content, empathize with others' emotions, and make meaning out of a complex social world. Constructive internal reflection and positive constructive daydreaming provide the emotional and cognitive "play spaces" to understand the social world by providing a variety of alternative possible worlds. Empathy, perspective taking, and multiculturalism allow learners to perceive and feel alternative emotional states. They help us understand those around us so that we can, as Bruner (1986) argued, "regulate [our] relations with each other." Meaning making, a deep understanding of others' stories or one's own circumstances, may be a necessary prerequisite to feelings of inspiration to be one's best-self.

Aligned with Bruner, meaning making is a process of creation, not discovery. These processes together shape students' abilities to understand intricate social scenarios and feel complex emotions. By aiding students in effectively switching between decontextualized cognition and personally relevant cognition and ensuring that there are protected times in which students can productively struggle with social-emotional understanding, we will produce students who not only perform better on traditional academic metrics, but who also have a better understanding of their social-emotional world, and who will lead us into new creative territories.

Appendix

Reprinted from: Immordino-Yang, M. H., Christodoulou, J. A., & Singh, V. (2012). Rest is not idleness: Implications of the brain's default mode for human development and education. *Perspectives on Psychological Science*, 7(4), 352–364.

REFERENCES

Addis, D. R., Wong, A. T., & Schacter, D. L. (2007). Remembering the past and imagining the future: Common and distinct neural substrates during event construction and elaboration. *Neuropsychologia*, **45**, 1363–1377.

Aiello, D. A., Jarosz, A. F., Cushen, P. J., & Wiley, J. (2012). Firing the executive: When an analytic approach to problem solving helps and hurts. *The Journal of Problem Solving*, **4**(2), 7.

Allen, M., Smallwood, J., Christensen, J., Gramm, D., Rasmussen, B., et al. (2013). The balanced mind: The variability of task-unrelated thoughts predicts error monitoring. *Frontiers in Human Neuroscience*, **7**, 743. doi:10.3389/fnhum.2013.00743

Andrews-Hanna, J. R., Smallwood, J., & Spreng, R. N. (2014). The default network and self-generated thought: Component processes, dynamic control, and clinical relevance. *Annals of the New York Academy of Sciences*, **1316**, 29–52.

Batson, C. D. (2009). Two forms of perspective taking: Imagining how another feels and imagining how you would feel. In K. D. Markman,

W. M. Klein & J. A. Suhr (Eds.), *The handbook of imagination and mental simulation* (pp. 267–279). New York: Psychology Press.

Baumeister, R. F., & Masicampo, E. J. (2010). Conscious thought is for facilitating social and cultural interactions: How mental simulations serve the animal–culture interface. *Psychological Review*, **117**(3), 945.

Beaty, R. E., Benedek, M., Kaufman, S. B., & Silvia, p. J. (2015). Default and executive network coupling supports creative idea production. *Nature Scientific Reports*, **5**, 10964. doi:10.1038/srep10964

Beaty, R. E., Benedek, M., Wilkins, R. W., Jauk, E., Fink, et al. (2014). Creativity and the default network: A functional connectivity analysis of the creative brain at rest. *Neuropsychologia*, **64**, 92–98.

Bruner, J. (1986). *Actual minds, possible worlds*. Cambridge, MA: Harvard University Press.

Cocchi, L., Zalesky, A., Fornito, A., & Mattingley, J. B. (2013). Dynamic cooperation and competition between brain systems during cognitive control. *Trends in Cognitive Sciences*, **17**, 494–501.

Cox, C. M. (1926). *The early mental traits of three hundred geniuses* (Vol. **2**). Stanford, CA: Stanford University Press.

D'Argembeau, A., Stawarczyk, D., Majerus, S., Collette, F., Van der Linden, M., et al. (2010). The neural basis of personal goal processing when envisioning future events. *Journal of Cognitive Neuroscience*, **22**(8), 1701–1713.

Davis, M. A. (2009). Understanding the relationship between mood and creativity: A meta-analysis. *Organizational Behavior and Human Decision Processes*, **108**(1), 25–38.

Decety, J., Chen, C., Harenski, C., & Kiehl, K. A. (2013). An fMRI study of affective perspective taking in individuals with psychopathy: imagining another in pain does not evoke empathy. *Frontiers in Human Neuroscience*, **7**, 489. doi:10.3389/fnhum.2013.00489

Depue, B. E., Curran, T., & Banich, M. T. (2007). Prefrontal regions orchestra suppression of emotional memories via a two-phase process. *Science*, **317**, 215–219.

Duckworth, A. L., & Seligman, M. E. (2005). Self-discipline outdoes IQ in predicting academic performance of adolescents. *Psychological Science*, **16**(12), 939–944.

Dweck, C. (2006). *Mindset: The new psychology of success*. New York: Random House.

Dwyer, D. B., Harrison, B. J., Yücel, M., Whittle, S., Zalesky, A., et al. (2014). Large-scale brain network dynamics supporting adolescent cognitive control. *Journal of Neuroscience*, **34**, 14096–14107.

Ericsson, K. A., & Charness, N. (1994). Expert performance: Its structure and acquisition. *American Psychologist*, **49**, 725–747.

Ericsson, K. A., Krampe, R. T., & Tesch-Römer, C. (1993). The role of deliberate practice in the acquisition of expert performance. *Psychological Review*, **100**, 363–406.

Esposito, F., Bertolino, A., Scarabino, T., Latorre, V., et al. (2006). Independent component model of the default-mode brain function: Assessing the impact of active thinking. *Brain Research Bulletin*, **70**(4), 263–269.

Flavell, J. H. (1979). Metacognition and cognitive monitoring: A new area of cognitive–developmental inquiry. *American Psychologist*, **34**(10), 906–911.

Forbes, C. E., Leitner, J. B., Duran-Jordan, K., Magerman, A. B., Schmader, T., & Allen, J. J. (2014). Spontaneous default mode network phase-locking moderates performance perceptions under stereotype threat. *Social Cognitive and Affective Neuroscience*, **10**(7), 994–1002.

Forbes, C. E., & Schmader, T. (2010). Retraining attitudes and stereotype to affect motivation and cognitive capacity under stereotype threat. *Journal of Personality and Social Psychology*, **99**(5), 740–754.

Fox, M. D., Snyder, A. Z., Vincent, J. L., Corbetta, M., Van Essen, D. C., & Raichle, M. E. (2005). The human brain is intrinsically organized into dynamic, anticorrelated functional networks. *Proceedings of the National Academy of Sciences, USA*, **102**, 9673–9678.

Fredricks, J. A., Blumenfeld, P. C., & Paris, A. H. (2004). School engagement: Potential of the concept, state of the evidence. *Review of Educational Research*, **74**(1), 59–109.

Fredrickson, B. L. (2004). The broaden-and-build theory of positive emotions. *Philosophical Transactions – Royal Society of London Series B, Biological Sciences*, 1367–1378.

Frey, C. B., & Osborne, M. A. (2013). *The future of employment: How susceptible are jobs to computerization?* Oxford: University of Oxford, Oxford Martin School.

Furnham, A., & Bachtiar, V. (2008). Personality and intelligence as predictors of creativity. *Personality and Individual Differences*, **45**(7), 613–617.

Gerlach, K. D., Spreng, R. N., Madore, K. P., & Schacter, D. L. (2014). Future planning: Default network activity couples with frontoparietal control network and reward-processing regions during process and outcome simulations. *Social Cognitive and Affective Neuroscience*, **9**(12), 1942–1951.

Gini, G., Albiero, P., Benelli, B., & Altoe, G. (2008). Determinants of adolescents' active defending and passive bystanding behavior in bullying. *Journal of Adolescence*, **31**(1), 93–105.

Goleman, D. (2013). *Focus: The hidden driver of excellence*. New York: Harper-Collins.

Greicius, M. D., Krasnow, B., Reiss, A. L., & Menon, V. (2003). Functional connectivity in the resting brain: A network analysis of the default mode hypothesis. *Proceedings of the National Academy of Sciences*, **100**(1), 253–258.

Greicius, M. D., & Menon, V. (2004). Default-mode activity during a passive sensory task: Uncoupled from deactivation but impacting activation. *Journal of Cognitive Neuroscience*, **16**(9), 1484–1492.

Gresky, D. M., Ten Eyck, L. L., Lord, C. G., & McIntyre, R. B. (2005). Effects of salient multiple identities on women's performance under mathematics stereotype threat. *Sex Roles*, **53**(9–10), 703–716.

Hare, T. A., Camerer, C., & Rangel, A. (2009). Self-control in decision-making involves modulation of the vmPFC valuation system. *Science*, **324**, 646–648.

Horstmanshof, L., & Zimitat, C. (2007). Future time orientation predicts academic engagement among first-year university students. *British Journal of Educational Psychology*, **77**(3), 703–718.

Immordino-Yang, M. H. (2010). Toward a microdevelopmental, interdisciplinary approach to social emotion. *Emotion Review*, **2**(3), 217–220.

Immordino-Yang, M. H. (2011a). Me, my "self" and you: Neuropsychological relations between social emotion, self-awareness, and morality. *Emotion Review*, **3**(3), 313–315.

Immordino-Yang, M. H. (2011b). Musings on the neurobiological and evolutionary origins of creativity via a developmental analysis of one child's poetry. *LEARNING Landscapes*, **5**(1), 133–139.

Immordino-Yang, M. H., Christodoulou, J. A., & Singh, V. (2012). Rest is not idleness: Implications of the brain's default mode for human development and education. *Perspectives on Psychological Science*, **7**(4), 352–364.

Immordino-Yang, M. H., & Damasio, A. (2007). We feel, therefore we learn: The relevance of affective and social neuroscience to education. *Mind, Brain, and Education*, **1**(1), 3–10.

Immordino-Yang, M. H., McColl, A., Damasio, H., & Damasio, A. (2009). Neural correlates of admiration and compassion. *Proceedings of the National Academy of Sciences USA*, **106**(19), 8021–8026.

Immordino-Yang, M. H., Yang, X. F., & Damasio, H. (2014). Correlations between social-emotional feelings and anterior insula activity are independent from visceral states but influenced by culture. *Frontiers in Human Neuroscience*, **8**(728), 1–15.

Jung, R. E., Mead, B. S., Carrasco, J., & Flores, R. A. (2013). The structure of creative cognition in the human brain. *Frontiers in Human Neuroscience*, **7**(330), 1–13.

Kane, M. J., Brown, L. H., McVay, J. C., Silvia, P. J., Myin-Germeys, I., & Kwapil, T. R. (2007). For whom the mind wanders, and when: An experience-sampling study of working memory and executive control in daily life. *Psychological Science*, **18**(7), 614–621.

Kane, M. J., & McVay, J. C. (2012). What mind wandering reveals about executive-control abilities and failures. *Current Directions in Psychological Science*, **21**(5), 348–354.

Kaufman, S. B. (2013a). *Ungifted: Intelligence redefined*. New York: Basic Books.

Kaufman, S. B. (2013b). Opening up openness to experience: A four-factor model and relations to creative achievement in the arts and sciences. *Journal of Creative Behavior*, **47**, 233–255.

Kaufman, S. B., Quilty, L. C., Grazioplene, R. G., Hirsh, J. B., Gray, J. R., Peterson, J. B., & DeYoung, C. G. (2015). Openness to experience and intellect differentially predict creative achievement in the arts and sciences. *Journal of Personality*, **84**(2), 248–258.

Killingsworth, M. A., & Gilbert, D. T. (2010). A wandering mind is an unhappy mind. *Science*, **330**(6006), 932

Kilpatrick, L. A., Suyenobu, B. Y., Smith, S. R., Bueller, J. A., Goodman, T., et al. (2011). Impact of mindfulness-based stress reduction training on intrinsic brain connectivity. *Neuroimage*, **56**(1), 290–298.

Kucyi, A., & Davis, K. D. (2014). Dynamic functional connectivity of the default mode network tracks daydreaming. *Neuroimage*, **100**, 471–480.

Lamm, C., Decety, J., & Singer, T. (2011). Meta-analytic evidence for common and distinct neural networks associated with directly experienced pain and empathy for pain. *Neuroimage*, **54**(3), 2492–2502.

Lee, C. S., Therriault, D. J., & Linderholm, T. (2012). On the cognitive benefits of cultural experience: Exploring the relationship between studying abroad and creative thinking. *Applied Cognitive Psychology*, **26**(5), 768–778.

Lee, H., & Kim, K. H. (2011). Can speaking more languages enhance your creativity? Relationship between bilingualism and creative potential among Korean American students with multicultural link. *Personality and Individual Differences*, **50**(8), 1186–1190.

Leikin, M. (2013). The effect of bilingualism on creativity: Developmental and educational perspectives. *International Journal of Bilingualism*, **17**(4), 431–447.

Levinson, D. B., Smallwood, J., & Davidson, R. J. (2012). The persistence of thought evidence for a role of working memory in the maintenance of task-unrelated thinking. *Psychological Science*, **23**(4), 375–380.

Lewis, J., Neil A., & Oyserman, D. (2015). When does the future begin? Time metrics matter, connecting present and future selves. *Psychological Science*, **26**(6), 816–825.

Li, Y., Liu, Y., Li, J., Qin, W., Li, K., Yu, C., & Jiang, T. (2009). Brain anatomical network and intelligence. *PLoS Computational Biology*, **5**(5), e1000395. doi:10.1371/journal.pcbi.1000395

McMillan, R. L., Kaufman, S. B., & Singer, J. L. (2013). Ode to positive constructive daydreaming. *Frontiers in Psychology*, **4**, 626. doi:10.3389/fpsyg.2013.00626

Miyake, A., Kost-Smith, L. E., Finkelstein, N. D., Pollock, S. J., Cohen, G. L., & Ito, T. A. (2010). Reducing the gender achievement gap in college science: A classroom study of values affirmation. *Science*, **330**(6008), 1234–1237.

Mooneyham, B. W., and Schooler, J. W. (2013). The costs and benefits of mind-wandering: A review. *Canadian Journal of Experimental Psychology*, **67**, 11–18.

Morris, M., Chiu, C.Y., & Liu, Z. (2015). Polycultural psychology. *Annual Review of Psychology*, **66**, 631–659.

Mrazek, M. D., Franklin, M. S., Phillips, D. T., Baird, B., & Schooler, J. W. (2013). Mindfulness training improves working memory capacity and GRE performance while reducing mind wandering. *Psychological Science*, **24**(5), 776–781.

Nickerson, A. B., Mele, D., & Princiotta, D. (2008). Attachment and empathy as predictors of roles as defenders or outsiders in bullying interactions. *Journal of School Psychology*, **46**(6), 687–703.

Nusbaum, E. C., & Silvia, P. J. (2011). Are openness and intellect distinct aspects of openness to experience? A test of the O/I model. *Personality and Individual Differences*, **51**(5), 571–574.

Ochsner, K. N., Ludlow, D. H., Knierim, K., Hanelin, J., Ramachandran, T., Glover, G. C., & Mackey, S. C. (2006). Neural correlates of individual differences in pain-related fear and anxiety. *Pain*, **120**(1), 69–77.

Ochsner, K. N., Silvers, J. A., & Buhle, J. T. (2012). Functional imagining studies of emotion regulation: A synthetic review and evolving model of the cognitive control of emotion. *Annals of the New York Academy Sciences*, **1251**(1), 1–24.

Oettingen, G., & Schwörer, B. (2013). Mind wandering via mental contrasting as a tool for behavior change. *Frontiers in Psychology*, **4**, 562. doi:10.3389/fpsyg.2013.00562

Oyserman, D., Bybee, D., & Terry, K. (2006). Possible selves and academic outcomes: How and when possible selves impel action. *Journal of Personality and Social Psychology*, **91**(1), 188–204.

Oyserman, D., Bybee, D., Terry, K., & Hart-Johnson, T. (2004). Possible selves as roadmaps. *Journal of Research in Personality*, **38**(2), 130–149.

Oyserman, D., & Destin, M. (2010). Identity-based motivation: Implications for intervention. *The Counseling Psychologist*, **38**(7), 1001–1043.

Oyserman, D., Johnson, E., & James, L. (2011). Seeing the destination but not the path: Effects of socioeconomic disadvantage on school-focused possible self content and linked behavioral strategies. *Self and Identity*, **10**(4), 474–492.

Oyserman, D., Novin, S., Flinkenflogel, N., & Krabbendam, L. (2014). Rethinking the culture-brain interface: Integrating culture-as-situated-cognition and neuroscience prediction models. *Culture and Brain*, **2**(1) 1–26.

Peetz, J., Wilson, A. E., & Strahan, E. J. (2009). So far away: The role of subjective temporal distance to future goals in motivation and behavior. *Social Cognition*, **27**(4), 475–495.

Pennebaker, J. W., & Seagal, J. D. (1999). Forming a story: The health benefits of narrative. *Journal of Clinical Psychology*, **55**(10), 1243–1254.

Peters, J., & Buchel, C. (2010). Episodic future thinking reduces reward delay discounting through an enhancement of prefrontal-mediotemporal interactions. *Neuron*, **66**, 138–148.

Piccoli, T., Valente, G., Linden, D. E., Re, M., Esposito, F., Sack, A. T., & Di Salle, F. (2015). The Default Mode Network and the Working Memory Network are not anti-correlated during all phases of a working memory task. *PLoS ONE*, **10**(4), e0123354. doi:10.1371/journal.pone.0123354

Pletzer, B., Kronbichler, M., Nuerk, H. C., & Kerschbaum, H. H. (2015). Mathematics anxiety reduces default mode network deactivation in response to numerical tasks. *Frontiers in Human Neuroscience*, **9**, 1–12.

Qin, P., & Northoff, G. (2011). How is our self related to midline regions and the default-mode network? *Neuroimage*, **57**(3), 1221–1233.

Raichle, M. E., & Snyder, A. Z. (2007). A default mode of brain function: A brief history of an evolving idea. *Neuroimage*, **37**(4), 1083–1090.

Ramirez, G., & Beilock, S. L. (2011). Writing about testing worries boosts exam performance in the classroom. *Science*, **331**(6014), 211–213.

Reeve, J., & Lee, W. (2014). Students' classroom engagement produces longitudinal changes in classroom motivation. *Journal of Educational Psychology*, **106**(2), 527–544.

Riggio, R. E., Tucker, J., & Coffaro, D. (1989). Social skills and empathy. *Personality and Individual Differences*, **10**(1), 93–99.

Ritter, S. M., Damian, R. I., Simonton, D. K., van Baaren, R. B., Strick, M., Derks, J., & Dijksterhuis, A. (2012). Diversifying experiences enhance cognitive flexibility. *Journal of Experimental Social Psychology*, **48**(4), 961–964.

Rotenstein, V., Bansal, S., Yang, X., & Immordino-Yang, M. H. (2014, April). Social and Non Social Media Use Are Oppositely Related to Empathic Concern in Adolescents. Poster presented at the University of Southern California Undergraduate Symposium, Los Angeles, CA.

Rowling, J. K. (2008, June 5). The fringe benefits of failure, and the importance of imagination. *Harvard Gazette*. Retrieved April 20, 2015 from http://news .harvard.edu/gazette/story/2008/06/text-of-j-k-rowling-speech/

Runco, M. A., Millar, G., Acar, S., & Cramond, B. (2010). Torrance tests of creative thinking as predictors of personal and public achievement: A fifty-year follow-up. *Creativity Research Journal*, **22**(4), 361–368.

Rydell, R. J., Beilock, S. L., & McConell, A. R. (2009). Multiple social identities and stereotype threat: Imbalance, accessibility, and working memory. *Journal of Personality and Social Psychology*, **96**(5), 949–966.

Schultz, L. H., Barr, D. J., & Selman, R. L. (2001). The value of a developmental approach to evaluating character development programmes: An outcome study of Facing History and Ourselves. *Journal of Moral Education*, **30**(1), 3–27.

Seligman, M. E. P., & Csikszentmihalyi, M. (2000). Positive psychology: An introduction. *American Psychologist*, **55**, 5–14.

Seligman, M. E. P., Railton, P., Baumeister, R. F., & Sripada, C. (2013). Navigating into the future or driven by the past. *Perspectives on Psychological Science*, **8**, 119–141.

Singer, J. L. (1961). Imagination and waiting ability in young children. *Journal of Personality*, **29**(4), 396–413.

Singer, T., & Lamm, C. (2009). The social neuroscience of empathy. *Annals of the New York Academy of Sciences*, 1156(1), 81–96.

Smallwood, J. (2013). Distinguishing how from why the mind wanders: a process–occurrence framework for self-generated mental activity. *Psychological Bulletin*, **139**(3), 519–535.

Smallwood, J., McSpadden, M., & Schooler, J. W. (2008). When attention matters: The curious incident of the wandering mind. *Memory & Cognition*, **36**(6), 1144–1150.

Smallwood, J., Nind, L., & O'Connor, R. C. (2009). When is your head at? An exploration of the factors associated with the temporal focus of the wandering mind. *Consciousness and Cognition*, **18**(1), 118–125.

Smallwood, J., & Schooler, J. W. (2015). The science of mind wandering: Empirically navigating the stream of consciousness. *Annual Review of Psychology*, **66**, 487–518.

Song, M., Liu, Y., Zhou, Y., Wang, K., Yu, C., & Jiang, T. (2009). Default network and intelligence difference. Conference Proceedings IEEE Engineering in Medicine & Biology Society, 2212–2215.

Spreng, R. N., DuPre, E., Selarka, D., Garcia, J., Gojkovic, S., et al. (2014). Goal-congruent default network activity facilitates cognitive control. *Journal of Neuroscience*, **34**, 14108–14114.

Steiner-Adair, C., & Barker, T. H. (2013). *The big disconnect: Protecting childhood and family relationships in the digital age*. New York: Harper Business.

Tamir, D. I., & Mitchell, J. P. (2011). The default network distinguishes construals of proximal versus distal events. *Journal of Cognitive Neuroscience*, **23**(10), 2945–2955.

Taylor, V. A., Daneault, V., Grant, J., Scavone, G., Breton, E., et al. (2012). Impact of meditation training on the default mode network during a restful state. *Social Cognitive and Affective Neuroscience*, **8**(1), 4–14.

Torrance, E. P. (1993). The Beyonders in a thirty-year longitudinal study of creative achievement. *Roeper Review*, **15**, 131–135.

Torrance, E. P. (2003). The millennium: A time for looking forward and looking back. *Journal of Secondary Gifted Education*, **15**, 6–12.

Torrance, E. P. (2004). Great expectations: Creative achievements of the sociometric stars in a 30-year study. *Journal of Advanced Academics*, **16**, 5–13.

van Noorden, T. H., Haselager, G. J., Cillessen, A. H., & Bukowski, W. M. (2014). Empathy and involvement in bullying in children and adolescents: A systematic review. *Journal of Youth and Adolescence*, **44**(3), 637–657.

von Stumm, S., Hell, B., & Chamorro-Premuzic, T. (2011). The hungry mind intellectual curiosity is the third pillar of academic performance. *Perspectives on Psychological Science*, **6**(6), 574–588.

Wang, K., Yu, C., Xu, L., Qin, W., Li, K., Xu, L., & Jiang, T. (2009). Offline memory reprocessing: Involvement of the brain's default network in spontaneous thought processes. *PLoS ONE*, **4**, e4867. doi: 10.1371/journal.pone.0004867

Wiley, J., & Jarosz, A. F. (2012). Working memory capacity, attentional focus, and problem solving. *Current Directions in Psychological Science*, **21**(4), 258–262.

Wilson, A. E., Gunn, G. R., & Ross, M. (2009). The role of subjective time in identity regulation. *Applied Cognitive Psychology*, **23**(8), 1164–1178.

Yang, X.-F., Bossmann, J., Schiffhauer, B., Jordan, M., & Immordino-Yang, M. H. (2013). Intrinsic default mode network connectivity predicts spontaneous verbal descriptions of autobiographical memories during social processing. *Frontiers in Psychology*, **3** (592), 1–10.

Yang, X.-F., Pavarini, G., Schnall, S., & Immordino-Yang, M. H. (2012, May). Spontaneous gaze aversion during interview-induced moral elevation predicts subsequent default network activation. Poster presented at the 2012 Association for Psychological Science Convention, Chicago, IL.

Yi, X., Plucker, J. A., & Guo, J. (2015). Modeling influences on divergent thinking and artistic creativity. *Thinking Skills and Creativity*, **16**, 62–68.

Zhiyan, T., & Singer, J. L. (1997). Daydreaming styles, emotionality, and the big five personality dimensions. *Imagination, Cognition, and Personality*, **16**, 399–414.

CHAPTER 18

Four Faces of Creativity at School

Maciej Karwowski and Dorota M. Jankowska

The Maria Grzegorzewska University

Introduction

Over the decades of the development of creative education, scholars have devoted a great amount of attention to understanding children's and young people's creative potential. This potential was usually defined through cognitive characteristics – mainly divergent thinking (Runco, 2015), creative imagination (Dziedziewicz & Karwowski, 2015; Jankowska & Karwowski, 2015), or problem solving skills (Voss & Means, 1989). However, creativity requires more than just abilities. Certain personality traits – especially openness and independence (Feist, 1998) – as well as intrinsic motivation (Amabile, 1993) or creative self-efficacy (Beghetto, 2006) may be perceived as elements of the complex mosaic of creative potential (Karwowski, 2015; Karwowski & Lebuda, 2016; Lubart, Zenasni, & Barbot, 2013).

In this chapter we briefly sketch a new model of creativity, understood as a dynamic interplay between creative abilities and those personality traits that, we believe, are crucial to creative activity, namely openness and independence. This leads us to the typological approach and four distinct types of creativity, briefly described later in the chapter. We explore these characteristics and focus especially on the usefulness of this approach for teaching creativity.

Teachers' perceptions of creativity are complex, but too often they are not complex enough. When asked what child creativity is, a great majority of teachers would probably define it with reference to at least one aspect of creative thinking. Most frequently, it would probably be originality ("non-schematic thinking," "creates new solutions") or fluency ("has lots of ideas"). Sometimes they would probably also refer to creative imagination ("fertile imagination," "fancy"), as well as openness to experience ("curious about the unknown," "eager to take up new challenges"). Indeed, decades of research into teachers' implicit theories of creativity show that the characteristics of creative students they list most frequently mainly refer

337

to students' cognitive functioning, followed by personality and motivation (Andiliou & Murphy, 2010). Unique or original, imaginative, curious, and open to experience are those characteristics of students that occur in most of these analyses (Andiliou & Murphy, 2010; Chan & Chan, 1999). This leads to the conclusion that teachers' perception of a creative student is dominated by individual (cognitive and personality) characteristics rather than by activity, process, or product factors (Gralewski & Karwowski, 2016). We presume, however, that a too linear understanding of creativity – regardless of its types, contexts, and dimensions – may in fact limit attempts to develop creative potential, especially in the case of young children. When teachers' naive theories excessively focus on the person, they are dangerously close to the fixed mindset – the conviction that a child possesses a particular trait or not, and that not much can be done if the child does not exhibit it (Dweck, 2006; Karwowski, 2014; Plucker, Beghetto, & Dow, 2004). Creativity in childhood – especially mini-c creativity – is clearly linked with the process of learning (Beghetto, 2016; Beghetto & Kaufman, 2009). To satisfy their natural curiosity, children engage in many activities and gain new experiences as they do so. These pursuits may be early manifestations of openness to experience or willingness to emphasize individual independence. This is why it seems so important to conduct a profile analysis of creativity incorporating signs of creative potential in both intellectual and personality spheres. This chapter aims at presenting the usefulness of such an approach.

Towards a Typological Approach to Creativity

Creative abilities (mainly divergent thinking and creative imagination), openness, and independence are associated with one another, but these associations are usually, at best, moderate (Feist, 1998; Feist & Brady, 2004; McCrae, 1987). Therefore, although on the one hand it seems reasonable to combine them while describing creative people, on the other, such combination should not be treated as a single dimension of creativity (a continuum, as is the case with the adaptors-innovators theory; Kirton, 1976). Instead, we propose a typological approach to creativity (TAC; Karwowski, 2010a).

The understanding of creativity as a multifaceted phenomenon alone is, obviously, not new. Similar, multidimensional approaches are present in the literature (i.e., Lubart et al., 2013) – for example, such an understanding of creativity forms the foundation of the Test for Creative Thinking – Drawing Production (Jellen & Urban, 1989), based on a componential

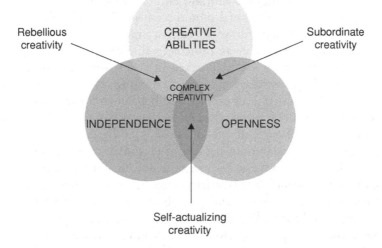

Figure 18.1 Typological model of creativity

model of creativity (Urban, 2005), with creativity seen as composed of abilities (divergent thinking, general abilities, specific knowledge, and abilities) as well as motivational and personality characteristics (tolerance of ambiguity, motivation, and task involvement).

The typological approach to creativity (TAC; Karwowski, 2010a) focuses on the relationship between three dimensions crucial to creative activity and achievement, namely: (1) creative abilities – cognitive characteristics that determine the effectiveness of generating, developing, and implementing solutions characterized by a high degree of originality and value, or divergent thinking and creative imagination, among other things; (2) openness – appreciation of intellect, learning, and willingness to meet new people and cultures; and (3) independence – nonconformity and low agreeableness, as well as readiness to oppose the situationally induced impact of the group and external factors (see Figure 18.1). These dimensions are continuous: individuals are not creatively gifted and lacking this gift, open and rigid, or dependent and independent, but they differ in the intensity of these characteristics.

The proposed model emphasizes the special role played by four basic types of creativity: complex (high creative abilities, openness, and independence), rebellious (high creative abilities and independence combined with low openness), subordinate (high creative abilities and openness combined with low independence), and self-actualizing (high openness and independence combined with low creative abilities).

We postulate that this model should serve as a heuristic representation when analyzing different forms of creativity rather than being treated as a typology that shows stable and unchangeable categories. The types we describe in this section are not carved in stone; on the contrary, they are flexible and open to development and progress. Hence, even when we characterize the most typical profiles and behaviors of each of the types, this does not mean that people – including students – should be perceived as representatives of one and only one type. Membership in each of these categories may change in time, because of personality development (Lucas & Donnellan, 2011), but also because of educational interventions.

Such an understanding of creativity – treated as a complex characteristic that determines the chances and probability of getting involved in creative activity and succeeding in it – may be of special importance when it comes to the development of children and young people as well as to their school functioning. To understand the mechanisms governing the transition from mini-c creativity to little-c creativity, or even to Pro-c and Big-C creativity (Kaufman & Beghetto, 2009), is one of key tasks for educational psychology of creativity. Creative potential should be considered as a necessary but insufficient condition of creative achievement. Perseverance (Prabhu, Sutton, & Sauser, 2008), maturity and coherence of identity (Helson & Pals, 2000), synergy of intrinsic and extrinsic motivation (Amabile, 1993, 1997), appropriate level of intelligence (Karwowski, Dul, Gralewski, Jauk, Jankowska, Gajda, Chruszczewski, & Benedek, 2016; Karwowski & Gralewski, 2013), domain-specific knowledge (Simonton, 2009), and environmental support (Sternberg & Lubart, 1995) – all these and many other factors add to its fulfillment. Yet very likely, all those moderators and mediators of the relationship between creative potential and creative achievement may additionally be moderated by the creativity type the given individual shows.

Initial empirical analyses of the TAC (Karwowski, 2010a) show differences between the types of creativity in both social characteristics (i.e., socioeconomic status, parental attitudes, family situation, perceived climate for creativity at school, teacher leadership perception) and psychological characteristics (i.e., differences in creative self-efficacy, values, personality, interests), as well as in the effectiveness of school functioning. What follows is a short summary of the key findings.

Complex creativity. Complex creativity children usually form a group of no more than 3 or 4 pupils in a 30-pupil classroom, and are characterized by high openness, independence, and creative abilities. Research shows (Karwowski, 2010a) that such individuals are also characterized by a high level of social competencies and considerable extraversion. They are confident about their own creative abilities (hence their high creative self-efficacy; Beghetto, 2006) and consider creativity to be an important part of their self-description (consequently, they also exhibit high creative personal identity; Jaussi, Randel, & Dionne, 2007). In line with these observations, such people also value intellectual autonomy and emotional independence highly while attaching less importance to maintaining social order. So, even if sometimes they are indeed rebels, they are constructive rebels who offer their own valuable solutions during classes. They are usually intrinsically motivated (Amabile, 1993); in the activities they undertake, they are more driven by the pleasure that stems from the activity itself than by rewards and external reinforcements. They do well at school but rarely are top of the class, and they tend to perceive the climate at their schools and classrooms as not very creative (Karwowski, 2010a).

The complex creativity type is clearly linked with the family's social and economic status. Not only is the parents' education higher in this group of people than in the overall population, but an overrepresentation of individuals from large cities and private schools is visible here. Individuals exhibiting this type of creativity are most frequently the only children or the oldest ones in their families. Parental attitudes also make this group different from the others both mothers and fathers are perceived as loving, and their parental attitudes are commonly characterized by a low degree of protective and controlling approach.

Rebellious creativity. Students representing the rebellious creativity type form a group of two to three individuals in a typical classroom (composed of approximately 30 pupils), and they are much more frequently boys than girls. Individuals from this creativity type are characterized by relatively low social competence, which in fact makes it harder for them to function effectively. In conflict situations – inevitable at school and in life – they mostly apply avoidance strategies or go for confrontation (Karwowski, 2010a). Demotivation is a problem in activating their creative potential; the level of both intrinsic and extrinsic motivation in this group is clearly lower than among other students. It is therefore difficult to arouse enthusiasm in students characterized by this type of creativity and encourage them to take action, regardless of whether one uses rewards or more intrinsically rooted arguments. Creativity is not one of the values they appreciate the most, although they do enjoy intellectual autonomy and agency – dimensions that are important for creativity. When we add average creative self-efficacy, this profile of creativity becomes complete. Consequently, we are dealing with individuals who have the cognitive potential to function creatively, but their low openness, coupled with high nonconformity, may form a barrier preventing the development their creativity. This type clearly shows that creative abilities alone are not enough for creative potential to be actualized when an individual lacks creative self-efficacy and creative personal identity as well as intrinsic motivation (Karwowski, 2010a).

Representatives of this group report being rejected by fathers and mothers more often than the average; they also report being less intensely loved by their mothers. Adverse family relationships and a feeling of rejection is the clearest strain of family characteristics in this group. These young people perceive school with similar aversion – most often they describe the climate there as bad, both in the sphere of relationships with others and in how much support they receive in the tasks they undertake (Karwowski, 2010a).

Subordinate creativity. About 4 pupils in an average 30-pupil class may be described as subordinately creative. Cognitively (creative abilities) and in terms of personality (openness), students representing this type seem to have all that is necessary to identify and solve problems. However, their conformism makes their functioning in many situations more difficult, especially when those situations contain the elements of risk. This profile represents the essence of an adaptive style of creativity (see Kirton, 1976); this is why such individuals improve something rather than change reality in a revolutionary way.

More often than the general population, these students come from families characterized by low socioeconomic status, and the attitudes of their parents (especially mothers) are exhibiting stronger protective behaviors. They rate the climate of the schools and classes they learn in positively and highly, so they adapted well there. They also highly appreciate the leadership of their teachers (Karwowski, 2010a). They generally do well at school, which may partially be due to their high level of conscientiousness (Gajda, Karwowski, & Beghetto, forthcoming). Moreover, they are characterized by a high level of intrinsic motivation. In conflict situations, they most frequently apply strategies of cooperation and compromise. They do not seek to dominate; instead, they value partner relationships and peace. Therefore, these individuals are well adapted to the surrounding reality, and although they are endowed with creative potential, they do not seek to achieve it at all costs, nor do they create in a revolutionary way. Therefore, one should not expect them to engage in activities that radically depart from the status quo, but when they work in a group under the right leadership, they are able to achieve valuable creative results (Karwowski, 2010a).

Self-actualizing creativity. The type of self-actualizing creativity children includes individuals who are open and independent but lack creative abilities that enable effective problem-solving and developing creative ideas. On average, the group includes 2 or 3 pupils in every 30-pupil class. These are individuals who value openness as well as independence in functioning and relations with others more than creative activity. They are also characterized by developed social skills – they do particularly well in situations of social exposure. In relation to the entire population, this group is distinguished by a slightly higher level of intrinsic motivation; consequently, these students want to act for the pleasure that stems from the process of acting, although the action is not always associated with creativity. This is validated by the fact that they do not value creativity so much. Instead, among the dimensions they do value highly there are emotional independence and social position (Karwowski, 2010a). Among different parental attitudes, the only difference between this group and the general population is that individuals characterized by self-actualizing creativity more frequently consider their fathers to be less demanding. Students characterized by the self-actualizing creativity profile usually do not value creativity very highly and do not exhibit an especially high creative self-efficacy; as a result, they infrequently undertake creative activities. This is why, when one wants to develop their creative potential, one should motivate them to undertake activities in domains that are associated with creativity, encourage them to boldly offer non-typical solutions, and to emphasize the importance of intellectual autonomy in group work. The strengths of this type of creativity (openness, developed social skills, high degree of intrinsic motivation) should be used to increase the willingness of these individuals to engage in creative activity. The effectiveness of stimulating creative abilities is well corroborated, and there are many ways to stimulate the creative potential of this group (Scott, Leritz, & Mumford, 2004).

Identification of Students' Type of Creativity

Not only are people not equally creative, but they are not creative in the same ways, either. While our estimates show that the four types of creativity described in the preceding section make up the total of almost half of an average class, more or less one out of ten individuals may be identified as a complexly creative child. Consequently, in an average class, there are likely to be two-to-three students characterized by this particular profile of creativity. But how does one identify the remaining types of creativity?

The profiled identification of creativity we encourage makes it possible to determine the type of creativity that a particular student usually exhibits. We believe that individual dimensions (intellectual and personality related) should be rated in comparison with other students, but also in a more ipsative way: showing the individual's strengths and weaknesses. As a consequence of such assessment, it is possible to plan the stimulation of creative potential in a way that is concordant with the profile of individual differences.

Responding to the demand for methods that make it possible to conduct profile assessment of creativity, we developed the Types of Creativity Questionnaire (TCQ) (Karwowski, 2015a) for older students. This questionnaire enables valid and reliable measurement of creative abilities, openness, and independence, and makes it possible to determine which types of creativity individuals represent. Currently, we are also working on the Types of Creativity Observation Scale for the assessment of younger pupils. This instrument is composed of two observation sheets that include statements that describe particular behaviors of a child (at home, in a kindergarten, or at school). As in the case of TCQ, these behaviors are indicators of creative abilities, openness, and independence. Sheets are completed by one of a particular child's parents and a teacher.

Supporting Students' Creativity: Holding Types in Mind

The typological approaches we propose make up a particular, potentially supportive system thanks to which teachers can better understand (and support) students' creativity. However, as is the case with any typology, it can bring benefits, but it can also carry some risks. The first example of the latter is associated with unreflective ascription of particular creativity types to students and consideration of these identifiers as unchangeable. It is important to remember that any type of support must aim at development of students' creative potential. However, even the type we defined as "complex creativity" cannot be considered as the point of arrival and the final step toward the development of students' creativity. It is therefore a mistake to think that students who fit in with the complex creativity type, characterized by high openness, independence, and creative abilities, do not require any special support anymore. First of all, a type is a theoretical classification category whose aim is to facilitate identification of strengths and those areas that require support, which requires application of some generalizations. After all, in practice, we infrequently come across the so-called *flat profile* that is characterized by low internal variability, and this is why even in case of complex creativity one can identify differences in the intensity of individual elements of a creative potential. Finally, even a relatively harmonious profile of complex creativity can still be developed further. It is important to note, after all, that even a very high level of creative potential does not yet warrant eminent creative achievement. Transfer from potential to its fulfillment in particular areas of life is the main task of those who work with students characterized by this profile.

It happens that pupils characterized by high creative potential are not aware of their own abilities, and for this reason they do not search for occasions to develop them. In case of rebellious creativity, we are dealing with pupils who have the potential for creative functioning, but their low openness and high level of nonconformism is occasionally a source of overall demotivation that pervades their functioning. They need someone who would suggest to them the domain where they could grow, or who would indicate a challenging problem for them to solve. Of course, this person can be a teacher, although this task is not at all easy. The key to success may be to understand the causes of the pupils' lack of motivation and openness that blocks their desire to act. Ordinarily, these causes are lack of self-confidence and/or lack of goals. Pupils who lack self-confidence usually focus on what they would like to do rather than what they have already achieved. Frequently, low social competencies result from this lack of confidence. Another reason for forsaking creative activities may be the fear of failure, which could seriously tarnish the image of independent individuals. This is why we think that it is worth to begin working with these pupils from building elements of creative identity. Sometimes, it is enough to indicate the current results of their creative activities and emphasize their value, cost-effectiveness, and benefits. However, activities that aim at realizing the potential of these pupils are usually a long process of building appropriate motivational orientations (it is unfortunately usually longer than stimulation of the development of the cognitive aspects of creativity).

Working with pupils characterized by the subordinate creativity profile (with high level of conformism), teachers should emphasize the element of "being creatively against," which includes alternative views and courage of proposing changes. It is of course not about encouraging destructive resistance, but reformist discord that expresses itself in autonomy, ability to make independent decisions, and sense of agency. This is where another question arises, however: How to encourage subordinate pupils to question the status quo? Apparently, it is worth to attract their attention to issues they find important and worth getting involved in. Subjective importance of the confronted problem may alleviate their internal emphasis of acceptance and "obedient" acceptance and, consequently, encourage a creative search for changes. It is often also worth to impose on them the role of group leaders in certain tasks in order to weaken their conformism and warm them up to taking risky decisions. Certainly, sensing the right moment to change the support strategy and support progressive expansion of the space for their independence in such a way that their developing independence aims at posing questions and discovering new problems is the most difficult thing while working with pupils characterized by subordinate creativity.

Putting Theory into Practice

Probably the most important practical questions that stem from this chapter are those that stress practical consequences of the typology we proposed, namely: How to develop students' creativity at school if it can have very different profiles? How to individualize stimulating activities? What level of support to provide in order to increase the probability of reforging the students' potential into tangible future creative achievements?

Individualization of activities that develop creativity during classes is a constant challenge for creative education. The typological approach we described was already applied, while conducting a unique creativity training known as "Creativity Compass" (Dziedziewicz, Gajda, & Karwowski, 2014; Jankowska, Gajda, & Karwowski, 2015).

The Creativity Compass program is directed at teachers who work with children aged 6–12 – especially those teachers who are interested in developing creativity and who search for practical tools that become useful when discussing multicultural issues. Among other things, its purpose is to stimulate the development of creative abilities, openness, and independence, which foster dealing with new and poorly defined situations. The activities in this program are of a fictionalized character – their leitmotif is mentally traveling to different countries, towns, and regions. The activities in this program are grouped into three stages. The first one (interest) aims at initiating the topic and encouraging children to undertake creative activity. It usually has the form of an open question that builds the climate of curiosity and openness and encourages children to formulate their own opinions and judgments (e.g., "Why do cats on the Isle of Man have no tails?"). Additionally, this stage is also a creative warm-up that stimulates the development of divergent thinking and creative imagination. Then comes the group work or pair work stage (searching), which refers to such thematic threads as the history of a given country, its legends and tales, culture, traditions and customs, national symbols, monuments, and tourist attractions. Thanks to the initial assessment of creativity profiles, in this stage the teacher can organize group work in a way that maximizes the potential of peer tutoring. Thus, the teacher does not consider natural differences in the various aspects of creative potential as barriers in effecting the program, but as good conditions to design an educational situation in which students can become creativity tutors for one another. And so, to provide an example, learning cooperation between a student profiled as showing self-actualizing creativity with his or her peer profiled as exhibiting subordinate creativity may prevent senseless destruction and, instead, develop openness in the former child while teaching the latter how to take risks and trigger independence. In this form of cooperation, the teacher's role should be to discreetly monitor tutoring for students to feel secure in both roles (the tutor and the tutored). At the end of each meeting of the Creativity Compass program, there comes the stage of exploration, which is a reflective summary of the knowledge gained about other cultural circles during the previous activities. The example of this program shows that multifaceted (i.e., cognitive, personality-related, and motivational) stimulation of creativity makes it possible to stimulate various types of creativity while creating space for the individualization of training activities (Dziedziewicz et al., 2014; Jankowska et al., 2015).

An important consequence that stems from the observed differences between the types is the significance of the role of social factors in the fostering of creativity. The importance of social and educational space and, most of all, parental attitudes is enormous, and it is these elements that significantly influence whether the student that a given teacher works with will be classified as belonging to the complex creativity or subordinate creativity group.

Perseverance and motivation are as important as the attitudes that stimulate the family environment. When dealing with motivation, it is worth considering not just a conviction about the role of intrinsic motivation but also the possibility of synergetic interaction between intrinsic and extrinsic motivations. With regard to creative attitude, the hypothesis of motivational synergy, posed by Amabile (1993, 1997) and confirmed in other studies (Karwowski & Gralewski, 2011), assumes that extrinsic motivation may be positively related to creativity, but only when intrinsic motivation is high. It is then that synergetic cooperation between the two types of motivation occurs. Amabile (1993) offers detailed mechanisms that fuel synergetic and nonsynergetic extrinsic motivation and indicates how the climate of the surroundings can stimulate both synergetic and nonsynergetic types of extrinsic motivation (Amabile, 1997).

The "creative self-efficacy – identity – values" triad is another important element that makes it possible to reforge creative potential into achievements and differentiates the creativity types. Actual creativity is impossible without the individual having a sense of being actually capable of it and without this person's high valuation of creativity. Creative self-efficacy mediates the relations between creative abilities and creative achievements (Chen, forthcoming; Karwowski & Barbot, 2016; Karwowski & Lebuda, forthcoming), whereby individuals who are more creative are also more aware of their strengths, which translates into their achievements (Tierney & Farmer, 2011). Jaussi, Randel, and Dionne (2007) propose to analyze not just creative self-efficacy but also the place creativity occupies in the overall system of personal identity (see also Karwowski, 2012; Karwowski, Lebuda, Wiśniewska, & Gralewski, 2013). What is important is not just whether individuals consider themselves to be a creative but also whether and to what extent it is important for them. When one is creative and considers oneself as such, and when this is at the same time very important for him or her, then chances for involvement in creative activities and for succeeding in them increase (see Helson & Pals, 2000).

Certainly, the elements mentioned above are just selected factors that foster creative achievements. Longitudinal studies of the relations between creative potential and creative achievements (Cramond, Matthews-Morgan, Bandalos, & Zuo, 2005; Feist & Barron, 2003; Helson & Pals, 2000; Plucker, 1999; Runco, 1999) provide a large number of predictors, mediators, and moderators of outstanding success in creativity, located at various levels of analysis and constantly interacting.

Conclusion

The typological approach to students' creativity stems from a rich tradition of similar theories – from Kirton's (1976) adaption-innovation theory to Galenson's (2011) finders and seekers. Thus, we concur with the underlying assumption that it is worthwhile to ask not only "How much creative abilities do you have?" but also "What is your style of creativity?" At the same time, however, we do believe that one continuum is unable to fully cover the richness of creativity; it does not matter whether we are talking about adaptors and innovators, finders and seekers, or any other dichotomy (Glǎveanu, 2015). Instead of another one-dimensional theory, we propose a typological model of creativity, with four distinct types, characterized by clearly different profiles (see Sternberg, Kaufman, & Pretz, 2002, for an even more complex approach). People with high creative abilities, openness, and independence represent the "complex creativity" type, but they are rare. On the other hand, teachers often perceive creativity negatively (Westby & Dawson, 1995) – likely because they tend to focus on the type we described as "rebellious creativity." The people of this creative type – highly talented or original and nonconformist but not very open – are clearly salient in the class, but usually not very productive. This category of creative rebels is not very welcome at school (Karwowski, 2010b), but they sometimes revolutionize the field they explore. Quite the opposite type was labeled as representing "subordinate creativity" – as having a clear profile of high openness and creative abilities combined with high conformity. Such people are "good students" (Karwowski, 2010b, forthcoming) and are conceptually close to Kirton's (1976) adaptors. They function well at school, are well adapted, and coexist with their peers effectively. The question is whether they will be able to persuade others that their creative ideas are worth implementing while dealing with real-life problems. Perhaps the most interesting category is the one we called "self-actualizing creativity" – people who are highly open and nonconformist while having relatively low creative abilities. Their personality profile fits almost perfectly into the classic descriptions of "creative personality" in early works of humanistic psychology (Fromm, 1959; Maslow, 1959). Such a profile may suggest "scribbler's creativity" or "creative potential without chances for real achievement" (Nicholls, 1972). However, there are dozens of proofs that creative abilities are quite easily developed and that creativity trainings are very effective (Dziedziewicz et al., 2013, 2014; Karwowski & Soszyński, 2008; Scott et al., 2004). Therefore, low initial creative abilities are not necessarily a problem – in fact, it is just a matter of practice to develop them.

The typological model of creativity stems from two different streams of research on creativity presented in the creativity literature. The first one focuses on the characteristics of creative people, exploring the rich complexity and domain-specificity of their characteristics (Baer, 2014; Feist, 1998). The second one stems from studies on teachers' implicit theories of creativity as well as common misunderstandings and biases found among teachers (e.g., Gralewski & Karwowski, 2013, 2016; Karwowski, 2007; Scott, 1999). We do believe that teachers usually define creativity by focusing only on its certain aspects and, consequently, having an incomplete picture of creative students.

Several consequences of the typological theory of creativity seem important. We need not only to develop valid and reliable measures of creativity types (works on this are in progress) but also to fully understand the school functioning of different types and the most efficient ways of stimulating their creativity, as it is very likely that "typical" creativity training is not equally effective for all types. It is also of special importance to understand how individuals representing different types cooperate while learning or solving ill-defined problems and to provide teachers with guidance on how to lead them most effectively. Future works should resolve these issues and shed some lights on our understanding of different types of creativity.

Authors' Note and Acknowledgment

The preparation of this chapter was supported by a grant from the Polish Ministry of Science and Higher Education (Iuventus Plus Program-0193/IP3/2015/73).

REFERENCES

Amabile, T. M. (1993). Motivational synergy: Toward new conceptualizations of intrinsic and extrinsic motivation in the workplace. *Human Resource Management Review*, **3**, 185–201.

Amabile, T. M. (1997). Entrepreneurial creativity through motivational synergy. *Journal of Creative Behavior*, **31**, 18–26.

Andiliou, A., & Murphy, P. K. (2010). Examining variations among researchers' and teachers' conceptualizations of creativity: A review and synthesis of contemporary research. *Educational Research Review*, **5**, 201–219.

Baer, J. (2014). The crisis in creativity research stems from too little fragmentation, not too much. *Creativity: Theories – Research – Applications*, **2**, 200–205.

Beghetto, R. A. (2006). Creative self-efficacy: Correlates in middle and secondary students. *Creativity Research Journal*, **18**, 447–457.

Beghetto, R. A. (2016). Creative learning: A fresh look. *Journal of Cognitive Education and Psychology*, 15, 6–23.

Chan, D. W., & Chan, L. (1999). Implicit theories of creativity: Teachers' perception of students characteristics in Hog-Kong. *Creativity Research Journal*, **12**, 185–195.

Cramond, B., Matthews-Morgan, J., Bandalos, D., & Zuo, L. (2005). A report on the 40-year follow-up of the Torrance Tests of Creative Thinking. *Gifted Child Quarterly*, **49**, 283–291.

Chen, B. B. (forthcoming). The creative self-concept as a mediator between openness to experience and creative behaviour. *Creativity: Theories-Research-Applications*.

Dweck, C. (2006). *Mindset: The new psychology of success.* New York: Random House.

Dziedziewicz, D., Gajda, A., & Karwowski, M. (2014). Developing intercultural competence and creativity. *Thinking Skills and Creativity,* **13**, 32–42.

Dziedziewicz, D., & Karwowski, M. (2015). Development of children's creative visual imagination: A theoretical model and enhancement programmes. *Education 3–13.* doi:10.1080/03004279.2015.1020646

Dziedziewicz, D., Olędzka, D., & Karwowski, M. (2013). Developing 4- to 6-year-old children's figural creativity using a doodle-book program. *Thinking Skills and Creativity,* **9**, 85–95.

Feist, G. J. (1998). A meta-analysis of personality in scientific and artistic creativity. *Personality and Social Psychology Review,* **2**, 290–309.

Feist, G. J., & Barron, F. X. (2003). Predicting creativity from early to late adulthood: Intellect potential, and personality. *Journal of Research in Personality,* **37**, 62–88.

Feist, G. J., & Brady, T. R. (2004). Openness to experience, non-conformity, and the preference for abstract art. *Empirical Studies of the Arts,* **22**, 77–89.

Fromm, E. (1959). The creative attitude. In H. H. Anderson (Eds.), *Creativity and its cultivation* (pp. 44–54). New York: Harper & Brothers.

Gajda, A., Karwowski, M., & Beghetto (forthcoming). Creativity and academic achievement: A meta-analysis. *Journal of Educational Psychology,* http://dx .doi.org/10.1037/edu0000133.

Galenson, D. W. (2011). *Old masters and young geniuses: The two life cycles of artistic creativity.* Princeton, NJ: Princeton University Press.

Gläveanu, V. P. (2015). The status of the social in creativity studies and the pitfalls of dichotomic thinking.*Creativity: Theories – Research – Applications,* 2, 94–111.

Gralewski, J., & Karwowski, M. (2013). Polite girls and creative boys? Students' gender moderates accuracy of teachers' ratings of creativity. *Journal of Creative Behavior,* **47**, 290–304.

Gralewski, J., & Karwowski, M. (2016). Are teachers' implicit theories of creativity related to the recognition of their students' creativity? *Journal of Creative Behavior,* doi: 10.1002/jocb.140.

Helson, R., & Pals, J. L. (2000). Creativity potential, creative achievement, and personal growth. *Journal of Personality,* **68**, 1–27.

Jankowska, D. M., Gajda, A., & Karwowski, M. (2015). How to develop children's creativity and intercultural sensitivity: Around Creativity Compass program. In A. G. Tan & C. Perleth (Eds.), *Creativity, culture, and development* (pp. 133–147). Singapore: Springer.

Jankowska, D. M., & Karwowski, M. (2015). Measuring creative imagery abilities. *Frontiers in Psychology,* 6, 1591, http://doi.org/10.3389/fpsyg.2015.01591.

Jaussi, K. S, Randel, A. E., & Dionne, S. D. (2007). I am, I think I can, and I do: The role of personal identity, self-efficacy, and cross-application of experiences in creativity at work. *Creativity Research Journal,* **19**, 247–258.

Jellen, H. G., & Urban, K. K. (1989). Assessing creative potential worldwide: The first cross-cultural application of the test for creative thinking-drawing production (TCT-DP). *Gifted Education International*, **6**, 78–86.

Karwowski, M. (2007). Teachers' nominations of students' creativity: Should we believe them? Are the nominations valid? *Social Sciences*, **2**, 264–269.

Karwowski, M. (2010a). Kreatywność – feeria rozumień, uwikłań, powodów. Teoretyczno-empiryczna prolegomena. [Creativity: a feeria of understandings, entanglements, conditions]. In. M. Karwowski & A. Gajda (Eds.), *Kreatywność (nie tylko) w klasie szkolnej* [Creativity not only in the classroom] (pp. 12–45). Warszawa: Wydawnictwo Akademii Pedagogiki Specjalnej.

Karwowski, M. (2010b). Are creative students really welcome in the classroom? Implicit theories of "good" and "creative" student' personality among Polish teachers. *Social and Behavioural Sciences Journal*, **2**, 1233–1237.

Karwowski, M. (2012). Did curiosity kill the cat? Relationship between trait curiosity, creative self-efficacy and creative personal identity. *Europe's Journal of Psychology*, **8**, 547–558.

Karwowski, M. (2014). Creative mindset: Measurement, correlates, consequences. *Psychology of Aesthetics, Creativity, and the Arts*, **8**, 62–70.

Karwowski, M. (2015a). Notes on creative potential and its measurement. *Creativity: Theories – Research – Applications*, **2**, 4–17.

Karwowski, M. (2015b). Types of creativity questionnaire. Unpublished manuscript.

Karwowski, M. (forthcoming). Subordinated and rebellious creativity at school. In R. A. Beghetto & B. Sriraman (Eds.), *Creative contradictions in education: Cross disciplinary paradoxes and perspectives*. Dordrecht, The Netherlands: Springer.

Karwowski, M. & Barbot, B. (2016). Creative self-beliefs: Their nature, development, and correlates. In J. C. Kaufman & J. Baer (Eds.), *Cambridge companion to reason and development* (pp. 302–326). New York: Cambridge University Press.

Karwowski, M., Dul, J., Gralewski, J., Jauk, E., Jankowska, D. M., Gajda, A., & Benedek, M. (2016). Intelligence as the necessary condition for creativity? Beyond the threshold hypothesis. *Intelligence*, **57**, 105–117.

Karwowski, M., & Gralewski, J. (2011). Zmotywowana kreatywność. Synergia motywacyjna postawy twórczej młodzieży. [Motivated creativity. Motivational synergy of youths' creative attitude]. *Chowanna*, **2**, 45–58.

Karwowski, M., & Gralewski, J. (2013). Threshold hypothesis: Fact or artifact? *Thinking Skills and Creativity*, **8**, 25–33.

Karwowski, M., & Lebuda, I. (2016). The big five, the huge two and creative self-beliefs: A meta-analysis. *Psychology of Aesthetics, Creativity, and the Arts*, **10**, 214–232.

Karwowski, M., & Lebuda, I. (forthcoming). Creative self-concept: A surface characteristic of creative personality. In G. Feist, R. Reiter-Palmon, & J. C. Kaufman (Eds.), *Cambridge Handbook of Creativity and Personality Research*. New York: Cambridge University Press.

Karwowski, M., Lebuda, I., Wisniewska, E., & Gralewski, J. (2013). Big Five personality factors as the predictors of creative self-efficacy and creative personal identity: Does gender matter. *Journal of Creative Behavior*, **47**, 215–232.

Karwowski, M., & Soszyński, M. (2008). How to develop creative imagination? *Thinking Skills and Creativity*, **3**, 163–171.

Kaufman, J. C. (2009). *Creativity 101*. New York: Springer.

Kaufman, J. C., & Beghetto, R. A. (2009). Beyond big and little: The four C model of creativity. *Review of General Psychology*, **13**, 1–12.

Kirton, M. J. (1976). Adaptors and innovators: A description and measure. *Journal of Applied Psychology*, **61**, 622–629.

Lubart, T., Zenasni, F., & Barbot, B. (2013). Creative potential and its measurement. *International Journal for Talent Development and Creativity*, **1**, 41–51.

Lucas, R. E., & Donnellan, M. B. (2011). Personality development across the life span: Longitudinal analyses with a national sample from Germany. *Journal of Personality and Social Psychology*, **101**, 847–861.

Maslow, A. (1959). Creativity in self-actualizing people. In. H. H. Anderson (Ed.), *Creativity and its cultivation* (pp. 83–95). New York: Harper & Brothers.

McCrae, R. R. (1987). Creativity, divergent thinking, and openness to experience. *Journal of Personality and Social Psychology*, **52**(6), 1258–1265.

Nicholls, J. G. (1972). Creativity in the person who will never produce anything original and useful: The concept of creativity as a normally distributed trait. *American Psychologist*, **27**, 717–727.

Plucker, J. (1999). Is the proof in the pudding? Reanalyses of Torrance's (1958 to present) longitudinal study data. *Creativity Research Journal*, **12**, 103–114.

Plucker, J. A., Beghetto, R. A., & Dow, G. T. (2004). Why isn't creativity more important to educational psychologists? Potentials, pitfalls, and future directions in creativity research. *Educational Psychologist*, **39**, 83–96.

Prabhu, V., Sutton, C., & Sauser, W. (2008). Creativity and certain personality traits: Understanding the mediating effect of intrinsic motivation. *Creativity Research Journal*, **20**, 53–66.

Runco, M. A. (1999). A longitudinal study of exceptional giftedness and creativity. *Creativity Research Journal*, **12**, 161–164.

Runco, M. A. (2015). A commentary on the social perspective on creativity. *Creativity: Theories – Research – Applications*, **2**, 21–32.

Scott, C. L. (1999). Teachers' biases toward creative children. *Creativity Research Journal*, **12**, 321–328.

Scott, G., Leritz, L. E., & Mumford, M. D. (2004). The effectiveness of creativity training: A quantitative review. *Creativity Research Journal*, **16**, 361–388.

Silvia, P. J., Nusbaum, E. C., Berg, C., Martin, C., & O'Connor, A. (2009). Openness to experience, plasticity, and creativity: Exploring lower-order, higher-order, and interactive effects. *Journal of Research in Personality*, **43**, 1087–1090.

Simonton, D. K. (2009). Varieties of (scientific) creativity: A hierarchical model of domain-specific disposition, development, and achievement. *Perspectives on Psychological Science*, **4**, 441–452.

Sternberg, R. J., Kaufman, J. C., & Pretz, J. E. (2002). *The creativity conundrum: A propulsion model of kinds of creative contributions.* New York: Psychology Press.

Sternberg, R. J., & Lubart, T. I. (1995). *Defying the crowd: Cultivating creativity in a culture of conformity.* New York: Free Press.

Tierney, P., & Farmer, S. M. (2011). Creative self-efficacy development and creative performance over time. *Journal of Applied Psychology,* **96**(2), 277–293.

Urban, K. K. (2005). Assessing creativity: The test for creative thinking – drawing production (TCT-DP). *International Education Journal,* **6**, 272–280.

Voss, J. F., & Means, M. L. (1989). Toward a model of creativity based upon problem solving in the social sciences. In J. A. Glover, R. R. Ronning, & C. R. Ronning (Eds.), *Handbook of creativity* (pp. 399–410). New York: Plenum Press.

Westby, E. L., & Dawson, V. L. (1995). Creativity: Asset or burden in the classroom? *Creativity Research Journal,* **8**, 1–10.

CHAPTER 19

Teaching for Creativity

Robert J. Sternberg

Cornell University

What Is Creativity?

Creativity is a habit (Sternberg, 2006; Tharp, 2005). Habits can be good or bad. My four-year-old daughter Brittany sucks her thumb: That's a bad habit. Creativity, however, is a good habit. The problem is that schools sometimes treat it as a bad habit (Craft, 2005), of the order of sucking one's thumb. And the world of conventional standardized tests we have invented does just that (Sternberg, 1997b; 2010a; Sternberg, Jarvin, & Grigorenko, 2011). If students try being creative on standardized tests, they will get slapped down just as soon as they get their score. That will teach them not to do it again.

Oddly enough, a distinguished psychometric tester, J. P. Guilford, was one of the first to try to incorporate creativity into the school curriculum (Guilford, 1950), but his efforts show little fruit today, although more and more educators recognize the importance of teaching for creativity (Plucker & Beghetto, 2015; Reis & Renzulli, 2014). Disciples of Guilford such as MacKinnon (1962) and Torrance (1962) had little more success, although again, there are signs that their efforts may yet bear fruit.

It may sound paradoxical that creativity – a novel response – is a habit – a routine response. But creative people are creative largely not as a result of any particular inborn trait, but rather through an attitude toward life (Maslow, 1967; Schank, 1988): They habitually respond to problems in fresh and novel ways, rather than allowing themselves respond mindlessly and automatically (Sternberg, 2010c; 2013b; Sternberg & Lubart, 1992, 1995a, 1995b, 1995c).

Like any habit, creativity can either be encouraged or discouraged. The main things that promote the habit are (1) opportunities to engage in it, (2) encouragement when people avail themselves of these opportunities, and (3) rewards when people respond to such encouragement and think and behave creatively. You need all three. Take away the opportunities, encouragement, or rewards, and you will take away the creativity. In this respect, creativity is no different from any other habit, good or bad.

Suppose, for example, you want to encourage good eating habits. You can do so by (1) providing opportunities for students to eat well in school and at home, (2) encouraging students to avail themselves of these opportunities, and then (3) praising young people who do in fact use the opportunities to eat well. Or suppose you want to discourage smoking. You can do so by (1) taking away opportunities for engaging in it (e.g., by prohibiting it in various places or by making prices of cigarettes so high one can scarcely afford to buy them), (2) discouraging smoking (e.g., advertisements showing how smoking kills), and (3) rewarding people who do not smoke (e.g., with praise or even preferred rates for health and life insurance policies).

This may sound too simple. It is not. Creative people routinely approach problems in novel ways (Albert & Runco, 1999; Baer & Kaufman, 2006; Kaufman & Beghetto, 2009; Plucker, Kaufman, & Beghetto, 2015). Creative people habitually (1) look for ways to see problems that other people don't look for, (2) take risks that other people are afraid to take, (3) have the courage to defy the crowd and to stand up for their own beliefs, and (4) seek to overcome obstacles and challenges to their views that other people give in to, among other things (Kaufman, 2009; Sternberg & Lubart, 1995b, 1995c; see also Sternberg, 1999, 2015; Sternberg & Grigorenko, 2007).

Educational practices that seem to promote learning may inadvertently suppress creativity, for the same reasons that environmental circumstances can suppress any habit (Sternberg & Williams, 1996). These practices often take away the opportunities for, encouragement of, and rewards for creativity. The increasingly massive and far-reaching use of conventional standardized tests is one of the most effective, if unintentional, vehicles this country has created for suppressing creativity. I say "conventional" because the problem is not with standardized tests per se, but rather with the kinds of tests we use. And teacher-made tests can be just as much of a problem.

Conventional standardized tests encourage a certain kind of learning and thinking – in particular, the kind of learning and thinking for which there is a right answer and many wrong answers (Gardner, 1991, 2006, 2011a, 2011b; Sternberg, 1997b, 2003a, 2003b, 2010a). To create a multiple-choice or short-answer test, you need a right answer and many wrong ones. Problems that do not fit into the right answer–wrong answer format do not lend themselves well to multiple-choice and short-answer testing. Put another way, problems that require divergent thinking are inadvertently devalued by the use of standardized tests. This is not to say knowledge is unimportant. On the contrary, one cannot think creatively and soundly unless one has the knowledge with which to think creatively. Creativity represents a balance between knowledge and freeing oneself of that knowledge (Johnson-Laird, 1988). Knowledge is a necessary but in no way sufficient condition for creativity (Sternberg & Lubart, 1995a). The problem is that schooling often stops short of encouraging creativity, with teachers content as long as students have the knowledge.

Examples are legion (see Sternberg & Grigorenko, 2007). If one is studying history, one might take the opportunity to think creatively about how we can learn from the mistakes of the past to do better in the future. Or one might think creatively about what would have happened had a certain historical event not come to pass (e.g., the Allies winning World War II). But there is no single "right" answer to such questions, so they are not likely to appear on a conventional standardized test. In science, one can design an experiment, but again, designing an experiment does not neatly fit into a multiple-choice format. In literature, one can imagine alternative endings to stories, or what the stories would be like if they took place in a different era. In mathematics, students can invent and think with novel number systems. In foreign language, students can invent dialogues with people from other cultures. But the emphasis in most tests is on the display of knowledge, and often inert knowledge, which may sit in students' heads but may at the same time be inaccessible for actual use.

Essay tests might seem to provide a solution to such problems, and they might, but as they are typically used, they do not. Increasingly, essay tests can be and are scored by a machine. Often, human raters of essays provide ratings that correlate more highly with machine grading than with the grading of other humans. Why? Because they are scored against one or more implicit prototypes or models of what a "correct" answer should be. The more the essay conforms to one or more prototypes, the higher the grade. Machines can detect conformity to prototypes better than humans do, so essay graders of the kind being used today succeed in a limited form of essay evaluation. Thus, the essays that students are being given often do not encourage creativity – rather, they discourage creativity in favor of model answers that conform to one or more prototypes. In the end, essay tests can end up rewarding uncreative students who spit back facts just as well as they do creative students (Sternberg, 1994).

Oddly enough, then, "accountability" movements that are being promoted as fostering solid education are, in at least one crucial respect, doing the opposite (Sternberg, 2004): They are discouraging creativity at the expense of conformity. The problem is the very narrow notion of accountability involved. But proponents of this notion of accountability often make it sound as though those who oppose them oppose any accountability, whereas, in fact, they instead may oppose only the narrow form of accountability conventional tests generate. The tests are not "bad" or "wrong" per se – just limited in what they assess (Sternberg, 2012). But they are treated as though they assess broader ranges of skills than they actually do. Curiously, governments may have a stake in such narrow, but not broad, forms of accountability.

Governments often wish to encourage conformity – after all, they see themselves as promoting order, usually order with respect to themselves – and so they inadvertently may prefer an educational agenda that promotes a model of an educated person that minimizes or excludes creative (i.e., nonconforming) thinking. Their goal is not necessarily to punish creativity, but rather to ensure their own stability and longevity. The punishment and extinction of creativity is merely a by-product. Thus, they may promote education, but not a kind of education that fosters creative thinking. They may also fail to promote active critical thinking, which also potentially puts their longevity at risk. Sometimes, they will allow creative or critical thinking, so long as it is not applied to their own policies. It is easy for a government or other powerful organization to slip into the view that critics are "traitors" who must be ridiculed or punished. Inert knowledge is much safer to stability because it gives the appearance of education without most of the substance.

Creativity is socialized through thousands upon thousands of acts of teachers, parents, and other authority figures. So is conformity. If people have been socialized over the years to think in conforming ways, and if they have been rewarded for conforming, no single school or governmental initiative is likely to change the way people think and act. Conformity may be so much a part of the social fabric that people give it up only reluctantly.

Whereas creativity is seen as departure from a mean, conformity is seen as adherence to that mean. Societies often speak of the "tall-poppy" phenomenon, whereby tall poppies – those that stick out – are cut down to size. If one grows up in a society that cuts down the tall poppies, or does what it can to ensure that the poppies never grow tall in the first place, it will be difficult to generate creative behavior. People in such societies will be so afraid of departure from the mean that they will be unwilling to be creative, whatever their creative abilities might be. They may also think that being creative is the province of the mentally ill. Although there are associations between creativity and mental illness (Kaufman, 2001a,

2001b), the overwhelming majority of creative people are mentally well, not ill!

Why is creativity even important? It is important because the world is changing at a far greater pace than it ever has before, and people need constantly to cope with novel kinds of tasks and situations. Learning in this era must be lifelong, and people constantly need to be thinking in new ways (Sternberg, 1997a). The problems we confront, whether in our families, communities, or nations, are novel and difficult, and we need to think creatively and divergently to solve these problems. The technologies, social customs, and tools available to us in our lives are replaced almost as quickly as they are introduced. We need to think creatively to thrive – and, at times, even to survive.

But this often is not how we are teaching students to think – quite the contrary. So we may end up with "walking encyclopedias" who show all the creativity of an encyclopedia. In a recent best seller, a man decided to become the smartest person in the world by reading an encyclopedia cover to cover. The fact that the book sold so well is a testament to how skewed our conception has become of what it means to be smart. Someone could memorize that or any other encyclopedia, but not be able to solve even the smallest novel problem in his or her life.

If we want to encourage creativity, we need to promote the creativity habit. That means we have to stop treating it as a bad habit. We have to resist efforts to promote a conception of accountability that encourages students to accumulate inert knowledge with which they learn to think neither creatively nor critically (Pang, 2015).

The Investment Theory of Creativity

Together with Todd Lubart, I have proposed an *investment theory of creativity* as a means of understanding the nature of creativity (Sternberg, 2012; Sternberg & Lubart, 1991, 1995a, 1995b). According to this theory, creative people are ones who are willing and able to "buy low and sell high" in the realm of ideas. Buying low means pursuing ideas that are unknown or out of favor but that have growth potential. Often, when these ideas are first presented, they encounter resistance. The creative individual persists in the face of this resistance, and eventually sells high, moving on to the next new, or unpopular, idea.

According to the investment theory, creativity requires a confluence of six distinct but interrelated resources: intellectual abilities, knowledge, styles of thinking, personality, motivation, and environment. Although levels of these resources are sources of individual differences, often the decision to use the resources is the more important source of individual differences. Ultimately, creativity is not about one thing, but about a system of things (Csikszentmilhalyi, 1988, 1990, 1999, 2013).

Intellectual abilities. Intellectual abilities are generally acknowledged to be necessary but not sufficient for creativity (Renzulli, 1986). Three intellectual skills are particularly important: (1) the synthetic ability to see problems in new ways and to escape the bounds of conventional thinking; (2) the analytic ability to recognize which of one's ideas are worth pursuing and which are not; and (3) the practical-contextual ability to know how to persuade others of – to sell other people on – the value of one's ideas. The confluence of these three abilities is also important. Analytic ability used in the absence of the other two abilities results in powerful critical but not creative thinking. Synthetic ability in the absence of the other two abilities results in new ideas that are not subjected to the scrutiny required to make them work. And practical-contextual ability in the absence of the other two may result in the transmittal of ideas not because the ideas are good, but rather because the ideas have been well and powerfully presented. To be creative, one must first *decide* to generate new ideas, analyze these ideas, and sell the ideas to others.

Knowledge. Concerning knowledge, on the one hand, one needs to know enough about a field to move it forward. One cannot move beyond where a field is if one does not know where it is. On the other hand, knowledge about a field can result in a closed and entrenched perspective, resulting in a person's not moving beyond the way in which he or she has seen problems in the past (Frensch & Sternberg, 1989). Thus, one needs to decide to use one's past knowledge, but also decide not to let the knowledge become a hindrance rather than a help.

Knowledge most becomes a hindrance when it leads to dogmatism (Ambrose, Sternberg, & Sriraman, 2012a, 2012b). One would hope, of course, that education would lead to a broadening of worldview. But many times it does not. In some schools, motivated by a particularly ideology, religion, or worldview, students actually become less open-minded, creative, and broad in their thinking. Students are taught not to question, but to give pat and often memorized answers.

We might like to think that such schools are to be found primarily abroad – for example, schools that consist solely of memorizing religious texts or even that teach kids to become terrorists or suicide bombers. Such schools have little incentive to encourage open-minded thinking. But such schools are to be found in the United States as well. Children grow up with religious or ideological beliefs that simply do not allow them to ask questions, for example, about the causes of the world's increasingly erratic climate or of the sudden run of earthquakes in some states that hardly ever had them before. Moreover, in some schools, students will be taught that the world was created at a specific time – for example, 6,000 years ago (Cosner, 2015). Such teaching scarcely encourages students to explore different views of the world and its origins.

Thinking styles. Thinking styles are related to creativity (Kogan, 1973; Zhang & Sternberg, 2009, 2012). With regard to thinking styles, a legislative style is particularly important for creativity, that is, a preference for thinking and a decision to think in new ways (Sternberg, 1997c). This preference needs to be distinguished from the ability to think creatively: Someone may like to think along new lines, but not think well, or vice versa. It also helps, to become a major creative thinker, if one is able to think globally as well as locally, distinguishing the forest from the trees and thereby recognizing which questions are important and which ones are not.

Personality. Numerous research investigations have supported the importance of certain personality attributes for creative functioning (Barron, 1969, 1988). These attributes include, but are not limited to, willingness to overcome obstacles, willingness to take sensible risks, willingness to tolerate ambiguity, and self-efficacy. In particular, buying low and selling high typically means defying the crowd, so that one has to be willing to stand up to conventions if one wants to think and act in creative ways. Note that none of these attributes are fixed. One can *decide* to overcome obstacles, take sensible risks, and so forth (Sternberg, 2000).

Motivation. Intrinsic, task-focused motivation is also essential to creativity. The research of Teresa Amabile (1996, 1999) and others (see, e.g., Hennessey, 2015) has shown the importance of such motivation for creative work, and has suggested that people rarely do truly creative work in an area unless they really love what they are doing and focus on the work rather than the potential rewards. Motivation is not something inherent in a person: One decides to be motivated by one thing or another.

Environment. Finally, one needs an environment that is supportive and rewarding of creative ideas (Sternberg & Lubart, 1995a; Sternberg & Williams, 1996). One could have all of the internal resources needed in order to think creatively, but without some environmental support (such as a forum for proposing those ideas), the creativity that a person has within him or her might never be displayed.

Confluence. Concerning the confluence of components, creativity is hypothesized to involve more than a simple sum of a person's level on each component (Sternberg & Lubart, 1991). First, there may be thresholds for some components (e.g., knowledge) below which creativity is not possible regardless of the levels on other components. Second, partial compensation may occur in which a strength on one component (e.g., motivation) counteracts a weakness on another component (e.g., environment). Third, interactions may also occur between components, such as intelligence and motivation, in which high levels of either component could multiplicatively enhance creativity.

Creative ideas are both novel and valuable, but they are often rejected because the creative innovator stands up to vested interests and defies the crowd. The crowd does not maliciously or wilfully reject creative notions. Rather, it does not realize, and often does not want to realize, that the proposed idea represents a valid and advanced way of thinking. Society generally perceives opposition to the status quo as annoying, offensive, and reason enough to ignore innovative ideas.

Evidence abounds that creative ideas are often rejected. Initial reviews of major works of literature and art are often negative. Toni Morrison's *Tar Baby* received negative reviews when it was first published, as did Sylvia Plath's *The Bell Jar*. The first exhibition in Munich of the work of Norwegian painter Edvard Munch opened and closed the same day because of the strong negative response from the critics. Some of the greatest scientific papers have been rejected not just by one but by several journals before being published. For example, John Garcia, a distinguished biopsychologist, was immediately denounced (see Garcia, 1981) when he first proposed that a form of learning called classical conditioning could be produced in a single trial of learning (Garcia & Koelling, 1966).

From the investment view, then, the creative person buys low by presenting a unique idea and then attempting to convince other people of its value. After convincing others that the idea is valuable, which increases the perceived value of the investment, the creative person sells high by leaving the idea to others and moving on to another idea. People typically want others to love their ideas, but immediate universal applause for an idea usually indicates that it is not particularly creative.

Research Supporting the Investment Theory

Research within the investment framework has yielded support for this model (Lubart & Sternberg, 1995; Sternberg, 2010a). This research has used tasks such as (1) writing short-stories using unusual titles (e.g., the octopus's sneakers), (2) drawing pictures with unusual themes (e.g., the earth from an insect's point of view), (3) devising creative advertisements for boring products (e.g., cufflinks), and (4) solving unusual scientific problems (e.g., how we could tell if someone had been on the moon within the past month). This research showed creative performance to be moderately domain-specific, and to be predicted by the combination of resources specified by the theory.

In another study, creativity was measured using open-ended measures (Sternberg & The Rainbow Project Collaborators, 2005, 2006). These performance tasks were expected to tap an important aspect of creativity that might not be measured using multiple-choice items alone, because open-ended measures require more spontaneous and free-form responses.

For each of the tasks, participants were given a choice of topic or stimuli on which to base their creative stories or cartoon captions. Each of the creativity performance tasks were rated on criteria that were determined a priori as indicators of creativity.

Participants were given five cartoons, minus their captions, purchased from the archives of the *New Yorker*. The participants' task was to choose three cartoons and to provide a caption for each . Two trained judges rated all the cartoons for cleverness, humor, originality, and task appropriateness on five-point scales. A combined creativity score was formed by summing the individual ratings on each dimension except task appropriateness, which, theoretically, is not a pure measure of creativity per se.

Participants were further asked to write two stories, spending about 15 minutes on each, choosing from the following titles: "A Fifth Chance," "2983," "Beyond the Edge," "The Octopus's Sneakers," "It's Moving Backwards," and "Not Enough Time" (Lubart & Sternberg, 1995; Sternberg & Lubart, 1995a). A team of six judges was trained to rate the stories. Each judge rated the stories for originality, complexity, emotional evocativeness, and descriptiveness on five-point scales.

Participants also were presented with five sheets of paper, each containing a set of 11 to 13 images linked by a common theme (keys, money, travel, animals playing music, and humans playing music). There were no restrictions on the minimum or maximum number of images that needed to be incorporated into the stories. After choosing one of the pages, the participant was given 15 minutes to formulate a short story and dictate it into a cassette recorder.

Six judges were trained to rate the stories. As with the written stories, each judge rated the stories for originality, complexity, emotional evocativeness, and descriptiveness on five-point scales.

Rasch reliability indices for the composite person ability estimates for the Written and Oral Stories were very good (.79 and .80, respectively). The judges for both the Written and Oral Stories varied greatly in terms of their severity of ratings for the stories. For the Written Stories, the judges also ranged in their fit to the model, although the reliability was still sound (rater reliability = .94). For the Oral Stories, all the judges fit the model very well, so their differences could be reliably modeled (rater reliability = .97).

Creativity-based performance tests formed a unique factor in a factor analysis. Furthermore, the creativity tests significantly and substantially increased prediction of first-year college grade-point averages for more than 700 highly diverse students from 13 colleges and universities across the United States that varied widely in quality and geographic location. The tests also substantially decreased ethnic-group differences. The reason is that different groups are socialized to be intelligent in different ways. For example, American Indians performed relatively poorly in comparison with other ethnic groups on the analytical measure of the battery but had the highest scores on oral storytelling.

How Can We Develop Creativity in Students?

Teaching creatively means encouraging students to (a) create, (b) invent, (c) discover, (d) imagine if . . . , (e) suppose that . . . , (f) predict. Teaching for creativity requires teachers not only to support and encourage creativity but also to role-model it and to reward it when it is displayed (Sternberg & Grigorenko, 2007; Sternberg & Lubart, 1995; Sternberg & Williams, 1996). In other words, teachers need not only to talk the talk but also to walk the walk. Consider some examples of instructional or assessment activities that encourage students to think creatively.

1. Create an alternative ending to the short story you just read that represents a different way things might have gone for the main characters in the story. [Literature]
2. Invent a dialogue between an American tourist in Paris and a Frenchman he encounters on the street from whom he is asking directions on how to get to the Rue Pigalle. [French]
3. Discover the fundamental physical principle that underlies all of the following problems, each of which differs from the others in the "surface structure" of the problem but not in its "deep structure. . . ." [Physics]

4. Imagine if the government of China keeps evolving over the course of the next 20 years in much the same way it has been evolving. What do you believe the government of China will be like in 20 years? [Government/Political Science]
5. Suppose that you were to design one additional instrument to be played in a symphony orchestra for future compositions. What might that instrument be like, and why? [Music]
6. Predict changes that are likely to occur in the vocabulary or grammar of spoken Spanish in the border areas of the Rio Grande over the next 100 years as a result of continuous interactions between Spanish and English speakers. [Linguistics]

Consider 12 keys for developing the creativity habit in students (see also Sternberg & Grigorenko, 2007; Sternberg & Williams, 1996).

Redefine Problems

Redefining a problem means taking a problem and turning it on its head (Sternberg & Smith, 1988). Many times in life individuals have a problem and they just do not see how to solve it. They are stuck in a box. Redefining a problem essentially means extricating oneself from the box. This process is the synthetic part of creative thinking.

There are many ways teachers and parents can encourage students to define and redefine problems for themselves, rather than – as is so often the case – doing it for them. Teachers and parents can promote creative performance by encouraging their students to define and redefine *their own* problems and projects. Adults can encourage creative thinking by having students choose their own topics for papers or presentations, choose their own ways of solving problems, and sometimes having them choose again if they discover that their selection was a mistake. Teachers and parents should also allow their students to pick their own topics, subject to the adults' approval, on projects the students do. Approval ensures that the topic is relevant to the lesson and has a chance of leading to a successful project.

Adults cannot always offer students choices, but giving choices is the only way for students to learn how to choose. Giving students latitude in making choices helps them develop taste and good judgment, both of which are essential elements of creativity.

At some point everyone makes a mistake in choosing a project or in the method they select to complete it. Teachers and parents should remember that an important part of creativity is the analytic part – learning to recognize a mistake – and give students the chance and the opportunity to redefine their choices.

Question and Analyze Assumptions

Everyone has assumptions. Often one does not know he or she has these assumptions because they are widely shared. Creative people question assumptions and eventually lead others to do the same. Questioning assumptions is part of the analytical thinking involved in creativity. When Copernicus suggested that Earth revolves around the sun, the suggestion was viewed as preposterous because everyone could see that the sun revolves around Earth. Galileo's ideas, including the relative rates of falling objects, caused him to be banned as a heretic.

Sometimes it is not until many years later that society realizes the limitations or errors of their assumptions and the value of the creative person's thoughts. The impetus of those who question assumptions allows for cultural, technological, and other forms of advancement.

Teachers can be role models for questioning assumptions by showing students that what they assume they know they really do not know. Of course, students should not question every assumption. There are times to question and try to reshape the environment, and there are times to adapt to it. Some creative people question so many things so often that others stop taking them seriously. Everyone must learn which assumptions are worth questioning and which battles are worth fighting. Sometimes it is better for individuals to leave the inconsequential assumptions alone so that they have an audience when they find something worth the effort.

Teachers and parents can help students develop this talent by making questioning a part of the daily exchange. It is more important for students to learn what questions to ask – and how to ask them – than to learn the answers. Adults can help students evaluate their questions by discouraging the idea that the adults ask questions and the students simply answer them. Adults need to avoid perpetuating the belief that their role is to teach students the facts, and instead help students understand that what matters is the students' ability to use facts. This can help students learn how to formulate good questions and how to answer questions.

Society tends to make a pedagogical mistake by emphasizing the answering and not the asking of questions. The good student is perceived as the one who rapidly furnishes the right answers. The expert in a field thus becomes the extension of the expert student – the one who knows and can recite a lot of information. As John Dewey recognized, how one thinks is often more important than what one thinks. Schools need to teach students how to ask the right questions (questions that are good, thought-provoking, and interesting) and lessen the emphasis on rote learning.

Do Not Assume That Creative Ideas Sell Themselves: Sell Them

Everyone would like to assume that their wonderful, creative ideas will sell themselves. But as Galileo, Edvard Munch, Toni Morrison, Sylvia Plath, and millions of others have discovered, they do not. On the contrary, creative ideas are usually viewed with suspicion and distrust. Moreover, those who propose such ideas may be viewed with suspicion and distrust as well. Because people are comfortable with the ways they already think, and because they probably have a vested interest in their existing way of thinking, it can be extremely difficult to dislodge them from their current way of thinking.

Thus, students need to learn how to persuade other people of the value of their ideas. This selling is part of the practical aspect of creative thinking. If students do a science project, it is a good idea for them present it and demonstrate why it makes an important contribution. If they create a piece of artwork, they should be prepared to describe why they think it has value. If they develop a plan for a new form of government, they should explain why it is better than the existing form of government. At times, teachers may find themselves having to justify their ideas about teaching to their principal. They should prepare their students for the same kind of experience.

Encourage Idea Generation

As mentioned earlier, creative people demonstrate a "legislative" style of thinking: They like to generate ideas. The environment for generating ideas can be constructively critical, but it must not be harshly or destructively critical. Students need to acknowledge that some ideas are better than others. Adults and students should collaborate to identify and encourage any creative aspects of ideas that are presented. When suggested ideas do not seem to have much value, teachers should not just criticize. Rather, they should suggest new approaches, preferably ones that incorporate at least some aspects of the previous ideas that seemed in themselves not to have much value. Students should be praised for generating ideas, regardless of whether some are silly or unrelated, while being encouraged to identify and develop their best ideas into high-quality projects.

Recognize That Knowledge Is a Double-Edged Sword and Act Accordingly

On the one hand, one cannot be creative without knowledge. Quite simply, one cannot go beyond the existing state of knowledge if one does not know what that state is. Many students have ideas that are creative with respect to themselves, but not with respect to the field because others have had the same ideas before. Those with a greater knowledge base can be creative in ways that those who are still learning about the basics of the field cannot be.

At the same time, those who have an expert level of knowledge can experience tunnel vision, narrow thinking, and entrenchment (Adelson, 1984; Frensch & Sternberg, 1989). Experts can become so stuck in a way of thinking that they become unable to extricate themselves from it. When a person believes that he or she knows everything there is to know, he or she is unlikely to ever show truly meaningful creativity again.

The upshot of this is that I tell my students and my own students that the teaching-learning process is a two-way process. I have as much to learn from my students and my students as they have to learn from me. I have knowledge they do not have, but they have flexibility I do not have – precisely because they do not know as much as I do. By learning from, as well as teaching to, one's students, one opens up channels for creativity that otherwise would remain closed.

Encourage Students to Identify and Surmount Obstacles

Buying low and selling high means defying the crowd. And people who defy the crowd – people who think creatively – almost inevitably encounter resistance. The question is not whether one will encounter obstacles; that obstacles will be encountered is a fact. The question is whether the creative thinker has the fortitude to persevere and to go against the crowd (Simonton, 1976, 1984, 1988, 1994). I have often wondered why so many people start off their careers doing creative work and then vanish from the radar screen. I think I know at least one reason why: Sooner or later, they decide that being creative is not worth the resistance and punishment. The truly creative thinkers pay the short-term price because they recognize that they can make a difference in the long term. But often it is a long while before the value of creative ideas is recognized and appreciated.

Teachers can prepare students for these types of experiences by describing obstacles that they, their friends, and well-known figures in society have faced while trying to be creative; otherwise, students may think that they are the only ones confronted by obstacles. Teachers should include stories about people who were not supportive, about bad grades for unwelcome ideas, and about frosty receptions to what they may have thought were their best ideas. To help students deal with obstacles, teachers can remind them of the many creative people whose ideas were initially shunned and help them develop an inner sense of awe of the creative act. Suggesting that students reduce their concern over what others think is also valuable. However, it is often difficult for students to lessen their dependence on the opinions of their peers.

When students attempt to surmount an obstacle, they should be praised for the effort, whether or not they were entirely successful. Teachers and parents alike can point out aspects of the students' attack that were successful and why, and suggest other ways to confront similar obstacles. Having the class brainstorm about ways to confront a given obstacle can get them thinking about the many strategies people can use to confront problems. Some obstacles are within oneself, such as performance anxiety. Other obstacles are external, such as others' bad opinions of one's actions. Whether internal or external, obstacles must be overcome.

Encourage Sensible Risk-Taking

When creative people defy the crowd by buying low and selling high, they take risks in much the same way as do people who invest. Some such investments simply may not pan out. Moreover, defying the crowd means risking the crowd's wrath. But there are levels of sensibility to keep in mind when defying the crowd. Creative people take sensible risks and produce ideas that others ultimately admire and respect as trendsetting. In taking these risks, creative people sometimes make mistakes, fail, and fall flat on their faces.

I emphasize the importance of sensible risk-taking because I am not talking about risking life and limb for creativity. To help students learn to take sensible risks, adults can encourage them to take some intellectual risks with courses, with activities, and with what they say to adults – to develop a sense of how to assess risks.

Nearly every major discovery or invention entailed some risk. When a movie theater was the only place to see a movie, someone created the idea of the home video machine. Skeptics questioned if anyone would want to see videos on a small screen. Another initially risky idea was the home computer. Many wondered if anyone would have enough use for a home computer to justify the cost. These ideas were once risks, and are now ingrained in our society.

Few students are willing to take many risks in school because they learn that taking risks can be costly. Perfect test scores and papers receive praise and open up future possibilities. Failure to attain a certain academic standard is perceived as deriving from a lack of ability and motivation and may lead to scorn and lessened opportunities. Why risk taking hard courses or saying things that teachers may not like when that may lead to low grades or even failure? Teachers may inadvertently advocate students to only learn to "play it safe" when they give assignments without choices and allow only particular answers to questions. Thus, teachers need not only to encourage sensible risk-taking but also to reward it.

Encourage Tolerance of Ambiguity

People often like things to be in black and white. People like to think that a country is good or bad (ally or enemy), or that a given idea in education works or does not work. The problem is that there are a lot of gray areas in creative work. Artists working on new paintings and writers working on new books often report feeling scattered and unsure in their thoughts. They often need to figure out whether they are even on the right track. Scientists often are not sure whether the theory they have developed is exactly correct. These creative thinkers need to tolerate the ambiguity and uncertainty until they get the idea just right.

A creative idea tends to come in bits and pieces and develops over time. However, the period in which the idea is developing tends to be uncomfortable. Without time or the ability to tolerate ambiguity, many may jump to a less than optimal solution. When a student has almost the right topic for a paper or almost the right science project, it is tempting for teachers to accept the near miss. To help students become creative, teachers need to encourage them to accept and extend the period in which their ideas do not quite converge. Students need to be taught that uncertainty and discomfort are a part of living a creative life. Ultimately, they will benefit from their tolerance of ambiguity by coming up with better ideas.

Help Students Build Self-Efficacy

Many people often reach a point where they feel as if no one believes in them. I reach this point frequently, feeling that no one values or even appreciates what I am doing. Because creative work often does not get a warm reception, it is extremely important that the creative people believe in the value of what they are doing. This is not to say that individuals should believe that every idea they have is a good idea. Rather, individuals need to believe that, ultimately, they have the ability to make a difference.

The main limitation on what students can do is what they think they can do. All students have the capacity to be creators and to experience the joy associated with making something new, but first they must be given a strong base for creativity. Sometimes teachers and parents unintentionally limit what students can do by sending messages that express or imply limits on students' potential accomplishments. Instead, these adults need to help students believe in their own ability to be creative.

I have found that probably the best predictor of success among my students is not their ability, but their belief in their ability to succeed. If students are encouraged to succeed and to believe in their own ability to succeed, they very likely will find the success that otherwise would elude them.

Help Students Find What They Love to Do

Teachers must help students find what excites them to unleash their students' best creative performances. Teachers need to remember that this may not be what really excites them. People who truly excel creatively in a pursuit, whether vocational or avocational, almost always genuinely love what they do.

Helping students find what they really love to do is often hard and frustrating work. Yet, sharing the frustration with them now is better than leaving them to face it alone later. To help students uncover their true interests, teachers can ask them to demonstrate a special talent or ability for the class, and explain that it does not matter what they do (within reason), only that they love the activity.

In working with my students and my students, I try to help them find what interests *them,* whether or not it particularly interests me. Often, their enthusiasm is infectious, and I find myself drawn into new areas of pursuit simply because I allow myself to follow my students rather than always expecting them to follow me.

I often meet students who are pursuing a certain career interest not because it is what they want to do, but because it is what their parents or other authority figures expect them to do. I always feel sorry for such students because I know that although they may do good work in that field, they almost certainly will not do great work. It is hard for people to do great work in a field that simply does not interest them.

Teach Students the Importance of Delaying Gratification

Part of being creative means being able to work on a project or task for a long time without immediate or interim rewards. Students must learn that rewards are not always immediate and that there are benefits to delaying gratification (Mischel, Shoda, & Rodriguez, 1989). The fact of the matter is that, in the short term, people are often ignored when they do creative work or even punished for doing it.

Many people believe that they should reward students immediately for good performance, and that students should expect rewards. This style of teaching and parenting emphasizes the here and now and often comes at the expense of what is best in the long term.

An important lesson in life – and one that is intimately related to developing the discipline to do creative work – is to learn to wait for rewards (Mischel, Shoda, & Rodriguez, 1989). The greatest rewards are often those that are delayed. Teachers can give their students examples of delayed gratification in their lives and in the lives of creative individuals and help them apply these examples to their own lives.

Hard work often does not bring immediate rewards. Students do not immediately become expert baseball players, dancers, musicians, or sculptors. And the reward of becoming an expert can seem very far away. Students often succumb to the temptations of the moment, such as watching television or playing video games. The people who make the most of their abilities are those who wait for a reward and recognize that few serious challenges can be met in a moment. Students may not see the benefits of hard work, but the advantages of a solid academic performance will be obvious when they apply to college.

The short-term focus of most school assignments does little to teach students the value of delaying gratification. Projects are clearly superior in meeting this goal, but it is difficult for teachers to assign home projects if they are not confident of parental involvement and support. By working on a task for many weeks or months, students learn the value of making incremental efforts for long-term gains.

Emphasize the Importance of the Ethical Use of Creativity

Creativity, like any other set of skills, can be used for good or bad ends. Put another way, creativity has a dark as well as a bright side (Sternberg, 2010b). If one looks at modern-day wars, they show creativity at its darkest. It is being used for destructive rather than constructive ends (Sternberg, 2013a). Students need to be shown how creativity can be used to make the world a better place to live, and they need to understand the consequences of creativity when it is used destructively.

Provide an Environment That Fosters Creativity

There are many ways teachers can provide an environment that fosters creativity. The most powerful way for teachers to develop creativity in students is to *role model creativity*. Students develop creativity not when they are told to, but when they are shown how (Amabile, 1996).

The teachers most people probably remember from their school days are not those who crammed the most content into their lectures. The teachers most people remember are those teachers whose thoughts and actions served as a role model. Most likely they balanced teaching content with teaching students how to think with and about that content.

Occasionally, I will teach a workshop on developing creativity and someone will ask exactly what he or she should do to develop creativity. Bad start. A person cannot be a role model for creativity unless he or she thinks and teaches creatively him- or herself. Teachers need to think carefully about their values, goals, and ideas about creativity and show them in their actions.

Teachers also can stimulate creativity by helping students *cross-fertilize in their thinking* to think across subjects and disciplines. The traditional school environment often has separate classrooms and classmates for different subjects and seems to influence students into thinking that learning occurs in discrete boxes: the math box, the social studies box, and the science box. However, creative ideas and insights often result from integrating material across subject areas, not from memorizing and reciting material.

Teaching students to cross-fertilize draws on their skills, interests, and abilities, regardless of the subject. If students are having trouble understanding math, teachers might ask them to draft test questions related to their special interests. For example, teachers might ask the baseball fan to devise geometry problems based on a game. The context may spur creative ideas because the student finds the topic (baseball) enjoyable and it may counteract some of the anxiety caused by geometry. Cross-fertilization motivates students who are not interested in subjects taught in the abstract.

One way teachers can enact cross-fertilization in the classroom is to ask students to identify their best and worst academic areas. Students can then be asked to come up with project ideas in their weak area based on ideas borrowed from one of their strongest areas. For example, teachers can explain to students that they can apply their interest in science to social studies by analyzing the scientific aspects of trends in national politics.

Teachers also need to *allow students the time to think creatively*. This society is a society in a hurry. People eat fast food, rush from one place to another, and value quickness. Indeed, one way to say someone is smart is to say that the person is *quick*, a clear indication of our emphasis on time. This is also indicated by the format of the standardized tests used – lots of multiple-choice problems squeezed into a brief time slot.

Most creative insights do not happen in a rush. People need time to understand a problem and to toss it around. If students are asked to think creatively, they need time to do it well. If teachers stuff questions into their tests or give their students more homework than the latter can complete, they are not allowing the students time to think creatively.

Teachers also should *instruct and assess for creativity*. If teachers give only multiple-choice tests, students quickly learn the type of thinking that teachers value, no matter what they say. If teachers want to encourage creativity, they need to include at least some opportunities for creative thought in assignments and tests. Questions that require factual recall, analytic thinking, and creative thinking should be asked. For example, students might be asked to learn about a law, analyze the law, and then think about how the law might be improved.

Teachers also need *to reward creativity*. It is not enough to talk about the value of creativity. Students are used to authority figures who say one thing and do another. They are exquisitely sensitive to what teachers value when it comes to the bottom line, namely the grade or evaluation.

Creative efforts also should be rewarded. For example, teachers can assign a project and remind students that they are looking for them to demonstrate their knowledge, analytical and writing skills, and creativity. Teachers should let students know that creativity does not depend on the teacher's agreement with what students write, but rather the agreement with ideas they express that represent a synthesis between existing ideas and their own thoughts. Teachers need to care only that the ideas are creative from the student's perspective, not necessarily creative with regard to the state-of-the-art findings in the field. Students may generate an idea that someone else has already had, but if the idea is original to the student, the student has been creative.

Teachers also need *to allow mistakes.* Buying low and selling high carries a risk. Many ideas are unpopular simply because they are not good. People often think a certain way because that way works better than other ways. But once in a while, a great thinker comes along – a Freud, a Piaget, a Chomsky, or an Einstein – and shows us a new way to think. These thinkers made contributions because they allowed themselves and their collaborators to take risks and make mistakes.

Although being successful often involves making mistakes along the way, schools are often unforgiving of mistakes. Errors on schoolwork are often marked with a large and pronounced X. When a student responds to a question with an incorrect answer, some teachers pounce on the student for not having read or understood the material, which results in classmates snickering. In hundreds of ways and in thousands of instances over the course of a school career, students learn that it is not all right to make mistakes. The result is that they become afraid to risk the independent and the sometimes-flawed thinking that leads to creativity.

When students make mistakes, teachers should ask them to analyze and discuss these mistakes. Often, mistakes or weak ideas contain the germ of correct answers or good ideas. In Japan, teachers spend entire class periods asking students to analyze the mistakes in their mathematical thinking. For the teacher who wants to make a difference, exploring mistakes can be an opportunity for learning and growing.

Another aspect of teaching students to be creative is teaching them *to take responsibility for both successes and failures.* Teaching students how to take responsibility means teaching students to (1) understand their creative process, (2) criticize themselves, and (3) take pride in their best creative work. Unfortunately, many teachers and parents look for – or allow students to look for – an outside enemy responsible for failures.

It sounds trite to say that teachers should teach students to take responsibility for themselves, but sometimes there is a gap between what people know and how they translate thought into action. In practice, people differ widely in the extent to which they take responsibility for the causes and consequences of their actions. Creative people need to take responsibility for themselves and for their ideas.

Teachers also can work *to encourage creative collaboration.* Creative performance often is viewed as a solitary occupation. We may picture the writer writing alone in a studio, the artist painting in a solitary loft, or the musician practicing endlessly in a small music room. In reality, people often work in groups. Collaboration can spur creativity. Teachers can encourage students to learn by example by collaborating with creative people.

Students also need to learn how *to imagine things from other viewpoints.* An essential aspect of working with other people and getting the most out of collaborative creative activity is to imagine oneself in other people's shoes. Individuals can broaden their perspective by learning to see the world from different points of view. Teachers and parents should encourage their students to see the importance of understanding, respecting, and responding to other people's points of view. This is important, as many bright and potentially creative students never achieve success because they do not develop practical intelligence. They may do well in school and on tests, but they may never learn how to get along with others or to see things and themselves as others see them.

Teachers also need to help students recognize person-environment fit. What is judged as creative is an interaction between a person and the environment. The very same product that is rewarded as creative in one time or place may be scorned in another.

By building a constant appreciation of the importance of person-environment fit, teachers prepare their students for choosing environments that are conducive to their creative success. Encourage students to examine environments to help them learn to select and match environments with their skills.

Creativity, then, is in large part a habit that adults can encourage in students or in themselves. It remains only for teachers to help foster this habit.

Conclusion

Creativity is as much a habit in and an attitude toward life as it is a matter of ability. Creativity is often obvious in young students, but it may be harder to find in older students and adults because their creative potential has been suppressed by a society that encourages intellectual conformity. Yet, anyone can decide to adopt the creativity habit. Start right now!

REFERENCES

Adelson, B. (1984). When novices surpass experts: The difficulty of a task may increase with expertise. *Journal of Experimental Psychology: Learning, Memory, and Cognition,* **10**(3), 483–495.

Albert, R. S., & Runco, M. A. (1999). A history of research on creativity. In R. J. Sternberg (Ed.), *Handbook of creativity* (pp. 16–31). New York: Cambridge University Press.

Amabile, T. M. (1996). *Creativity in context*. Boulder, CO: Westview.

Amabile, T. M. (1999). How to kill creativity. In *Harvard business review on breakthrough thinking* (pp. 1–28). Cambridge, MA: Harvard University Press.

Ambrose, D., Sternberg, R. J., & Sriraman, B. (Eds.). (2012a). *Confronting dogmatism in gifted education*. New York: Taylor & Francis.

Ambrose, D., Sternberg, R. J., & Sriraman, B. (2012b). Considering the effects of dogmatism on giftedness and talent development. In D. Ambrose, R. J. Sternberg, & B. Sriraman (Eds.), *Confronting dogmatism in gifted education* (pp. 1–11). New York: Taylor & Francis.

Baer, J., & Kaufman, J. C. (2006). Creativity research in English-speaking countries. In J. C. Kaufman & R. J. Sternberg (Eds.), *The international handbook of creativity* (pp. 10–38). New York: Cambridge University Press.

Barron, F. (1969). *Creative person and creative process*. New York: Holt, Rinehart & Winston.

Barron, F. (1988). Putting creativity to work. In R. J. Sternberg (Ed.), *The nature of creativity* (pp. 76–98). New York: Cambridge University Press.

Cosner, L. (2015). How does the Bible teach 6000 years? http://creation.com/6000-years.

Craft, A. (2005). *Creativity in schools: Tensions and dilemmas*. London: Routledge.

Csikszentmihalyi, M. (1988). Society, culture, and person: A systems view of creativity. In R. J. Sternberg (Ed.), *The nature of creativity* (pp. 325–339). New York: Cambridge University Press.

Csikszentmihalyi, M. (1990). The domain of creativity. In M. A. Runco & R. S. Albert (Eds.), *Theories of creativity* (pp. 190–212). Newbury Park, CA: Sage.

Csikszentmihalyi, M. (1999). Implications of a systems perspective for the study of creativity. In R. J. Sternberg (Ed.), *Handbook of creativity* (pp. 313–335). New York: Cambridge University Press.

Csikszentmihalyi, M. (2013). *Creativity: The psychology of discovery and invention*. New York: HarperCollins.

Frensch, P. A., & Sternberg, R. J. (1989). Expertise and intelligent thinking: When is it worse to know better? In R. J. Sternberg (Ed.), *Advances in the psychology of human intelligence* (Vol. 5, pp. 157–188). Hillsdale, NJ: Lawrence Erlbaum Associates.

Garcia, J. (1981). Tilting at the paper mills of academe. *American Psychologist*, 36(2), 149–158.

Garcia, J., & Koelling, R. A. (1966). The relation of cue to consequence in avoidance learning. *Psychonomic Science*, 4, 123–124.

Gardner, H. (1983). *Frames of mind: The theory of multiple intelligences*. New York: Basic.

Gardner, H. (1991). *The unschooled mind*. New York: Basic Books.

Gardner, H. (2006). *Multiple intelligences: New horizons*. New York: Perseus.

Gardner, H. (2011a). *Creating minds*. New York: Basic Books.

Gardner, H. (2011b). *Frames of mind: The theory of multiple intelligences*. New York: Basic.

Guilford, J. P. (1950). Creativity. *American Psychologist*, **5**, 444–454.

Hennessey, B. A. (2015). If I were Secretary of Education: A focus on intrinsic motivation and creativity in the classroom. *Psychology of Aesthetics, Creativity, and the Arts*, **9**(2), 187–192.

Johnson-Laird, P. N. (1988). Freedom and constraint in creativity. In R. J. Sternberg (Ed.), *The nature of creativity* (pp. 202–219). New York: Cambridge University Press.

Kaufman, J. C. (2001a). Genius, lunatics, and poets: Mental illness in prize-winning authors. *Imagination, Cognition, and Personality*, **20**(4), 305–314.

Kaufman, J. C. (2001b). The Sylvia Plath effect: Mental illness in eminent creative writers. *Journal of Creative Behavior*, **35**(1), 37–50.

Kaufman, J. C. (2009). *Creativity 101*. New York: Springer.

Kaufman, J. C., & Beghetto, R. A. (2009). Beyond big and little: The Four C model of creativity. *Review of General Psychology*, **13**, 1–12.

Kogan, N. (1973). Creativity and cognitive style: A life-span perspective. In P. B. Baltes & K. W. Schaie (Eds.), *Life-span developmental psychology: Personality and socialization* (pp. 145–178). New York: Academic Press.

Lubart, T. I., & Sternberg, R. J. (1995). An investment approach to creativity: Theory and data. In S. M. Smith, T. B. Ward, & R. A. Finke (Eds.), *The creative cognition approach* (pp. 269–302). Cambridge, MA: MIT Press.

Maslow, A. (1967). The creative attitude. In R. L. Mooney & T. A. Rasik (Eds.), *Explorations in creativity* (pp. 43–57). New York: Harper & Row.

MacKinnon, D. W. (1962). The nature and nurture of creative talent. *American Psychologist*, 17, 484–495.

Mischel, W., Shoda, Y., & Rodriguez, M. L. (1989). Delay of gratification in children. *Science*, **244**, 933–938.

Pang, W. (2015). Promoting creativity in the classroom: A generative view. *Psychology of Aesthetics, Creativity, and the Arts*, **9**(2), 122–127.

Plucker, J. A., & Beghetto, R. A. (2015). Editorial: Introduction to the special issue. *Psychology of Aesthetics, Creativity, and the Arts*, **9**(2), 113–114.

Plucker, J. A., Kaufman, J. C., & Beghetto, R. A. (2015). *What we know about creativity*. Washington, DC: Partnership for 21st Century Skills.

Reis, S., & Renzulli, J. S. (2014). *The schoolwide enrichment model* (3rd ed.). Waco, TX: Prufrock Press.

Renzulli, J. S. (1986). The three-ring conception of giftedness: A developmental model for creative productivity. In R. J. Sternberg & J. E. Davidson (Eds.), *Conceptions of giftedness* (pp. 53–92). New York: Cambridge University Press.

Schank, R. C. (1988). *The creative attitude*. New York: Macmillan.

Simonton, D. K. (1976). Biographical determinants of achieved eminence: A multivariate approach to the Cox data. *Journal of Personality and Social Psychology*, **33**, 218–226.

Simonton, D. K. (1984). *Genius, creativity, and leadership*. Cambridge, MA: Harvard University Press.

Simonton, D. K. (1988a). Age and outstanding achievement: What do we know after a century of research? *Psychological Bulletin*, **104**, 251–267.

Simonton, D. K. (1988b). *Scientific genius*. New York: Cambridge University Press.

Simonton, D. K. (1994). *Greatness: Who makes history and why?* New York: Guilford.

Sternberg, R. J. (1994). Allowing for thinking styles. *Educational Leadership*, **52**(3), 36–40.

Sternberg, R. J. (1997a). The concept of intelligence and its role in lifelong learning and success. *American Psychologist*, **52**, 1030–1037.

Sternberg, R. J. (1997b). *Successful intelligence*. New York: Plume.

Sternberg, R. J. (1997c). *Thinking styles*. New York: Cambridge University Press.

Sternberg, R. J. (Ed.). (1999) *Handbook of creativity*. New York: Cambridge University Press.

Sternberg, R. J. (2000). Creativity is a decision. In A. L. Costa (Ed.), *Teaching for intelligence II* (pp. 85–106). Arlington Heights, IL: Skylight Training and Publishing Inc.

Sternberg, R. J. (2003a). Creative thinking in the classroom. *Scandinavian Journal of Educational Research*, 47(3), 326–338.

Sternberg, R. J. (2003b). Teaching for successful intelligence: Principles, practices, and outcomes. *Educational and Child Psychology*, **20**(2), 6–18.

Sternberg, R. J. (2004). Good intentions, bad results: A dozen reasons why the No Child Left Behind (NCLB) Act is failing our nation's schools. *Education Week*, **24**(9), 42, 56.

Sternberg, R. J. (2006). Creativity is a habit. *Education Week*, **25**(24), 47–64.

Sternberg, R. J. (2010a). *College admissions for the 21st century*. Cambridge, MA: Harvard University Press.

Sternberg, R. J. (2010b). The dark side of creativity and how to combat it. In D. H. Cropley, A. J. Cropley, J. C. Kaufman, & M. A. Runco (Eds.), *The dark side of creativity* (pp. 316–328). New York: Cambridge University Press.

Sternberg, R. J. (2010c). Teach creativity, not memorization. *Chronicle of Higher Education*, **57**(8), A29.

Sternberg, R. J. (2012). The assessment of creativity: An investment-based approach. *Creativity Research Journal*, **24**(1), 3–12.

Sternberg, R. J. (2013a). Creativity, ethics, and society. *International Journal on Creativity and Talent Development*, **1**(1), 15–24.

Sternberg, R. J. (2013b). Viewing creativity as a decision: A vehicle for success in life. *Inspire: The Gifted Magazine for Educators*, **9**, 4–9.

Sternberg, R. J. (2015). Teaching for creativity: The sounds of silence. *Psychology of Aesthetics, Creativity, and the Arts*, **9**(2), 115–117.

Sternberg, R. J., & Grigorenko, E. L. (2004). Successful intelligence in the classroom. *Theory into Practice*, **43**(4), 274–280.

Sternberg, R. J., & Grigorenko, E. L. (2007). *Teaching for successful intelligence* (2nd ed.). Thousand Oaks, CA: Corwin.

Sternberg, R. J., Jarvin, L., & Grigorenko, E. L. (2011). *Explorations of the nature of giftedness*. New York: Cambridge University Press.

Sternberg, R. J., & Lubart, T. I. (1991). An investment theory of creativity and its development. *Human Development*, **34**(1), 1–31.

Sternberg, R. J., & Lubart, T. I. (1992). Buy low and sell high: An investment approach to creativity. *Current Directions in Psychological Science*, 1(1), 1–5.

Sternberg, R. J., & Lubart, T. I. (1995a). *Defying the crowd: Cultivating creativity in a culture of conformity*. New York: Free Press.

Sternberg, R. J., & Lubart, T. I. (1995b). Ten keys to creative innovation. *R & D Innovator*, **4**(3), 8–11.

Sternberg, R. J., & Lubart, T. I. (1995c). Ten tips toward creativity in the workplace. In C. M. Ford & D. A. Gioia (Eds.), *Creative action in organizations: Ivory tower visions and real world voices* (pp. 173–180). Newbury Park, CA: Sage Publications.

Sternberg, R. J., & The Rainbow Project Collaborators. (2005). Augmenting the SAT through assessments of analytical, practical, and creative skills. In W. Camara & E. Kimmel (Eds.), *Choosing students: Higher education admission tools for the 21st century* (pp. 159–176). Mahwah, NJ: Lawrence Erlbaum Associates.

Sternberg, R. J., & The Rainbow Project Collaborators. (2006). The Rainbow Project: Enhancing the SAT through assessments of analytical, practical and creative skills. *Intelligence*, **34**(4), 321–350.

Sternberg, R. J., & Williams, W. M. (1996). *How to develop student creativity*. Alexandria, VA: Association for Supervision and Curriculum Development.

Sternberg, R. J., & Smith, E. E. (Eds.). (1988). *The psychology of human thought*. New York: Cambridge University Press.

Tharp, T. (2005). *The creative habit: Learn it and use it for life*. New York: Simon & Schuster.

Torrance, E. P. (1962). *Guiding creative talent*. Englewood Cliffs, NJ: Prentice-Hall.

Zhang, L.-F., & Sternberg, R. J. (2009). Intellectual styles and creativity. In T. Rickards, M. A. Runco, & S. Moger (Eds.), *The Routledge companion to creativity* (pp. 256–266). New York: Routledge.

Zhang, L.-F., Sternberg, R. J., & Rayner, S. (Eds.). (2012). *Handbook of intellectual styles*. New York: Springer.

CHAPTER 20

A Coda for Creativity in the Classroom
Take-Home Points and Final Insights

James C. Kaufman and Ronald A. Beghetto

University of Connecticut

As you have seen, essay and chapter authors approached the assignment in several different ways. Some of them talked about their own personal journey with creativity in schools and classrooms. Others used specific, concrete examples of creativity-nurturing curriculum and activities. Some discussed their experiences teaching courses on creativity and the importance of developing new programs to encourage creativity. Still others drew from the latest research and theory to make recommendations for best practices.

A central, recurring theme in the book is the importance of recognizing that creativity can (and should) be cultivated in classrooms (be they early elementary or higher education). The contributors have provided various compelling reasons for why nurturing creativity is an international educational priority. These reasons include everything from complementing academic learning to better prepare future generations to work together to solve increasingly complex personal, social, and global challenges. Many authors also commented on why they feel creativity is often stifled in classroom settings. Unlike other critiques of the educational system, however, the authors in this volume also offer concrete ideas, strategies, and suggestions for addressing the challenges facing teachers interested in promoting creativity. Moreover, the authors in this volume do not blindly advocate for more creativity. Many highlight the risks and costs involved in creative teaching and learning. Taken together, the critiques, insights, and suggestions represent a more balanced treatment of what it means to nurture creativity in the classroom. Some of the ideas and concepts presented are provocative and meant to challenge the way we think about creativity. Others are aspirational and serve as goals we can all strive to attain. Still others are very concrete and actionable – strategies, ideas, and tips that can be incorporated immediately in teachers' existing curriculum and teaching practices. In what follows we offer our own synthesis of key points that personally resonated with us as educators. We then highlight some other important themes and ideas that recur in these chapters.

Our list of the key points:

1. The power of being able to learn and share classroom ideas with other cultures. One example of this, from Niu and Zhou, is China's concept of the "Good Teacher" in which the teacher occupies a high place in society and is given societal support and confirmation of the importance of their work (see also Renzulli).

2. The importance of being aware of limiting and creativity-stifling myths and misconceptions. Plucker and Dow highlight (and dispel) several false myths pertaining to creativity being inextricably linked to madness or the view that there is a necessarily disruptive or dangerous component to being creative (see also Beghetto & J. Kaufman).

3. Renzulli emphasizes that teaching is a creative act in itself. Teachers who want to nurture creativity in students must model creativity in their curricula. He further provides many ideas for how teachers can accomplish these goals (see also Beghetto & J. Kaufman)

4. Baer and Garret argue for the importance of developing domain-specific knowledge as means for preparing students to be creative in that specific area – as opposed to using general creativity techniques and tactics (see also Niu & Zhou; Skiba, Tan, Sternberg, & Grigorenko).

5. Hennessey writes about the importance of supporting students' intrinsic motivation and enjoyment while learning and also highlights the potential negative effect of rewards on student creativity (see also Niu & Zhou; Piirto; Renzulli; Sternberg). Baer and Garrett similarly consider how the need to give feedback and rewards can be balanced with the need to enhance intrinsic student motivation.

6. Reisman offers many valuable classroom tools rooted in classic creativity concepts (such as divergent and convergent thinking) that can be used to support teachers who want to spur student imagination (see also Renzulli).

7. Cropley describes how important it is to integrate creativity into the preparation of engineers, moving away from traditional models that paint creativity as a complementary but separate entity.

8. Skiba, Tan, Sternberg, and Grigorenko stress the importance of embedding creativity in the academic curriculum and highlight important advances in establishing curriculum-based measures of creativity (see also Baer & Garret).

9. Gotlieb, Jahner, Immordino-Yang, and S. Kaufman suggest how the social-emotional imagination plays a central role in making meaning

from a complex social world and how empathy, perspective-taking, and multiculturalism allow learners to develop and exercise their imagination.

10. Everyday creativity is important and of value. Beghetto and J. Kaufman say that most people and activities can be creative, not only the elect or elite (see also Plucker & Dow), and argue for the inclusion of creativity in the everyday curriculum (see also Skiba, Tan, Sternberg, & Grigorenko).

11. Karwowski and Jankowska present a new model that emphasizes creativity's nuance and many facets. The interaction of creative abilities, openness, and independence may result in rebellious, subordinate, self-actualizing, or complex creativity.

12. Beghetto and J. Kaufman stress that the reason creativity sometimes gets a bad reputation is not that teachers dislike creativity, but that anyone may dislike poorly timed creativity. There are times to be creative and times to wait.

13. Just as improvisation enhances ensemble musical comedy or theatrical performances, Sawyer argues, so too will creative classroom teaching come from the allowance of unplanned and seemingly tangential thoughts and ideas (see also Piirto; Reisman).

14. Sternberg writes of the importance of supportive mentors and environment (see also Glăveanu, Branco, & Neves-Pereira; Piirto). Renzulli adds that one way to encourage creativity is by finding students a wide variety of resources – including mentors who will connect them to potentially meaningful subjects or topics – and offering a chance for students' creative ideas to reach an audience.

15. Glăveanu, Branco, and Neves-Pereira emphasize the importance of supporting creativity and prosocial values in active collaborations between teachers and students, students and peers, and the larger community outside the classroom (see also Gotlieb, Jahner, Immordino-Yang, & S. Kaufman).

16. Broadening conceptions of creativity in classroom by exploring potentially limiting self-beliefs about the nature of creativity is particularly important for prospective and practicing teachers, students, and parents (Beghetto & J. Kaufman). This point is in alignment with Plucker and Dow's idea that examining one's own beliefs about creativity (and identifying misconceptions) is a necessary first step toward creating conditions for creativity enhancement (see also Gotlieb, Jahner, Immordino-Yang, & S. Kaufman).

17. Hennessey says that at a time when it may be especially difficult for teachers to highlight creativity, it is even more important for individual teachers to support creativity at a "grassroots level" (see also Beghetto & J. Kaufman; Reisman; Sawyer).

18. When assessing academic and creative ability/potential, Sternberg writes, it is important to be very careful to use the best possible assessments; many of the most commonly used assessments are not the best ones available (see also Baer & Garrett; Sawyer).

19. Piirto argues for the need to help students develop strong self-discipline, which can both increase creative productivity and enhance persistence in following a creative idea (see also Sternberg). Piirto also stresses the important point that nurturing creativity in the classroom results from a partnership between educators and their students – helping ensure that creativity becomes a meaningful part of students' and teachers' lives (see also Glăveanu, Branco, & Neves-Pereira).

20. Sawyer proposes that creativity should go beyond arts education and be present in all types of curriculum (including math and science) via the fostering of learning environments that emphasize active learning and knowledge building.

These are but a few of the themes in this book. We hope that this book was as enjoyable, provocative, and fun to read for you as it has been for us (both times around). We continue to write about creativity in the classroom (with John Baer, we wrote the recent *Teaching for Creativity in the Common Core Classroom,* from Teacher's College Press; Ron published *Big Wins, Small Steps* for Corwin Press; and the second edition of James's *Creativity 101* just came out from Springer). We would also love to keep hearing stories of teachers coming up with new ways to be creative in the classroom (and, indeed, are interested in working on a future volume filled with best creative practices); feel free to e-mail us at ronald.beghetto@uconn.edu or james.kaufman@uconn.edu.

Index